The Tailoring Book

The Tailoring Book

A step-by-step guide to creating bespoke garments

Alison Smith MBE

Contents

Introduction

Welcome to *The Tailoring Book*! Sewing is my passion and I adore creating tailored pieces. To me, a tailored wardrobe means a collection of stylish, structured, and well-fitting garments. This book takes you through the essentials of a tailored wardrobe, from a simple pencil skirt and classic trousers, to the complexities of princess-line and darted jackets. I'm not aiming to turn you into a Savile Row tailor, but into a home sewer with the confidence to tailor-make your own beautiful, bespoke garments. If you can already make a skirt, let me stretch your skills and show you how to make a canvas-lined jacket or camel coat.

These are techniques that I teach in my sewing classes every week, and I am delighted to be able to share them with you. This book will help you discover new fabrics (especially linings and interfacings), and expand the skillset you already use in your dressmaking and sewing. You'll find instructions on how to download the patterns that will enable you to construct a total of ten garments, including a fully-canvassed menswear blazer. I will also show you three ways to tailor jackets and coats, from speed tailoring, and hybrid techniques used in ready-to-wear jackets and coats, to couture-canvas methods. All techniques have comprehensive step-by-step instructions, and list all the materials you will need. So gather your tools and fabrics, and let's get started!

Alison Smith

What is tailoring?

The art of tailoring can be traced back over many centuries, when clothing featured an underlayer of padding, rather than following the contours of the body. By the 1500s, makers of traditional menswear – the tailors – had developed construction techniques quite different to those used in dressmaking. By the 1800s, good fit became the main criterion of a tailored garment. The understructure of jackets now featured multiple thin underlayers of canvas, that not only gave structure but also subtle shaping through the lapel and collar. Today, the use of a canvas understructure is used by custom tailors – think Savile Row in London and haute couturiers in Paris. The advent of fusible interfacings in the 1950s soon led to their use in ready-to-wear suits. By the 1960s fusible interfacing

fabrics were available to the home sewer. The ten garment projects in this book will help you explore three distinct tailoring methods: fusible or "speed" tailoring, hybrid tailoring, and couture canvas tailoring.

Pencil skirt This fully lined skirt with stylish chino pockets is a great beginner tailor's project. Take time making the toile to get the perfect fit (see pp.222–227).

Straight-leg trousers With a fly front, a shaped waistband, and pockets, these trousers contain all the elements of a classic tailored trouser (see pp.228–235).

Wide-leg trousers A reflection on the 1920s and 1930s style, these flowy trousers are still on trend today (see pp.236–239).

Classic shirt A tailored shirt is a joy to sew once you know how! With run and fell seams, cuffs and plackets, plus a collar and stand, the construction techniques apply to both mens- and womenswear (see pp.240–245).

Five-button waistcoat The finishing touch under a tailored jacket, this is a traditional menswear garment created using modern fusible techniques (see pp.246–251).

Princess-line jacket This fully lined jacket is constructed using speed tailoring methods, but the techniques are true to traditional tailoring (see pp.252–259).

Unlined summer jacket A deconstructed version of the princess-line jacket, this is a great first tailoring project (see pp.260–265).

Darted blazer If you have tried speed tailoring, it's time to stretch your skills as you hand-tailor this classic menswear jacket, using canvas and pad stitching to shape your garment (see pp.266–275).

Camel coat A timeless piece in any wardrobe, a tailored camel coat will take you anywhere. This project requires hybrid tailoring methods, combining the use of fusibles and canvas (see pp.276–283).

Knee-length coat This shorter version of the camel coat also features hybrid tailoring, together with patch pockets and a velvet collar (see pp.284–291).

How to use this book

This book contains all the information you need to tailor your own clothes. There are patterns and step-by-step instructions for ten classic garments. Additional guidance, if needed, can be found in sections on key tailoring techniques, tools, fabrics, and pattern alterations.

THE GARMENTS SECTION

GARMENT OVERVIEWS

An overview of each of the garments gives the key techniques that will be used when making each piece, all of which can be found in the techniques and tailoring methods sections. It also provides guidance on the difficulty level of each project, lists what materials you will need, outlines key construction elements, and provides advice on fabric choices along with relevant swatch images. At the top of the page, you will see the title of the corresponding downloadable project pattern (see pp.12–13 for instructions on downloading the patterns).

GARMENT STEP-BY-STEP INSTRUCTIONS

The first step given for each classic garment is to make a toile. This is an essential starting point when crafting bespoke clothing and ensures you achieve the perfect fit.

Clear step-by-step instructions, along with annotated images, will guide you seamlessly through the process of constructing your tailored garment, from start to finish.

OTHER USEFUL SECTIONS

TOOLS AND MATERIALS

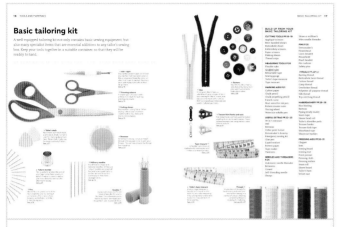

All the essential tools and materials you may need are contained in a gallery at the beginning of the book. Full-colour photographs and clear text explain the uses of each.

FABRICS

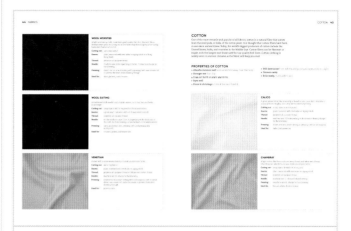

These galleries showcase more than 40 tailoring fabrics, along with linings, facings, and tapes, explaining the uses of each. Use them to find more information on the suggested fabrics for your garment or to find inspiration for future projects.

TAILORING TECHNIQUES

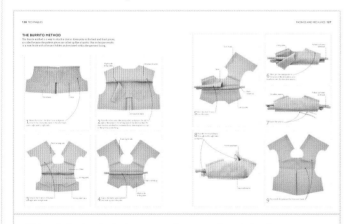

All key tailoring techniques are shown and explained, step-by-step, in a section on techniques, and another on the principle methods of tailoring. Turn to these pages for extra guidance when completing a project, or use as a general reference for tailoring queries.

PATTERN ALTERATION

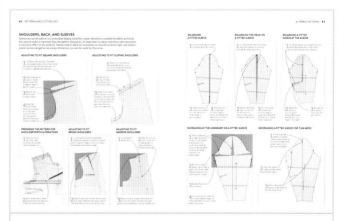

A chapter on pattern alterations teaches you to customize patterns to fit your body shape – for example, shortening sleeves or lengthening a top. These techniques can be used with the patterns you download to use alongside this book or with commercial patterns.

Downloading the patterns

To create any of the garments in this book, you will first need to download and prepare the corresponding pattern. Head to our website, dk.com/the-tailoring-book, to choose from a selection of ten classic patterns, each in a range of sizes that can later be adapted to suit your own unique body size and shape.

FIND YOUR SIZE

Find your size by taking your bust, waist, and hip measurements and finding the closest set of measurements in the table below. If you are between sizes, choose the larger of the two.

SIZE (WOMENSWEAR)	6-8	8-10	10-12	12-14	14-16	16-18	18-20	20-22	22-24
BUST	82cm (32¼in)	84.5cm (33¼in)	87cm (34¼in)	92cm (36¼in)	97cm (38in)	102cm (40in)	107cm (42in)	112cm (44in)	117cm (46in)
WAIST	62cm (24½in)	64.5cm (25¼in)	67cm (26¼in)	72cm (28¼in)	77cm (30¼in)	82cm (32¼in)	87cm (34¼in)	92cm (36¼in)	97cm (38 in)
HIP	87cm (34¼in)	89.5cm (35¼in)	92cm (36¼in)	97cm (38in)	102cm (40in)	107cm (42in)	112cm (44in)	117cm (46in)	122cm (48in)

The Five-button Waistcoat (see pp.246–251) and Darted Blazer (see pp.266–275) are menswear patterns. For these patterns, measure your chest, waist, and hips.

SIZE (MENSWEAR)	38	40	42	44	46	48	50	52	54
CHEST	97cm (38in)	102cm (40in)	107cm (42in)	112cm (44in)	117cm (46in)	122cm (48in)	127cm (50in)	132cm (52in)	137cm (54in)
WAIST	81cm (32in)	87cm (34¼in)	92cm (36¼in)	99cm (39in)	107cm (42in)	112cm (44in)	117cm (46in)	122cm (48in)	127cm (50in)
HIP	99cm (39in)	104cm (41in)	109cm (43in)	114cm (45in)	119cm (47in)	124cm (49in)	130cm (51in)	135cm (53in)	140cm (55in)

SEAM ALLOWANCE

Seam allowance is the amount of fabric that is taken up by the seam. It is usually given as the distance between the cutting line and the stitching line.

The patterns in this section include 1.5cm (⅝in) seam allowance. This means that to make a garment that is the correct size and shape, you will need to cut along the line on the pattern, and stitch 1.5cm (⅝in) inside the cutting line. An easy way to remember to do this is to mark a stitching line onto the pattern pieces before you begin.

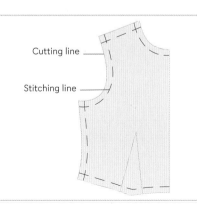

Cutting line

Stitching line

VARIED SIZES

You may have noticed that your size in the table differs from what you would buy in a store. In general, dressmaking sizes tend to be smaller than store sizes. It is always a good idea to make a garment in a toile first (see pp.78–79) to make sure that the size is right and the garment fits. Note that the amount of fabric you need will vary depending on the garment sizing.

THE TAILORING BOOK WEBSITE

All the garment projects featured in this book can be made using patterns downloaded from **dk.com/the-tailoring-book**.

THE PATTERNS

The website features ten patterns that correspond to the projects in this book. These patterns are:

Pencil skirt (see pp.222–227)
Straight-leg trousers (see pp.228–235)
Wide-leg trousers (see pp.236–239)
Classic shirt (see pp.240–245)
Five-button waistcoat (see pp.246–251)
Princess-line jacket (see pp.252–259)
Unlined summer jacket (see pp.260–265)
Darted blazer (see pp.266–275)
Camel coat (see pp.276–283)
Knee-length coat (see pp.284–291)

To make these garments, download the corresponding classic garment pattern, then follow the steps shown in each individual project.

This single-breasted wool coat epitomizes effortless elegance with its simple shape, a deep back vent, and single welt pockets with flaps. Fully lined, it is constructed using hybrid tailoring techniques; a combination of fusible methods and machine pad stitching.

Camel coat

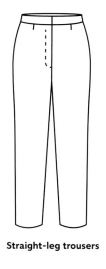

These ankle-grazing trousers are so flattering and versatile, featuring front and back darts, a shaped split waistband, hip pockets, a faced fly, and back welt pockets that enhance the trouser's sleek symmetry.

Straight-leg trousers

This classic fitted jacket features fusible underlinings, jetted pockets, and collar and revers with a contemporary curved finish. The two-piece sleeve has a faux vent mirroring the curved finished edge.

Princess-line jacket

HOW TO DOWNLOAD YOUR PATTERN

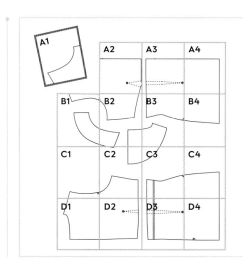

1 Start by checking which pattern is needed to make the garment. The pattern name is listed on the first page of the project instructions, for instance, on page 223, the pattern name is **Pencil skirt pattern**.

2 Then go to **dk.com/the-tailoring-book**. Find the correct PDF for your garment and your size. Download the PDF to your computer, and print it out. The pages will be labelled in the order that they fit together.

3 Trim the white margins from the printed pages, and tape the pages together, using the letters and gridlines as a guide. Cut out the pattern pieces.

PATTERN MARKINGS

The following markings are used on the patterns.

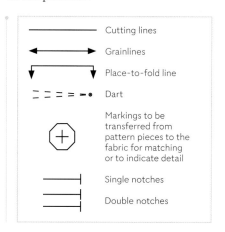

———	Cutting lines
◄——►	Grainlines
▼———▼	Place-to-fold line
= = = —•	Dart
⊕	Markings to be transferred from pattern pieces to the fabric for matching or to indicate detail
⊢——⊣	Single notches
⊨——⊨	Double notches

Tools and materials

As well as a basic sewing kit – tape measure, sharp scissors, pins, needles, threads, and a seam ripper – a tailor's toolkit should include a sturdy sewing machine, a decent iron, and preferably an overlocker. There are many other handy gadgets available to complement the basics and help perfect your tailoring projects.

Basic tailoring kit

A well-equipped tailoring kit not only contains basic sewing equipment, but also many specialist items that are essential additions to any tailor's sewing box. Keep your tools together in a suitable container, so that they will be readily to hand.

◀ Seam ripper
Also called a stitch ripper, to remove any stitches that have been sewn in the wrong place. Keep the cover on when not in use to protect the sharp point and replace annually as they do go blunt.
See p.18

◀ Trimming scissors
A smaller pair of scissors with a 10cm (4in) blade for layering and clipping seams.
See p.19

◀ Cutting shears
Required for cutting fabric. When buying, select a pair that feels comfortable in your hand and that is not too heavy.
See p.19

◀ Tailor's chalk
Also known as French chalk, a solid piece of tailor's chalk is used for marking placement lines. These chalk marks can be easily brushed off fabric.
See p.21

◀ Beeswax
When hand sewing, run your thread through the wax and press in with your fingers. This will help prevent the thread from tangling.
See p.22

▲ Tailor's thimble
This is useful to protect the end of your finger when hand sewing. A tailor's thimble is open-ended to give more dexterity and tactility when hand sewing.
See p.23

◀ Millinery needles
In addition to sharps and between needles, millinery or "straw" needles are essential for hand sewing and tacking, as they are very long, thin, and sharp, so they don't damage fabric.
See p.24

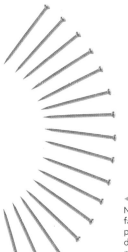

◀ Pins
Needed by every tailor to hold the fabric together prior to sewing it permanently. The choice of pin depends on the fabric and the project being sewn.
See p.25

Needles ▶
A good selection of different types of needles for sewing by hand. This will enable you to tackle any hand-sewing project. Keep them safe in a needle twist.
See p.24

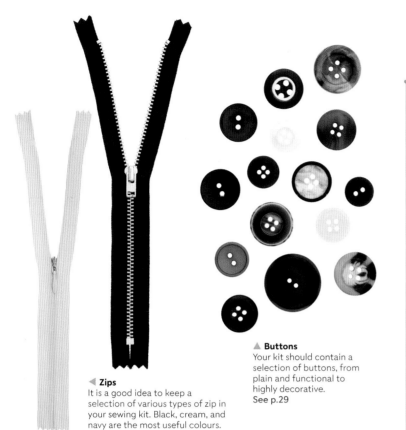

Buttons
Your kit should contain a selection of buttons, from plain and functional to highly decorative.
See p.29

◀ **Zips**
It is a good idea to keep a selection of various types of zip in your sewing kit. Black, cream, and navy are the most useful colours. Both concealed and metal zips are used in tailored garments.

◀ **Trouser/skirt hooks and eyes**
Flat metal hooks and bars used to fasten waistbands on skirts and trousers. These hidden fasteners are designed to create little or no bulk.
See p.29

Tape measure ▶
A flexible tape measure marked with centimetres and inches is an essential item.
See p.20

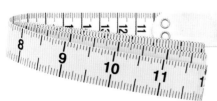

▲ **Tailor's tape measure**
A tailor's tape measure is flexible and moulds to the body for accurate measuring. It has a long metal end to end to aid the measurement of the inside leg.
See p.20

Threads ▶
A selection of threads for hand sewing and machine/overlocker sewing in a variety of colours. Basting or tacking thread is essential for tailoring.
See pp.26–27

BUILD UP FROM YOUR BASIC TAILORING KIT

CUTTING TOOLS PP.18–19
Appliqué scissors
Bent-handled shears
Buttonhole chisel
Embroidery scissors
Paper scissors
Pinking shears
Thread snips

MEASURING TOOLS P.20
Flexible ruler
Gridded ruler
Retractable tape
Sewing gauge
Tailor's tape measure
Tape measure

MARKING AIDS P.21
Carbon paper
Chalk pencil
Chalk propelling pencil
French curve
Heat-sensitive ink pen
Pattern master ruler
Tracing wheel
Water/air-soluble pen

USEFUL EXTRAS PP.22–23
14-in-1 measure
Awl
Beeswax
Collar point turner
Dressmaker's dummy
Emergency sewing kit
Glue pen
Liquid sealant
Pattern paper
Tape maker
Tweezers

NEEDLES AND THREADERS P.24
Automatic needle threader
Betweens
Crewel
Self-threading needle
Sharps

Straw or milliner's
Wire needle threader

PINS P.25
Dressmaker's
Flowerhead
Glass-headed
Household
Pearl-headed
Pin cushion
Safety pins

THREADS PP.26–27
Basting thread
Buttonhole twist thread
Cotton thread
Gimp thread
Overlocker thread
Polyester all-purpose thread
Silk thread
Top-stitching thread

HABERDASHERY PP.28–29
Bias binding
Buttons
Piping (ready made)
Seam tape
Sleeve head roll
Tailor's shoulder pads
Trouser hooks
Trouser kick tape
Waistband tape
Waistcoat buckles

PRESSING AIDS PP.30–31
Clapper
Iron
Ironing board
Ironing mat
Point presser
Pressing cloth
Pressing mitten
Seam roll
Sleeve board
Tailor's ham
Velvet mat

Cutting tools

There are many types of cutting tools, but one rule applies to all: buy good-quality products that can be re-sharpened. Cutting shears should fit the span of your hand so that you can comfortably open the whole of the blade with one action, which is very important for clean and accurate cutting lines. A seam ripper is essential for removing misplaced stitches or for unpicking seams for mending.

▼ **Thread snips**
Store these with your sewing machine to clip the ends of thread as you sew.

Appliqué scissors ▲
Use these scissors to trim upper fabric layers. The duck bill prevents snipping into the under layer.

Paper scissors ▼
Keep a pair of scissors to be used only for cutting paper, as paper may dull your sewing scissors.

Seam ripper ▶
A sharp, pointed hook to slide under a stitch, with a small cutting blade at the base to cut the thread. Various sizes of seam ripper are available, to cut through light to heavyweight fabric seams.

Buttonhole chisel ▶
A smaller version of a carpenter's chisel, to cut cleanly and accurately through buttonholes. As this is so sharp it must be used with a self-healing cutting mat.

▲ **Embroidery scissors**
Small and very sharp scissors used to get into corners and clip threads close to the fabric.

▼ **Trimming scissors**
These scissors have a 10cm (4in) blade and are used to trim away surplus fabric and neaten ends of machining.

Pinking shears ▶
A sharp pair of pinking shears will aid clipping and trimming corners and linings.

◀ **Bent-handled shears**
This type of shear has a blade that can sit flat against the table when cutting out, due to the angle between the blade and handle. Popular for cutting long, straight edges.

▼ **Cutting shears**
The most popular type of shear, used for cutting large pieces of fabric. The length of the blade can vary from 20–30cm (8–12in).

Measuring tools and marking aids

A selection of different measuring and marking tools will help to ensure precise measurements for that perfect fit. Some of these tools are also useful for pattern adjustment.

MEASURING TOOLS

There are many tools available to help you measure everything from the width of a seam or hem, to body dimensions. One of the most basic yet invaluable measuring tools is the tape measure. Be sure to keep yours in good condition – once it stretches or gets snipped on the edges it will no longer be accurate and should be replaced. A selection of rulers and curves helps when marking and altering patterns.

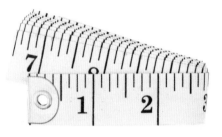

▲ **Tape measure**
Available in various colours and widths. Try to choose one that is the same width as standard seam allowance (1.5cm/⅝in), because it will prove exceedingly useful.

▲ **Sewing gauge**
A handy small tool about 15cm (6in) long, marked in centimetres and inches, with a sliding tab. Use as an accurate measure for small measurements such as hems.

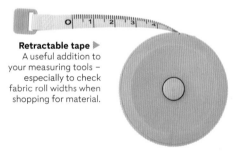

Retractable tape ▶
A useful addition to your measuring tools – especially to check fabric roll widths when shopping for material.

▲ **Tailor's tape measure**
A tailor's tape measure is flexible and malleable, allowing you to measure every curve with accuracy. The long metal end plate makes it easy to take a trouser in-seam measurement.

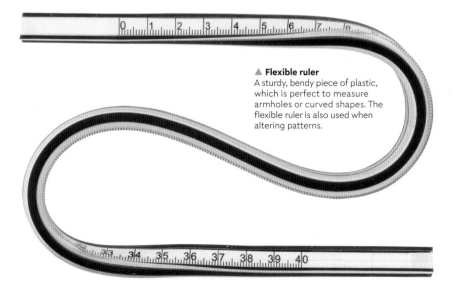

▲ **Flexible ruler**
A sturdy, bendy piece of plastic, which is perfect to measure armholes or curved shapes. The flexible ruler is also used when altering patterns.

▼ **Gridded ruler**
These are available in various sizes and widths and help with measuring bias strips, pattern alterations, and ascertaining straight grain.

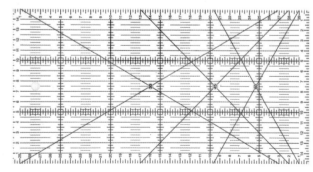

MARKING AIDS

Marking certain parts of your work, to make sure that things such as pockets and darts are placed correctly and seamlines are straight, is an important part of tailoring. With some marking tools, such as pens and a tracing wheel and carbon paper, it is always a good idea to test on a scrap of fabric first to make sure that the mark made will not be permanent.

▼ Chalk propelling pencil
Chalk leads of different colours can be inserted into this propelling pencil, making it a very versatile marking tool. The leads can be sharpened.

▲ Pattern master and French curve
These rulers aid pattern alterations, enabling you to draw smooth curves and mark out seam allowances. They are particularly useful in shaping armholes, collars, and necklines.

◄ Tailor's chalk
Also known as French chalk, this solid piece of chalk in either a square or triangular shape is available in a large variety of colours. The chalk easily brushes off fabric.

◄ Water/air-soluble pen
This resembles a felt marker pen. Marks made can be removed from the fabric with either a spray of water or by leaving to air-dry. Be careful – if you press over the marks, they may become permanent.

◄ Chalk pencil
Available in blue, pink, and white. As it can be sharpened like a normal pencil, it will draw accurate lines on fabric.

◄ Tracing wheel and carbon paper
These items are used together to mark fabric and are especially useful when making a toile (see pp.86–87). However, take care when using these tools on fine or pale fabric as the markings could show through and may not be easily removed.

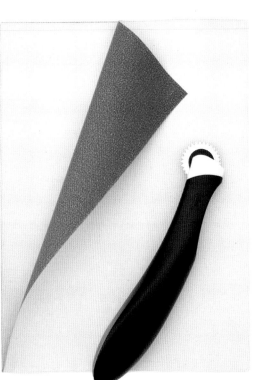

Heat-sensitive ink pen ►
This pen draws clear fine lines on fabric and will vanish once ironed. However, test it first as the ink can reappear in cold conditions.

Useful extras

There are many more accessories that can be purchased to help with your tailoring projects, and knowing which products to choose and for which job can be daunting. The tools shown here are not essential, but can be useful aids.

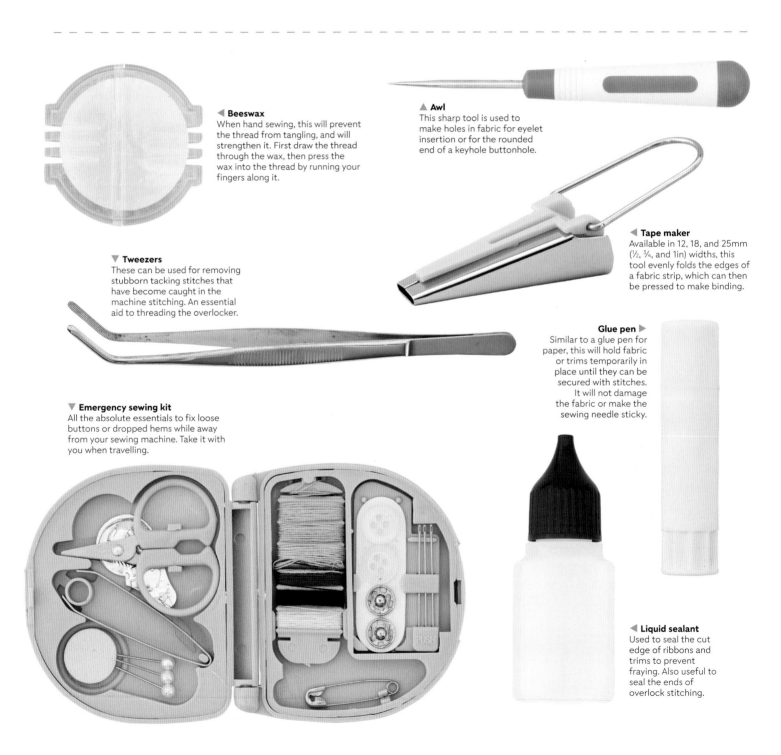

◀ **Beeswax**
When hand sewing, this will prevent the thread from tangling, and will strengthen it. First draw the thread through the wax, then press the wax into the thread by running your fingers along it.

▲ **Awl**
This sharp tool is used to make holes in fabric for eyelet insertion or for the rounded end of a keyhole buttonhole.

◀ **Tape maker**
Available in 12, 18, and 25mm (½, ¾, and 1in) widths, this tool evenly folds the edges of a fabric strip, which can then be pressed to make binding.

▼ **Tweezers**
These can be used for removing stubborn tacking stitches that have become caught in the machine stitching. An essential aid to threading the overlocker.

Glue pen ▶
Similar to a glue pen for paper, this will hold fabric or trims temporarily in place until they can be secured with stitches. It will not damage the fabric or make the sewing needle sticky.

▼ **Emergency sewing kit**
All the absolute essentials to fix loose buttons or dropped hems while away from your sewing machine. Take it with you when travelling.

◀ **Liquid sealant**
Used to seal the cut edge of ribbons and trims to prevent fraying. Also useful to seal the ends of overlock stitching.

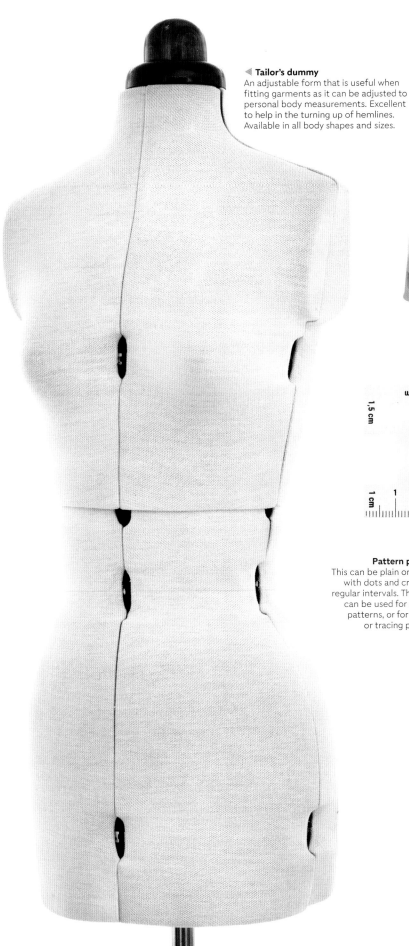

◄ Tailor's dummy
An adjustable form that is useful when fitting garments as it can be adjusted to personal body measurements. Excellent to help in the turning up of hemlines. Available in all body shapes and sizes.

▲ Collar point turner
This is excellent for pushing out those hard-to-reach corners in collars and cuffs.

◄ Thimble
An essential item for many sewers, to protect the middle finger from the end of the needle. Choose a thimble that fits your finger comfortably as there are many varieties to choose from.

▼ 14-in-1 measure
A strange-looking tool that has 14 different measurements on it. Use to turn hems or edges accurately. Available in both metric and imperial.

Pattern paper ►
This can be plain or printed with dots and crosses at regular intervals. The paper can be used for drafting patterns, or for altering or tracing patterns.

Needles and pins

Choosing the appropriate pins and needles is so important, as the wrong choice can damage fabric or leave small holes. Needles are made from steel and pins from steel or occasionally brass. Look after them by keeping pins in a pin cushion and needles in a needle case – if kept together in a small container they could become scratched and blunt.

NEEDLES AND THREADERS

Needles are available for all types of fabrics and projects. A good selection of needles should be to hand at all times, whether it be for emergency mending of tears, or sewing on buttons, or adding trimmings to special-occasion wear. With a special needle threader, inserting the thread through the eye of the needle is simplicity itself.

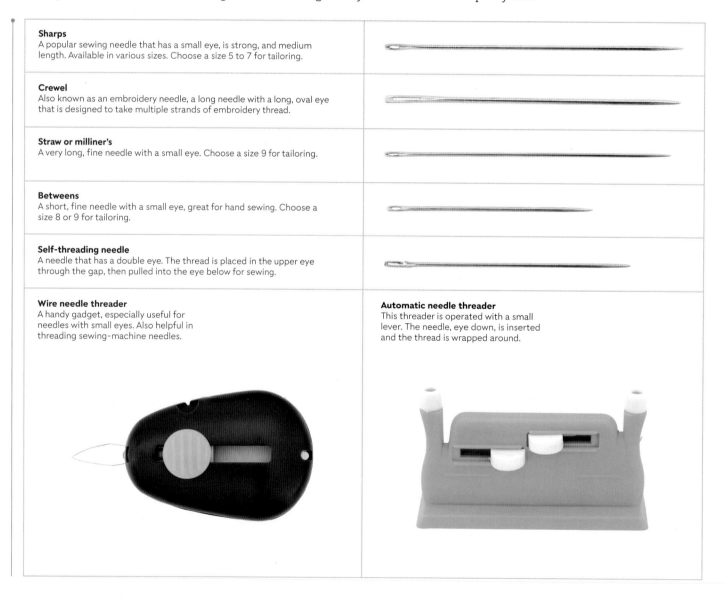

Sharps
A popular sewing needle that has a small eye, is strong, and medium length. Available in various sizes. Choose a size 5 to 7 for tailoring.

Crewel
Also known as an embroidery needle, a long needle with a long, oval eye that is designed to take multiple strands of embroidery thread.

Straw or milliner's
A very long, fine needle with a small eye. Choose a size 9 for tailoring.

Betweens
A short, fine needle with a small eye, great for hand sewing. Choose a size 8 or 9 for tailoring.

Self-threading needle
A needle that has a double eye. The thread is placed in the upper eye through the gap, then pulled into the eye below for sewing.

Wire needle threader
A handy gadget, especially useful for needles with small eyes. Also helpful in threading sewing-machine needles.

Automatic needle threader
This threader is operated with a small lever. The needle, eye down, is inserted and the thread is wrapped around.

PINS

A selection of various pins is important. Most tailors have a favourite sort to work with, but it's best to choose fine, thin pins for fine shirtings and silks, and longer pins with heads for thicker woollen fabrics.

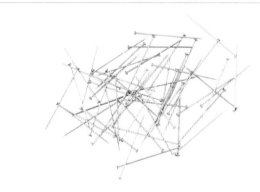

Household
General-purpose pins of a medium length and thickness. Can be used for all types of sewing.

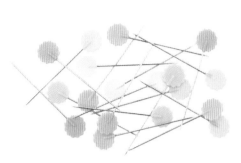

Flowerhead
A long pin of medium thickness with a flat, flower-shaped head. It is designed to be pressed over, as the head lays flat on the fabric.

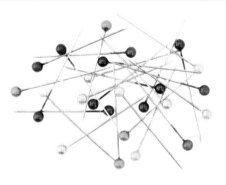

Pearl-headed
Longer than household pins, with a coloured pearl head. They are easy to pick up and use.

Glass-headed
Similar to pearl-headed pins but shorter. They have the advantage that they can be pressed over without melting.

Dressmaker's
Similar to a household pin in shape and thickness, but slightly longer. These are the pins for beginners to choose.

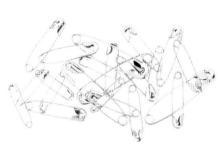

Safety pins
Available in a huge variety of sizes and made either of brass or stainless steel. Used for holding two or more layers together.

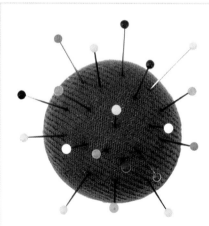

Pin cushion
Choose a fabric cover: a foam cushion may blunt pins. Magnetic ones should not be put on a computerized sewing machine.

Threads

With so many threads available, it is good to know which ones you need for tailoring. An all-purpose thread is essential, as is a basting (tacking) thread. Threads vary in fibre content, from pure cotton to rayon to polyester; some are very fine while others are thick and coarse. Choose the correct type of thread to perfect your project, and avoid problems with the stitch quality of your sewing machine.

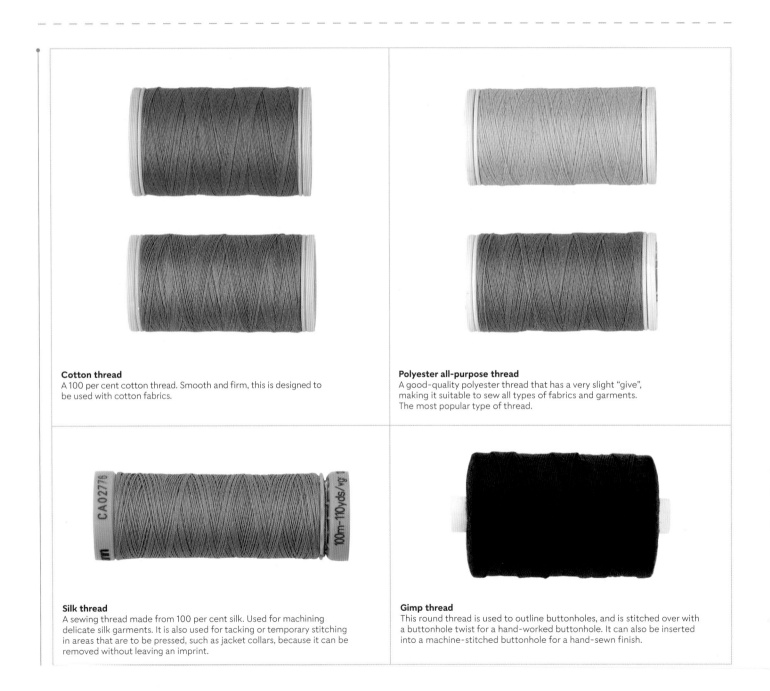

Cotton thread
A 100 per cent cotton thread. Smooth and firm, this is designed to be used with cotton fabrics.

Polyester all-purpose thread
A good-quality polyester thread that has a very slight "give", making it suitable to sew all types of fabrics and garments. The most popular type of thread.

Silk thread
A sewing thread made from 100 per cent silk. Used for machining delicate silk garments. It is also used for tacking or temporary stitching in areas that are to be pressed, such as jacket collars, because it can be removed without leaving an imprint.

Gimp thread
This round thread is used to outline buttonholes, and is stitched over with a buttonhole twist for a hand-worked buttonhole. It can also be inserted into a machine-stitched buttonhole for a hand-sewn finish.

Buttonhole twist thread
A strong, bold thread used for hand-sewn buttonholes. This may be silk or polyester and is around three times the diameter of normal sewing silk.

Top-stitching thread
A thicker polyester thread used for decorative top-stitching and buttonholes. Also for hand sewing buttons on thicker fabrics.

Overlocker thread
A dull yarn on a larger reel designed to be used on the overlocker. This type of yarn is normally not strong enough to use on the sewing machine.

Basting thread
When constructing tailored garments, a cotton basting or tacking thread can be used to temporarily hold layers together.

Tailor's haberdashery

Haberdashery for tailoring can be quite specific and often relates to a type of garment. Some of these items may not be commonly used in general dressmaking, but you may find them useful additions to your tailoring kit. All of these items should be available from any good haberdashery shop.

Piping (ready made) ▶
A cotton or polyester cord covered with a bias fabric. Has a flange to enable it to be sewn into a seam.

▲ **Trouser kick tape**
A woven tape with a reinforced edge. It is sewn onto the inside edge of a trouser hem to strengthen and prevent wear.

◀ **Seam tape**
A stable woven cotton or polycotton tape used to prevent stretching. Available in various widths.

◀ **Bias binding**
Bias cut fabric in either cotton or polyester. Available in different widths and is pre-folded, edges to centre.

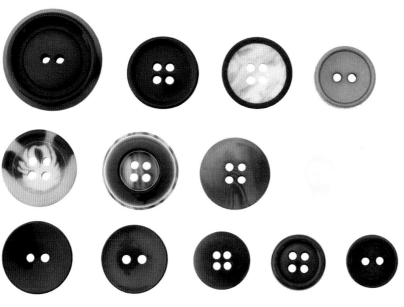

▲ Waistcoat buckles
A buckle designed to "cinch" the waistcoat at the back to give shape. Self-locking to hold the belt in place.

Trouser hooks ▶
Flat hooks and bars to fasten the waistband of skirts or trousers without any additional bulk.

▲ Buttons
Buttons are essential for jackets and coats and are available in a variety of sizes, materials, and colours. Choose matching large and small buttons for cuffs and centre fronts.

◀ Tailor's shoulder pads
A half-moon shaped pad made from felted wool type fabric and cotton wadding. Available in grey and ivory. Different thicknesses are available.

◀ Waistband tape
A specialist tape featuring a gripper strip, to hold a shirt in place. This is used primarily in smart suit or evening dress trouser waistbands.

◀ Sleeve head roll
A grey or ivory felted fabric, folded over a strip of canvas or sponge on the one edge. Inserted into sleeve heads to lift the shoulder and give a rounded look.

Pressing aids

Pressing your tailored garments will not only smooth out wrinkles, it will enhance the sharp, crisp lines of the garment, helping you to achieve a polished and professional finish.

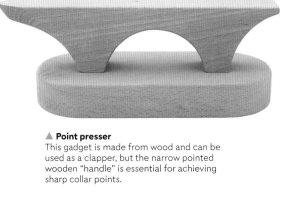

▲ Point presser
This gadget is made from wood and can be used as a clapper, but the narrow pointed wooden "handle" is essential for achieving sharp collar points.

▲ Iron
Choose a good-quality steam iron that has some weight to it. Specialist steam generator tailoring irons are available for domestic use.

Clapper ▶
A heavy piece of wood to be used after steaming. It will hold the steam in your fabric to help set a crisp edge.

◀ Ironing mat
A useful extra, this mat provides a heat-resistant flat surface, ideal for pressing small items.

◀ Velvet mat
A pressing mat with a tufted side to aid the pressing of pile fabrics, such as velvet.

◀ Pressing cloth
Choose a cloth made from silk organza, as you can see through it and it prevents shine on fabric.

◀ **Seam roll**
A long sausage-shaped padded roll for pressing inside trouser legs and shirt sleeves. Also used for pressing straight seams to avoid the seam imprinting on the fabric.

◀ **Tailor's ham**
This ham-shaped cushion is for aiding the pressing of princess curves and darts.

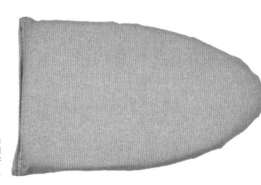

Pressing mitten ▶
With this on your hand you can press all those awkward inner corners, and protect your hand from hot steam if you are ironing or steaming garments.

▼ **Ironing board**
Essential for pressing pattern pieces and finished garments. Make sure the board is height-adjustable.

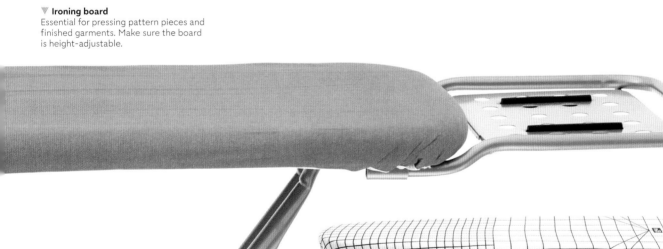

▲ **Sleeve board**
A sleeve board is useful for pressing sleeves and trouser legs, as well as small pieces of fabric such as collars.

Sewing machine

A sewing machine will quickly speed up any job, whether it be a quick repair or a huge home-sewing project. Most sewing machines today are aided by computer technology for stitch quality, and ease of use. If possible spend time trying out a sewing machine before you buy, to really get a feel for it.

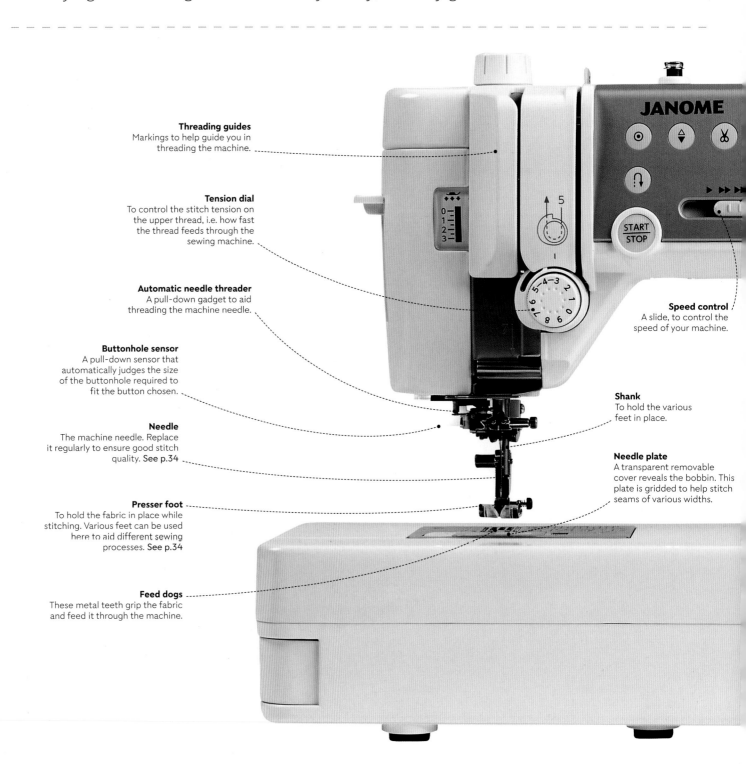

Threading guides
Markings to help guide you in threading the machine.

Tension dial
To control the stitch tension on the upper thread, i.e. how fast the thread feeds through the sewing machine.

Automatic needle threader
A pull-down gadget to aid threading the machine needle.

Buttonhole sensor
A pull-down sensor that automatically judges the size of the buttonhole required to fit the button chosen.

Needle
The machine needle. Replace it regularly to ensure good stitch quality. See p.34

Presser foot
To hold the fabric in place while stitching. Various feet can be used here to aid different sewing processes. See p.34

Feed dogs
These metal teeth grip the fabric and feed it through the machine.

Speed control
A slide, to control the speed of your machine.

Shank
To hold the various feet in place.

Needle plate
A transparent removable cover reveals the bobbin. This plate is gridded to help stitch seams of various widths.

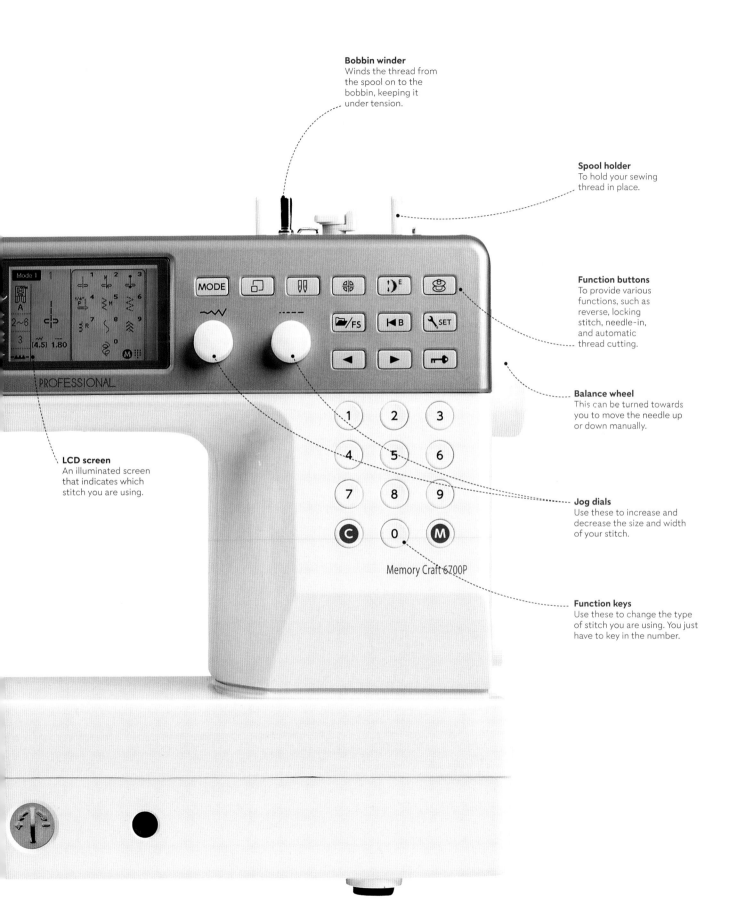

Bobbin winder
Winds the thread from the spool on to the bobbin, keeping it under tension.

Spool holder
To hold your sewing thread in place.

Function buttons
To provide various functions, such as reverse, locking stitch, needle-in, and automatic thread cutting.

Balance wheel
This can be turned towards you to move the needle up or down manually.

LCD screen
An illuminated screen that indicates which stitch you are using.

Jog dials
Use these to increase and decrease the size and width of your stitch.

Function keys
Use these to change the type of stitch you are using. You just have to key in the number.

SEWING-MACHINE ACCESSORIES

Many accessories can be purchased for your sewing machine to make certain sewing processes so much easier. There are different machine needles not only for different fabrics but also for different types of threads. There is also a huge number of sewing-machine feet, and new feet are constantly coming on to the market. Those shown here are the most useful for tailoring projects.

Plastic bobbin
The bobbin is for the lower thread. Some machines take plastic bobbins, others metal. Always check which sort of bobbin your machine uses as the incorrect choice can cause stitch problems.

Metal bobbin
Also known as a universal bobbin, this is used on many types of sewing machine. Be sure to check that your machine needs a metal bobbin before you buy.

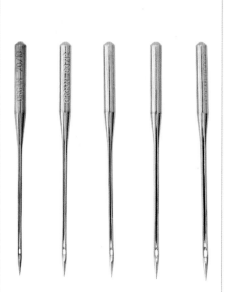

Machine needles
There are different types of sewing machine needles to cope with different fabrics. Machine needles are sized from 60 to 100, a 60 being a very fine needle.

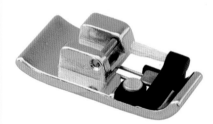

Overedge foot
A foot that runs along the raw edge of the fabric and holds it stable while an overedge stitch is worked.

Run and fell seam foot
This clever foot folds the fabric under as you sew to give a neat, even, flat fell seam.

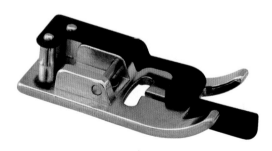

Stitch in the ditch foot
This foot guides the needle along the ditch line of a seam and is useful for securing waistband linings.

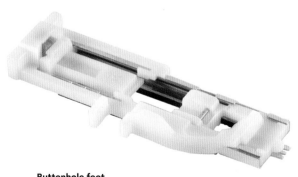

Buttonhole foot
This extends and the button is placed in the back of the foot. The machine will stitch a buttonhole to fit due to the buttonhole sensor.

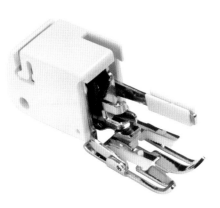

Walking foot
This strange-looking foot "walks" across the fabric, so that the upper layer of fabric does not push forward. Great for matching checks and stripes and also for difficult fabrics.

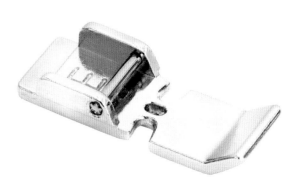

Zip foot
This foot fits to either the right- or left-hand side of the needle to enable you to stitch close to a zip.

Concealed zip foot
A foot that is used to insert a concealed zip – the foot holds open the coils of the zip, enabling you to stitch behind them.

Pin tuck foot
A foot with grooves underneath to allow multiple pin tucks to be sewn.

Piping foot
A deep groove in this foot allows a piping cord to fit underneath, enabling close stitching to the cord.

Blind hem foot
Use this foot in conjunction with the blind hem stitch to create a neat hemming stitch.

Overlocker

This machine is often used in conjunction with the sewing machine as it gives a very professional finish to your work. The overlocker has two upper threads and two lower threads (the loopers), with a knife that removes the edge of the fabric. Used extensively for neatening the edges of fabric, it can also be used for construction of stretch knits.

OVERLOCKER STITCHES

As the overlocker works, the threads wrap around the edge to give a professional finish. The 3-thread stitch is used primarily for neatening. A 4-thread stitch can also be used for neatening, as well as for construction due to its having the extra thread.

3-THREAD OVERLOCK STITCH

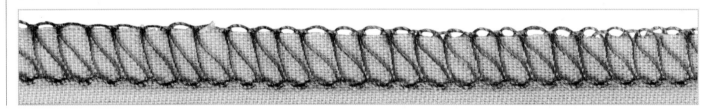

4-THREAD OVERLOCK STITCH

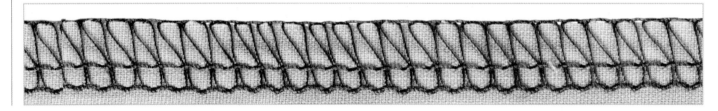

OVERLOCKER ACCESSORIES

You can purchase additional feet for the overlocker, such as a cording foot to aid decorative techniques.

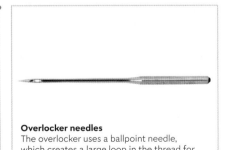

Overlocker needles
The overlocker uses a ballpoint needle, which creates a large loop in the thread for the loopers to catch and produce a stitch. If a normal sewing machine needle is used it could damage the overlocker.

Overlocker foot
The standard foot used for most processes.

Cording foot
A foot with a coil on one side through which a thin cord or fishing line is fed. Use in conjunction with a rolled hem setting for decorative effects.

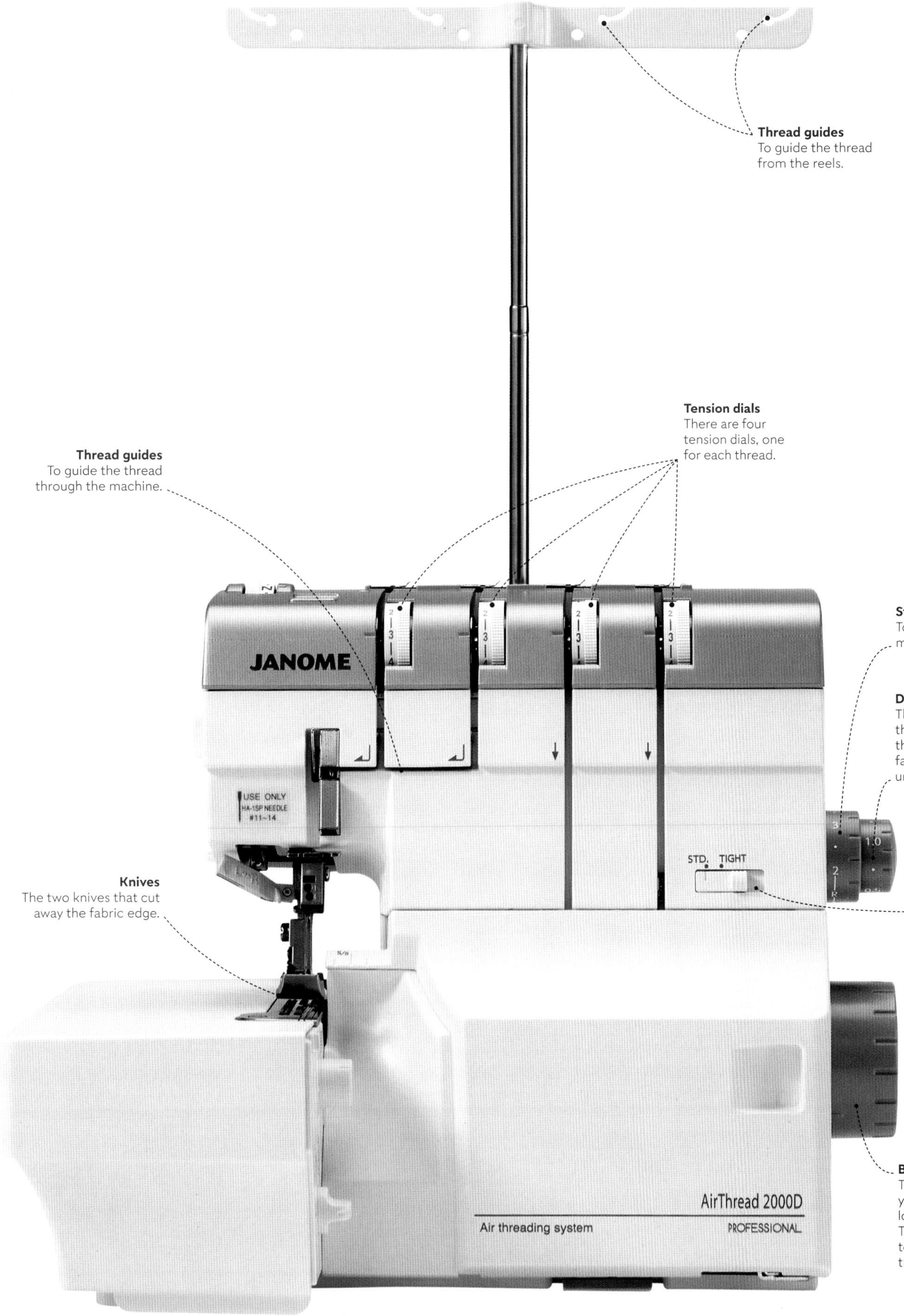

Thread guides
To guide the thread from the reels.

Tension dials
There are four tension dials, one for each thread.

Thread guides
To guide the thread through the machine.

Stitch length
To set the size of the machine stitch.

Differential feed
This dial controls the ratio between the two layers of fabric feeding under the foot.

JANOME

USE ONLY
HA-1SP NEEDLE
#11~14

STD. TIGHT

Knives
The two knives that cut away the fabric edge.

Lower looper pre-tension setting slider
This should be on STD when threading the machine. Slide to TIGHT for rolled hems and picot hems.

AirThread 2000D

Air threading system   PROFESSIONAL

Balance wheel
Turn this towards you to raise and lower the needles. Turn it backwards to disengage the threads.

Fabrics

Your choice of fabric will define the quality of your tailored garment. It will influence the drape, fit, and overall look of the garment and its functionality. Look for natural fibres, which will keep you warm in winter and cool in summer. You may also need to take fabric care into consideration as some suitings and silks are dry-clean only.

WOOL

A natural fibre, wool comes primarily from sheep – Australian merino sheep's wool is considered to be the best. However, we also get wool fibres from goats (angora, mohair, and cashmere), camels (camel hair), and llamas (alpaca). A wool fibre is either short and fluffy, when it is known as a woollen yarn, or it is long, strong, and smooth, when it is called worsted. The term virgin (or new) wool denotes wool fibres that are being used for the first time. Wool may be reprocessed or reused, and is often mixed with other fibres.

PROPERTIES OF WOOL

- ▶ **Comfortable to wear** in all climates as it is available in many weights and weaves
- ▶ **Warm in the winter** and cool in the summer, because it will breathe with your body
- ▶ **Absorbs moisture** better than other natural fibres – will absorb up to 30 per cent of its weight before it feels wet
- ▶ **Flame-resistant**

- ▶ **Relatively crease-resistant**
- ▶ **Ideal to tailor** as it can be easily shaped with steam
- ▶ **Often blended** with other fibres to reduce the cost of a fabric
- ▶ **Felts** if exposed to excessive heat, moisture, and pressure
- ▶ **Will be bleached** by sunlight with prolonged exposure
- ▶ **Can be damaged** by moths

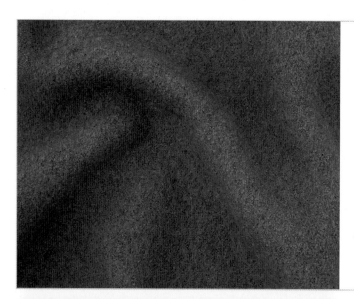

BOILED WOOL

Made from heat-treated wool or a wool blend, this does not fray or lose its shape. Known for its warmth and durability. It is also known for shrinking (if not bought pre-shrunk), so always test first by placing in a dryer set on a low temperature with a damp towel.

Cutting out:	a nap layout is not required
Seams:	walking foot; plain and neatened edges should not be required but some layering to reduce bulk may be required
Thread:	silk for pure wool; polycotton all-purpose thread for wool blends
Needle:	machine size 14/16 ballpoint needle depending on thickness of the fabric; sharps for hand sewing
Pressing:	wool setting with a pressing cloth; steam-press by holding the iron 2.5cm (1in) above the fabric for approximately 5 seconds
Used for:	coats, jackets, capes, and smaller items such as berets

CASHMERE

Wool from the Kashmir goat, and the most luxurious of all the wools. A soft yet hard-wearing fabric available in different weights.

Cutting out:	as cashmere often has a slight pile, use a nap layout
Seams:	plain, neatened with overlocker stitch or pinking shears (a zigzag stitch would curl the edge of the seam)
Thread:	a silk thread is ideal, or a polyester all-purpose thread
Needle:	machine size 12/14, depending on the thickness of the fabric; sharps for hand sewing
Pressing:	steam iron on a steam setting, with a pressing cloth and seam roll
Used for:	jackets, coats, knitted cashmere yarn for sweaters, cardigans, underwear

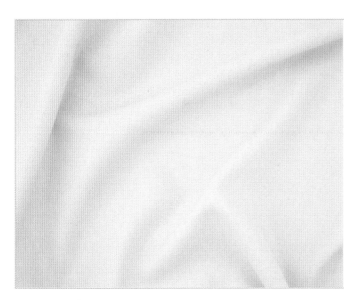

CHALLIS

A fine wool fabric, made from a worsted yarn that has an uneven surface texture. Challis is often printed as well as plain.

Cutting out: a nap layout is not required unless the fabric is printed

Seams: plain, neatened with overlocker or zigzag stitch; a run and fell seam can also be used

Thread: polyester all-purpose thread

Needle: machine size 11/12; sharps for hand sewing

Pressing: steam iron on a steam setting, with a pressing cloth; fabric will stretch while warm so handle with care

Used for: dresses, jackets, garments with pleating or draping detail

CREPE

A soft fabric made from a twisted yarn that produces an uneven surface. Crepe will have stretched on the bolt and is prone to shrinkage so it is important to pre-shrink it by steaming prior to use.

Cutting out: a nap layout is not required

Seams: plain, neatened with overlocker stitch (a zigzag stitch may curl the edge of the seam)

Thread: polyester all-purpose thread

Needle: machine size 12; sharps or milliner's for hand sewing

Pressing: steam iron on a wool setting; a pressing cloth is not always required

Used for: all types of clothing

FELTED WOOL

A woven fabric that has been washed and dried at a high temperature. During this process the wool shrinks and becomes thicker and gains a puffy texture, giving it a soft and fluffy feel.

Cutting out: for plain fabrics a nap layout is not required. Patterns, such as plaids, may need a nap layout

Seams: plain, neatened edges should not be required but some layering to reduce bulk may be required

Thread: silk or cotton

Needle: machine size 14/16 ballpoint needle depending on the thickness of fabric; 14/16 sharps for hand sewing

Pressing: wool setting with a pressing cloth

Used for: coats, jackets, waistcoats, and smaller items such as slippers and hats

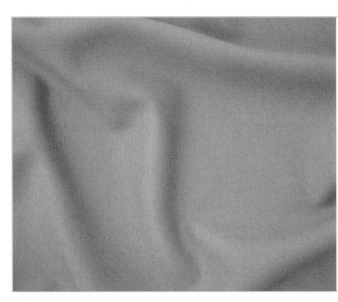

FLANNEL

A wool with a lightly brushed surface, featuring either a plain or a twill weave. Used in the past for underwear.

Cutting out: use a nap layout

Seams: plain, neatened with overlocker or zigzag stitch or a Hong Kong finish

Thread: polyester all-purpose thread

Needle: machine size 14; sharps for hand sewing

Pressing: steam iron on a wool setting with a pressing cloth; use a seam roll as the fabric is prone to marking

Used for: coats, jackets, skirts, trousers

GABARDINE

A hard-wearing suiting fabric with a distinctive weave. Gabardine often has a sheen and is prone to shine. It can be difficult to handle as it is springy and frays badly.

Cutting out: a nap layout is advisable as the fabric has a sheen

Seams: plain, neatened with overlocker or zigzag stitch

Thread: polyester all-purpose thread or 100 per cent cotton thread

Needle: machine size 14; sharps for hand sewing

Pressing: steam iron on a wool setting; use just the toe of the iron and a silk organza pressing cloth as the fabric will mark and may shine

Used for: jackets, trousers

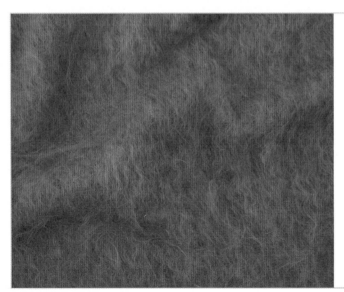

MOHAIR

From the wool of the Angora goat. A long, straight, and very strong fibre that produces a hairy cloth or yarn for knitting.

Cutting out: use a nap layout, with the fibres brushing down the pattern pieces in the same direction, from neck to hem

Seams: plain, neatened with overlocker stitch or pinking shears

Thread: polyester all-purpose thread

Needle: machine size 14; sharps for hand sewing

Pressing: steam iron on a wool setting; "stroke" the iron over the wool, moving in the direction of the nap

Used for: jackets, coats, knitted mohair yarns for sweaters

TARTAN

An authentic tartan belongs to a Scottish clan, and each has its own unique design that can only be used by that clan. The fabric is made using a twill weave from worsted yarns.

Cutting out: check the design for even/uneven checks as it may need a nap layout or even a single layer layout

Seams: lain, matching the pattern and neatened with overlocker or zigzag stitch

Thread: polyester all-purpose thread

Needle: machine size 14; sharps for hand sewing

Pressing: steam iron on a wool setting; may require a pressing cloth, so test first

Used for: traditionally kilts, but these days also skirts, trousers, jackets

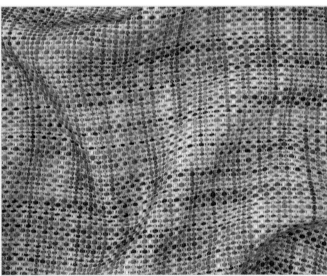

TWEED, MODERN

A mix of chunky and nobbly wool yarns. Modern tweed is often found in contemporary colour palettes as well as plain, and with interesting fibres in the weft such as metallics and paper. It is much favoured by fashion designers.

Cutting out: use a nap layout

Seams: plain, neatened with overlocker or zigzag stitch; the fabric is prone to fraying

Thread: polyester all-purpose thread

Needle: machine size 14; sharps for hand sewing

Pressing: steam iron on a wool setting; a pressing cloth may not be required

Used for: jackets, coats; also skirts, dresses

TWEED, TRADITIONAL

A rough fabric with a distinctive warp and weft, usually in different colours, and often forming a small check pattern. Traditional tweed is associated with the English countryside.

Cutting out: a nap layout is not required unless the fabric features a check

Seams: plain, neatened with overlocker or zigzag stitch; can also be neatened with pinking shears

Thread: polyester all-purpose thread or 100 per cent cotton thread

Needle: machine size 14; sharps for hand sewing

Pressing: steam iron on a steam setting; a pressing cloth may not be required

Used for: jackets, coats, skirts

WOOL WORSTED

A light and strong cloth, made from good-quality thin, firm filament fibres. Always steam prior to cutting out as the fabric may shrink slightly after having been stretched around a bolt.

Cutting out: use a nap layout

Seams: plain, neatened with overlocker or zigzag stitch or a Hong Kong finish

Thread: polyester all-purpose thread

Needle: machine size 12/14 depending on fabric; milliner's or sharps for hand sewing

Pressing: steam iron on a wool setting with a pressing cloth; use a seam roll to prevent the seam from showing through

Used for: skirts, jackets, coats, trouser

WOOL SUITING

A traditional cloth used in suits. A plain weave, but it may feature checks or pinstripes.

Cutting out: a nap layout will be required for checks and stripes

Seams: a plain seam neatened with a 3-thread overlock stitch

Thread: polyester all-purpose thread

Needle: on the machine a size 12 or 14, depending on the thickness of the cloth. For hand sewing a straw/milliners or betweens needle

Pressing: use a good steam iron, pressing cloth, and pressing aids as required

Used for: trousers, jackets, and waistcoats

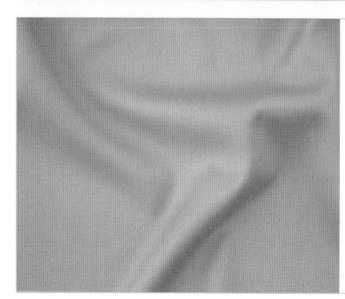

VENETIAN

A wool with a satin weave, making a luxurious, expensive fabric.

Cutting out: use a nap layout

Seams: plain, neatened with overlocker or zigzag stitch

Thread: polyester all–purpose thread or 100 per cent cotton thread

Needle: machine size 14; sharps for hand sewing

Pressing: steam iron on a steam setting with a silk organza cloth to avoid shine; use a seam roll under the seams to prevent them from showing through

Used for: jackets, coats,

COTTON

One of the most versatile and popular of all fabrics, cotton is a natural fibre that comes from the seed pods, or bolls, of the cotton plant. It is thought that cotton fibres have been in use since ancient times. Today, the world's biggest producers of cotton include the United States, India, and countries in the Middle East. Cotton fibres can be filament or staple, with the longest and finest used for top-quality bed linen. Cotton clothing is widely worn in warmer climates as the fabric will keep you cool.

PROPERTIES OF COTTON

▸ **Absorbs moisture well** and carries heat away from the body

▸ **Stronger wet** than dry

▸ **Does not build up static electricity**

▸ **Dyes well**

▸ **Prone to shrinkage** unless it has been treated

▸ **Will deteriorate** from mildew and prolonged exposure to sunlight

▸ **Creases easily**

▸ **Soils easily,** but launders well

CALICO

A plain-weave fabric that is usually unbleached and quite firm. Available in many different weights, from very fine to extremely heavy.

Cutting out:	a nap layout is not required
Seams:	plain, neatened with overlocker or zigzag stitch
Thread:	polyester all-purpose thread
Needle:	machine size 11/14 depending on thickness of thread; sharps for hand sewing
Pressing:	steam iron on a steam setting; a pressing cloth is not required
Used for:	toiles (test garments)

CHAMBRAY

A light cotton that has a coloured warp thread and white weft thread. Chambray can also be found as a check or a striped fabric.

Cutting out:	a nap layout should not be required
Seams:	plain, neatened with overlocker or zigzag stitch
Thread:	polyester all-purpose thread
Needle:	machine size 11; sharps for hand sewing
Pressing:	smachine size 11; sharps for hand sewing
Used for:	blouses, shirts, children's wear

CORDUROY

A soft pile fabric with distinctive stripes (known as wales or ribs) woven into it. The name depends on the size of the ribs: baby or pin cord has extremely fine ribs; needle cord has slightly thicker ribs; corduroy has 10–12 ribs per 2.5cm (1in); and elephant or jumbo cord has thick, heavy ribs.

Cutting out:	use a nap layout with the pile on the corduroy brushing up the pattern pieces from hem to neck, to give depth of colour
Seams:	plain, stitched using a walking foot and neatened with overlocker or zigzag stitch
Thread:	polyester all-purpose thread
Needle:	machine size 12/16; sharps or milliner's for hand sewing
Pressing:	steam iron on a cotton setting; use a seam roll under the seams with a pressing cloth
Used for:	trousers, skirts

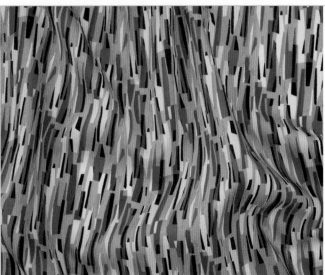

COTTON LAWN

A plain-weave fabric woven from fine, high-density yarns, which results in a silky, smooth feel.

Cutting out:	a nap layout is not required unless the fabric has a one-way print
Seams:	plain, neatened with overlocker or zigzag stitch; French
Thread:	pure cotton thread; or a polyester all-purpose thread
Needle:	machine size 11; or a milliner's size 9 for hand sewing
Pressing:	steam iron on a cotton setting; a pressing cloth should not be required
Used for:	blouses, shirts, dresses, children's wear, interlining

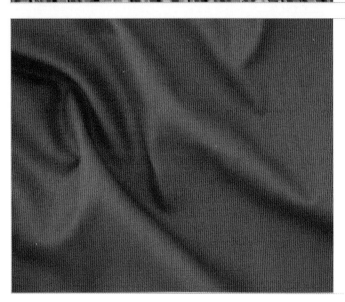

DRILL

A hard-wearing twill or plain-weave fabric with the same colour warp and weft. Drill frays badly on the cut edges.

Cutting out:	a nap layout is not required
Seams:	run and fell; or plain, neatened with overlocker or zigzag stitch
Thread:	polyester all-purpose thread with top-stitching thread for detail top-stitching
Needle:	machine size 14; sharps for hand sewing
Pressing:	steam iron on a cotton setting; a pressing cloth is not required
Used for:	casual jackets, trousers

GINGHAM

A fresh, two-colour cotton fabric that features a check of various sizes. A plain weave made by having groups of white and coloured warp and weft threads.

Cutting out: usually an even check, so nap layout is not required but recommended; pattern will need matching

Seams: plain, neatened with overlocker or zigzag stitch

Thread: polyester all-purpose thread

Needle: machine size 11/12; sharps for hand sewing

Pressing: steam iron on a cotton setting; a pressing cloth should not be required

Used for: children's wear, dresses, shirts

MADRAS

A check fabric made from a fine cotton yarn, usually from India. Often found in bright colours featuring an uneven check. An inexpensive cotton fabric.

Cutting out: use a nap layout and match the check

Seams: plain, neatened with overlocker or zigzag stitch

Thread: polyester all-purpose thread

Needle: machine size 12/14; sharps for hand sewing

Pressing: steam iron on a cotton setting; a pressing cloth is not required

Used for: shirts, skirts

MUSLIN

A fine, plain, open-weave cotton. Can be found in colours but usually sold as natural/unbleached or white. Makes great pressing cloths and interlinings. Washing prior to use is recommended.

Cutting out: a nap layout is not required

Seams: 4-thread overlock stitch or plain seam, neatened with overlocker or zigzag stitch; a French seam could also be used

Thread: polyester all–purpose thread

Needle: machine size 11; milliner's for hand sewing

Pressing: steam iron on a cotton setting; a cloth is not required

Used for: pressing cloth, linings, interlinings, toiles (test garments)

SEERSUCKER

A woven cotton that has a bubbly appearance woven into it, due to stripes of puckers. Do not over-press, or the surface effect will be damaged.

Cutting out:	use a nap layout, due to puckered surface effect
Seams:	plain, neatened with overlocker or zigzag stitch
Thread:	polyester all-purpose thread
Needle:	machine size 11/12; milliner's for hand sewing
Pressing:	steam iron on a cotton setting (be careful not to press out the wrinkles)
Used for:	summer clothing, skirts, shirts, children's wear

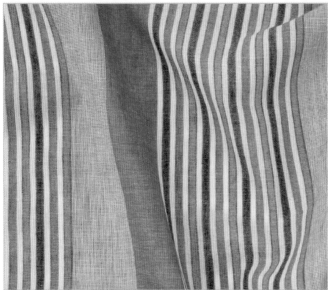

SHIRTING

A closely woven, fine cotton with coloured warp and weft yarns making stripes or checks.

Cutting out:	use a nap layout if fabric has uneven stripes
Seams:	plain, neatened with overlocker or zigzag stitch; a run and fell seam can also be used
Thread:	polyester all-purpose thread
Needle:	machine size 12; milliner's for hand sewing
Pressing:	steam iron on a cotton setting; a pressing cloth is not required
Used for:	shirts

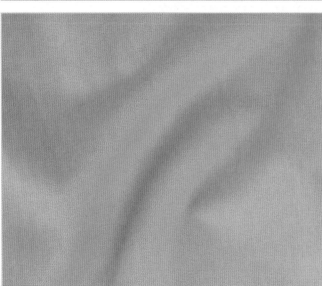

VELVET

A pile-weave fabric, made by using an additional yarn that is then cut to produce the pile. Difficult to handle and can be easily damaged if seams have to be unpicked.

Cutting out:	use a nap layout with the pile brushing up from hem to neck, to give depth of colour
Seams:	plain, stitched using a walking foot (stitch all seams from hem to neck) and neatened with overlocker or zigzag stitch
Thread:	polyester all-purpose thread
Needle:	machine size 14; milliner's for hand sewing
Pressing:	only if you have to; use a velvet board, a little steam, the toe of the iron, and a silk organza cloth
Used for:	jackets, coats

LINEN

Linen is a natural fibre that is derived from the stem of the flax plant. It is available in a variety of qualities and weights, from very fine linen to heavy suiting weights. Coarser than cotton, it is sometimes woven with cotton as well as being mixed with silk.

PROPERTIES OF LINEN

▶ **Cool and comfortable** to wear

▶ **Absorbs moisture well**

▶ **Shrinks** when washed

▶ **Does not ease well**

▶ **Has a tendency to crease**

▶ **Prone to fraying**

▶ **Resists moths** but is damaged by mildew

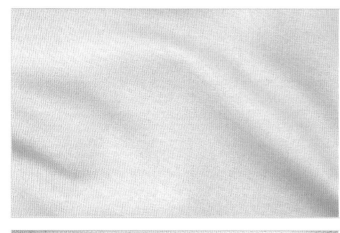

COTTON AND LINEN MIX

Two fibres may have been mixed together in the yarn or there may be mixed warp and weft yarns. It has lots of texture in the weave.

Cutting out: a nap layout should not be required

Seams: plain, neatened with overlocker or zigzag stitch

Thread: polyester all-purpose thread

Needle: machine size 14; sharps for hand sewing

Pressing: a steam iron on a steam setting with a silk organza pressing cloth

Used for: summer-weight jackets, tailored dresses

FANCY WEAVE LINEN

A linen woven with additional decorative yarns such as metallicor lurex.

Cutting out: a nap layout is not required

Seams: plain, neatened with overlocker or a zigzag stitch

Thread: polyester all-purpose thread with a top-stitch thread for top-stitching

Needle: machine size 14; sharps for hand sewing

Pressing: press carefully as decorative yarns may melt; use a pressing cloth

Used for: dresses, jackets

SUITING LINEN

A heavier yarn is used to produce a linen suitable for suits for men and women. Can be a firm, tight weave or a looser weave.

Cutting out: a nap layout is not required

Seams: plain, neatened with overlocker or a zigzag stitch

Thread: polyester all-purpose thread with a top-stitch thread for top-stitching

Needle: machine size 14; sharps for hand sewing

Pressing: steam iron on a cotton setting (steam is required to remove creases)

Used for: suits, trousers, coats

SILK FABRICS

Often referred to as the queen of all fabrics, silk is made from the fibres of the silkworm's cocoon. This strong and luxurious fabric dates back thousands of years to its first development in China, and the secret of silk production was well protected by the Chinese until 300 CE. Silk fabrics can be very fine or thick and chunky. They need careful handling as some silk fabrics can be easily damaged.

PROPERTIES OF SILK

- ▶ **Keeps you warm** in winter and cool in summer
- ▶ **Absorbs moisture** and dries quickly
- ▶ **Dyes well,** producing deep, rich colours
- ▶ **Static electricity** can build up and fabric may cling
- ▶ **Will fade in prolonged** strong sunlight

- ▶ **Prone to shrinkage**
- ▶ **Best dry-cleaned**
- ▶ **Weaker when wet** than dry
- ▶ **May water-mark**

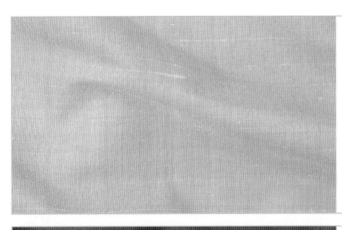

DUPION

Woven using a textured yarn that produces irregularities in the weave.

Cutting out:	use a nap layout to prevent shadowing
Seams:	plain, neatened with overlocker or zigzag stitch
Thread:	polyester all-purpose thread
Needle:	machine size 12; milliner's for hand sewing
Pressing:	steam iron on a wool setting with a pressing cloth as fabric may water-mark
Used for:	dresses, skirts, jackets, special-occasion wear

DUPION, HAND-WOVEN

The most popular of all the silks. A distinctive weft yarn with many nubbly bits. Available in hundreds of colours. Easy to handle, but it does fray badly.

Cutting out:	use a nap layout as the fabric shadows
Seams:	plain, neatened with overlocker or zigzag stitch
Thread:	polyester all-purpose thread
Needle:	machine size 12; milliner's for hand sewing
Pressing:	steam iron on a wool setting, with a pressing cloth to avoid water-marking
Used for:	dresses, special-occasion wear, jackets

HABUTAI

Originally from Japan, a smooth, fine silk that can have a plain or a twill weave. Fabric is often used for silk painting.

Cutting out:	a nap layout is not required
Seams:	French
Thread:	polyester all-purpose thread
Needle:	machine size 9/11; very fine milliner's or betweens for hand sewing
Pressing:	steam iron on a wool setting
Used for:	lining, shirts, blouses

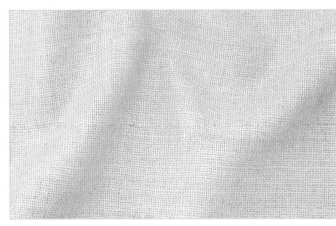

MATKA

A silk suiting fabric with an uneven-looking yarn. Matka can be mistaken for linen.

Cutting out: use a nap layout as silk may shadow

Seams: plain, neatened with overlocker or zigzag stitch or a Hong Kong finish

Thread: polyester all-purpose thread

Needle: machine size 12/14; milliner's for hand sewing

Pressing: steam iron on a wool setting with a pressing cloth; a seam roll is recommended to prevent the seams from showing through

Used for: dresses, jackets, trousers

ORGANZA

A sheer fabric with a crisp appearance that will crease easily.

Cutting out: a nap layout is not required

Seams: French or use a seam for a difficult fabric

Thread: polyester all-purpose thread

Needle: machine size 11; milliner's or betweens for hand sewing

Pressing: steam iron on a wool setting; a pressing cloth should not be required

Used for: sheer blouses, shrugs, interlining, interfacing

SATIN

A silk with a satin weave that can be very light to quite heavy in weight.

Cutting out: use a nap layout in a single layer as fabric is slippery

Seams: French; on thicker satins, use a seam for a difficult fabric

Thread: polyester all-purpose thread (not silk thread as it becomes weak with wear)

Needle: machine size 11/12; milliner's or betweens for hand sewing

Pressing: steam iron on a wool setting with a pressing cloth as fabric may water-mark

Used for: blouses, dresses, special-occasion wear

SILK AND WOOL MIX

A fabric made by mixing wool and silk fibres or wool and silk yarns. The fabric made may be fine in quality or thick, like a coating.

Cutting out: use a nap layout

Seams: plain, neatened with overlocker or zigzag stitch

Thread: polyester all-purpose thread

Needle: machine size 11/14, depending on fabric; sharps for hand sewing

Pressing: steam iron on a wool setting; seams will require some steam to make them lie flat

Used for: suits, skirts, trousers, coats

SYNTHETIC FABRICS

The term synthetic applies to any fabric that is not 100 per cent natural. Many of these fabrics have been developed over the last hundred years, which means they are new compared to natural fibres. Some synthetic fabrics are made from natural elements mixed with chemicals, while others are made entirely from non-natural substances. The properties of synthetic fabrics vary from fabric to fabric.

PROPERTIES OF SYNTHETIC FABRICS

▶ **Durable** and usually launder well

▶ **Can be prone to static** and "cling" to the body

▶ **Can dye well** and are often digitally printed

▶ **Mix well with natural fibres**

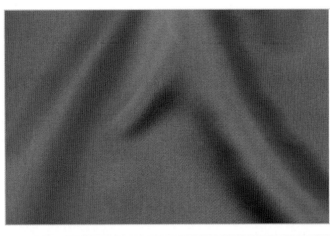

ACETATE

Introduced in 1924, acetate is made from cellulose and chemicals. The fabric has a slight shine and is widely used for linings. Acetate can also be woven into fabrics such as acetate taffeta, acetate satin, and acetate jersey.

Properties of acetate:	• Dyes well • Can be heat-set into pleats	• Washes well
Cutting out:	use a nap layout due to sheen on fabric	
Seams:	plain, neatened with overlocker or zigzag stitch, or 4-thread overlock stitch	
Thread:	polyester all-purpose thread	
Needle:	machine size 11; sharps for hand sewing	
Pressing:	steam iron on a cool setting (fabric can melt)	
Used for:	special-occasion wear, linings	

POLYESTER

One of the most popular of the man-made fibres, polyester was introduced in 1951 as a man's washable suiting. Polyester fibres are made from petroleum by-products and can take on any form, from a very fine sheer fabric to a thick, heavy suiting.

Properties of polyester	• Non-absorbent • Can build up static	• Does not crease • May "pill"
Cutting out:	a nap layout is only required if the fabric is printed	
Seams:	French, plain, or 4-thread overlock, depending on the weight of the fabric	
Thread:	polyester all-purpose thread	
Needle:	machine size 11/14; sharps for hand sewing	
Pressing:	steam iron on a wool setting	
Used for:	workwear, school uniforms, shirts, trousers, jackets	

RAYON

Also known as viscose and often referred to as artificial silk, this fibre was developed in 1889. It is made from wood pulp or cotton linters mixed with chemicals. Rayon can be knitted or woven and made into a wide range of fabrics. It is often blended with other fibres.

Properties of rayon:	• Absorbent • Non-static	• Dyes well • Frays badly
Cutting out:	a nap layout is only required if the fabric is printed	
Seams:	plain, neatened with overlocker or zigzag stitch	
Thread:	polyester all-purpose thread	
Needle:	machine size 12/14; sharps for hand sewing	
Pressing:	steam iron on a silk setting	
Used for:	dresses, blouses, jackets	

ECO-FRIENDLY FABRICS

Traditional fabric production methods may have a negative impact on the environment, with some using harmful chemicals or large amounts of water. Haberdasheries now sell a growing number of eco-friendly fabrics. Such fabrics are produced using raw ingredients that do not use pesticides, synthetic fertilizers, or chemicals that damage the environment and wildlife. They may also use fibres from sustainable and renewable sources, such as hemp and bamboo, and can be easier to recycle, too.

WHAT MAKES A FABRIC ECO-FRIENDLY?

▶ **Eco-fabrics are fabrics** that use plant-based, biodegradable raw materials, and are produced using ethical and environmentally sustainable methods. Unlike traditional textile production, eco-fabric production does not utilize chemicals that may harm the environment and wildlife.

▶ **Not all natural fibres** are necessarily eco-friendly – it is all down to the way they are produced. For example, much bamboo viscose is manufactured in a way that is harmful to both workers and the environment. However, bamboo fabrics produced in a closed-loop system reuse chemicals rather than releasing them. Even better are those that use natural enzymes – this process results in a soft yarn used to make bamboo linen.

▶ **Some eco-fabrics** are made solely from recycled textiles, helping to reuse some of the 13 million tonnes of clothing thrown out each year.

BIO LINEN

A fabric made from the flax plant, which requires less water during the growing process than cotton. This fabric is absorbent and breathable, which means it is cool to wear in the summer but provides an insulating layer during the colder months. It is washed with bio enzymes, rather than chemicals, making it soft.

Cutting out:	a nap layout is only required if the fabric is printed
Seams:	plain, neatened with a 3-thread overlocker or zigzag stitch; a run and fell seam could also be used
Thread:	polyester all-purpose thread
Needle:	machine size 11/12; sharps for hand sewing
Pressing:	steam iron on a cotton setting; a pressing cloth should not be required
Used for:	skirts, shirts, tunics, trousers, shorts, dresses

LYOCELL

Lyocell is a relatively new fibre, made from the wood pulp of trees like eucalyptus, oak, birch, and bamboo. It is 100 per cent biodegradable and compostable.

Properties of lyocell:	• Sustainable	• Breathes with your body
	• Soft to wear	• Does not crease excessively
	• Strong and durable	
Disadvantages:	• Still more expensive than viscose as it's a new fibre requiring specific manufacturing processes.	
Cutting out:	cut a nap layout if possible and use fine pins	
Seams:	depending on the fabric – for wovens use a plain seam neatened with the overlocker or a french seam. On a knit use a 4-thread overlock seam	
Thread:	polyester all-purpose thread	
Needle:	size 14 needle for the sewing machine and a straw needle size 9 for hand sewing	
Pressing:	steam iron with a silk organza press cloth	
Used for:	sportswear, bedding, trousers, shirts	

ECO-VISCOSE

Viscose comes from wood pulp cellulose from fast-growing, regenerative trees. It absorbs moisture well but can shrink during washing, so it is advisable to wash prior to cutting.

Cutting out: a nap layout is only required if the fabric is printed; it has a tendency to move while cutting, so use a rotary cutter rather than scissors to cut out

Seams: plain, neatened with a 3-thread overlocker or zigzag stitch

Thread: polyester all-purpose thread

Needle: machine size 10/11; sharps for hand stitching; the use of a walking foot may make sewing easier

Pressing: medium heat setting; use a pressing cloth

Used for: blouses, dresses, skirts, coats, jackets

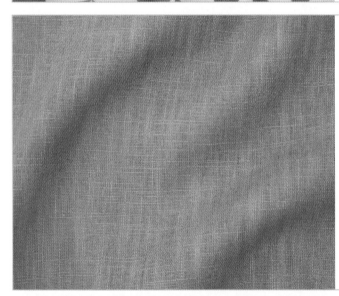

RAMIE

A hard-wearing fabric made from nettle fibres. It is often mixed with other fibres such as cotton, wool, and silk. It is a breathable fabric, similar in appearance to linen, and is cool to wear. Resistant to shrinking but creases easily. It is also bacteria resistant.

Cutting out: use a nap layout

Seams: plain, neatened with a 3-thread overlocker or zigzag stitch

Thread: polyester all-purpose thread

Needle: machine size 14; sharps for hand sewing

Pressing: use a high temperature and a pressing cloth

Used for: All types of garments

RECYCLED POLYESTER SATIN

While not made from natural fibres, recycled polyester is an eco-friendly, less wasteful alternative to virgin synthetic fabrics. It is made from recycled plastic bottles, which means less energy is required to make it than virgin polyester. It has a sheen on one side and a matt finish on the other. It is long lasting, soft to touch, and drapes well; however, it can be less durable than virgin polyester.

Cutting out: a nap layout is only required if the fabric is printed

Seams: plain, with a 3-thread overlocker or zigzag stitch

Thread: polyester all-purpose thread

Needle: machine size 14; sharps for hand sewing

Pressing: cool iron; swatch test advised

Used for: blouses, dresses, skirts, coats, jackets

FABRIC CONSTRUCTION

Most fabric is made by either knitting or weaving. A knitted fabric is constructed by interlocking looped yarns. For a woven fabric, horizontal and vertical yarns go under and over each other. The warp yarn, which is the strongest, runs vertically and the weft crosses it at right angles. There are also non-woven fabrics created by a felting process where tiny fibres are mixed and squeezed together, then rolled out.

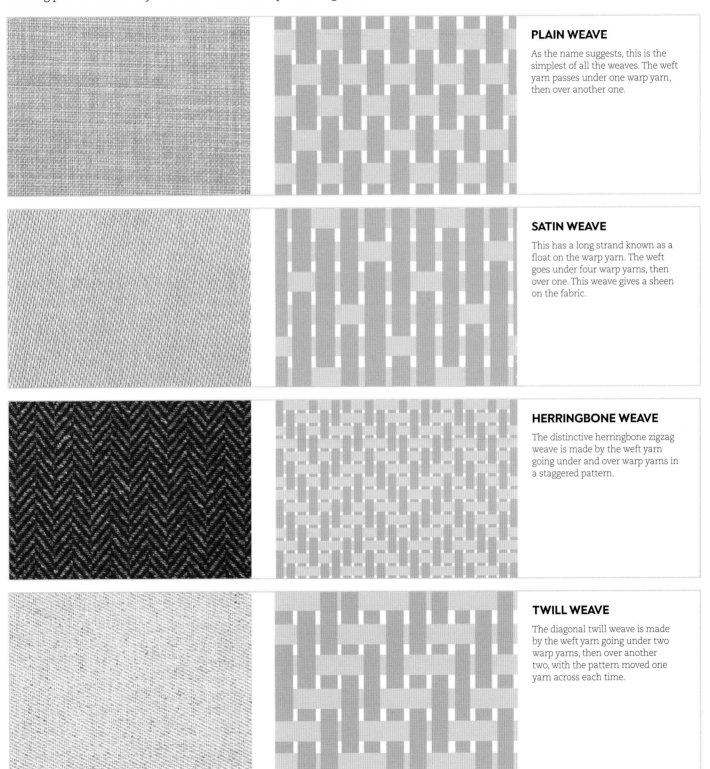

PLAIN WEAVE

As the name suggests, this is the simplest of all the weaves. The weft yarn passes under one warp yarn, then over another one.

SATIN WEAVE

This has a long strand known as a float on the warp yarn. The weft goes under four warp yarns, then over one. This weave gives a sheen on the fabric.

HERRINGBONE WEAVE

The distinctive herringbone zigzag weave is made by the weft yarn going under and over warp yarns in a staggered pattern.

TWILL WEAVE

The diagonal twill weave is made by the weft yarn going under two warp yarns, then over another two, with the pattern moved one yarn across each time.

Interlinings, interfacings, tapes, and linings

Interlinings, interfacings, and linings may all sound similar, but each fabric has its own unique job to do in tailoring. Sometimes these fabrics are used in combination, to create the structure required for a tailored garment. It's important that you understand the role of each fabric and how to apply it. Always test your chosen interfacing or interlining on some scrap fabric before applying to your garment.

INTERLININGS

An interlining (also known as underlining) is a sew-in fabric that is attached to the main fashion fabric prior to construction and the two fabrics are treated as one. The purpose of an interlining is to provide stability to a fragile fabric, to hide inner construction, or to provide structure. In certain tailored garments an interlining can play a vital role. The following fabrics are all ideal for interlining and are natural fibres.

HOW TO APPLY INTERLININGS

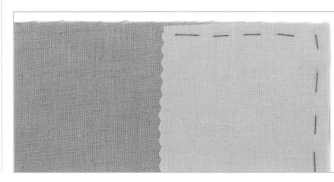

1 Lay the interlining on top of the fabric.

2 Pin at the edges, and press the two layers together to smooth the fabrics out.

3 Then tack around the raw edges, keeping it flat on the table at all times.

4 On large pieces it is advisable to also add vertical diagonal tacking stitches.

MUSLIN

A loose weave 100 per cent cotton fabric, also known as butter muslin. Wash before use as the weave may tighten a little. Provides a good base for canvas tailoring methods.

Cutting out:	cut on the straight grain, nap layout not required
Seams:	as this fabric will be mounted onto the fashion fabric, seam as appropriate to the fashion fabric, but normally a plain seam pressed open. Seam neatening will depend on the garment
Thread:	all-purpose polyester thread
Needle:	machine size 14, hand sewing straw needle size 9
Pressing:	press with a steam iron
Used for:	interlining wool, cotton, and linen fabrics for skirts, jackets, and lightweight dresses

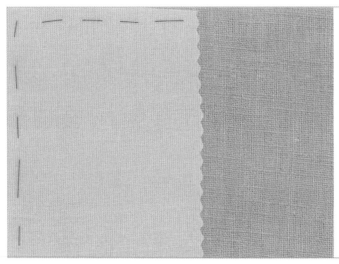

SILK ORGANZA

Silk organza (100 per cent silk) is a wonderful interlining as it gives shape and structure without weight.

Cutting out:	cut on the straight grain, nap layout not required
Seams:	the seam will depend on the fashion fabric and garment, but usually a plain seam pressed open
Thread:	all-purpose polyester thread
Needle:	machine size 14, hand sewing straw needle size 9
Pressing:	press with a steam iron, pressing cloth might be required
Used for:	interlining silk and silk blends, wool, fashion tweeds, and linen for skirts, jackets, and special-occasion wear

COTTON LAWN

A high thread count fine 100 per cent cotton fabric that is soft and durable.

Cutting out: cut on the straight grain, nap layout not required

Seams: the seam will depend on the fashion fabric and garment, but usually a plain seam pressed open

Thread: all-purpose polyester thread

Needle: machine size 12/14, hand sewing straw needle size 9

Pressing: press with a steam iron, pressing cloth might be required

Used for: interlining cottons and linens for special-occasion wear, skirts, bodices, and jackets.

FUSIBLE INTERFACINGS

Fusible interfacing is invaluable in some types of tailoring, used to provide structure and support in garment construction. Always cut fusible interfacings on the straight grain as they all stretch slightly selvedge to selvedge. Fusible interfacings fall into three categories – woven, knitted, and non-woven.

HOW TO APPLY A FUSIBLE INTERFACING

1 Place the fabric on the pressing surface, wrong side up, making sure it is straight and not wrinkled.

2 Place the sticky side (this feels gritty) of the chosen interfacing on the fabric.

3 Cover with a dry pressing cloth and spray the cloth with a fine mist of water.

4 Place a steam iron, on a steam setting, on top of the pressing cloth.

5 Leave the iron in place for at least 10 seconds before moving it to the next area of fabric.

6 Check to see if the interfacing is fused to the fabric by rolling the fabric. If the interfacing is still loose in places, repeat the pressing process.

7 When the fabric has cooled down, the fusing process will be complete. Then pin the pattern back on to the fabric and transfer the pattern markings as required.

WOVEN FUSIBLE INTERFACINGS

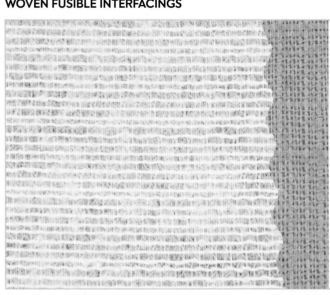

WEFT INSERTION

An interfacing with a dominant weft thread used specifically for tailoring. Remove any seam allowances darts prior to fusing.

Cutting out: always cut on the same grain as the pattern piece and remove the seam allowances and any darts

Pressing: fuse in place for 12 seconds

Used for: fuse to jacket and coat fronts, lapels, and waistbands

LIGHTWEIGHT WOVEN FUSIBLE

A very fine woven fusible made from polyester.

Cutting out: always cut on the same grain as the pattern piece and remove the seam allowances and any darts

Pressing: fuse in place for 8–10 seconds using a steam iron and a pressing cloth

Used for: use on fine fabrics such as chiffon, georgette, viscose, or lawn to give support with little weight. Can be used to support loose weave fashion tweeds. Also used in tailoring on jackets and coats

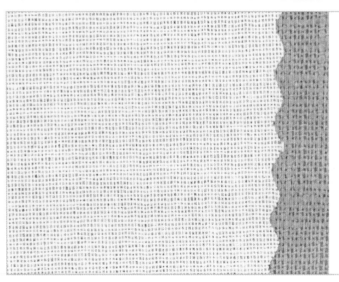

LIGHTWEIGHT COTTON FUSIBLE

A lightweight woven cotton fusible.

Cutting out: always cut on the same grain as the pattern piece and remove the seam allowances and any darts

Pressing: fuse in place for 10–12 seconds using a steam iron and a pressing cloth

Used for: use where more structure and support is required as has more weight than the lightweight woven, and for small area application such as collars and cuffs. Use with cottons, linens, and polyesters. Widely used in special occasion wear

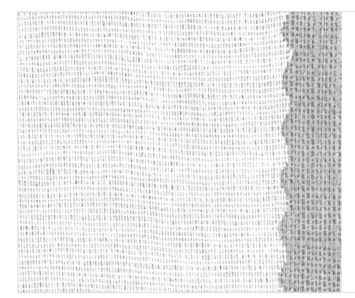

MEDIUM WEIGHT COTTON FUSIBLE

A heavier cotton woven interfacing than the opposite. It may have a brushed feel to it.

Cutting out: always cut on the same grain as the pattern piece

Pressing: fuse in place for 12 seconds using a steam iron and a pressing cloth

Used for: Use on small areas, such as cuffs and also on jackets and coats. Use on medium to heavy fabrics such as wool suitings and tweeds

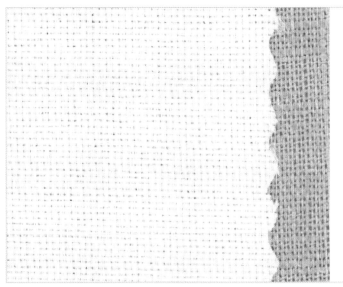

HEAVY POLYESTER WOVEN FUSIBLE

A polyester fusible interfacing with a distinctive weave.

Cutting out: always cut on the same grain as the pattern piece

Pressing: fuse in place for 8 seconds using a steam iron and a pressing cloth

Used for: small area application and tailored jacket fronts. Use on wool, tweed, suiting weight linens, acrylics, and polyester. Widely used in ready-to-wear garments

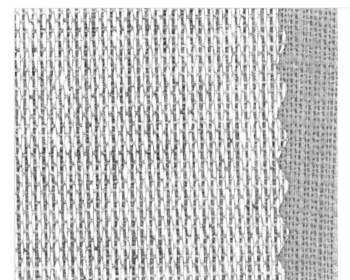

FUSIBLE CANVAS

A fusible version of a tailoring canvas. Fibre content will be mixed with some wool or cotton content.

Cutting out: cut on the grain or as appropriate to the jacket

Pressing: fuse in place for 12 seconds with a steam iron and pressing cloth

Used for: jacket front parts. Widely used in ready-to-wear

KNITTED FUSIBLE INTERFACING

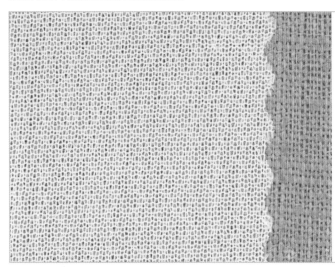

STRETCH KNIT FUSIBLE

A fine knitted fusible with lots of stretch selvedge to selvedge.

Cutting out: cut on the straight grain so the stretch goes around the body

Pressing: fuse in place for 8–10 seconds with a steam iron and pressing cloth

Used for: ideal for stretch fabrics. Also use on loosely woven tweeds and to support large sections on jackets and coats

NON-WOVEN FUSIBLE INTERFACING

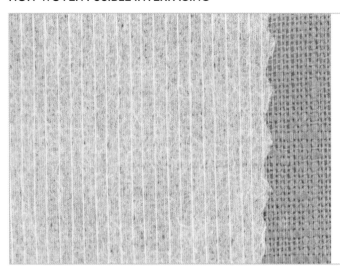

STITCH REINFORCED

A non-woven fusible with a lengthwise stitch running parallel to the selvedge.

Cutting out: cut on the straight grain or as appropriate to the pattern. Remove seam allowances and any darts to reduce the bulk on the seams

Pressing: fuse in place for 12 seconds using a steam iron and a pressing cloth

Used for: designed specifically for tailoring. The stitch reinforcement holds the fabric on grain. Use in any fabric suitable for a jacket or coat

LIGHTWEIGHT

A lightweight non-woven fusible interfacing that is semi sheer.

Cutting out: cut on the straight grain

Pressing: fuse in place for 8–10 seconds using a steam iron and a pressing cloth

Used for: small area application, shaped waistbands, centre fronts, and soft cuffs. Use on lightweight fabrics, cotton lawn, viscose, silk, and polyester

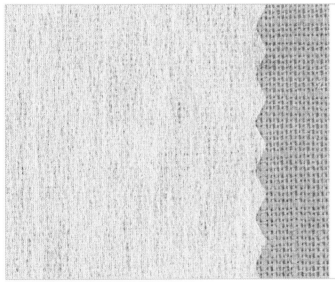

MEDIUM WEIGHT

A medium weight non-woven fusible that is a little denser than the lightweight.

Cutting out: cut on the straight grain

Pressing: fuse in place for 8–10 seconds using a steam iron and a pressing cloth

Used for: small area application such as collars, cuffs, and waistbands. Use on cottons, polycotton, twill weaves, lightweight wools, and linens

HEAVYWEIGHT

A heavyweight non-woven fusible interfacing on which the glue dots are more visible.

Cutting out: cut on the straight grain

Pressing: fuse in place for 10–12 seconds using a steam iron and a pressing cloth

Used for: small area application such as collars, cuffs, waistbands, and trouser hems. Use on wools, tweeds, and linens

FUSIBLE CHEST FELT

A fusible needle-punched felted fabric made from mixed fibres.

Cutting out: cut on the straight grain or as the pattern dictates

Pressing: fuse in place for 12 seconds with a steam iron and pressing cloth

Used for: jacket and coat fronts to create the chest plate

SEW-IN INTERFACINGS

These are tailoring interfacings that are sewn into the fashion fabric using pad stitching. They contain natural fibres so that they can be moulded into shape.

HOW TO APPLY SEW-IN INTERFACING

1 Place the interfacing on to the wrong side of the fabric, aligning the cut edges.

2 Pin in place.

3 Using a basic tacking stitch, tack the interfacing to the fabric or facing at 1cm (⅜in) within the seam allowance.

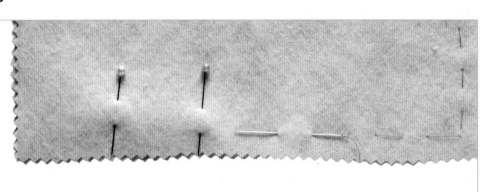

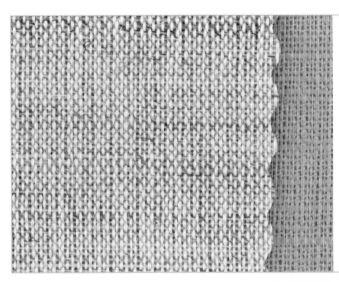

LIGHTWEIGHT/MEDIUM/HEAVY CANVAS

Sew-in tailoring canvas comes in various weights to suit all types of fabric and styles of suit or coat. Choose a canvas that is lighter than the fashion fabric.

Cutting out: cut on the straight grain or as appropriate to the pattern

Seams: overlaid seams

Thread: all-purpose polyester thread

Needle: a straw or betweens needle

Pressing: shape over a tailor's ham with a steam iron

Used for: shape, structure, and support in tailored jackets and coats. Used for chest plates and floating shoulders. Can also be used for hems and waistbands

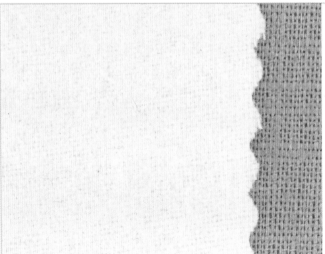

DOMETTE FOR CHEST PLATE

A soft woven brushed fabric of mixed fibres.

Cutting out: cut on the same grain as the pattern piece

Thread: all-purpose polyester thread

Needle: machine size 14, hand needle straw or betweens

Pressing: use a steam iron

Used for: chest plates on jackets and coats. Can also be used as a sleeve head

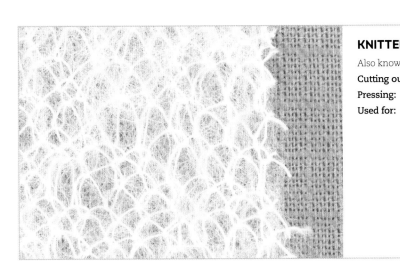

KNITTED DOMETTE

Also known as ice wool, this is a loosely knitted fabric.

Cutting out: cut on the same grain as the pattern piece

Pressing: press carefully so as not to stretch

Used for: primarily for sleeve heads and chest plates. Can also be used as an interlining for warmth

TAPES

In tailoring we use many tapes to create crisp edges; some of these are fusible and some are non-fusible, or "sew-in". Invaluable for tasks such as hemming and seam reinforcement, they can also aid stability and prevent stretch.

FUSIBLE TAPES

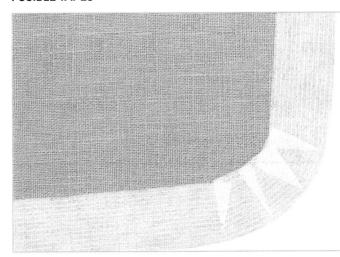

STRAIGHT GRAIN TAPE

A 2cm (¾in) wide straight grain tape. Fuse on leading front edges and shoulders to prevent stretch. Snip and overlap to place around curves.

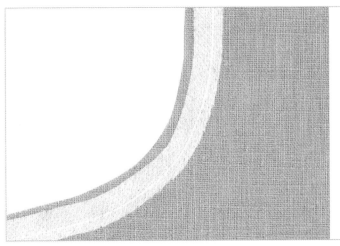

BIAS GRAIN TAPE

A 12mm (½in) wide fusible bias tape, that is stitch reinforced and has a chain stitch running through it 8mm (⁵⁄₁₆in) from the edge. Fuse for 8 seconds with a steam iron and pressing cloth, so that the chain stitch is on the stitching line of the garment and the 8mm part of the tape is in the seam allowance.

WAISTBAND TAPE

A fusible slotted tape to create a 2.5cm (1in) waistband. Fuse for 10 seconds with a steam iron and pressing cloth so that the centre of the tape corresponds to the centre of the waistband fabric.

NON-FUSIBLE TAPES

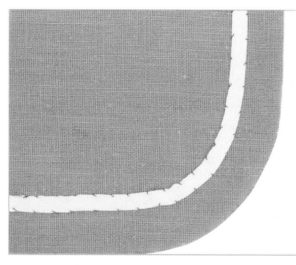

COTTON TAPE

A 6mm (¼in) wide cotton tape that does not stretch. Hand sew in place on either side, adjacent to the stitching line to give a defined sharp edge and prevent the fabric stretching. Shape the tape around curves with the iron prior to application.

KICK TAPE

A woven polyester tape with a narrow finished edge. It is sewn onto the hem edge of trousers to prevent wear against the shoe.

LININGS

Lining is added to a garment to hide the inner construction. It also makes the garment easier
to slip on, more durable, and helps to prevent creasing. Most linings have a satin weave so they
glide against the body. Choose a lining that has a natural element in the fibres for comfort.

ACETATE LINING

An acetate taffeta lining will breathe with your body as it is derived from cellulose.

Cutting out:	cut on the straight grain
Seams:	a plain seam neatened with the overlocker
Thread:	all-purpose polyester thread
Needle:	machine size 12/14, hand sewing sharps or straw needle
Pressing:	press carefully on 2 dots of the iron as a hot iron may wrinkle the fabric
Used for:	lining skirts, dresses, jackets, and coats

JACKET/COAT LININGS

Some linings are made specifically for tailored coats and jackets. These often have
a twill weave and feature a thicker yarn.

Cutting out:	cut on the straight grain
Seams:	a plain seam neatened with the overlocker
Thread:	all-purpose polyester thread
Needle:	machine size 14, hand sewing sharps or betweens needle
Pressing:	press carefully on 2 dots of the iron as a hot iron may wrinkle the fabric
Used for:	lining jackets and coats. Often too heavy for skirts

JACQUARD LINING

A decorative lining as the fabric is a jacquard weave. The designs vary but often
feature a floral or paisley pattern. May have more than one colour yarn.

Cutting out:	cut on the straight grain, paying attention to any direction in the weave
Seams:	a plain seam neatened with the overlocker
Thread:	all-purpose polyester thread
Needle:	machine size 14, hand sewing straws or betweens needle
Pressing:	press carefully on 2 dots of the iron as a hot iron may wrinkle the fabric
Used for:	lining jackets and coats – this is a lining that is meant to be seen!

Patterns and cutting out

Patterns for garments are today available from many sources, from instant downloads to those bought in a store. Always test your chosen pattern first in calico – this is known as a toile. Perfecting your cutting out technique will ensure your pattern pieces fit together perfectly.

Reading patterns

Most dressmakers buy a commercial paper pattern to make a garment. A pattern has three main components: the envelope, the pattern sheets, and the instructions. The envelope gives an illustration of the garment that can be made from the contents, together with fabric suggestions and other requirements. The pattern sheets are normally printed on tissue and contain a wealth of information, while the instructions tell you how to construct the garment.

READING A PATTERN ENVELOPE

The envelope front illustrates the garment that can be made from the contents of the envelope. The illustration may be a line drawing or a photograph. There may be different versions, known as views. On the reverse of the envelope there is usually an illustration of the back view and the standard body measurement chart that has been used for this pattern, plus a chart that will help you purchase the correct amount of fabric for each view. The reverse of the envelope also includes suggestions for suitable fabrics, together with the "notions", or haberdashery, which are all the bits and pieces you need to complete the project.

Number of pattern pieces.

Pattern code number for ordering.

Description of garment giving details of style and different views included in pattern.

List of pattern sizes in metric and imperial measurements for bust, waist, and hips in each size.

Suggested fabrics suitable for garment as well as advice on unsuitable fabrics.

Notions required for each view.

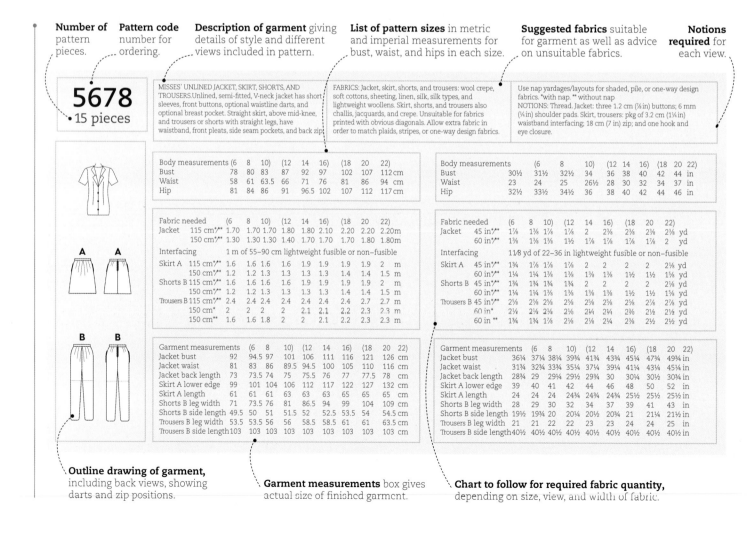

5678
• 15 pieces

MISSES' UNLINED JACKET, SKIRT, SHORTS, AND TROUSERS. Unlined, semi-fitted, V-neck jacket has short sleeves, front buttons, optional waistline darts, and optional breast pocket. Straight skirt, above mid-knee, and trousers or shorts with straight legs, have waistband, front pleats, side seam pockets, and back zip.

FABRICS: Jacket, skirt, shorts, and trousers: wool crepe, soft cottons, sheeting, linen, silk, silk types, and lightweight woollens. Skirt, shorts, and trousers also challis, jacquards, and crepe. Unsuitable for fabrics printed with obvious diagonals. Allow extra fabric in order to match plaids, stripes, or one-way design fabrics.

Use nap yardages/layouts for shaded, pile, or one-way design fabrics. *with nap. ** without nap
NOTIONS: Thread. Jacket: three 1.2 cm (⅞ in) buttons; 6 mm (¼ in) shoulder pads. Skirt, trousers: pkg of 3.2 cm (1¼ in) waistband interfacing; 18 cm (7 in) zip; and one hook and eye closure.

A A

B B

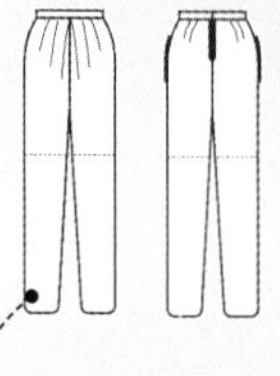

Body measurements	(6	8	10)	(12	14	16)	(18	20	22)	
Bust	78	80	83	87	92	97	102	107	112	cm
Waist	58	61	63.5	66	71	76	81	86	94	cm
Hip	81	84	86	91	96.5	102	107	112	117	cm

Body measurements	(6	8	10)	(12	14	16)	(18	20	22)	
Bust	30½	31½	32½	34	36	38	40	42	44	in
Waist	23	24	25	26½	28	30	32	34	37	in
Hip	32½	33½	34½	36	38	40	42	44	46	in

Fabric needed		(6	8	10)	(12	14	16)	(18	20	22)	
Jacket	115 cm*/**	1.70	1.70	1.70	1.80	1.80	2.10	2.20	2.20	2.20	m
	150 cm*/**	1.30	1.30	1.30	1.40	1.70	1.70	1.70	1.80	1.80	m
Interfacing		1 m of 55–90 cm lightweight fusible or non-fusible									
Skirt A	115 cm*/**	1.6	1.6	1.6	1.6	1.9	1.9	1.9	1.9	2	m
	150 cm*/**	1.2	1.2	1.3	1.3	1.3	1.3	1.4	1.4	1.5	m
Shorts B	115 cm*/**	1.6	1.6	1.6	1.6	1.9	1.9	1.9	1.9	2	m
	150 cm*/**	1.2	1.2	1.3	1.3	1.3	1.3	1.4	1.4	1.5	m
Trousers B	115 cm*/**	2.4	2.4	2.4	2.4	2.4	2.4	2.4	2.7	2.7	m
	150 cm*	2	2	2	2	2.1	2.1	2.2	2.3	2.3	m
	150 cm**	1.6	1.6	1.8	2	2	2.1	2.2	2.3	2.3	m

Fabric needed		(6	8	10)	(12	14	16)	(18	20	22)	
Jacket	45 in*/**	1⅞	1⅜	1⅞	1⅞	2	2⅜	2⅜	2⅜	2⅜	yd
	60 in*/**	1⅜	1⅜	1⅜	1½	1⅞	1⅞	1⅞	1⅞	2	yd
Interfacing		11/8 yd of 22–36 in lightweight fusible or non-fusible									
Skirt A	45 in*/**	1¾	1⅞	1⅞	1⅞	2	2	2	2	2⅛	yd
	60 in*/**	1¼	1¼	1⅜	1⅜	1⅜	1⅜	1½	1½	1⅝	yd
Shorts B	45 in*/**	1¾	1¾	1¾	1¾	2	2	2	2	2⅛	yd
	60 in*/**	1¼	1¼	1⅜	1⅜	1⅜	1⅜	1½	1½	1⅝	yd
Trousers B	45 in*/**	2⅝	2⅝	2⅝	2⅝	2⅝	2⅝	2⅝	2⅞	2⅞	yd
	60 in*	2⅛	2⅛	2⅛	2⅛	2¼	2¼	2⅜	2½	2½	yd
	60 in **	1¾	1¾	1⅞	2⅛	2⅛	2¼	2⅜	2½	2½	yd

Garment measurements	(6	8	10)	(12	14	16)	(18	20	22)	
Jacket bust	92	94.5	97	101	106	111	116	121	126	cm
Jacket waist	81	83	86	89.5	94.5	100	105	110	116	cm
Jacket back length	73	73.5	74	75	75.5	76	77	77.5	78	cm
Skirt A lower edge	99	101	104	106	112	117	122	127	132	cm
Skirt A length	61	61	61	63	63	63	65	65	65	cm
Shorts B leg width	71	73.5	76	81	86.5	94	99	104	109	cm
Shorts B side length	49.5	50	51	51.5	52	52.5	53.5	54	54.5	cm
Trousers B leg width	53.5	53.5	56	56	58.5	58.5	61	61	63.5	cm
Trousers B side length	103	103	103	103	103	103	103	103	103	cm

Garment measurements	(6	8	10)	(12	14	16)	(18	20	22)	
Jacket bust	36¼	37¼	38¼	39¾	41¾	43¾	45¼	47¾	49¾	in
Jacket waist	31¾	32¾	33¾	35¼	37¼	39¼	41¼	43¼	45¼	in
Jacket back length	28¾	29	29¼	29½	29¾	30	30¼	30½	30¾	in
Skirt A lower edge	39	40	41	42	44	46	48	50	52	in
Skirt A length	24	24	24	24¾	24¾	24¾	25½	25½	25½	in
Shorts B leg width	28	29	30	32	34	37	39	41	43	in
Shorts B side length	19½	19¾	20	20¼	20½	20¾	21	21¼	21½	in
Trousers B leg width	21	21	22	22	23	23	24	24	25	in
Trousers B side length	40½	40½	40½	40½	40½	40½	40½	40½	40½	in

Outline drawing of garment, including back views, showing darts and zip positions.

Garment measurements box gives actual size of finished garment.

Chart to follow for required fabric quantity, depending on size, view, and width of fabric.

SINGLE-SIZE PATTERNS

Some patterns contain a garment of one size only. If you are using a single-size pattern, cut around the tissue on the thick black cutting line before making any alterations.

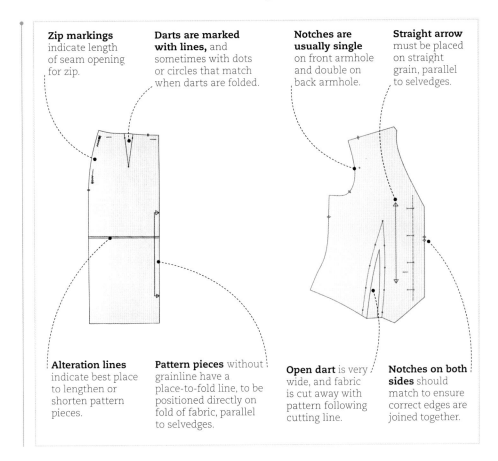

Zip markings indicate length of seam opening for zip.

Darts are marked with lines, and sometimes with dots or circles that match when darts are folded.

Notches are usually single on front armhole and double on back armhole.

Straight arrow must be placed on straight grain, parallel to selvedges.

Alteration lines indicate best place to lengthen or shorten pattern pieces.

Pattern pieces without grainline have a place-to-fold line, to be positioned directly on fold of fabric, parallel to selvedges.

Open dart is very wide, and fabric is cut away with pattern following cutting line.

Notches on both sides should match to ensure correct edges are joined together.

MULTI-SIZE PATTERNS

Many patterns today have more than one size printed on the tissue. Each size is clearly labelled and the cutting lines are marked with a different type of line for each size.

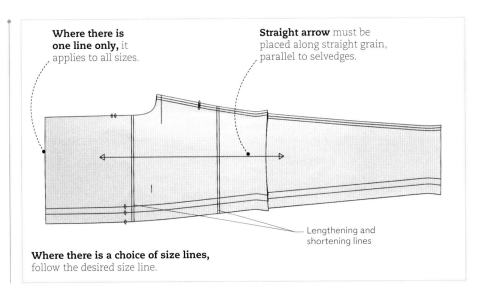

Where there is one line only, it applies to all sizes.

Straight arrow must be placed along straight grain, parallel to selvedges.

Lengthening and shortening lines

Where there is a choice of size lines, follow the desired size line.

PATTERN MARKINGS

Each pattern piece will have a series of lines, dots, and other symbols printed on it. These symbols help you to alter the pattern and join the pattern pieces together. The symbols are universal across all major paper patterns.

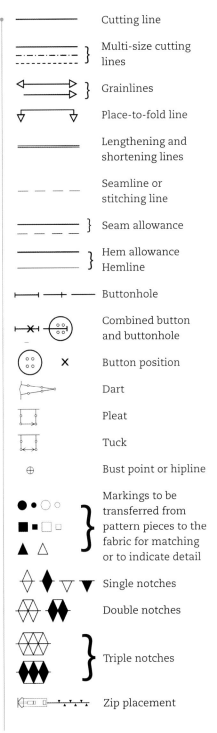

Cutting line

Multi-size cutting lines

Grainlines

Place-to-fold line

Lengthening and shortening lines

Seamline or stitching line

Seam allowance

Hem allowance
Hemline

Buttonhole

Combined button and buttonhole

Button position

Dart

Pleat

Tuck

Bust point or hipline

Markings to be transferred from pattern pieces to the fabric for matching or to indicate detail

Single notches

Double notches

Triple notches

Zip placement

Body measuring

Accurate body measurements are needed to determine the correct pattern size to use, and to know if any alterations are required. Pattern sizes are usually chosen by the hip or bust measurement; for tops follow the bust measurement, but for skirts or trousers use the hip measurement. If you are choosing a dress pattern, go by whichever of your measurements is the largest.

TAKING BODY MEASUREMENTS

- You will need a tape measure and ruler as well as a helper for some of the measuring, and a firm chair or stool.

- Wear close-fitting clothes such as a tight T-shirt or vest and leggings.

- Do not wear any shoes.

MEASURING YOUR HEIGHT

Tailoring paper patterns are typically designed for the average or standard height, around 165cm (5ft 5in) for women and 178cm (5ft 10in) for men. If you are shorter or taller than this you may need to adjust the pattern prior to cutting out your fabric.

1 Remove your shoes.

2 Stand straight, with your back against a wall.

3 Place a ruler flat on your head, touching the wall, and mark the wall at this point.

4 Step away and measure the distance from the floor to the marked point.

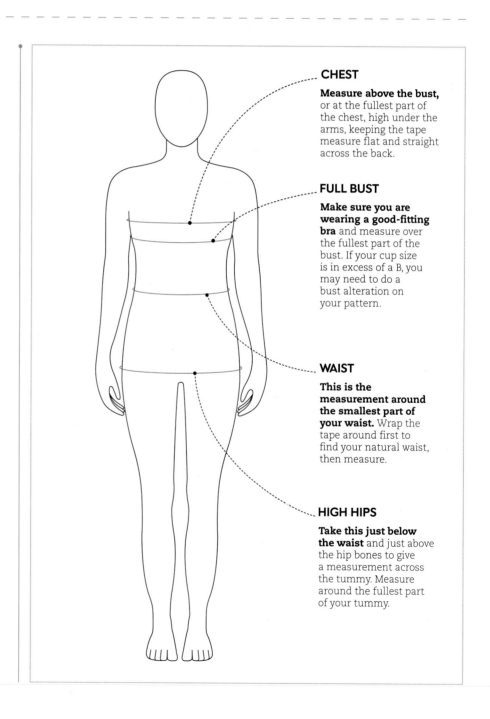

CHEST

Measure above the bust, or at the fullest part of the chest, high under the arms, keeping the tape measure flat and straight across the back.

FULL BUST

Make sure you are wearing a good-fitting bra and measure over the fullest part of the bust. If your cup size is in excess of a B, you may need to do a bust alteration on your pattern.

WAIST

This is the measurement around the smallest part of your waist. Wrap the tape around first to find your natural waist, then measure.

HIGH HIPS

Take this just below the waist and just above the hip bones to give a measurement across the tummy. Measure around the fullest part of your tummy.

SHOULDER

Hold the end of the tape measure at the base of your neck (where a necklace would lie) and measure to the dent at the end of your shoulder bone. To find this dent raise your arm slightly.

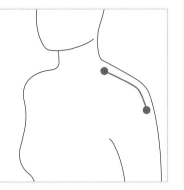

BACK WAIST

Take this measurement down the centre of the back, from the bony bit at the top of the spine, in line with the shoulders, to the waist.

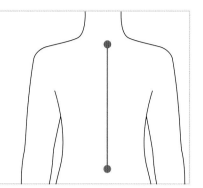

NECK

Measure around the neck – snugly but not too tightly – to determine collar size.

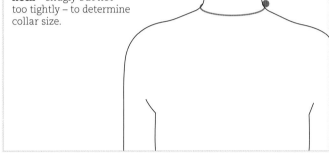

OUTSIDE LEG

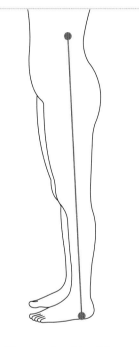

Measure the side of the leg from the waist, over the hip, and straight down the leg to the ankle bone.

INSIDE LEG

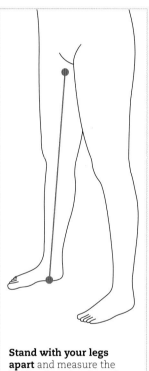

Stand with your legs apart and measure the inside of one leg from the crotch to the ankle bone.

ARM

Bend your elbow and place your hand on your hip, then measure from the end of the shoulder over the elbow to the wrist bone.

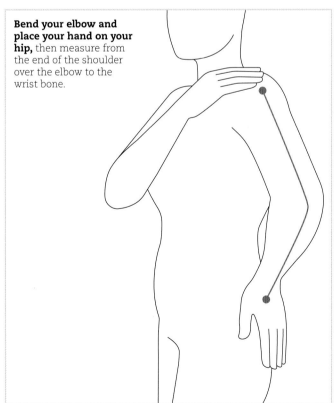

CROTCH DEPTH

Sit upright on a firm chair or stool and measure from the waist vertically down to the chair.

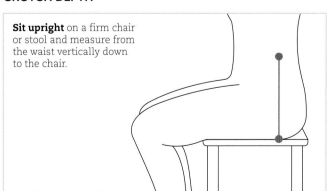

Altering patterns

It is unlikely that your body measurements will be exactly the same as those of your chosen pattern, so you will need to alter the pattern to accommodate your figure. Here is how to lengthen and shorten pattern pieces, and how to make specific alterations at the bust, waist and hips, shoulders and back, and to sleeves and trousers.

EQUIPMENT

▶ **In addition to scissors and pins or tape,** you will need a pencil, an eraser, a ruler that is clearly marked, and possibly a set square. For many alterations you will also need pattern paper.

▶ **After pinning or taping the piece of pattern tissue to the paper,** you can redraw the pattern lines. Trim away the excess tissue or paper before pinning the pattern pieces to the fabric for cutting out.

EASY MULTI-SIZE PATTERN ALTERATIONS

Using a multi-size pattern has many advantages because you can cut on different size lines for different parts of your body. For example, you can combine sizes to accommodate a larger hip or a thinner waist.

INDIVIDUAL PATTERN ADJUSTMENT

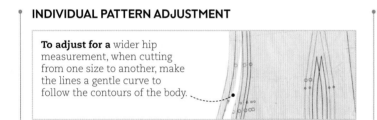

To adjust for a wider hip measurement, when cutting from one size to another, make the lines a gentle curve to follow the contours of the body.

BETWEEN SIZES

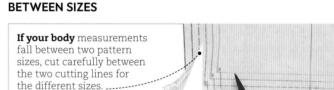

If your body measurements fall between two pattern sizes, cut carefully between the two cutting lines for the different sizes.

LENGTHENING AND SHORTENING PATTERNS

If you are shorter or taller, or your arms or legs are shorter or longer, than the pattern pieces, you will need to adjust the paper pattern prior to cutting out. There are lines printed on the pattern pieces that will guide you as to the best places to adjust. However, you will need to compare your body shape against the pattern. Alter the front and back by the same amount at the same points, and always check finished lengths.

FOR A FITTED SLEEVE

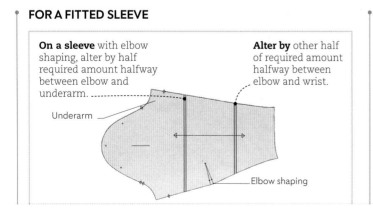

On a sleeve with elbow shaping, alter by half required amount halfway between elbow and underarm.

Underarm

Alter by other half of required amount halfway between elbow and wrist.

Elbow shaping

FOR A STRAIGHT SLEEVE

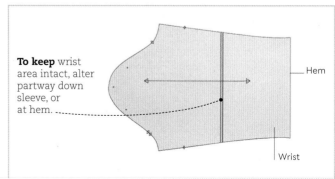

To keep wrist area intact, alter partway down sleeve, or at hem.

Hem

Wrist

FOR A BODICE

Alter back neck to waist length below bust dart but above waist (through waist dart if there is one).

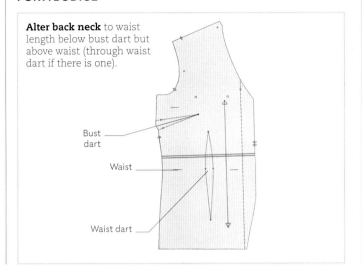

Bust dart

Waist

Waist dart

FOR A SKIRT

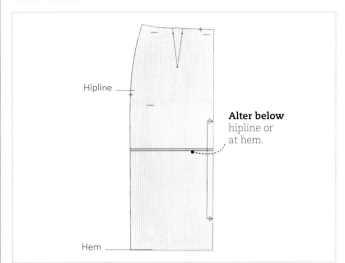

Hipline

Alter below hipline or at hem.

Hem

FOR SHAPED-LEG TROUSERS

For large alterations, divide amount and alter half above knee and half below.

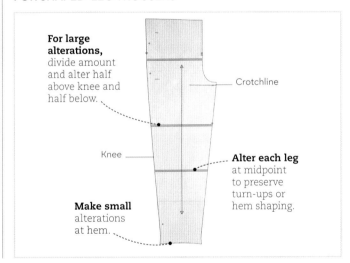

Crotchline

Knee

Alter each leg at midpoint to preserve turn-ups or hem shaping.

Make small alterations at hem.

FOR STRAIGHT TROUSERS

Increase crotch below tucks, but above crotchline.

Make large alterations midway down leg to retain leg width.

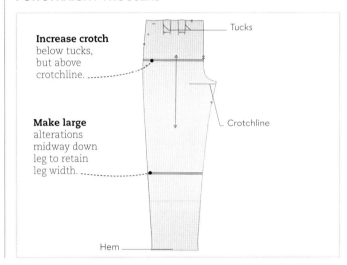

Tucks

Crotchline

Hem

HOW TO LENGTHEN A PATTERN PIECE

1 First work out the amount you want to add by comparing your measurements to those of the pattern.

2 Cut through the lengthening and shortening lines on the tissue paper, following the lines carefully.

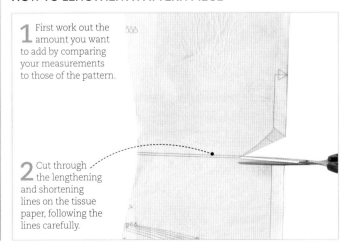

3 Place some pattern paper behind the tissue and spread the pattern pieces apart to leave a gap of the required amount. Make sure the gap is level along the cut lines.

4 Pin or tape the pattern pieces to the paper.

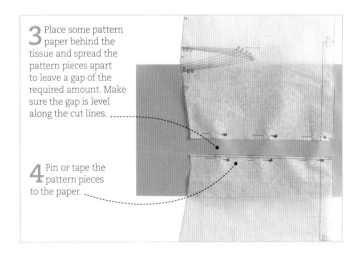

SHORTENING A PATTERN PIECE

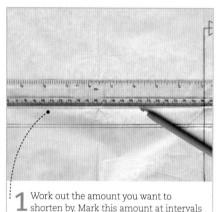

1 Work out the amount you want to shorten by. Mark this amount at intervals above the lengthening and shortening lines, then draw a line through the marks using the ruler as a guide.

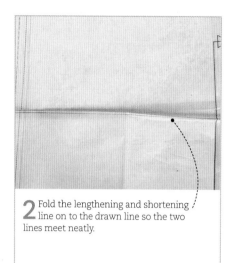

2 Fold the lengthening and shortening line on to the drawn line so the two lines meet neatly.

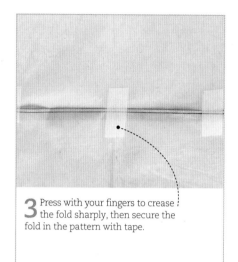

3 Press with your fingers to crease the fold sharply, then secure the fold in the pattern with tape.

LENGTHENING ACROSS DARTS

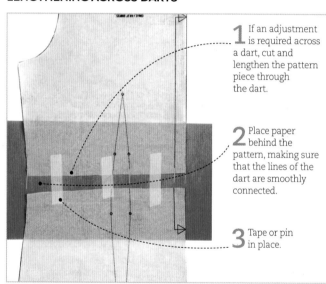

1 If an adjustment is required across a dart, cut and lengthen the pattern piece through the dart.

2 Place paper behind the pattern, making sure that the lines of the dart are smoothly connected.

3 Tape or pin in place.

SHORTENING ACROSS DARTS

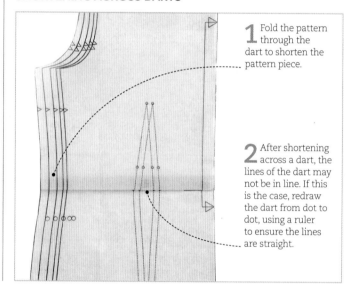

1 Fold the pattern through the dart to shorten the pattern piece.

2 After shortening across a dart, the lines of the dart may not be in line. If this is the case, redraw the dart from dot to dot, using a ruler to ensure the lines are straight.

LENGTHENING A HEM EDGE

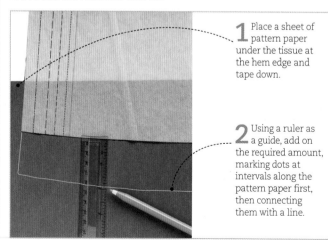

1 Place a sheet of pattern paper under the tissue at the hem edge and tape down.

2 Using a ruler as a guide, add on the required amount, marking dots at intervals along the pattern paper first, then connecting them with a line.

SHORTENING A HEM EDGE

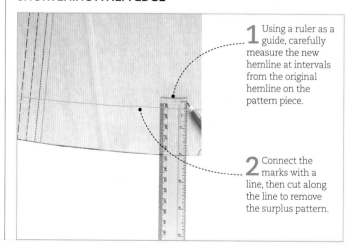

1 Using a ruler as a guide, carefully measure the new hemline at intervals from the original hemline on the pattern piece.

2 Connect the marks with a line, then cut along the line to remove the surplus pattern.

BUST

Some paper patterns today feature various cup sizes, but most are cut to accommodate a B cup, including those in this book. If you are larger than this, you will probably need to adjust your pattern before cutting out. As a general rule, when spreading the pattern pieces apart, try adjusting by 6mm (¼in) per cup size over a B cup.

RAISING A BUST DART

1 If you have a high bust you may need to raise the point of the darts. The bust point is nearly always marked on the pattern. Mark the desired new bust point on the pattern.

2 Redraw the dart, tapering it to the new, higher, point.

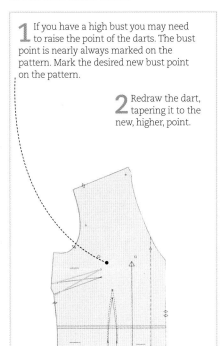

RAISING A BUST DART SUBSTANTIALLY

1 Mark the desired new bust point on the pattern.

2 Cut a rectangle out of the bust dart area and move it up to the new position.

3 Tape paper behind and redraw the side seam.

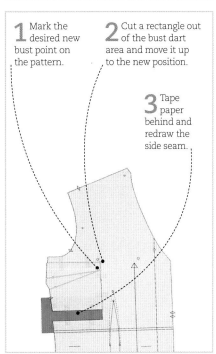

INCREASING A BUST DART FOR A FULL BUST

1 Cut the pattern vertically and horizontally straight through the bust point.

2 Spread the cut pattern pieces apart by about 6mm (¼in) per cup size over a B cup.

3 Tape paper behind and redraw the cutting lines as necessary.

Dart redrawn to original length

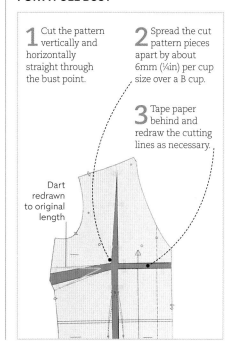

LOWERING A BUST DART

1 Mark the desired new bust point on the pattern.

2 Redraw the dart, tapering it to the new, lower, point.

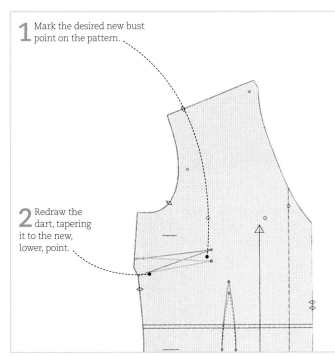

LOWERING A BUST DART SUBSTANTIALLY

1 Mark the desired new bust point on the pattern.

2 Cut a rectangle out of the bust dart area and move it to the new, lower position.

3 Tape paper behind and redraw the side seam.

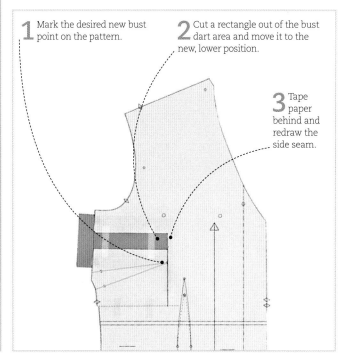

RAISING A CURVED BUST SEAM

1 Fold a pleat in the shoulder pattern to bring the bust point up by the required amount.

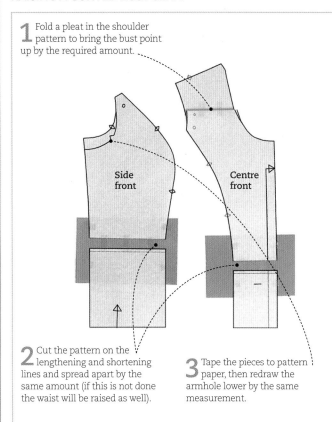

Side front

Centre front

2 Cut the pattern on the lengthening and shortening lines and spread apart by the same amount (if this is not done the waist will be raised as well).

3 Tape the pieces to pattern paper, then redraw the armhole lower by the same measurement.

LOWERING A CURVED BUST SEAM

1 Cut the shoulder pattern piece and spread apart by the required amount, then tape to a sheet of pattern paper.

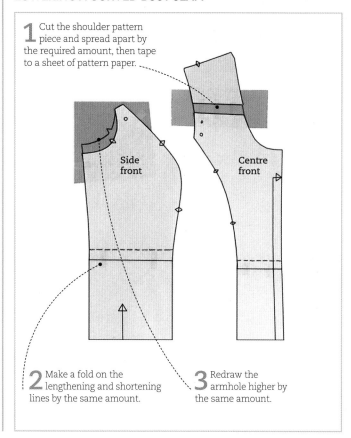

Side front

Centre front

2 Make a fold on the lengthening and shortening lines by the same amount.

3 Redraw the armhole higher by the same amount.

ADJUSTING A CURVED SEAM

1 For a larger bust, place a sheet of pattern paper under the bust curve on the side front piece.

2 Add onto this curve 6mm (¼in) per cup size over a B cup, for example 12mm (½in) for a D cup. Redraw the curve.

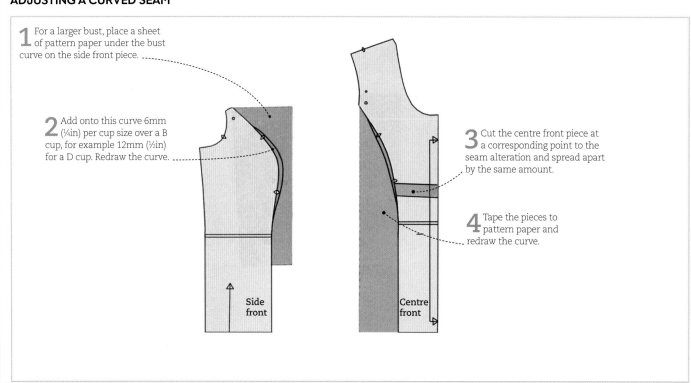

3 Cut the centre front piece at a corresponding point to the seam alteration and spread apart by the same amount.

4 Tape the pieces to pattern paper and redraw the curve.

Side front

Centre front

WAIST AND HIPS

Most people's waists and hips are out of proportion when compared to the measurements of a paper pattern.
To alter the pattern to suit your body shape, adjust the pieces for the waist first and then do the hip pieces.

INCREASING THE WAIST AT A SEAM

1 On a fitted skirt, increase the waist at the side seams. Divide the amount to be increased by four as there are four seamlines.

2 Tape pattern paper behind the tissue pieces and add the increase on at the waist edge.

3 Draw a new seamline from this point, tapering it back into the skirt side seam.

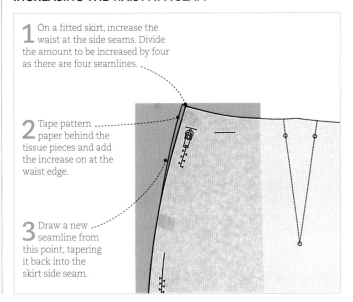

INCREASING THE WAIST ON A PANELLED SKIRT

1 As there are many seams on a gored skirt, divide the increase amount by the number of seamlines.

2 Tape the tissue pieces on to pattern paper and add one of these small amounts to each seamline at the waist.

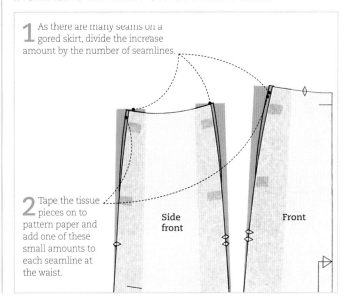

Side front

Front

INCREASING THE WAIST ON A PRINCESS SEAM DRESS

1 Place a sheet of pattern paper under the waist section of each of the pattern pieces.

2 Divide the amount to be increased by the number of seamlines.

3 Add one of these small amounts on to each seamline.

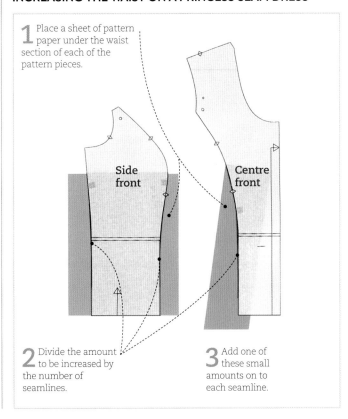

Side front

Centre front

DECREASING THE WAIST AT A SEAM

1 On a straight skirt, divide the amount to be decreased by four as there are four seamlines.

2 Mark the amount of decrease at the waist edge on the pattern pieces.

3 Redraw the side seams, tapering back into the pattern line.

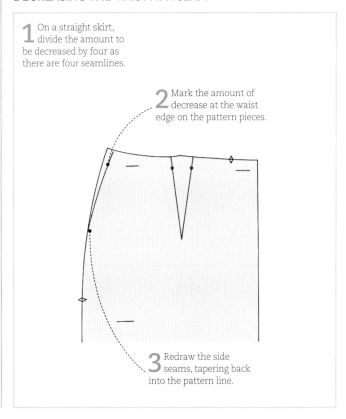

DECREASING THE WAIST ON A FITTED JACKET

1 To reduce the waist seam, you need to redraw the side seamline on each pattern piece. Divide the total decrease by four.

2 Measure one-quarter of the total amount to be decreased at the waist.

3 Draw a curved line from above and below to this point.

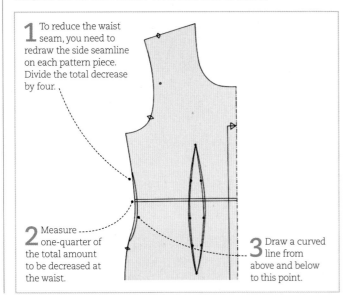

DECREASING THE WAIST ON A FITTED JACKET

1 Divide the total amount of reduction by the number of seamlines, then mark the required amount of decrease at the waist on each pattern piece.

2 Redraw the seams, curving each one in to the marked point.

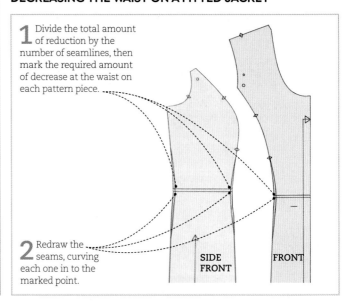

SIDE FRONT   FRONT

WIDENING A FITTED SKIRT AT THE HIPLINE

1 To increase the hip dimension on a fitted skirt, divide the amount of the increase by four. Place the tissue pieces on pattern paper and increase each side seam at the hip point by the required amount.

2 Redraw the seamline from the hip increase, gradually tapering into the waistline.

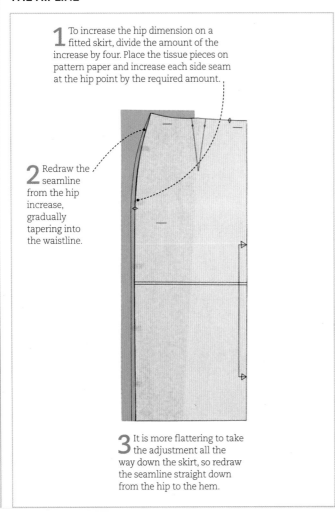

3 It is more flattering to take the adjustment all the way down the skirt, so redraw the seamline straight down from the hip to the hem.

ADJUSTING A FITTED SKIRT FOR EXTRA-LARGE HIPS

1 For an increase over 5cm (2in), cut each pattern piece vertically between the dart and the side seam.

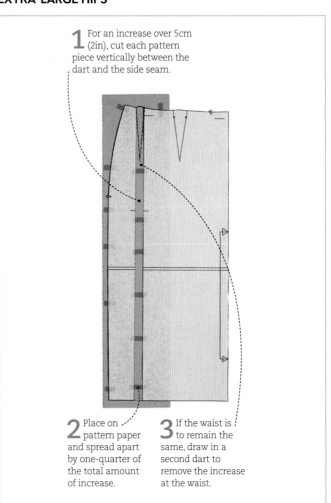

2 Place on pattern paper and spread apart by one-quarter of the total amount of increase.

3 If the waist is to remain the same, draw in a second dart to remove the increase at the waist.

ADJUSTING A FITTED SKIRT FOR PROMINENT HIPS

1 Place the tissue on pattern paper and add the required amount from the waist to the hip point as for a fitted skirt (see p.79), tapering the line back into the seam.

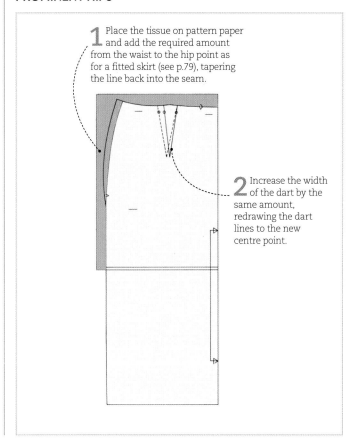

2 Increase the width of the dart by the same amount, redrawing the dart lines to the new centre point.

ADJUSTING A FITTED SKIRT FOR A LARGE BOTTOM

1 Cut through the skirt back pattern piece, vertically through the dart to the hem.

2 Cut across the hipline, but not through the side seam.

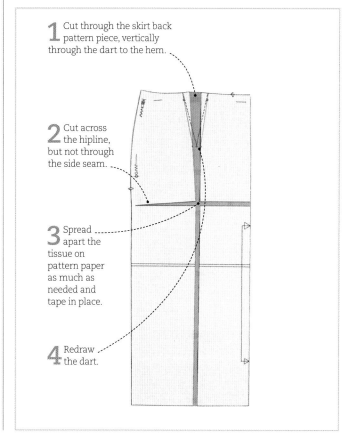

3 Spread apart the tissue on pattern paper as much as needed and tape in place.

4 Redraw the dart.

DECREASING THE HIPLINE ON A FITTED SKIRT

1 Divide the amount to be reduced by four and mark the reduction amount on each pattern piece at the hipline.

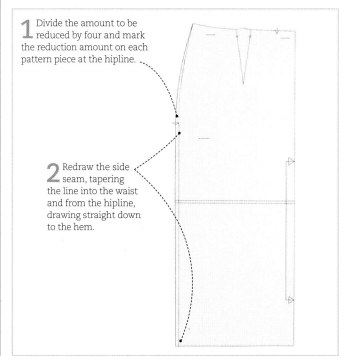

2 Redraw the side seam, tapering the line into the waist and from the hipline, drawing straight down to the hem.

ADJUSTING AT THE HIPLINE TO ALLOW FOR A HOLLOW BACK

1 A hollow back requires a shorter centre back seam. Draw a line on the pattern piece across the hipline, from the centre back.

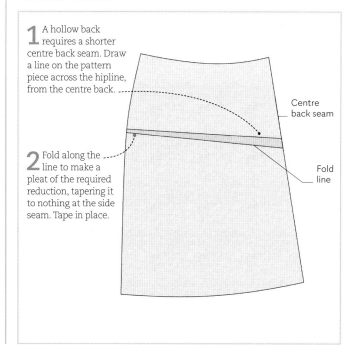

Centre back seam

Fold line

2 Fold along the line to make a pleat of the required reduction, tapering it to nothing at the side seam. Tape in place.

SHOULDERS, BACK, AND SLEEVES

Alterations can be made to accommodate sloping shoulders, square shoulders, rounded shoulders, and backs that may be wider or narrower than the pattern allowances. It's important to ensure that these alterations have a minimum effect on the armhole. Sleeves need to allow for movement, so should not be too tight, and pattern pieces can be enlarged as necessary. Alterations can also be made for thin arms.

ADJUSTING TO FIT SQUARE SHOULDERS

1 Starting at the armhole, slash the pattern piece about 3cm (1¼in) below and parallel with the shoulder line, not cutting through the neck seamline.

2 Spread the tissue apart to make the shoulder line straighter. Tape to pattern paper.

3 Redraw the line across the gap created.

4 Raise the armhole by the amount added at the shoulder. Adjust the front shoulder pattern pieces by the same amount as the back.

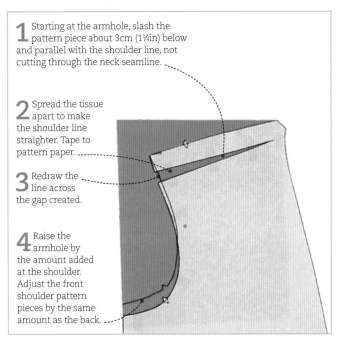

ADJUSTING TO FIT SLOPING SHOULDERS

1 Slash from the armhole across the pattern piece 3cm (1¼in) below the shoulder line and parallel with it.

2 Overlap the tissue by the required amount and tape in place.

3 Lower the armhole by the same amount, drawing a new seamline on the tissue. Adjust the front shoulder pattern pieces by the same amount as the back.

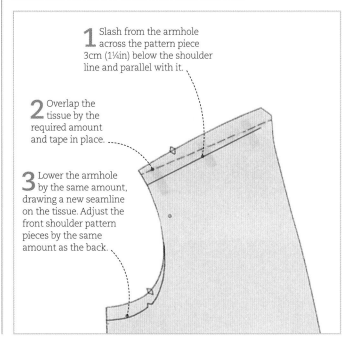

PREPARING THE PATTERN FOR SHOULDER WIDTH ALTERATIONS

1 Draw a vertical line 20cm (8in) long from the middle of the shoulder line.

2 Next, draw a second line horizontally from the end of this line to the armhole.

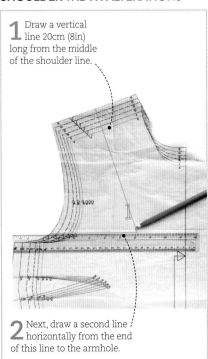

ADJUSTING TO FIT BROAD SHOULDERS

1 Cut along the lines that have been drawn and spread the pieces of tissue apart on pattern paper, to accommodate the increase in shoulder length.

2 Tape in place and redraw the shoulder line. Adjust the front shoulder pattern pieces by the same amount as the back.

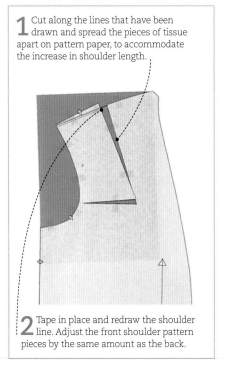

ADJUSTING TO FIT NARROW SHOULDERS

1 Cut along the drawn lines.

2 Slide the cut-out piece of tissue in to overlap the cut edges and reduce the shoulder length.

3 Tape on to pattern paper and redraw the shoulder line. Adjust the front shoulder pattern pieces by the same amount as the back.

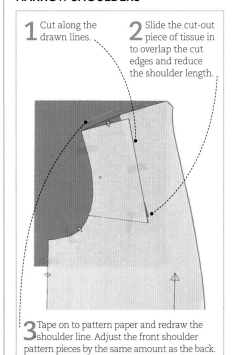

ENLARGING A FITTED SLEEVE

1 Cut the sleeve pattern piece vertically down the centre.

2 Spread apart as much as required to make the sleeve wider. Tape to pattern paper.

3 You may need to make the armhole slightly larger, by adding half this amount to each bodice side seam.

ENLARGING THE HEAD ON A FITTED SLEEVE

1 Cut the pattern piece vertically down the centre, not cutting through the wrist seamline.

2 Spread the tissue apart at the top by the required amount and taper to nothing at the wrist.

3 You may need to make the armhole slightly larger, by adding half this amount to each bodice side seam.

ENLARGING A FITTED SLEEVE AT THE ELBOW

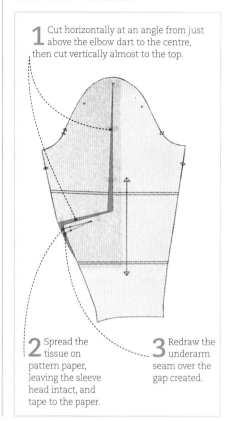

1 Cut horizontally at an angle from just above the elbow dart to the centre, then cut vertically almost to the top.

2 Spread the tissue on pattern paper, leaving the sleeve head intact, and tape to the paper.

3 Redraw the underarm seam over the gap created.

INCREASING AT THE UNDERARM ON A FITTED SLEEVE

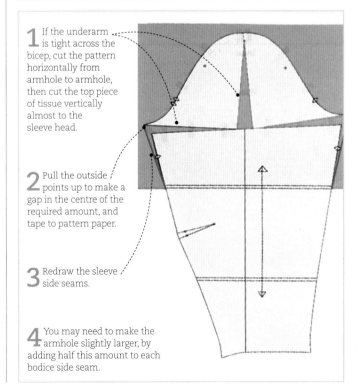

1 If the underarm is tight across the bicep, cut the pattern horizontally from armhole to armhole, then cut the top piece of tissue vertically almost to the sleeve head.

2 Pull the outside points up to make a gap in the centre of the required amount, and tape to pattern paper.

3 Redraw the sleeve side seams.

4 You may need to make the armhole slightly larger, by adding half this amount to each bodice side seam.

DECREASING A FITTED SLEEVE FOR THIN ARMS

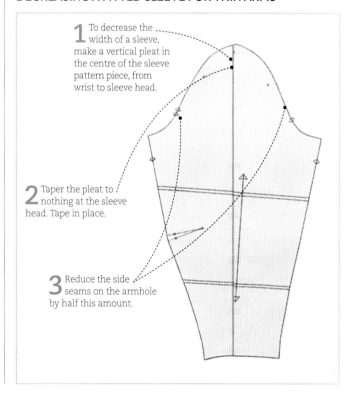

1 To decrease the width of a sleeve, make a vertical pleat in the centre of the sleeve pattern piece, from wrist to sleeve head.

2 Taper the pleat to nothing at the sleeve head. Tape in place.

3 Reduce the side seams on the armhole by half this amount.

TROUSERS

Trouser alterations, to accommodate a large stomach, wide hips, a prominent or flat bottom, can be more complicated than those on other pattern pieces, and need to be done in the correct order. Crotch depth alterations are done first, followed by width alterations, then crotch length alterations, and finally trouser leg length. The crotch depth line is only marked on the back pattern pieces.

INCREASING DEPTH AT CROTCH SEAM

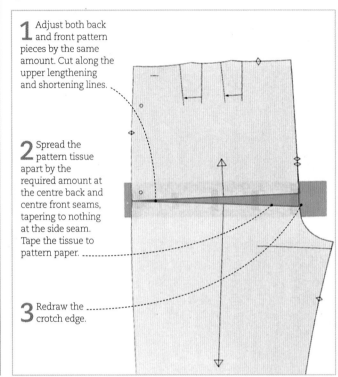

1 Adjust both back and front pattern pieces by the same amount. Cut along the upper lengthening and shortening lines.

2 Spread the pattern tissue apart by the required amount at the centre back and centre front seams, tapering to nothing at the side seam. Tape the tissue to pattern paper.

3 Redraw the crotch edge.

DECREASING DEPTH AT CROTCH SEAM

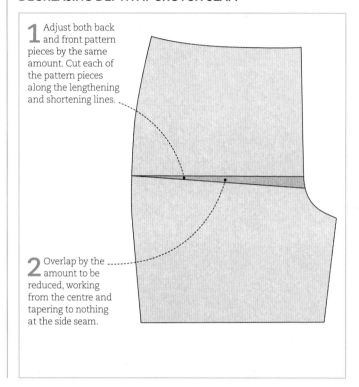

1 Adjust both back and front pattern pieces by the same amount. Cut each of the pattern pieces along the lengthening and shortening lines.

2 Overlap by the amount to be reduced, working from the centre and tapering to nothing at the side seam.

INCREASING THE WAISTLINE

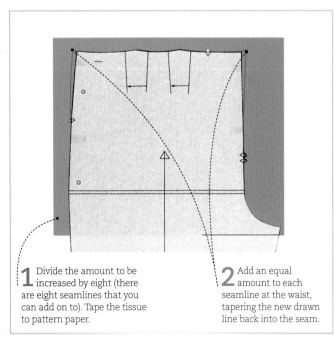

1 Divide the amount to be increased by eight (there are eight seamlines that you can add on to). Tape the tissue to pattern paper.

2 Add an equal amount to each seamline at the waist, tapering the new drawn line back into the seam.

DECREASING THE WAISTLINE

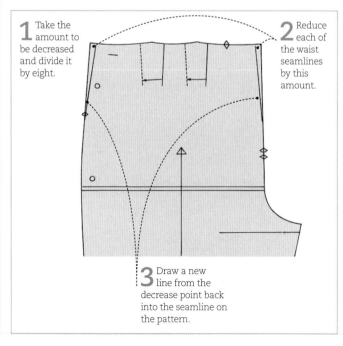

1 Take the amount to be decreased and divide it by eight.

2 Reduce each of the waist seamlines by this amount.

3 Draw a new line from the decrease point back into the seamline on the pattern.

INCREASING AT THE HIPLINE

1 Take the amount to be increased and divide it by four.

2 Place a sheet of pattern paper under the hip area on the side seam of each pattern piece.

3 Add the required amount to each of the seamlines at the hip, tapering the new seamline into the waist and thigh.

4 For straight trousers, draw the new seamline straight down from the hip to the hem.

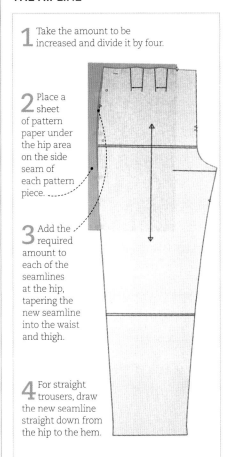

INCREASING THE BOTTOM OR TUMMY AREA

1 Adjust the back pattern pieces for a large bottom or the front pattern pieces for a full tummy. Cut through the pieces at the hipline.

2 Place the tissue on pattern paper and spread apart by the required amount, then tape the tissue to the paper.

3 Redraw the crotch edge. This adjustment may be in addition to a crotch depth adjustment.

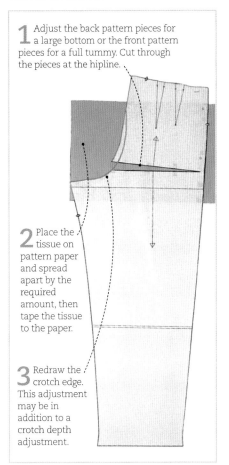

DECREASING AT THE HIPLINE

1 For fitted trousers, divide the amount to be decreased by four.

2 Reduce the side seam at the hipline on each pattern piece by one-quarter of the total reduction.

3 Taper the new drawn seamline to waist and thigh.

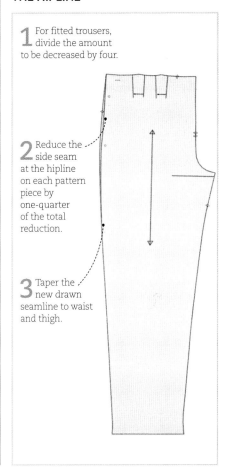

INCREASING LENGTH AT CROTCH POINT

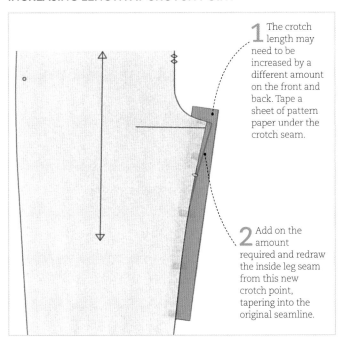

1 The crotch length may need to be increased by a different amount on the front and back. Tape a sheet of pattern paper under the crotch seam.

2 Add on the amount required and redraw the inside leg seam from this new crotch point, tapering into the original seamline.

DECREASING LENGTH AT CROTCH POINT

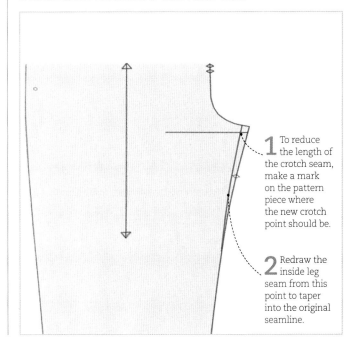

1 To reduce the length of the crotch seam, make a mark on the pattern piece where the new crotch point should be.

2 Redraw the inside leg seam from this point to taper into the original seamline.

Making a toile

When using a new pattern for the first time, or if you have made pattern alterations, it is always a good idea to try out the pattern in calico, to make a test garment called a toile. This will tell you if the garment is going to fit you, or whether more alterations are required. It is also a good opportunity to confirm that the style suits your figure type. You will need a helper, or failing that a dressmaker's dummy.

TOILE TOO BIG

When you try the toile on, if it is too big there will be surplus fabric. Pleat and pin out the surplus fabric, making the pleating equal on both the left- and right-hand sides of the garment. Take off the toile and measure the surplus amount. Alter the pattern pieces to match, by pinning out the surplus tissue.

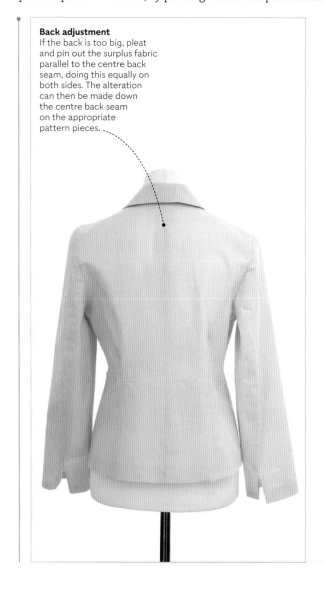

Back adjustment
If the back is too big, pleat and pin out the surplus fabric parallel to the centre back seam, doing this equally on both sides. The alteration can then be made down the centre back seam on the appropriate pattern pieces.

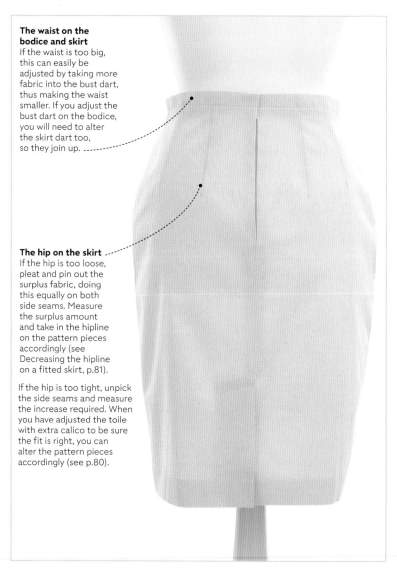

The waist on the bodice and skirt
If the waist is too big, this can easily be adjusted by taking more fabric into the bust dart, thus making the waist smaller. If you adjust the bust dart on the bodice, you will need to alter the skirt dart too, so they join up.

The hip on the skirt
If the hip is too loose, pleat and pin out the surplus fabric, doing this equally on both side seams. Measure the surplus amount and take in the hipline on the pattern pieces accordingly (see Decreasing the hipline on a fitted skirt, p.81).

If the hip is too tight, unpick the side seams and measure the increase required. When you have adjusted the toile with extra calico to be sure the fit is right, you can alter the pattern pieces accordingly (see p.80).

TOILE TOO SMALL

If the toile is too small, the fabric will "pull" where it is too tight. The garment shown below is too tight over the bust and also over the high hip area. The pattern will need adjusting to allow more fabric in these areas. It is also snug at the top of the sleeve, which will need adjusting.

HOW TO ADJUST A TOILE THAT IS TOO SMALL

If the toile is too tight, it will require more fabric to cover the contours of the body and you will need to make further alterations to the pattern pieces. For small increases (up to 4cm/1½in), you can adjust the toile as described below and then alter the pattern pieces accordingly, redrawing the seamlines. For more substantial increases, after altering the pattern pieces you will need to make up a new toile to try on.

1 Where the toile is too tight, unpick the side seam on either side, until the garment will hang without pulling.

2 Measure the gap between the stitching lines where the seam has been opened at the fullest point. It should be the same on both sides of the body.

3 Divide this measurement by four (four seams) – for example, if the gap is 4cm (1½in) at the fullest point, then 1cm (⅜in) needs to be added to each seamline.

4 Using a marker pen, mark directly on the toile the top and bottom of the alteration. Also mark the fullest point of the alteration.

5 When the toile has been removed, add calico to the seam in the given area at the fullest point, tapering back to the original seam at either end.

6 Try the toile on again to be sure your alterations have made it fit you properly, then measure them and make adjustments to the relevant pattern pieces.

The bust on the bodice
If a small increase is required in the bust, unpick the side seams and measure the increase required. Then make the required alteration to the pattern pieces. If a larger increase is required the whole pattern piece will need to be altered and a new front cut out (see Increasing a bust dart, p.77). To be sure the alteration is successful, make up a new toile bodice to try.

Sleeve adjustment
If the sleeve is tight at the top, or at the underarm, it is best to alter the pattern pieces (see p.83) and then to make up a new sleeve for the toile.

Shoulder adjustment
If the shoulder is too wide it will need a narrow shoulder adjustment (see p.82).

Cutting out

Cutting out can make or break your project. But first you need to examine the fabric in the shop, looking for any flaws, such as a crooked pattern, and checking to see if the fabric has been cut properly from the roll – that is at a right angle to the selvedge. If it has not been cut properly, you will need to straighten the edge before cutting out. If the fabric is creased, press it; if washable, wash it to avoid shrinkage later. After this preparation, lay the pattern pieces on the fabric, pin in place, and cut out.

FABRIC GRAIN AND NAP

It is important that pattern pieces are cut on the correct grain; this will make the fabric hang correctly. The grain is the direction in which the yarns or threads that make up the fabric lie. The majority of pattern pieces need to be placed with the straight of grain symbol running parallel to the warp yarn. Some fabrics have a nap due to the pile, which means the fabric shadows when it is smoothed in one direction. A fabric with a one-way design or uneven stripes is also described as having a nap. Fabrics with nap are generally cut out with the nap running down, whereas those without nap can be cut out at any angle.

GRAIN ON WOVEN FABRICS

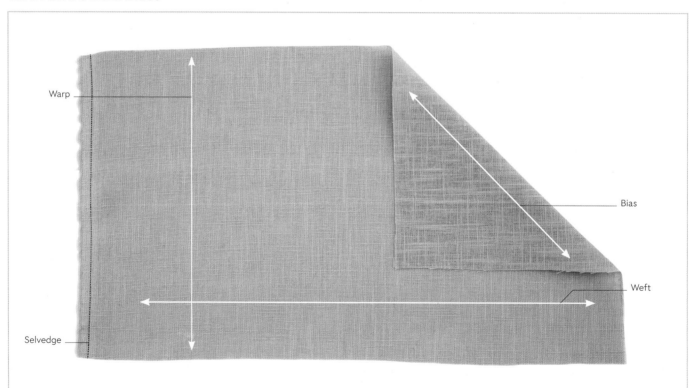

Warp yarns run the length of the fabric. They are stronger than weft yarns and less likely to stretch.

Weft yarns run crossways, over and under the warp yarns.

The bias grain is diagonal – running at 45 degrees to the warp and weft. A garment cut on the bias will follow the contours of the body.

The selvedge is the woven, non-frayable edge that runs parallel to the warp yarn.

NAP DUE TO PILE

Fabrics such as velvet, corduroy, and velour will show a difference in colour, depending on whether the nap is running up or down.

NAP DUE TO ONE-WAY DESIGN

A one-way pattern – in this case flowers – that runs lengthways in the fabric will be upside-down on one side when the fabric is folded back on itself.

NAP DUE TO STRIPES

If the stripes do not match on both sides when the fabric is folded back, they are uneven and the fabric will need a nap layout.

FABRIC PREPARATION

To check if the fabric has been cut properly from the roll, fold it selvedge to selvedge and see if it lies flat. If the cut ends are uneven and do not match, use one of the following methods to make the edge straight. Then press the fabric.

PULLING A THREAD TO OBTAIN A STRAIGHT EDGE

1 On a loose-woven fabric you can pull a weft thread to get a straight edge. First snip the selvedge, then find a single thread and tug it gently to pull it out.

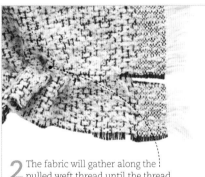

2 The fabric will gather along the pulled weft thread until the thread can be removed completely.

3 Carefully cut along the space left by the pulled-out weft thread.

CUTTING ON A STRIPE LINE TO OBTAIN A STRAIGHT EDGE

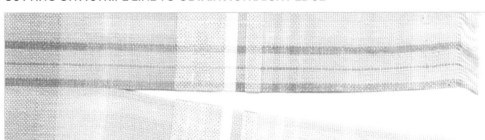

On checks and stripes, cut along the edge of one of the boldest stripes to achieve a straight edge.

PATTERN LAYOUT

Fabric is usually folded selvedge to selvedge. With the fabric folded, the pattern is pinned on top, and both the right- and left-side pieces are cut out at the same time. If pattern pieces have to be cut from single layer fabric, remember to cut matching pairs. For a fabric with a design it is a good idea to have the right side of the fabric on the outside so that you can arrange the pattern pieces to show off the design. If you have left- and right-side pattern pieces, they are cut on single fabric with the fabric right side up and the pattern right side up.

PINNING THE PATTERN TO THE FABRIC

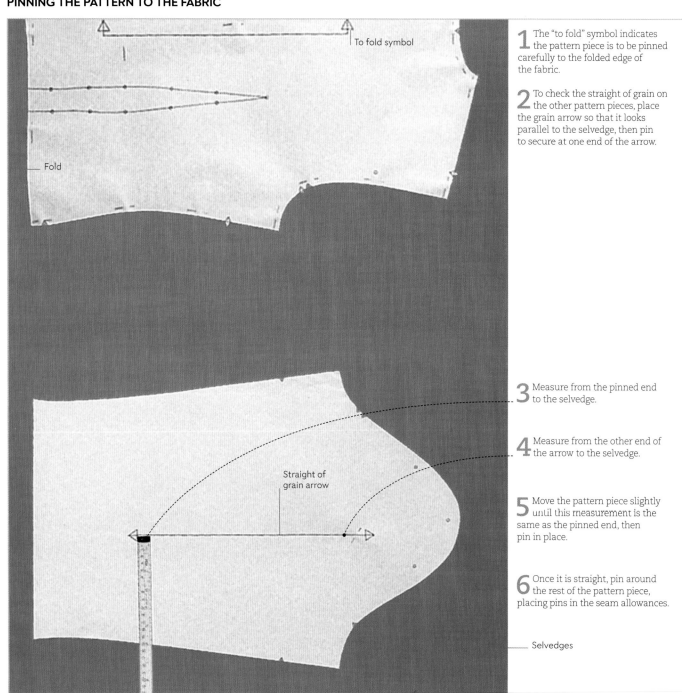

To fold symbol

Fold

Straight of grain arrow

Selvedges

1 The "to fold" symbol indicates the pattern piece is to be pinned carefully to the folded edge of the fabric.

2 To check the straight of grain on the other pattern pieces, place the grain arrow so that it looks parallel to the selvedge, then pin to secure at one end of the arrow.

3 Measure from the pinned end to the selvedge.

4 Measure from the other end of the arrow to the selvedge.

5 Move the pattern piece slightly until this measurement is the same as the pinned end, then pin in place.

6 Once it is straight, pin around the rest of the pattern piece, placing pins in the seam allowances.

GENERAL GUIDE TO LAYOUT

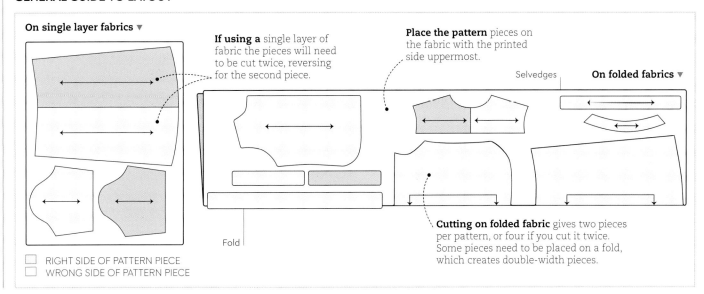

On single layer fabrics ▼

If using a single layer of fabric the pieces will need to be cut twice, reversing for the second piece.

Place the pattern pieces on the fabric with the printed side uppermost.

Selvedges

On folded fabrics ▼

Fold

Cutting on folded fabric gives two pieces per pattern, or four if you cut it twice. Some pieces need to be placed on a fold, which creates double-width pieces.

☐ RIGHT SIDE OF PATTERN PIECE
☐ WRONG SIDE OF PATTERN PIECE

LAYOUT ON A CROSSWAYS FOLD WITH A NAP

If a crossways fold is required in a fabric with a nap, fold the fabric with the wrong sides together, then cut into two pieces. Turn one around to make sure that the nap is running in the same direction on both pieces. Place the two pieces of fabric together, wrong side to wrong side.

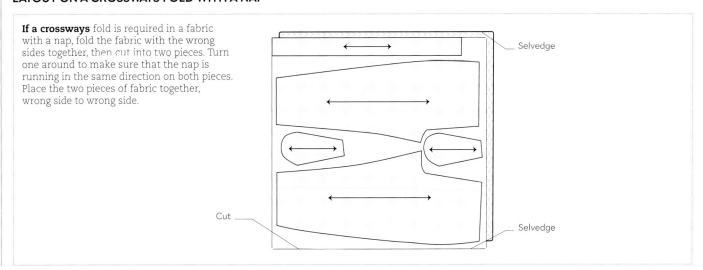

Selvedge

Cut

Selvedge

LAYOUT ON A PARTIAL FOLD

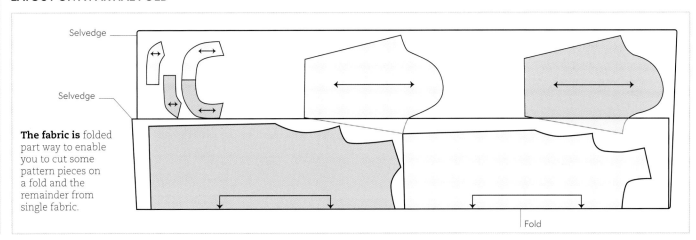

Selvedge

Selvedge

The fabric is folded part way to enable you to cut some pattern pieces on a fold and the remainder from single fabric.

Fold

STRIPES AND CHECKS

For fabrics with a stripe or check pattern, a little more care is needed when laying out the pattern pieces. If the checks and stripes are running across or down the length of the fabric when cutting out, they will run the same direction in the finished garment. So it is important to place the pattern pieces to ensure that the checks and stripes match and that they run together at the seams. If possible, try to place the pattern pieces so each has a stripe down the centre. With a checked fabric, be aware of the hemline placement on the pattern.

EVEN AND UNEVEN STRIPES

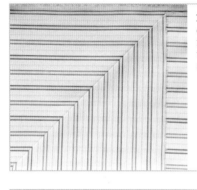

Even stripes When a corner of the fabric is folded back diagonally, the stripes will meet up at the fold.

Uneven stripes When a corner of the fabric is folded back diagonally, the stripes will not match at the fold.

EVEN AND UNEVEN CHECKS

Even checks When a corner of the fabric is folded back diagonally, the checks will be symmetrical on both of the fabric areas.

Uneven checks When a corner of the fabric is folded back diagonally, the checks will be uneven lengthways, widthways, or both.

MATCHING STRIPES OR CHECKS ON A SKIRT

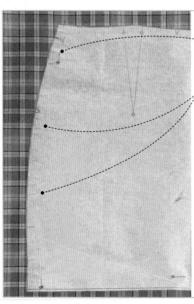

1 Place one of the skirt pattern pieces on the fabric and pin in place.

2 Mark on the pattern the position of the boldest lines of the checks or stripes.

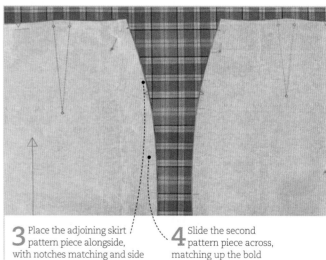

3 Place the adjoining skirt pattern piece alongside, with notches matching and side seams even. Transfer the marks to the second pattern piece.

4 Slide the second pattern piece across, matching up the bold lines. Pin in place.

MATCHING STRIPES OR CHECKS AT THE ARMHOLE

1 Mark the boldest lines of the stripes or checks around the armhole on the front bodice pattern.

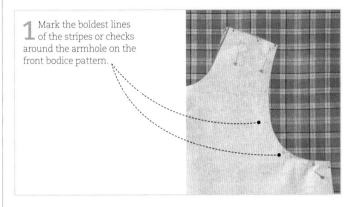

2 Place the sleeve pattern on to the armhole, matching the notches, and copy the marks on to the sleeve pattern.

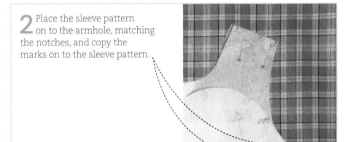

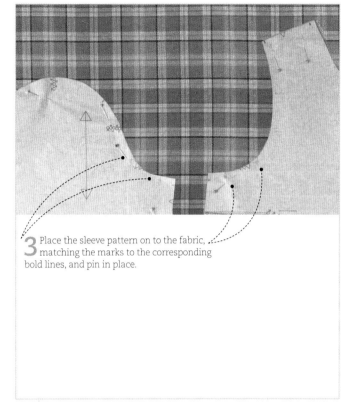

3 Place the sleeve pattern on to the fabric, matching the marks to the corresponding bold lines, and pin in place.

LAYOUT FOR UNEVEN CHECKS OR STRIPES ON UNFOLDED FABRIC

Hem foldline is placed on a prominent stripe

Centre back is aligned with a prominent lengthwise stripe

Pattern piece is cut out twice from single layer of fabric

Bars align on both collar pieces

Selvedge

LAYOUT FOR EVEN CHECKS ON FOLDED FABRIC

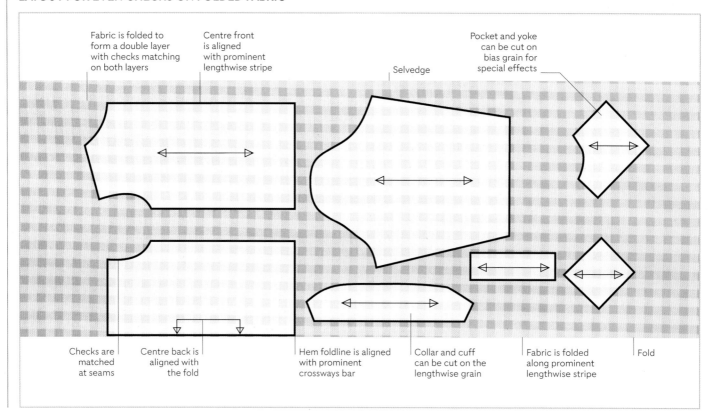

Fabric is folded to form a double layer with checks matching on both layers

Centre front is aligned with prominent lengthwise stripe

Selvedge

Pocket and yoke can be cut on bias grain for special effects

Checks are matched at seams

Centre back is aligned with the fold

Hem foldline is aligned with prominent crossways bar

Collar and cuff can be cut on the lengthwise grain

Fabric is folded along prominent lengthwise stripe

Fold

LAYOUT FOR EVEN STRIPES ON FOLDED FABRIC

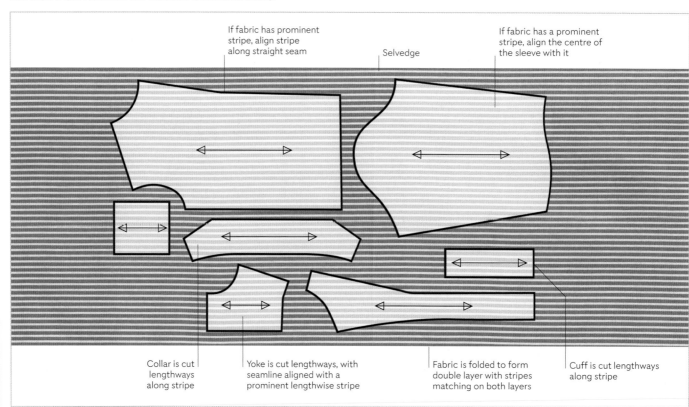

If fabric has prominent stripe, align stripe along straight seam

Selvedge

If fabric has a prominent stripe, align the centre of the sleeve with it

Collar is cut lengthways along stripe

Yoke is cut lengthways, with seamline aligned with a prominent lengthwise stripe

Fabric is folded to form double layer with stripes matching on both layers

Cuff is cut lengthways along stripe

LAYOUT FOR HIGHLY PATTERNED FABRIC

Large patterns require a nap layout

For centre front or back seams lay the pattern so the cutting line is placed on the same part of the design

Avoid a large part of the pattern falling on a prominent part of the body such as the point of bust dart

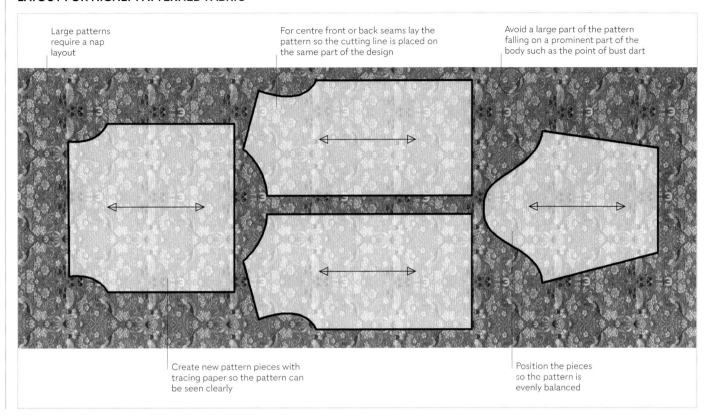

Create new pattern pieces with tracing paper so the pattern can be seen clearly

Position the pieces so the pattern is evenly balanced

CUTTING ON THE BIAS

Selvedge

To cut on the bias the straight of grainline must follow the true bias (45 degrees) of the fabric

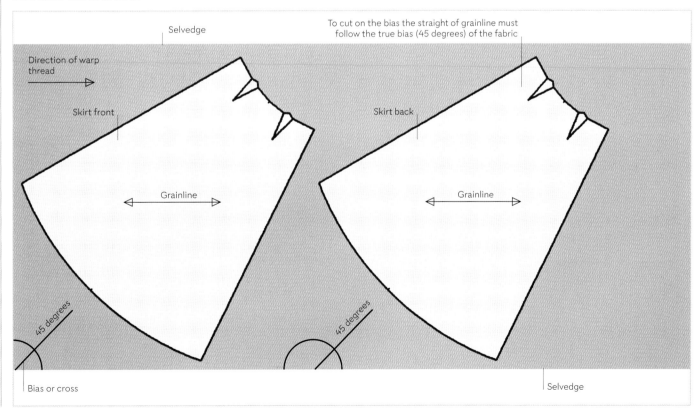

Direction of warp thread

Skirt front

Skirt back

Grainline

Grainline

45 degrees

45 degrees

Bias or cross

Selvedge

Cutting out accurately

Careful, smooth cutting around the pattern pieces will ensure that they join together accurately. Always cut out on a smooth, flat surface such as a table – the floor is not ideal – and be sure your scissors are sharp. Use the full blade of the scissors on long, straight edges, sliding the blades along the fabric; use smaller cuts around curves. Do not nibble or snip at the fabric.

HOW TO CUT

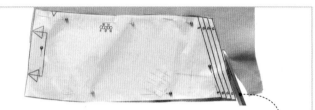

If you are right-handed, place your left hand on the pattern and fabric to hold them in place, and cut cleanly with the scissor blades at a right angle to the fabric.

MARKING NOTCHES

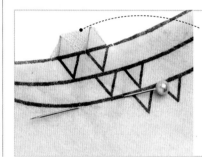

These symbols need to be marked on to the fabric as they are matching points. One of the easiest ways to do this is to cut out the mirror image of the notches in the fabric. Rather than cutting out double or triple notches separately, cut straight across from point to point.

MARKING DOTS

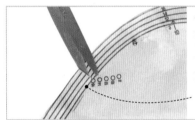

You can cut a small clip into the fabric to mark the dots that indicate the top of the shoulder on a sleeve. Alternatively, these can be marked with tailor's tacks (see opposite).

CLIPPING LINES

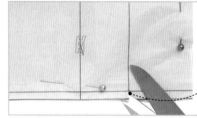

A small clip or snip into the fabric is a useful way to mark some of the lines that appear on a pattern, such as the centre front line and foldlines or notches and dart ends.

PATTERN MARKING

Once the pattern pieces have been cut out, but before you remove the pattern, you will need to mark the symbols shown on the pattern through to the fabric. There are various ways to do this. Tailor's tacks are good for circles and dots, or these can be marked with a water- or air-soluble pen. When using a pen, it's a good idea to test it on a piece of scrap fabric first. For lines, you can use trace tacks or a tracing wheel with dressmaker's carbon paper.

TRACE TACKS

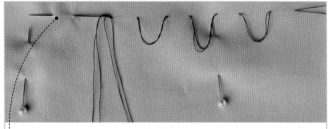

1 This is a really useful technique to mark centre front lines, foldlines, and placement lines. With double thread in your needle, stitch a row of loopy stitches, sewing along the line marked on the pattern.

2 Carefully pull away the tissue. Cut through the loops, then gently separate the layers of fabric to show the threads. Snip apart to leave thread tails in both of the fabric layers.

TAILOR'S TACKS

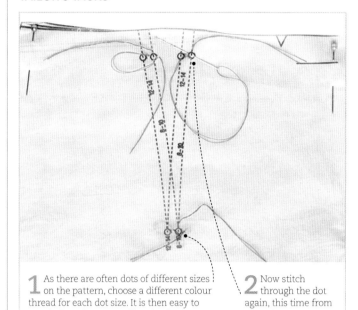

1 As there are often dots of different sizes on the pattern, choose a different colour thread for each dot size. It is then easy to match the colours as well as the dots. Have double thread in your needle, unknotted. Insert the needle through the dot from right to left, leaving a tail of thread. Be sure to go through the pattern and both layers of fabric.

2 Now stitch through the dot again, this time from top to bottom to make a loop. Cut through the loop, then snip off excess thread to leave a tail.

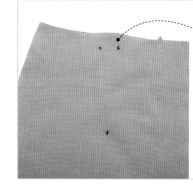

3 Carefully pull the pattern away. On the top side you will have four threads marking each dot. When you turn the fabric over, the dot positions will be marked with an X.

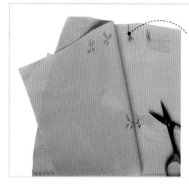

4 Gently turn back the two layers of fabric to separate them, then cut through the threads so that thread tails are left in both pieces of fabric.

TRACING PAPER AND WHEEL

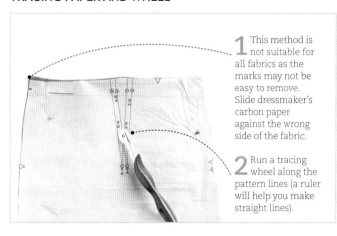

1 This method is not suitable for all fabrics as the marks may not be easy to remove. Slide dressmaker's carbon paper against the wrong side of the fabric.

2 Run a tracing wheel along the pattern lines (a ruler will help you make straight lines).

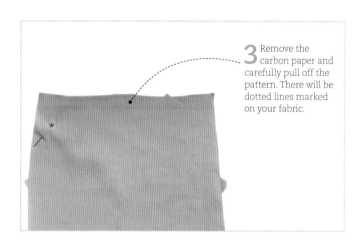

3 Remove the carbon paper and carefully pull off the pattern. There will be dotted lines marked on your fabric.

MARKER PENS

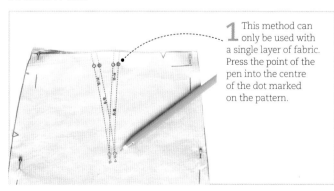

1 This method can only be used with a single layer of fabric. Press the point of the pen into the centre of the dot marked on the pattern.

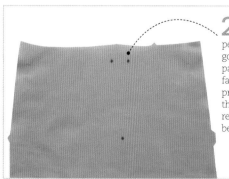

2 Carefully remove the pattern. The pen marks will have gone through the pattern on to the fabric. Be sure not to press the fabric before the pen marks are removed or they may become permanent.

Techniques

Tailoring employs its own special and unique techniques, many of which relate to hand sewing, and advanced construction methods – from making tucks and darts to creating crisp collars and inserting sleeves.

Stitches for hand sewing

Although modern sewing machines have eliminated the need for a lot of hand sewing, it is still necessary to use hand stitching to prepare the fabric prior to permanent stitching – these temporary pattern marking and tacking stitches will eventually be removed. Permanent hand stitching is used to finish a garment and to attach fasteners, as well as to help out with a quick repair.

THREADING THE NEEDLE

When sewing by hand, cut your piece of thread to be no longer than the distance from your fingertips to your elbow. If the thread is much longer than this, it will knot as you sew.

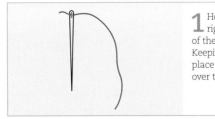

1 Hold your needle in your right hand and the end of the thread in your left. Keeping the thread still, place the eye of the needle over the thread.

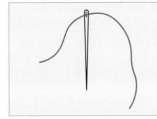

2 If the needle will not slip over the thread, dampen your fingers and run the moisture across the eye of the needle. Pull the thread through.

3 At the other end of the thread, tie a knot as shown (left) or secure the thread (shown right).

4 You are now ready to start sewing.

SECURING THE THREAD

The ends of the thread must be secured firmly, especially if the hand stitching is to be permanent. A knot (see left) is frequently used and is the preferred choice for temporary stitches. For permanent stitching a double stitch is a better option.

DOUBLE STITCH

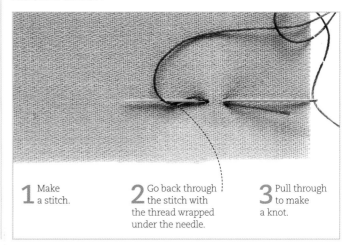

1 Make a stitch.

2 Go back through the stitch with the thread wrapped under the needle.

3 Pull through to make a knot.

BACKSTITCH

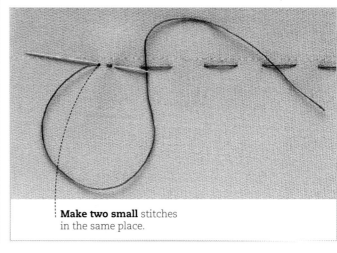

Make two small stitches in the same place.

TACKING STITCHES

Each of the many types of tacking stitches has its own individual use. Trace tacks are used to transfer pattern markings to fabric. Basic tacks and bar tacks hold two or more pieces of fabric together. Long-and-short tacks are an alternative version of the basic tacking stitch, often used when the tacking will stay in the work for some time. Thread chain tacks work in a similar way to bar tacks but are much finer as they are made by looping a single thread through itself. Diagonal tacks hold folds or overlaid fabrics together, while slip tacks are used to hold a fold in fabric to another piece of fabric.

BASIC TACKS

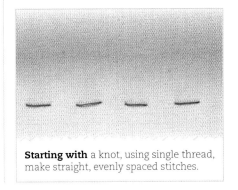

Starting with a knot, using single thread, make straight, evenly spaced stitches.

DIAGONAL TACKS

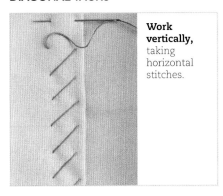

Work vertically, taking horizontal stitches.

SLIP TACKS

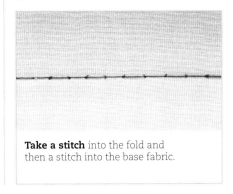

Take a stitch into the fold and then a stitch into the base fabric.

LONG-AND-SHORT TACKS

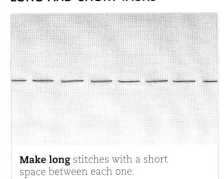

Make long stitches with a short space between each one.

BAR TACKS

1 Using double thread, make two or three loops between the two layers of fabric.

2 Work a buttonhole stitch (see p.103) across the loops.

THREAD CHAIN TACKS

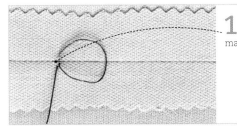

1 Start with a stitch in the fabric and make a loop.

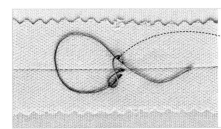

2 Make another loop from the thread and push through the first loop, then pull to tighten the first loop.

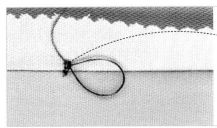

3 Repeat the process. Eventually you will have made a thread chain.

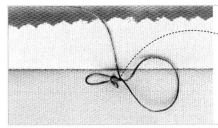

4 To finish, take a single thread through the last loop and pull to tighten. Use the thread end to stitch the loop as required.

HAND STITCHES

There are a number of hand stitches that can be used during construction of a garment. Some are for decorative purposes while others are more functional.

BACKSTITCH

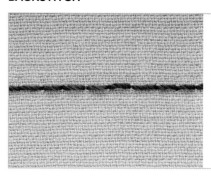

A strong stitch that could be used to construct a piece of work. Work from right to left. Bring the needle up, leaving a space, and then take the thread back to the end of the last stitch. Repeat.

RUNNING STITCH

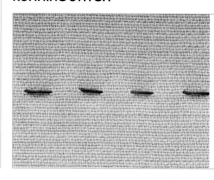

Very similar to tacking (see p.101), but used more for decorative purposes. Work from right to left. Run the needle in and out of the fabric to create even stitches and spaces.

PRICK STITCH

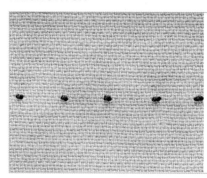

Often used to highlight the edge of a completed garment, such as a collar. Work from right to left. Make small stitches about 2mm (1⁄16in) long, with spaces between of at least three times that length.

WHIP STITCH

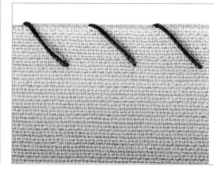

A diagonal stitch sewn with a single thread along a raw edge to prevent fraying. Work from right to left. Take a stitch through the edge of the fabric. The depth of the stitch depends on the thickness of the fabric – for a thin fabric take a shallow stitch.

HERRINGBONE STITCH

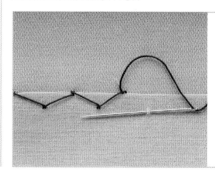

A very useful stitch as it is secure yet has some movement in it. It is used to secure hems and interlinings. Work from left to right. Take a small horizontal stitch into one layer and then the other, so the thread crosses itself.

FLAT FELL STITCH

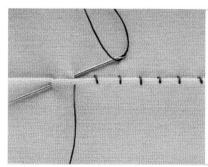

A strong, secure stitch to hold two layers permanently together. This stitch is often used to secure bias bindings and linings. Work from right to left. Make a short, straight stitch at the edge of the fabric.

SLIP HEM STITCH

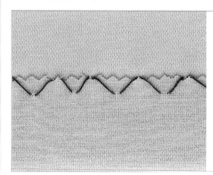

Also called a catch stitch, this is used primarily for securing hems. It looks similar to herringbone (above). Work from right to left. Take a short horizontal stitch into one layer and then the other.

BLIND HEM STITCH

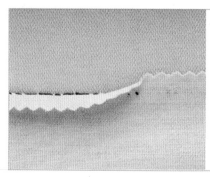

As the name suggests this is for hemming a garment. As the stitch is under the edge of the fabric it should be discreet. Work from right to left and use a slip hem stitch (left).

BUTTONHOLE STITCH

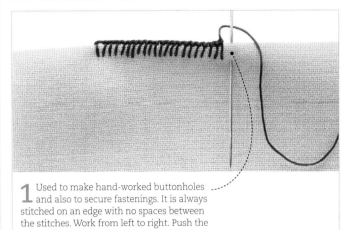

1 Used to make hand-worked buttonholes and also to secure fastenings. It is always stitched on an edge with no spaces between the stitches. Work from left to right. Push the needle from the top edge into the fabric.

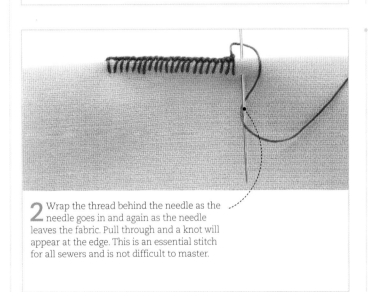

2 Wrap the thread behind the needle as the needle goes in and again as the needle leaves the fabric. Pull through and a knot will appear at the edge. This is an essential stitch for all sewers and is not difficult to master.

CROSS STITCH

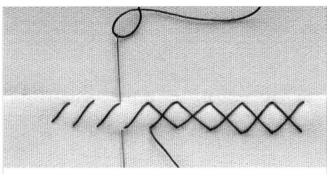

A temporary securing stitch used to hold pleats in place after construction. It can also be used to secure linings. Work a row of even diagonal stitches in one direction and then a row back over them to make crosses.

SLIP STITCH/LADDER STITCH

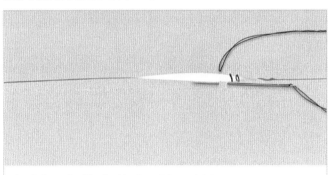

A stitch worked in double thread from right to left to secure a gap in a seam. Take a small horizontal stitch on one side and then a small horizontal stitch on the opposite side. When tightened, the gap is seamlessly closed.

BLANKET STITCH

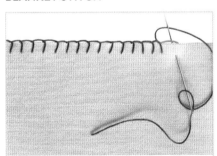

Similar to buttonhole stitch (above) but without the knot. Blanket stitch is useful to neaten edges and for decorative purposes. Always leave a space between the stitches. Push the needle into the fabric and, as it appears at the edge, wrap the thread under the needle.

FEATHER/BASEBALL STITCH

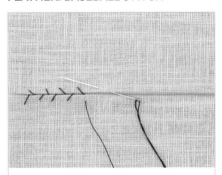

1 This stitch is worked from left to right and secures two edges together, that butt together or align. Take the stitch through the fold and then insert your needle diagonally through the opposite edge.

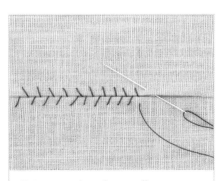

2 Repeat to give a chevron effect to secure the two edges together, either temporarily during the construction of a garment, or permanently.

HAND-STITCHED ARROWHEADS

An arrowhead is a triangular shape made by working straight stitches in a set order. This is a permanent stitch placed at an area of strain or stress, such as the top of a split.

PAD STITCHING

Pad stitching is used to secure canvas interfacing to jacket fronts. It is also used to secure two layers of canvas together, and will provide shape and structure. This stitch is all about needle control.

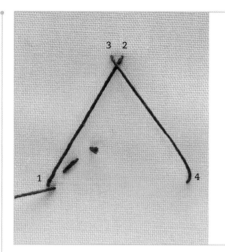

1 Mark a triangle with sides about 8mm (⁵⁄₁₆in) long on the fabric. Start with a knot. Bring the needle up through **1** and down through **2**.

2 Then bring the needle up through **3** and down through **4**. Repeat the stitch.

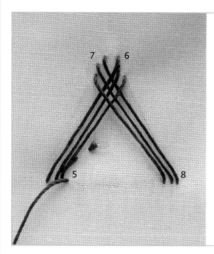

3 Continue the stitches, up through **5** and down through **6**, up through **7** and down through **8**.

4 Make about 10 alternating stitches to complete the arrowhead.

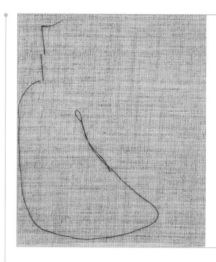

1 Similarly to diagonal tacks (see p.101) or basting, work this stitch vertically, horizontally, or diagonally in rows.

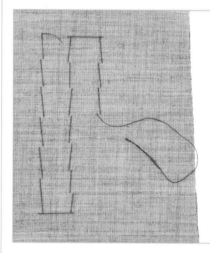

2 Sew the longer pad stitches between 2.5–3cm (1–1¼in) long and work in rows 2.5cm (1in) apart. Take the needle through the canvas and pick up a few threads of the under layer to make a stitch at 90 degrees. Do not go all the way through – this stitch does not show at all on the right side.

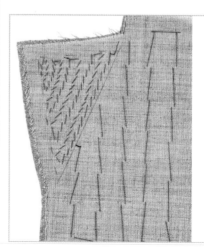

3 On lapels, the pad stitch should be worked much shorter and deeper. Again, pick up the under layer but do not go all the way through. The shorter version of this stitch is also a little tighter and will give a dimple effect on the underside of the lapel.

Machine stitches and seams

When making a garment, fabric is joined together using seams. The most common seam is a plain seam, which is suitable for a wide variety of fabrics and garments. However, there are many other seams to be used as appropriate, depending on the fabric and garment being constructed.

SECURING THE THREAD

Machine stitches need to be secured at the end of a seam to prevent them from coming undone. This can be done by hand, tying the ends of the thread, or using the machine with a reverse stitch or a locking stitch, which works three or four stitches in the same place.

TIE THE ENDS

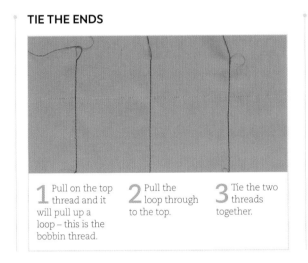

1 Pull on the top thread and it will pull up a loop – this is the bobbin thread.

2 Pull the loop through to the top.

3 Tie the two threads together.

REVERSE STITCH

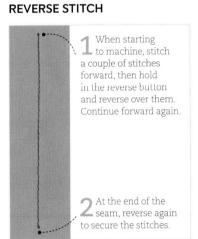

1 When starting to machine, stitch a couple of stitches forward, then hold in the reverse button and reverse over them. Continue forward again.

2 At the end of the seam, reverse again to secure the stitches.

LOCKING STITCH

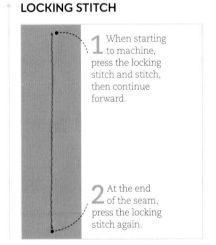

1 When starting to machine, press the locking stitch and stitch, then continue forward.

2 At the end of the seam, press the locking stitch again.

STITCHES MADE WITH A MACHINE

The sewing machine will stitch plain seams and decorative seams as well as buttonholes of various styles. The length and width of buttonholes can be altered to suit the garment.

STRAIGHT STITCH

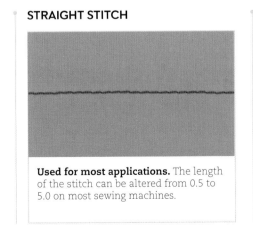

Used for most applications. The length of the stitch can be altered from 0.5 to 5.0 on most sewing machines.

ZIGZAG STITCH

To neaten seam edges and for securing and decorative purposes. Both the width and the length of this stitch can be altered.

3-STEP ZIGZAG STITCH

Made up of small, straight stitches. This stitch is decorative as well as functional. The stitch length and width can be altered.

BLIND HEM STITCH

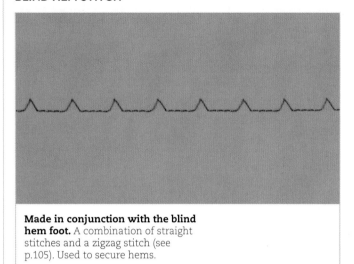

Made in conjunction with the blind hem foot. A combination of straight stitches and a zigzag stitch (see p.105). Used to secure hems.

OVEREDGE STITCH

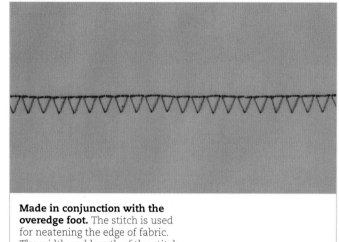

Made in conjunction with the overedge foot. The stitch is used for neatening the edge of fabric. The width and length of the stitch can be altered.

BASIC BUTTONHOLE STITCH

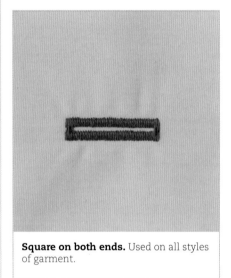

Square on both ends. Used on all styles of garment.

ROUND-END BUTTONHOLE STITCH

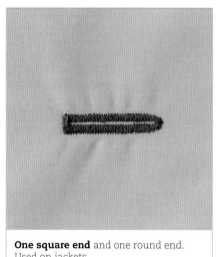

One square end and one round end. Used on jackets.

KEYHOLE BUTTONHOLE STITCH

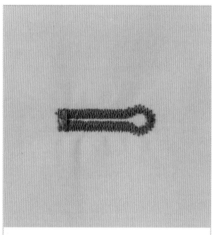

One square end and one end shaped like a loop. Used on jackets.

3-THREAD OVERLOCK STITCH

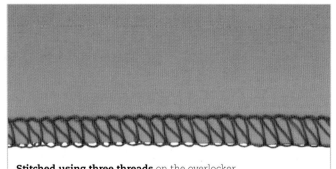

Stitched using three threads on the overlocker. Used to neaten the edge of fabric to prevent fraying.

4-THREAD OVERLOCK STITCH

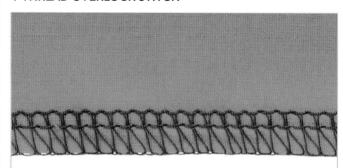

Made using four threads on the overlocker. Used to neaten edges on difficult fabrics or to construct a seam on stretch knits.

PLAIN SEAM

A plain seam is 1.5cm (⅝in) wide. It is important that the seam is stitched accurately at this measurement, otherwise the garment will end up being the wrong size and shape. There are guides on the plate of the sewing machine to help align the fabric correctly.

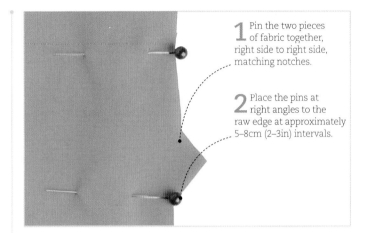

1 Pin the two pieces of fabric together, right side to right side, matching notches.

2 Place the pins at right angles to the raw edge at approximately 5–8cm (2–3in) intervals.

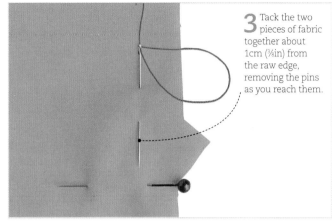

3 Tack the two pieces of fabric together about 1cm (⅜in) from the raw edge, removing the pins as you reach them.

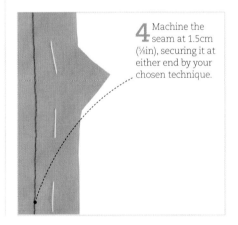

4 Machine the seam at 1.5cm (⅝in), securing it at either end by your chosen technique.

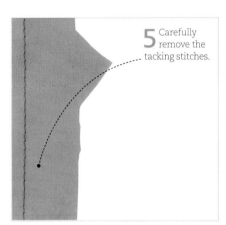

5 Carefully remove the tacking stitches.

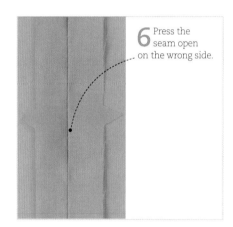

6 Press the seam open on the wrong side.

RUN AND FELL SEAM

Some garments require a strong seam that will withstand frequent washing and wear and tear. A run and fell seam, also known as a flat fell seam, is very strong. It is made on the right side of a garment and is used on the inside leg seam of jeans and on tailored shirts.

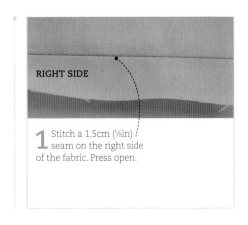

RIGHT SIDE

1 Stitch a 1.5cm (⅝in) seam on the right side of the fabric. Press open.

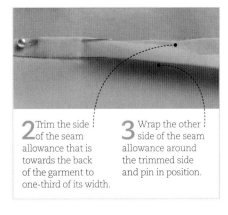

2 Trim the side of the seam allowance that is towards the back of the garment to one-third of its width.

3 Wrap the other side of the seam allowance around the trimmed side and pin in position.

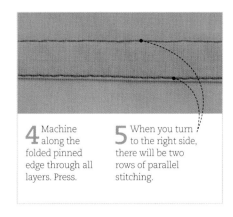

4 Machine along the folded pinned edge through all layers. Press.

5 When you turn to the right side, there will be two rows of parallel stitching.

SEAM NEATENING

It is important that the raw edges of the seam are neatened or finished – this will make the seam hard-wearing and prevent fraying. The method of neatening will depend on the style of item that is being made and the fabric you are using.

PINKED

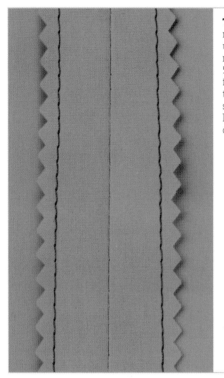

This method of neatening is ideal to use on fabrics that do not fray badly. Stitch 5mm (³⁄₁₆in) away from the raw edge, then use pinking shears to trim as little as possible off the edge.

ZIGZAGGED

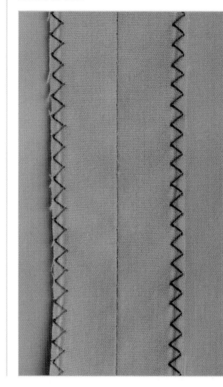

All sewing machines will make a zigzag stitch. It is an ideal stitch to use to stop the edges fraying and is suitable for all types of fabric. Stitch in from the raw edge, then trim back to the zigzag stitch. On most fabrics, use a stitch width of 2.0 and a stitch length of 1.5.

OVEREDGE STITCHED

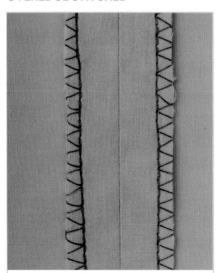

This is found on most sewing machines. Select the overedge stitch on your machine. Using the overedge machine foot and the pre-set stitch length and width, machine along the raw edge of the seam.

CLEAN FINISH

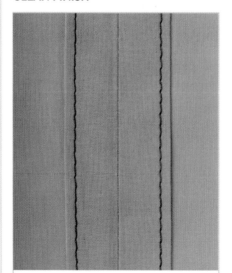

This is a very hard-wearing finish and is ideal for cottons and fine fabrics. Using a straight stitch, turn under the raw edge of the seam allowance by 3mm (¹⁄₈in) and straight stitch along the fold.

3-THREAD OVERLOCKED

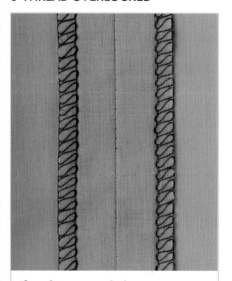

If you have an overlocker, you can neaten seams with a 3-thread overlock stitch. It is one of the most professional ways to finish seams and is suitable for all types of fabrics and items.

HONG KONG FINISH

This is a great finish to use on wools and linens, to neaten the seams on unlined jackets. It is made by wrapping the raw edge with bias-cut strips.

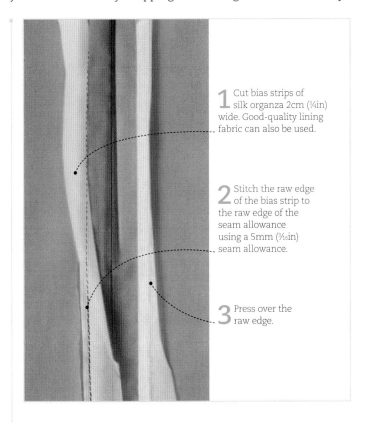

1 Cut bias strips of silk organza 2cm (¾in) wide. Good-quality lining fabric can also be used.

2 Stitch the raw edge of the bias strip to the raw edge of the seam allowance using a 5mm (³⁄₁₆in) seam allowance.

3 Press over the raw edge.

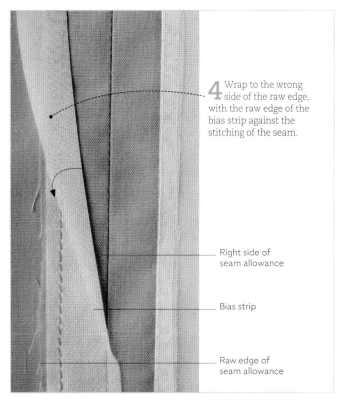

4 Wrap to the wrong side of the raw edge, with the raw edge of the bias strip against the stitching of the seam.

Right side of seam allowance

Bias strip

Raw edge of seam allowance

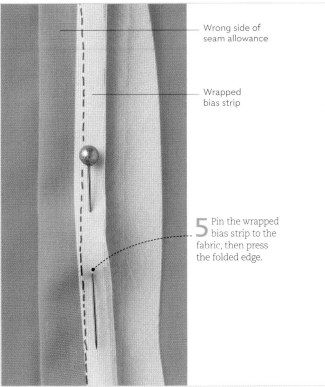

Wrong side of seam allowance

Wrapped bias strip

5 Pin the wrapped bias strip to the fabric, then press the folded edge.

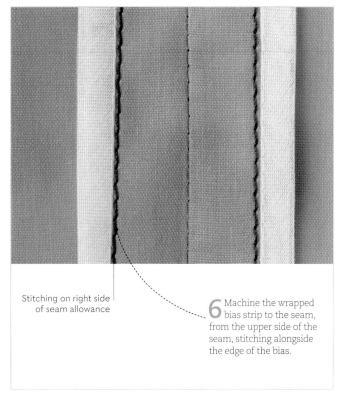

Stitching on right side of seam allowance

6 Machine the wrapped bias strip to the seam, from the upper side of the seam, stitching alongside the edge of the bias.

STITCHING CORNERS AND CURVES

Not all sewing is straight lines. The work may have curves and corners that require negotiation to produce sharp clean angles and curves on the right side. The technique for stitching a corner shown below applies to corners of all angles. On a thick fabric, the technique is slightly different, with a stitch taken across the corner, and on a fabric that frays badly the corner is reinforced with a second row of stitches.

STITCHING A CORNER

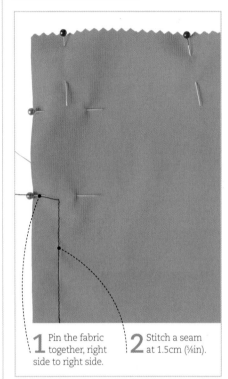

1 Pin the fabric together, right side to right side.

2 Stitch a seam at 1.5cm (⅝in).

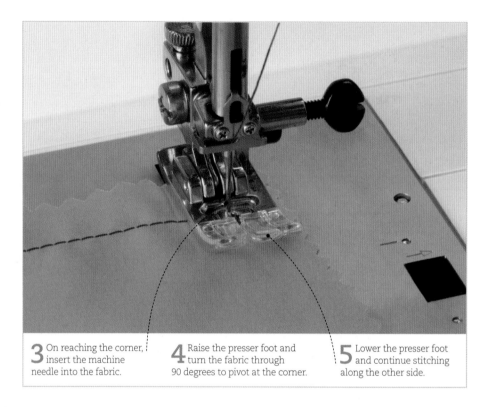

3 On reaching the corner, insert the machine needle into the fabric.

4 Raise the presser foot and turn the fabric through 90 degrees to pivot at the corner.

5 Lower the presser foot and continue stitching along the other side.

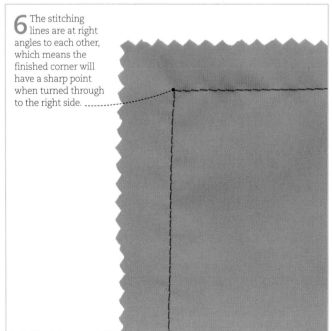

6 The stitching lines are at right angles to each other, which means the finished corner will have a sharp point when turned through to the right side.

STITCHING A CORNER ON HEAVY FABRIC

1 On a thick fabric it is very difficult to achieve a sharp point, so instead a single stitch is taken across the corner. First, stitch to the corner.

2 At the corner, insert the needle into the fabric, then lift the presser foot. Turn the fabric 45 degrees. Put the foot down again and make one stitch.

3 With the needle in the fabric, lift the foot and turn the fabric 45 degrees again. Lower the foot and continue stitching along the other side.

STITCHING A REINFORCED CORNER

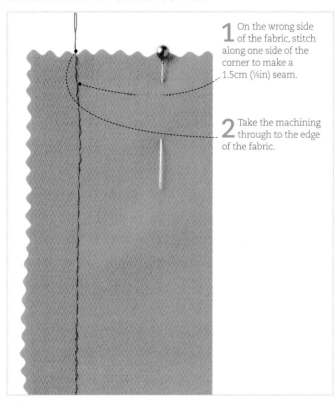

1 On the wrong side of the fabric, stitch along one side of the corner to make a 1.5cm (⅝in) seam.

2 Take the machining through to the edge of the fabric.

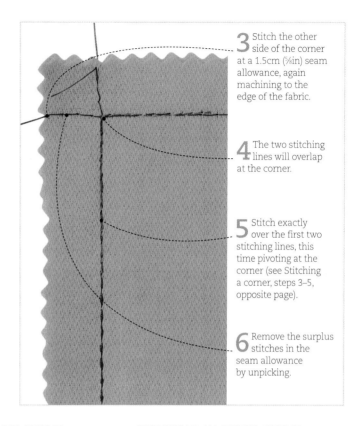

3 Stitch the other side of the corner at a 1.5cm (⅝in) seam allowance, again machining to the edge of the fabric.

4 The two stitching lines will overlap at the corner.

5 Stitch exactly over the first two stitching lines, this time pivoting at the corner (see Stitching a corner, steps 3–5, opposite page).

6 Remove the surplus stitches in the seam allowance by unpicking.

STITCHING AN INNER CORNER

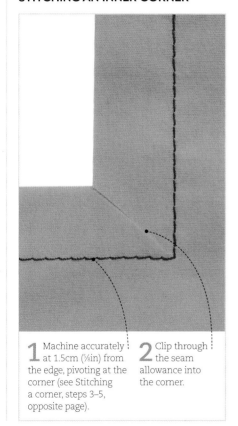

1 Machine accurately at 1.5cm (⅝in) from the edge, pivoting at the corner (see Stitching a corner, steps 3–5, opposite page).

2 Clip through the seam allowance into the corner.

STITCHING AN INNER CURVE

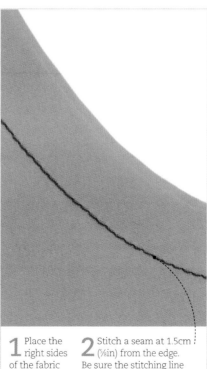

1 Place the right sides of the fabric together.

2 Stitch a seam at 1.5cm (⅝in) from the edge. Be sure the stitching line follows the curve (use the stitching guides on the needle plate to help).

STITCHING AN OUTER CURVE

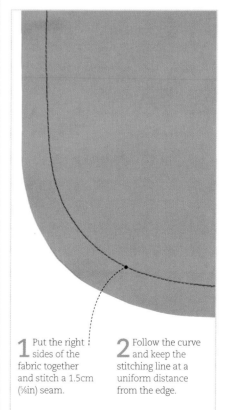

1 Put the right sides of the fabric together and stitch a 1.5cm (⅝in) seam.

2 Follow the curve and keep the stitching line at a uniform distance from the edge.

Reducing seam bulk

It is important that the seams used for construction do not cause bulk on the right side. To make sure this does not happen, the seam allowances need to be reduced in size by a technique known as layering a seam. They may also require V shapes to be removed, which is known as notching, or the seam allowance may be clipped.

LAYERING A SEAM

On the majority of fabrics, if the seam is on the edge of the work, the amount of fabric in the seam needs reducing. Leave the seam allowance that lies closest to the outside of the garment full width, but reduce the seam allowance that lies closest to the body.

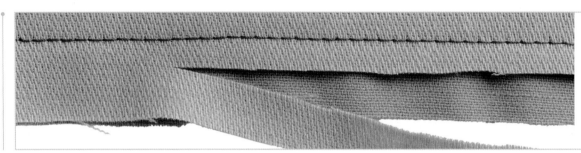

Cut along one side of the seam allowance to reduce the fabric in the seam allowance by half to one-third of its original width.

REDUCING SEAM BULK ON AN INNER CURVE

For an inner curve to lie flat, the seam will need to be layered and notched, then understitched to hold it in place.

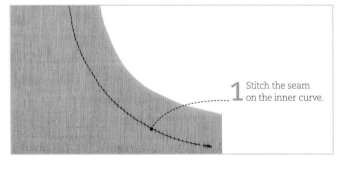

1 Stitch the seam on the inner curve.

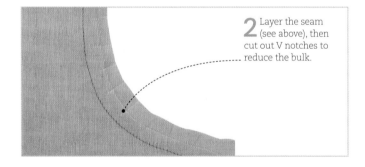

2 Layer the seam (see above), then cut out V notches to reduce the bulk.

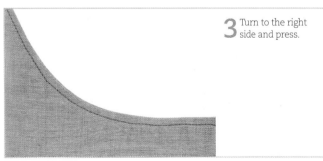

3 Turn to the right side and press.

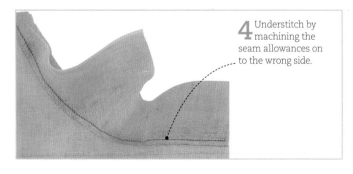

4 Understitch by machining the seam allowances on to the wrong side.

REDUCING SEAM BULK ON AN OUTER CURVE

An outer curve also needs layering and notching or clipping to allow the seam to be turned to the right side, after which it is understitched.

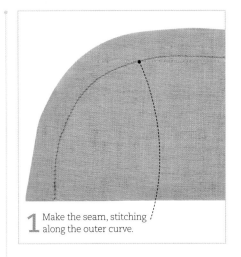

1 Make the seam, stitching along the outer curve.

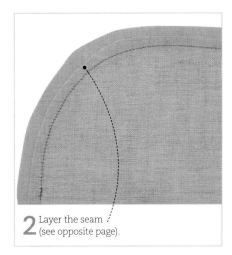

2 Layer the seam (see opposite page).

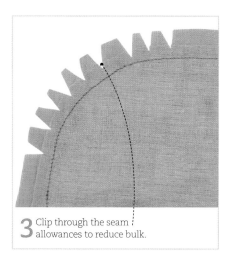

3 Clip through the seam allowances to reduce bulk.

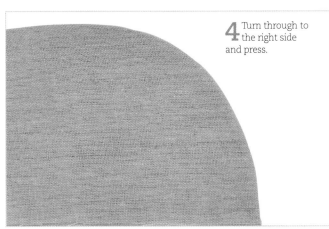

4 Turn through to the right side and press.

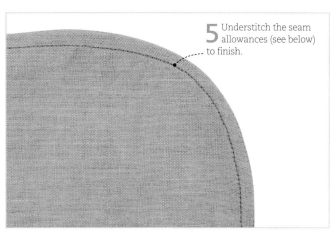

5 Understitch the seam allowances (see below) to finish.

FINISHING EDGES

Top-stitching and understitching are two methods to finish edges. Top-stitching is meant to be seen on the right side of the work, whereas understitching is not visible from the right side.

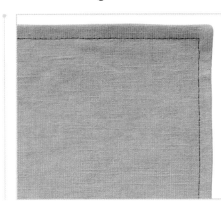

A top-stitch gives a decorative, sharp finish to an edge. Use a longer stitch length, of 3.0 or 3.5, and machine on the right side of the work, using the edge of the machine foot as a guide.

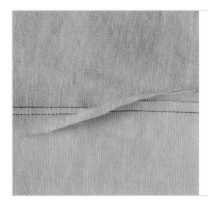

Understitching is used to secure a seam that is on the edge of a piece of fabric. It helps to stop the seam from rolling to the right side. First make the seam, then layer (see opposite page), turn to the right side and press. Working from the right side, machine the seam allowance to the facing or to the lining side of the fabric.

Darts

A dart is used to give shape to a piece of fabric so that it can fit around the contours of the body. Some darts are stitched following straight stitching lines and others are stitched following a slightly curved line. Always stitch a dart from the point to the wide end so you can sink the machine needle into the point accurately and securely.

PLAIN DART

This is the most common type of dart and is used to give shaping to the bust in the bodice. It is also found at the waist in skirts and trousers to give shape from the waist to the hip.

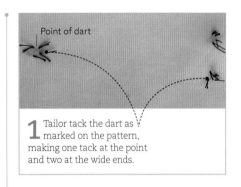

Point of dart

1 Tailor tack the dart as marked on the pattern, making one tack at the point and two at the wide ends.

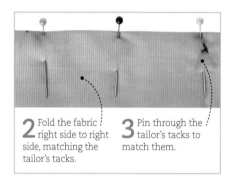

2 Fold the fabric right side to right side, matching the tailor's tacks.

3 Pin through the tailor's tacks to match them.

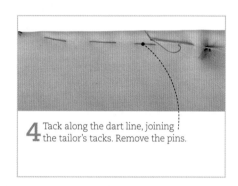

4 Tack along the dart line, joining the tailor's tacks. Remove the pins.

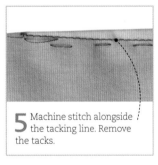

5 Machine stitch alongside the tacking line. Remove the tacks.

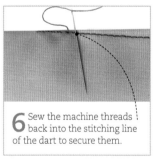

6 Sew the machine threads back into the stitching line of the dart to secure them.

7 Press the dart to one side (see opposite page).

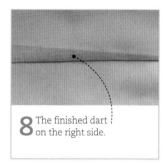

8 The finished dart on the right side.

SHAPING DARTS TO FIT

Our bodies have curves, and the straight line of the dart may not sit closely enough to our own personal shape. The dart can be stitched slightly concave or convex so it follows our contours. Do not curve the dart by more than 3mm (1/8in) from the straight line.

CONVEX DART

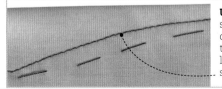

Use this for fuller shapes. Stitch the dart slightly inside the normal stitching line, to make a smooth convex curve.

CONCAVE DART

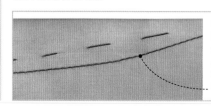

This is for thinner bodies as it takes up more fabric. Stitch the dart slightly outside the normal stitching line, in a smooth concave curve.

CONTOUR OR DOUBLE-POINTED DART

This type of dart is like two darts joined together at their wide ends.
It is used to give shape at the waist of a dress. It will contour the fabric
from the bust into the waist and then from the waist out towards the hip.

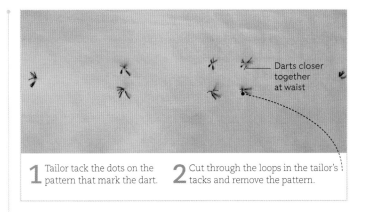

Darts closer
together
at waist

1 Tailor tack the dots on the pattern that mark the dart.

2 Cut through the loops in the tailor's tacks and remove the pattern.

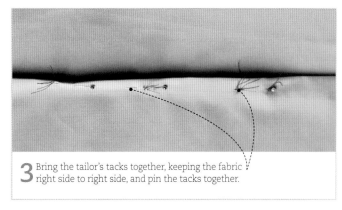

3 Bring the tailor's tacks together, keeping the fabric right side to right side, and pin the tacks together.

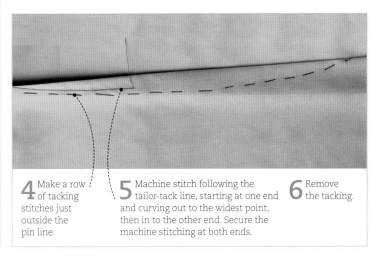

4 Make a row of tacking stitches just outside the pin line.

5 Machine stitch following the tailor-tack line, starting at one end and curving out to the widest point, then in to the other end. Secure the machine stitching at both ends.

6 Remove the tacking.

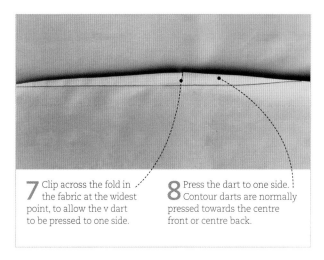

7 Clip across the fold in the fabric at the widest point, to allow the v dart to be pressed to one side.

8 Press the dart to one side. Contour darts are normally pressed towards the centre front or centre back.

PRESSING A DART

If a dart is pressed incorrectly it can spoil the look of a garment. For successful pressing
you will need a tailor's ham and a steam iron on a steam setting. A pressing cloth may
be required for delicate fabrics such as silk, satin, and chiffon, and for lining fabrics.

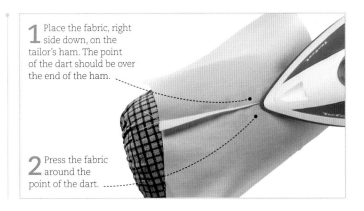

1 Place the fabric, right side down, on the tailor's ham. The point of the dart should be over the end of the ham.

2 Press the fabric around the point of the dart.

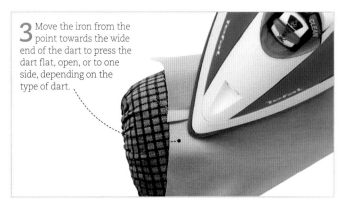

3 Move the iron from the point towards the wide end of the dart to press the dart flat, open, or to one side, depending on the type of dart.

BALANCED DART

This dart is used on thicker fabrics such as wool, crepe, or tweed, as well as on fabrics that mark when pressed. The addition of a balancing strip helps distribute the fabric on either side of the dart on the wrong side, making it less conspicuous on the worn garment.

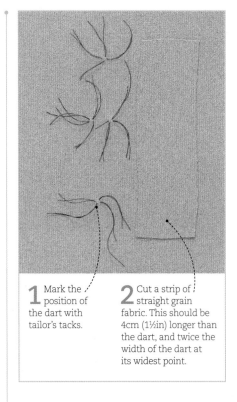

1 Mark the position of the dart with tailor's tacks.

2 Cut a strip of straight grain fabric. This should be 4cm (1½in) longer than the dart, and twice the width of the dart at its widest point.

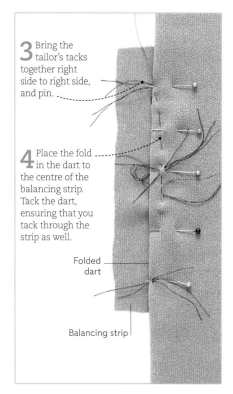

3 Bring the tailor's tacks together right side to right side, and pin.

4 Place the fold in the dart to the centre of the balancing strip. Tack the dart, ensuring that you tack through the strip as well.

Folded dart

Balancing strip

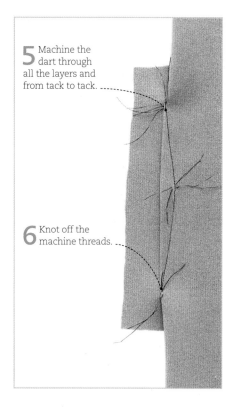

5 Machine the dart through all the layers and from tack to tack.

6 Knot off the machine threads.

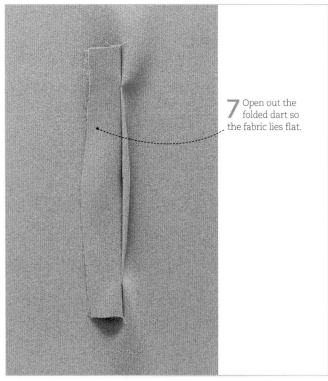

7 Open out the folded dart so the fabric lies flat.

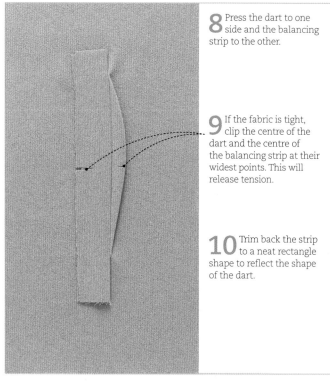

8 Press the dart to one side and the balancing strip to the other.

9 If the fabric is tight, clip the centre of the dart and the centre of the balancing strip at their widest points. This will release tension.

10 Trim back the strip to a neat rectangle shape to reflect the shape of the dart.

Tucks

A tuck is a decorative addition to any piece of fabric, and can be big and bold or very delicate. Tucks are made by stitching evenly spaced folds into the fabric on the right side, normally on the straight grain of the fabric. As the tucks take up additional fabric, it is advisable to make them prior to cutting out.

PLAIN TUCKS

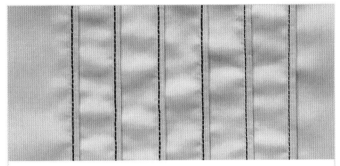

A plain tuck is made by marking and creasing the fabric at regular intervals. A row of machine stitches is then worked adjacent to each of the folds.

PIN TUCKS

These narrow, regularly spaced tucks are stitched very close to the foldline, which may require moving the machine needle closer to the fold. Use the pintuck foot on the sewing machine.

ADDING A TUCK ON A SHIRT BACK

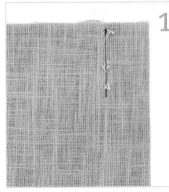

1 Mark the tuck with trace tacking.

2 Fold the fabric, right side to right side, bringing the rows of tacks together. Stitch along the markings. Remove the tacks and press either as shown or to one side.

ADDING A FRONT TUCK ON TROUSER LEGS

1 Mark the tuck lines.

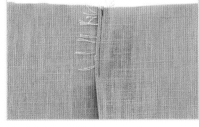

2 On the right side, fold along one line of tailor's tacks and place over the other line of tailor's tacks. Pin.

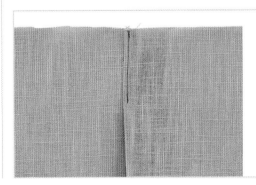

3 Machine along the tuck close to the folded edge.

Linings

A lining is placed inside a garment primarily to make the garment more comfortable to wear – it will prevent the garment from sticking to you. It will also make the garment last longer. Choose a good-quality lining made from rayon or acetate as these fabrics will breathe with your body. Polyester linings can be sticky to wear.

HAND INSERTED SLEEVE LINING

In tailoring it is advisable to insert a sleeve lining by hand. This will ensure the lining does not "pull" in the shoulder area and will enable more movement through the shoulder.

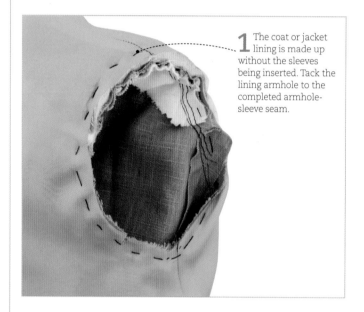

1 The coat or jacket lining is made up without the sleeves being inserted. Tack the lining armhole to the completed armhole-sleeve seam.

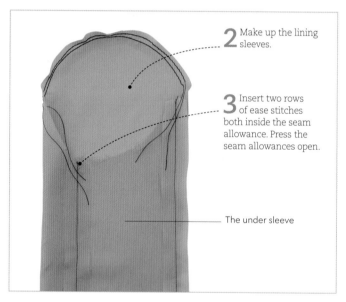

2 Make up the lining sleeves.

3 Insert two rows of ease stitches both inside the seam allowance. Press the seam allowances open.

The under sleeve

4 Place the lining sleeve into the jacket sleeve, wrong side to wrong side. Turn under the 1.5cm (⁵⁄₈in) sleeve seam allowance and pin to the armhole, matching seams and pattern markings.

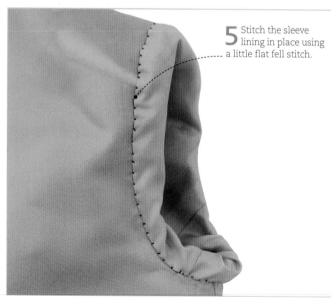

5 Stitch the sleeve lining in place using a little flat fell stitch.

LINING A SKIRT

Cut the lining out the same as the skirt, using the same pattern pieces, and join together, leaving a gap for the zip. Do not stitch in the darts.

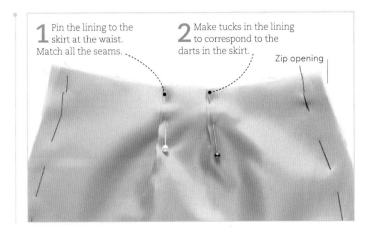

1 Pin the lining to the skirt at the waist. Match all the seams.

2 Make tucks in the lining to correspond to the darts in the skirt.

Zip opening

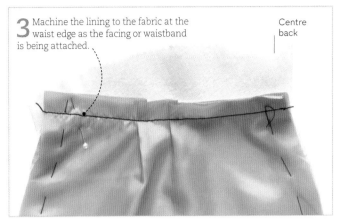

3 Machine the lining to the fabric at the waist edge as the facing or waistband is being attached.

Centre back

HEMMING A LINING

The lining on a skirt or dress should be slightly shorter – about 4cm (1½in) – than the finished garment, so that the lining does not show when you are walking or sitting.

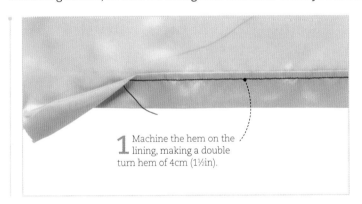

1 Machine the hem on the lining, making a double turn hem of 4cm (1½in).

2 Turn up the hem on the garment and stitch in place. The lining hem should sit about 4cm (1½in) from the hem fold.

LINING AROUND A SPLIT

If there is a split in a hemline, the lining will need to be stitched around it securely. First construct the skirt, with its split finished, corners mitred, and hemmed. Finish the lining hem in the same way.

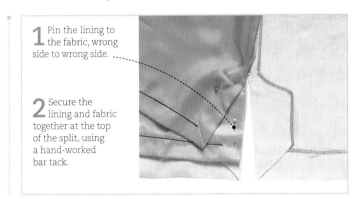

1 Pin the lining to the fabric, wrong side to wrong side.

2 Secure the lining and fabric together at the top of the split, using a hand-worked bar tack.

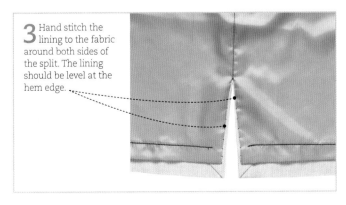

3 Hand stitch the lining to the fabric around both sides of the split. The lining should be level at the hem edge.

LINING AROUND A VENT

Some skirts and jackets feature a vent at the hemline, where the fabric overlaps to allow for movement. Lining around a vent can be tricky though, as the pattern pieces for the vent can be confusing.

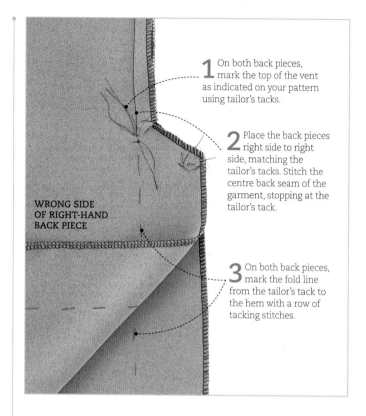

1 On both back pieces, mark the top of the vent as indicated on your pattern using tailor's tacks.

2 Place the back pieces right side to right side, matching the tailor's tacks. Stitch the centre back seam of the garment, stopping at the tailor's tack.

3 On both back pieces, mark the fold line from the tailor's tack to the hem with a row of tacking stitches.

WRONG SIDE OF RIGHT-HAND BACK PIECE

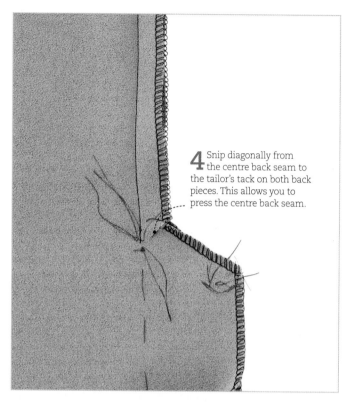

4 Snip diagonally from the centre back seam to the tailor's tack on both back pieces. This allows you to press the centre back seam.

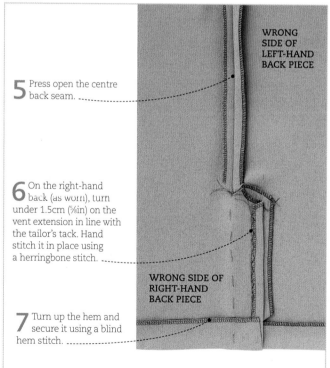

5 Press open the centre back seam.

6 On the right-hand back (as worn), turn under 1.5cm (⅝in) on the vent extension in line with the tailor's tack. Hand stitch it in place using a herringbone stitch.

7 Turn up the hem and secure it using a blind hem stitch.

WRONG SIDE OF LEFT-HAND BACK PIECE

WRONG SIDE OF RIGHT-HAND BACK PIECE

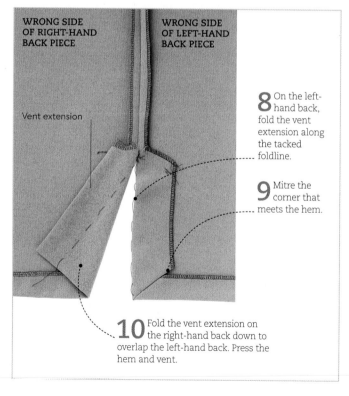

WRONG SIDE OF RIGHT-HAND BACK PIECE

WRONG SIDE OF LEFT-HAND BACK PIECE

Vent extension

8 On the left-hand back, fold the vent extension along the tacked foldline.

9 Mitre the corner that meets the hem.

10 Fold the vent extension on the right-hand back down to overlap the left-hand back. Press the hem and vent.

11 Cut the lining pieces according to your pattern.

12 On both back pieces, mark the vent as indicated on your pattern using tailor's tacks.

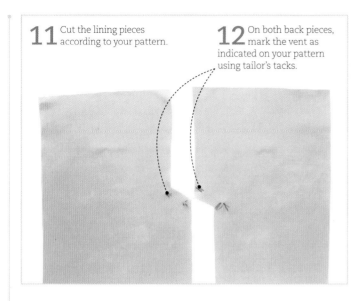

13 Neaten the centre back edges using a 3-thread overlock stitch or zigzag stitch.

14 Reinforce the inner corners as shown, stitching through the tailor's tacks about 2cm (¾in) from, and parallel to, the edge.

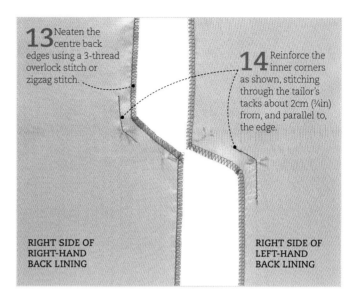

RIGHT SIDE OF RIGHT-HAND BACK LINING

RIGHT SIDE OF LEFT-HAND BACK LINING

15 Place the back lining pieces right side to right side, matching the tailor's tacks. Stitch the centre back seam of the garment, stopping at the tailor's tack.

16 Press the centre back seam open then snip diagonally from the centre back edge into the reinforced corners.

17 At the bottom edge, make a double-turn hem and machine it in place.

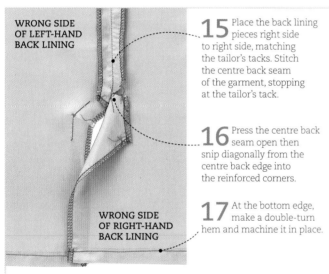

WRONG SIDE OF LEFT-HAND BACK LINING

WRONG SIDE OF RIGHT-HAND BACK LINING

18 Place the lining to the skirt wrong side to wrong side, matching them at the centre back seam. Pin in place.

19 On the right-hand back lining (as worn), turn under the edge of the opening by 1.5cm (⅝in) and pin to the seam on the skirt vent extension.

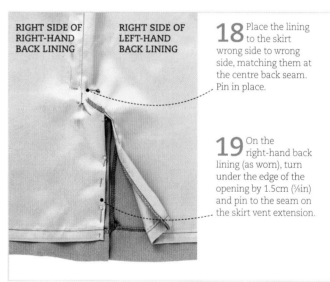

RIGHT SIDE OF RIGHT-HAND BACK LINING

RIGHT SIDE OF LEFT-HAND BACK LINING

20 On the left-hand back lining (as worn), turn under the edge of the opening by 1.5cm (⅝in). This should fit alongside the right-hand side of the vent. Pin in place.

21 At the top of the vent, push the seam allowance of the right-hand back lining under the diagonal part of the left-hand-back lining.

22 Fold the diagonal part under and pin.

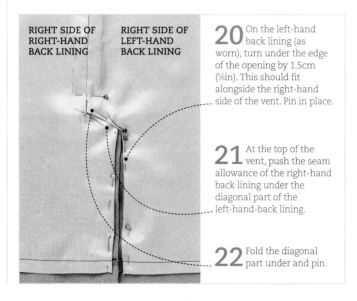

RIGHT SIDE OF RIGHT-HAND BACK LINING

RIGHT SIDE OF LEFT-HAND BACK LINING

23 Stitch the lining to the skirt around the vent using a flat fell stitch.

24 Machine diagonally from the centre back seam to the top of the vent, stitching through all layers. Pin in place.

25 Press to finish. The lining hem should remain unattached to the skirt hem.

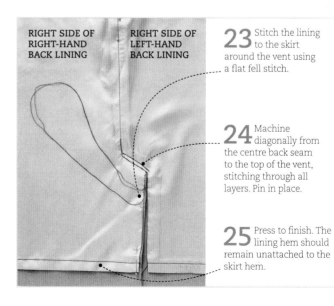

RIGHT SIDE OF RIGHT-HAND BACK LINING

RIGHT SIDE OF LEFT-HAND BACK LINING

Facings and necklines

The simplest way to finish the neck or armhole of a garment is to apply a facing. The neckline can be any shape to have a facing applied, from a curve to a square to a V, and many more. Some facings and necklines can add interest to the centre back or centre front of a garment.

ATTACHING A HAND-STITCHED FRONT FACING

On tailored jackets that feature canvas, the front facing is sometimes hand sewn in place for a couture finish.

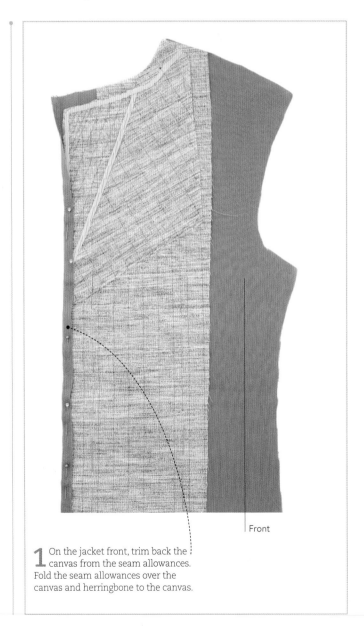

Front

1 On the jacket front, trim back the canvas from the seam allowances. Fold the seam allowances over the canvas and herringbone to the canvas.

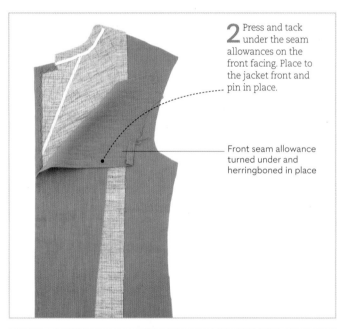

2 Press and tack under the seam allowances on the front facing. Place to the jacket front and pin in place.

Front seam allowance turned under and herringboned in place

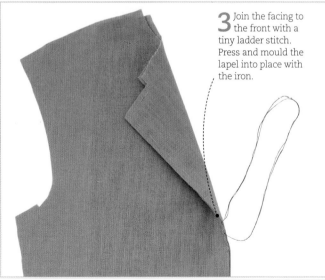

3 Join the facing to the front with a tiny ladder stitch. Press and mould the lapel into place with the iron.

APPLYING INTERFACING TO A FACING

All facings require interfacing. The interfacing is to give structure to the facing and to hold it in shape. A fusible interfacing is the best choice and it should be cut on the same grain as the facing. Choose an interfacing that is lighter in weight than the main fabric.

INTERFACING FOR HEAVY FABRIC

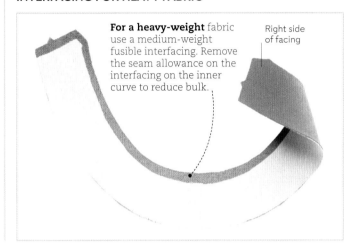

For a heavy-weight fabric use a medium-weight fusible interfacing. Remove the seam allowance on the interfacing on the inner curve to reduce bulk.

Right side of facing

INTERFACING FOR LIGHT FABRIC

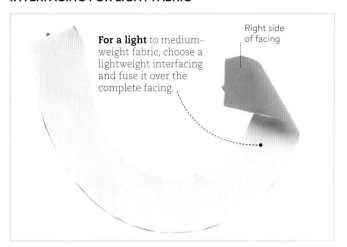

For a light to medium-weight fabric, choose a lightweight interfacing and fuse it over the complete facing.

Right side of facing

CONSTRUCTION OF A FACING

The facing may be in two or three pieces in order to fit around a neck or armhole edge. The facing sections need to be joined together prior to being attached. The photographs here show an interfaced neck facing in three pieces.

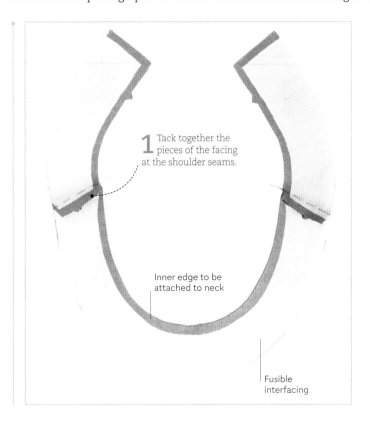

1 Tack together the pieces of the facing at the shoulder seams.

Inner edge to be attached to neck

Fusible interfacing

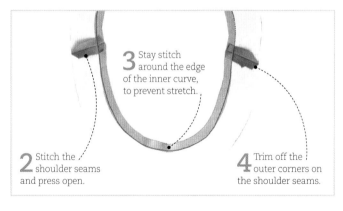

3 Stay stitch around the edge of the inner curve, to prevent stretch.

2 Stitch the shoulder seams and press open.

4 Trim off the outer corners on the shoulder seams.

5 The right side of the facing, ready to attach to the neckline.

NEATENING THE EDGE OF A FACING

The outer edge of a facing will require neatening to prevent it from fraying, and there are several ways to do this. Binding the lower edge of a facing with a bias strip makes the garment a little more luxurious and can add a designer touch inside the garment. You can make your own bias strip or buy one ready-made. Alternatively, the edge can be stitched or pinked (see opposite page).

HOW TO CUT BIAS STRIPS

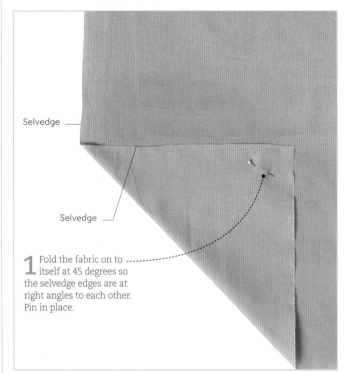

Selvedge

Selvedge

1 Fold the fabric on to itself at 45 degrees so the selvedge edges are at right angles to each other. Pin in place.

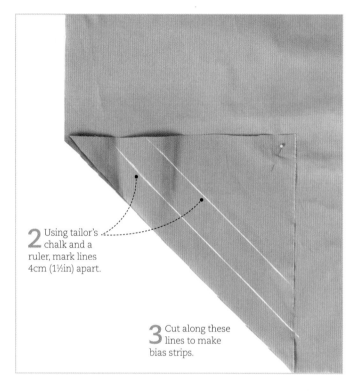

2 Using tailor's chalk and a ruler, mark lines 4cm (1½in) apart.

3 Cut along these lines to make bias strips.

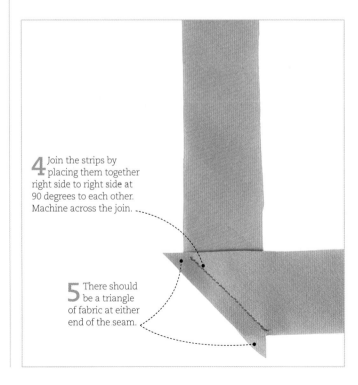

4 Join the strips by placing them together right side to right side at 90 degrees to each other. Machine across the join.

5 There should be a triangle of fabric at either end of the seam.

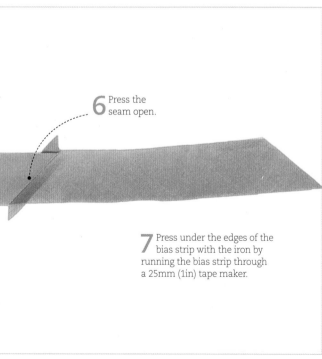

6 Press the seam open.

7 Press under the edges of the bias strip with the iron by running the bias strip through a 25mm (1in) tape maker.

NEATENING AN EDGE WITH A BIAS STRIP

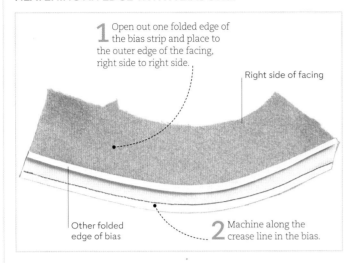

1 Open out one folded edge of the bias strip and place to the outer edge of the facing, right side to right side.

Right side of facing

Other folded edge of bias

2 Machine along the crease line in the bias.

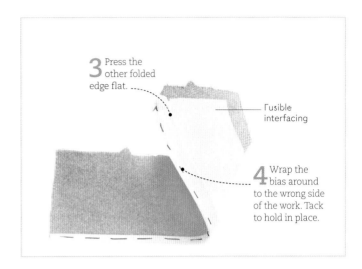

3 Press the other folded edge flat.

Fusible interfacing

4 Wrap the bias around to the wrong side of the work. Tack to hold in place.

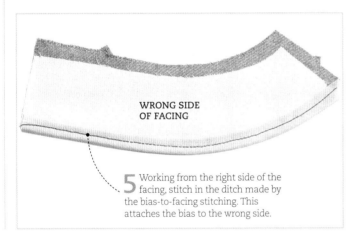

WRONG SIDE OF FACING

5 Working from the right side of the facing, stitch in the ditch made by the bias-to-facing stitching. This attaches the bias to the wrong side.

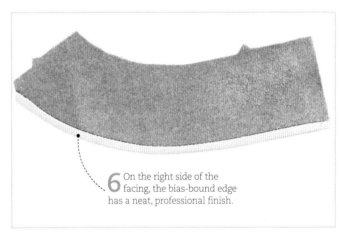

6 On the right side of the facing, the bias-bound edge has a neat, professional finish.

OTHER NEATENING METHODS

The following techniques are alternative popular ways to neaten the edge of a facing. Which one you choose depends upon the garment being made and the fabric used.

OVERLOCKED

Neaten the outer edge with a 3-thread overlock stitch.

PINKED

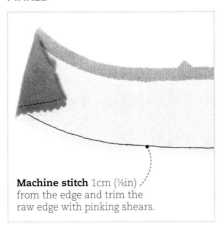

Machine stitch 1cm (⅜in) from the edge and trim the raw edge with pinking shears.

ZIGZAGGED

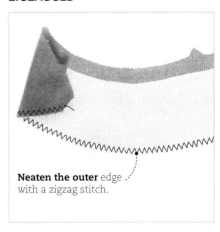

Neaten the outer edge with a zigzag stitch.

THE BURRITO METHOD

The burrito method is a way to attach a shirt or dress yoke to the back and front pieces, so-called because the pattern pieces are rolled up like a burrito. This technique results in a neat finish with all seams hidden and enclosed within the garment facing.

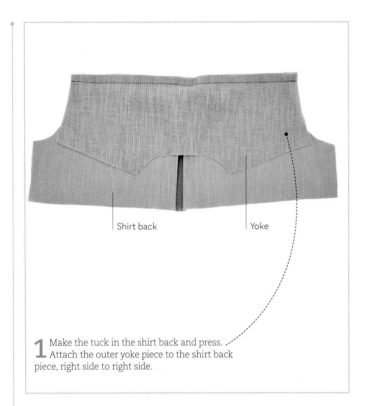

Shirt back

Yoke

1 Make the tuck in the shirt back and press. Attach the outer yoke piece to the shirt back piece, right side to right side.

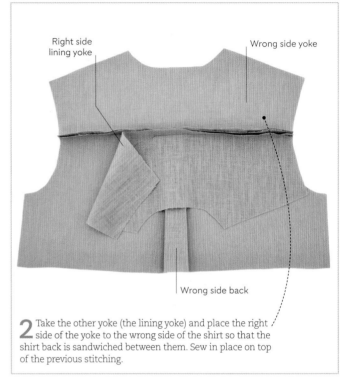

Right side lining yoke

Wrong side yoke

Wrong side back

2 Take the other yoke (the lining yoke) and place the right side of the yoke to the wrong side of the shirt so that the shirt back is sandwiched between them. Sew in place on top of the previous stitching.

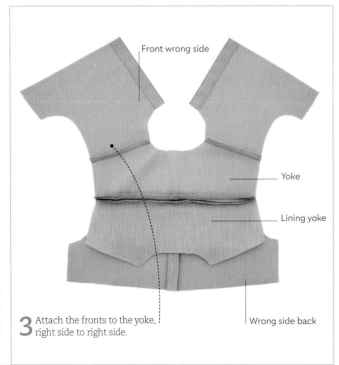

Front wrong side

Yoke

Lining yoke

Wrong side back

3 Attach the fronts to the yoke, right side to right side.

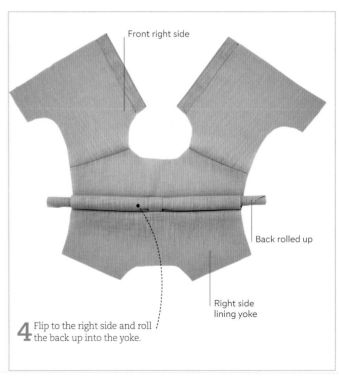

Front right side

Back rolled up

Right side lining yoke

4 Flip to the right side and roll the back up into the yoke.

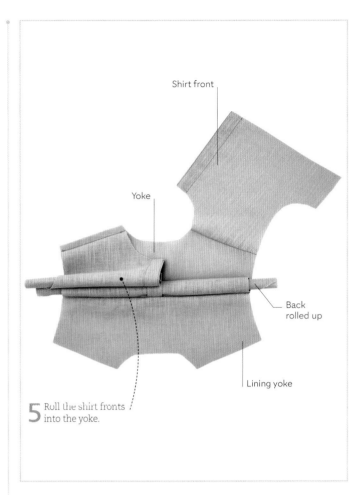

Shirt front

Yoke

Back rolled up

Lining yoke

5 Roll the shirt fronts into the yoke.

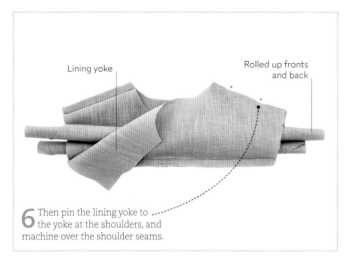

Lining yoke

Rolled up fronts and back

6 Then pin the lining yoke to the yoke at the shoulders, and machine over the shoulder seams.

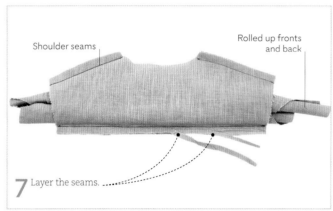

Shoulder seams

Rolled up fronts and back

7 Layer the seams.

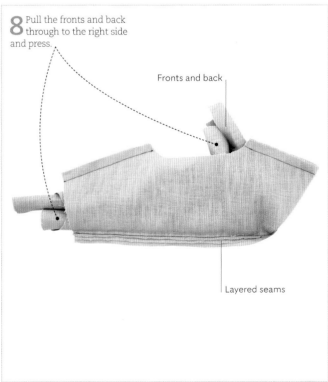

8 Pull the fronts and back through to the right side and press.

Fronts and back

Layered seams

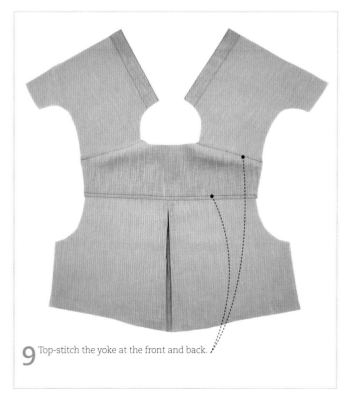

9 Top-stitch the yoke at the front and back.

Collars

All collars consist of a minimum of two pieces, the upper collar (which will be on the outside) and the under collar. Interfacing, which is required to give the collar shape and structure, is often applied to the upper collar to give a smoother appearance to the fabric.

FLAT COLLAR

A flat collar is the easiest of all the collars to construct, and the techniques used are the same for most other shapes of flat collar and facings.

1 Cut out the fabric for the collar accurately. Make sure the two halves match.

2 Cut out a fusible interfacing, being sure to cut on the same grain as the collar. Apply the interfacing to the upper collar.

3 Insert tailor's tacks at the centre front point of the collar where indicated by a dot on the pattern piece.

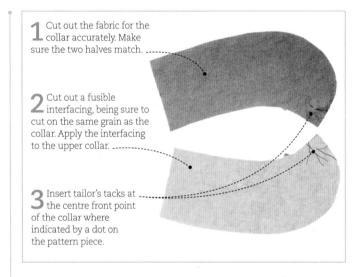

4 Pin the upper collar and under collar together, right side to right side. Match any notches and make sure the cut edges match.

5 Machine stitch 1.5cm (⅝in) along the outer curved edge to the lower edge of the collar. Make sure the machining at the centre front goes through the tailor's tack. If you have problems stitching a curve, mark the fabric first with chalk.

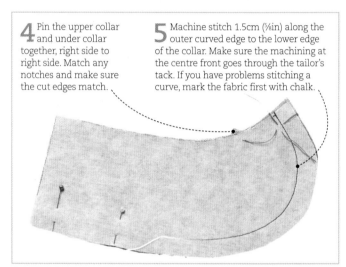

6 Trim the under collar seam allowance to half of its width, which will reduce the bulk.

7 Trim around the curve with pinking shears, reducing both layers. This will allow the fabric to turn.

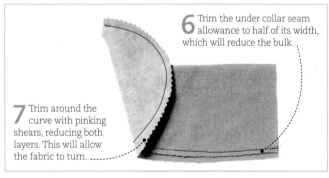

8 Press the seam allowance of the upper collar on to the collar.

9 While the collar is still warm from the steam iron, turn to the right side.

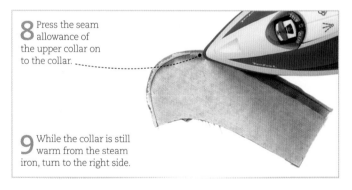

10 Working from the inside of the collar, push all the seam allowance towards the under collar.

11 Understitch as far through the curve as you can.

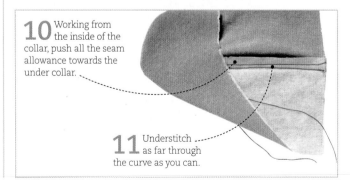

12 Press the curved edge flat on the right side, making sure the seam is pushed out completely.

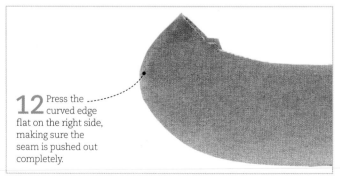

ATTACHING A FLAT COLLAR

A flat collar can be attached to the neckline by means of a facing. Depending upon the style of the garment, the facing may go all around the neck, which is usually found on garments with centre back openings, or just be at the front. The collar with no back facing has to be attached to the garment in stages.

FLAT ROUND COLLAR WITH NO BACK FACING

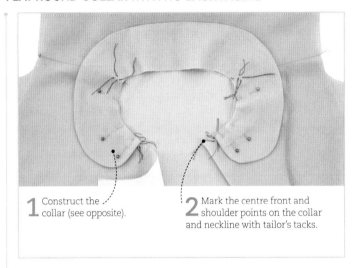

1 Construct the collar (see opposite).

2 Mark the centre front and shoulder points on the collar and neckline with tailor's tacks.

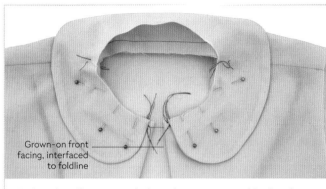

Grown-on front facing, interfaced to foldline

3 Place the collar to the neckline, matching the tailor's tacks. Pin in place.

4 Pin the under collar to the back neckline between the shoulders.

5 Machine just the under collar in place. The upper part of the collar should be loose.

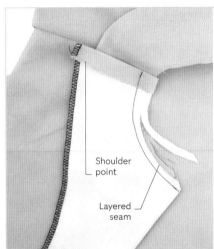

Shoulder point

Layered seam

6 Fold the front facing over the collar, right side to right side, from the centre front to the shoulder.

7 At the shoulder, turn under the seam allowance on the facing.

8 Pin and stitch through all the layers, from the fold at the centre front to the shoulder. Layer the seam.

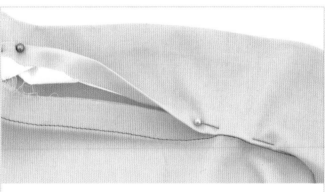

9 Snip through the upper collar seam allowance at the shoulder points.

10 Turn under the seam allowance on the upper collar and place the fold to the back neck machine stitching. Pin.

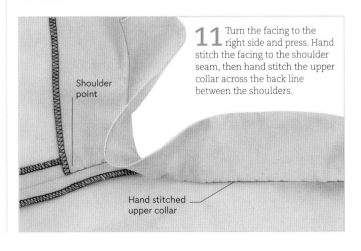

Shoulder point

Hand stitched upper collar

11 Turn the facing to the right side and press. Hand stitch the facing to the shoulder seam, then hand stitch the upper collar across the back line between the shoulders.

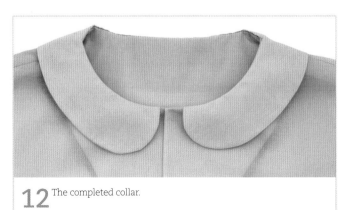

12 The completed collar.

FLAT ROUND COLLAR WITH A FULL FACING

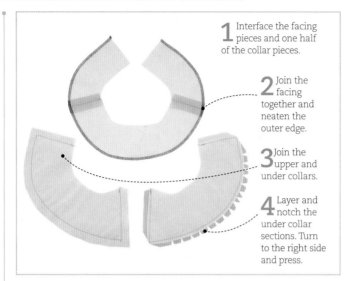

1 Interface the facing pieces and one half of the collar pieces.

2 Join the facing together and neaten the outer edge.

3 Join the upper and under collars.

4 Layer and notch the under collar sections. Turn to the right side and press.

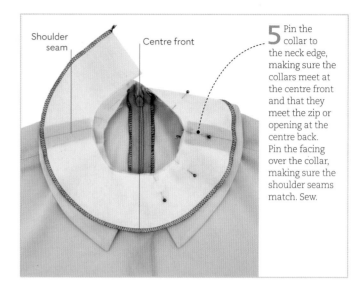

Shoulder seam   Centre front

5 Pin the collar to the neck edge, making sure the collars meet at the centre front and that they meet the zip or opening at the centre back. Pin the facing over the collar, making sure the shoulder seams match. Sew.

6 Layer the facing part of the seam, by two-thirds. Sew around the collar and neck edge, and then layer the collar by one-third. Notch.

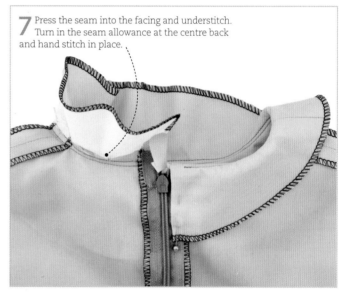

7 Press the seam into the facing and understitch. Turn in the seam allowance at the centre back and hand stitch in place.

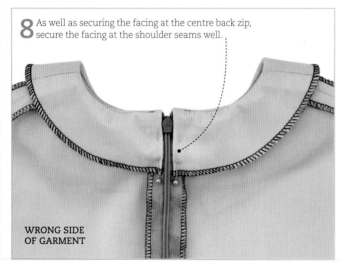

8 As well as securing the facing at the centre back zip, secure the facing at the shoulder seams well.

WRONG SIDE OF GARMENT

9 The finished collar and facing.

RIGHT SIDE OF GARMENT

STAND COLLAR

Also called a mandarin collar, this collar stands upright around the neck. It is normally cut from a straight piece of fabric, with shaping at the centre front edges. For a very close-fitting stand collar, the collar is cut with a slight curve.

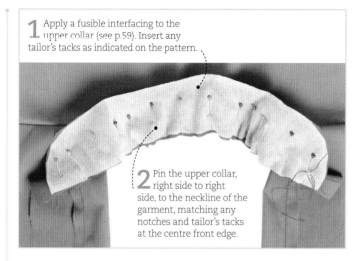

1 Apply a fusible interfacing to the upper collar (see p.59). Insert any tailor's tacks as indicated on the pattern.

2 Pin the upper collar, right side to right side, to the neckline of the garment, matching any notches and tailor's tacks at the centre front edge.

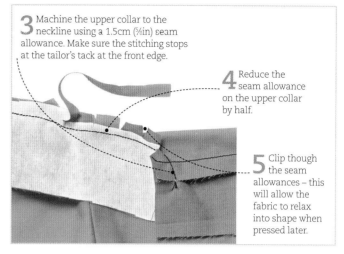

3 Machine the upper collar to the neckline using a 1.5cm (⅝in) seam allowance. Make sure the stitching stops at the tailor's tack at the front edge.

4 Reduce the seam allowance on the upper collar by half.

5 Clip though the seam allowances – this will allow the fabric to relax into shape when pressed later.

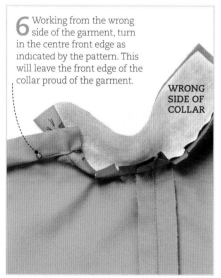

6 Working from the wrong side of the garment, turn in the centre front edge as indicated by the pattern. This will leave the front edge of the collar proud of the garment.

WRONG SIDE OF COLLAR

7 Pin the under collar to the upper collar, right side to right side, along the top edge.

8 Machine the two pieces together using a 1.5cm (⅝in) seam allowance.

9 At the centre front, the reduced neck seam allowance needs to be pointing up into the collar, so that the machining attaching the two collar sections together goes over it. Be sure the machining is in line with the centre front of the garment.

10 Reduce the seam allowance to half its width on the under collar side of the seam (the non-interfaced side).

11 Clip V shapes out of the seam allowance to reduce the bulk. Be careful not to cut through the stitching.

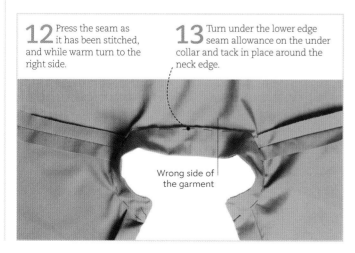

12 Press the seam as it has been stitched, and while warm turn to the right side.

13 Turn under the lower edge seam allowance on the under collar and tack in place around the neck edge.

Wrong side of the garment

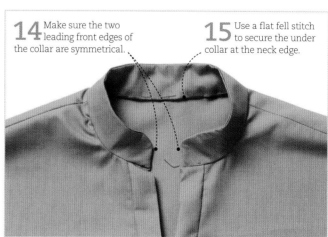

14 Make sure the two leading front edges of the collar are symmetrical.

15 Use a flat fell stitch to secure the under collar at the neck edge.

BLOUSE COLLAR WITH REVERS

A blouse collar can have rounded or pointed centre front edges, depending on the style of blouse chosen. A blouse collar forms a V neckline with revers. When constructing the collar, before fusing the interfacing to the upper collar, trim the corners of the interfacing to reduce bulk.

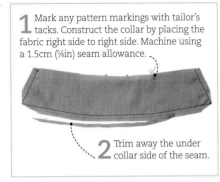

1 Mark any pattern markings with tailor's tacks. Construct the collar by placing the fabric right side to right side. Machine using a 1.5cm (⅝in) seam allowance.

2 Trim away the under collar side of the seam.

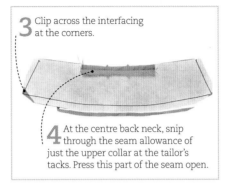

3 Clip across the interfacing at the corners.

4 At the centre back neck, snip through the seam allowance of just the upper collar at the tailor's tacks. Press this part of the seam open.

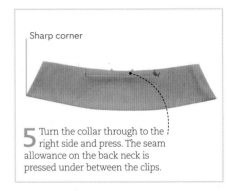

Sharp corner

5 Turn the collar through to the right side and press. The seam allowance on the back neck is pressed under between the clips.

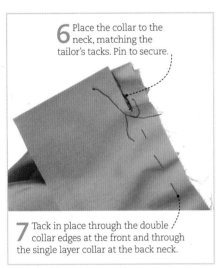

6 Place the collar to the neck, matching the tailor's tacks. Pin to secure.

7 Tack in place through the double collar edges at the front and through the single layer collar at the back neck.

8 Place the front facing over the front part of the collar, matching notches and tailor's tacks.

9 Machine in place, stitching across the back neck at the same time. Match at the shoulder seams.

Sharp point in stitching at centre front

10 Trim and layer the seam. Turn to the right side and press.

11 Turn under the raw edge of the upper collar at the back neck and tack in place, then hand stitch with a flat fell or blind hem stitch.

Rever

12 Press the collar and revers.

TWO-PIECE SHIRT COLLAR

A classic tailored shirt has a collar that consists of two pieces: a collar and a stand, both of which require interfacing. The stand fits close around the neck and the collar is attached to the stand.

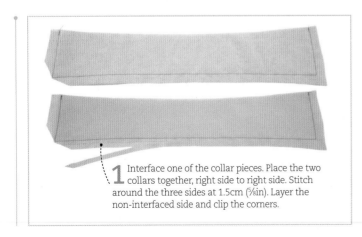

1 Interface one of the collar pieces. Place the two collars together, right side to right side. Stitch around the three sides at 1.5cm (⅝in). Layer the non-interfaced side and clip the corners.

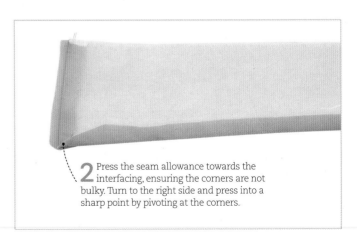

2 Press the seam allowance towards the interfacing, ensuring the corners are not bulky. Turn to the right side and press into a sharp point by pivoting at the corners.

3 Top-stitch the collar 1cm (⅜in) from the edge.

5 Layer the seam and notch through the curve.

The non-interfaced collar stand

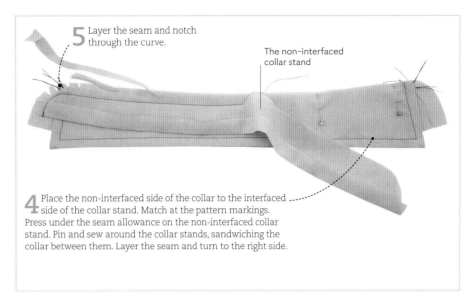

4 Place the non-interfaced side of the collar to the interfaced side of the collar stand. Match at the pattern markings. Press under the seam allowance on the non-interfaced collar stand. Pin and sew around the collar stands, sandwiching the collar between them. Layer the seam and turn to the right side.

6 Place the interfaced collar stand to the shirt neck edge. Match carefully at the centre front. Make sure the stand follows the line of the front edge. Machine just at the front edges first.

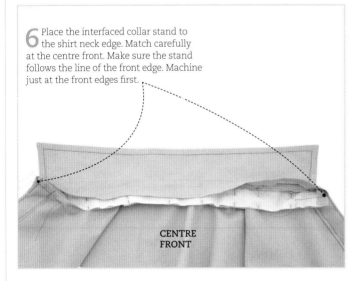

CENTRE FRONT

7 Now sew the rest of the collar stand to the neck edge. Layer the seam and clip if necessary. Press the seam towards the stand.

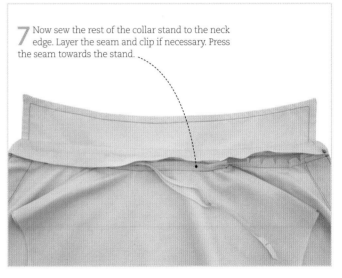

8 Fold down the pressed edge of the collar stand to the machine-stitched line. Hand stitch with a slip stitch to secure.

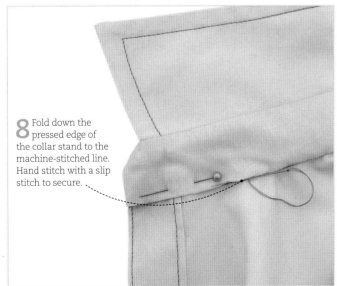

9 The completed collar.

MELTON UNDER COLLAR

Melton is a strong woollen fabric used in under collars to create crisp, sharp edges. It is
available for under collars ready pad stitched. or you can pad stitch a piece of melton fabric.
This technique is often used on coats and tailored jackets to give a professional finish

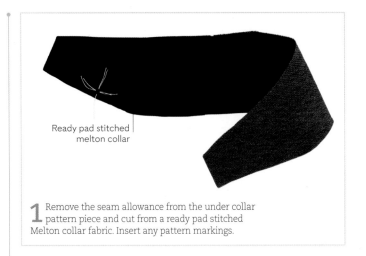

Ready pad stitched
melton collar

1 Remove the seam allowance from the under collar
pattern piece and cut from a ready pad stitched
Melton collar fabric. Insert any pattern markings.

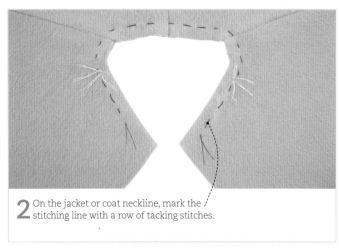

2 On the jacket or coat neckline, mark the
stitching line with a row of tacking stitches.

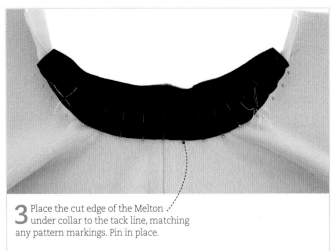

3 Place the cut edge of the Melton
under collar to the tack line, matching
any pattern markings. Pin in place.

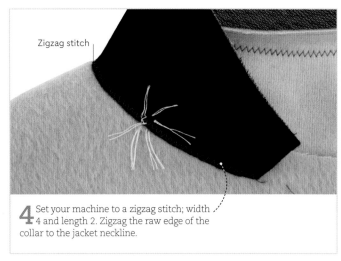

Zigzag stitch

4 Set your machine to a zigzag stitch; width
4 and length 2. Zigzag the raw edge of the
collar to the jacket neckline.

5 Attach the front facing
to the jacket.

The front facing

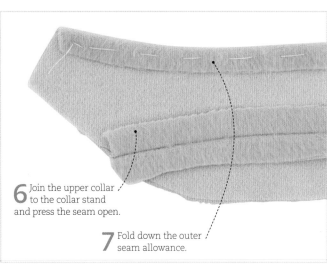

6 Join the upper collar
to the collar stand
and press the seam open.

7 Fold down the outer
seam allowance.

8 Turn the facing to the right side. Place the Melton under collar to the folded edge of the upper collar. Pin in place and stitch.

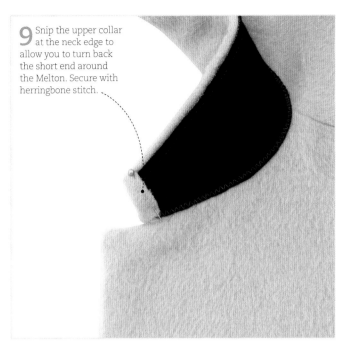

9 Snip the upper collar at the neck edge to allow you to turn back the short end around the Melton. Secure with herringbone stitch.

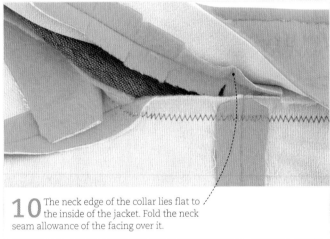

10 The neck edge of the collar lies flat to the inside of the jacket. Fold the neck seam allowance of the facing over it.

Collar stand

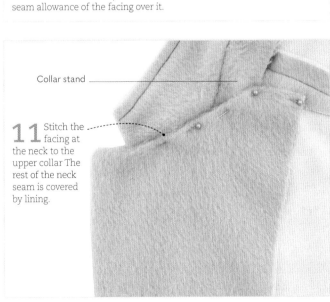

11 Stitch the facing at the neck to the upper collar The rest of the neck seam is covered by lining.

12 The completed collar.

COLLAR APPLICATION

A notched collar is a sign of a tailored jacket. This type of collar consists of an upper and under collar, and a facing that folds back to form the rever on either side. Careful stitching and accurate marking are required.

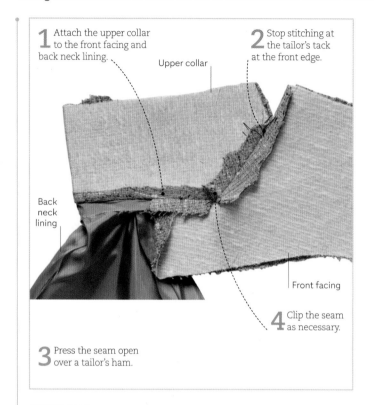

1 Attach the upper collar to the front facing and back neck lining.

Upper collar

2 Stop stitching at the tailor's tack at the front edge.

Back neck lining

Front facing

3 Press the seam open over a tailor's ham.

4 Clip the seam as necessary.

5 Join the under collar to the jacket front and back.

Under collar

JACKET FRONT

6 Stop stitching at the tailor's tack at the front edge.

7 Press the seam open. Clip as necessary.

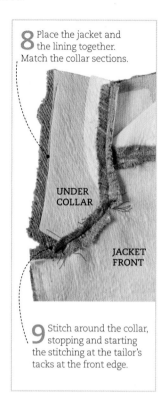

8 Place the jacket and the lining together. Match the collar sections.

UNDER COLLAR

JACKET FRONT

9 Stitch around the collar, stopping and starting the stitching at the tailor's tacks at the front edge.

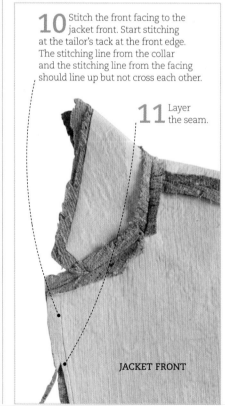

10 Stitch the front facing to the jacket front. Start stitching at the tailor's tack at the front edge. The stitching line from the collar and the stitching line from the facing should line up but not cross each other.

11 Layer the seam.

JACKET FRONT

12 On the inside, herringbone stitch the neck seams together.

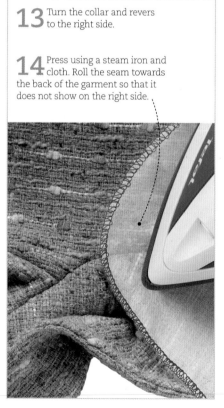

13 Turn the collar and revers to the right side.

14 Press using a steam iron and cloth. Roll the seam towards the back of the garment so that it does not show on the right side.

Sleeves

A few sleeves, such as the dolman, are cut as part of the garment, but most sleeves, including set-in and raglan, are made separately and then inserted into the armhole. Whichever type of sleeve is being inserted, always place it to the armhole and not the armhole to the sleeve – in other words, always work with the sleeve facing you.

FLAT SLEEVE CONSTRUCTION

On shirts and children's clothes, sleeves are inserted flat prior to the side seams being constructed. This technique can be difficult on firmly woven fabrics, because ease stitches are not normally used.

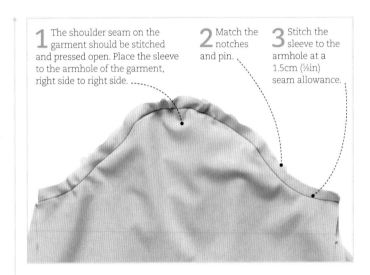

1 The shoulder seam on the garment should be stitched and pressed open. Place the sleeve to the armhole of the garment, right side to right side.

2 Match the notches and pin.

3 Stitch the sleeve to the armhole at a 1.5cm (⅝in) seam allowance.

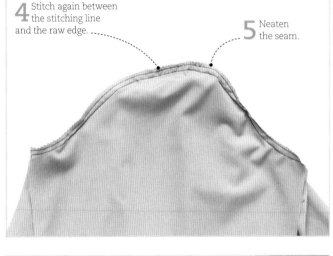

4 Stitch again between the stitching line and the raw edge.

5 Neaten the seam.

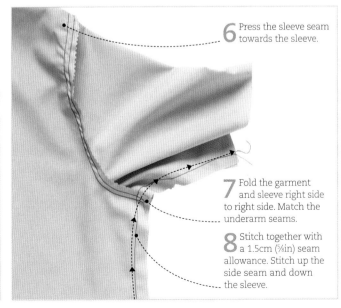

6 Press the sleeve seam towards the sleeve.

7 Fold the garment and sleeve right side to right side. Match the underarm seams.

8 Stitch together with a 1.5cm (⅝in) seam allowance. Stitch up the side seam and down the sleeve.

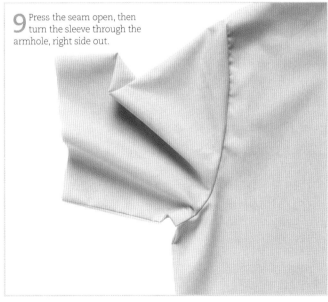

9 Press the seam open, then turn the sleeve through the armhole, right side out.

RAGLAN SLEEVE

A raglan sleeve can be constructed as a one-piece sleeve or a two-piece sleeve. The armhole seam on a raglan sleeve runs diagonally from the armhole to the neck.

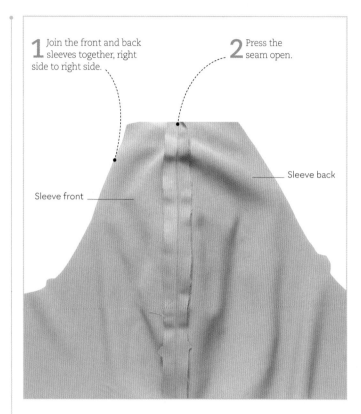

1 Join the front and back sleeves together, right side to right side.

2 Press the seam open.

Sleeve front

Sleeve back

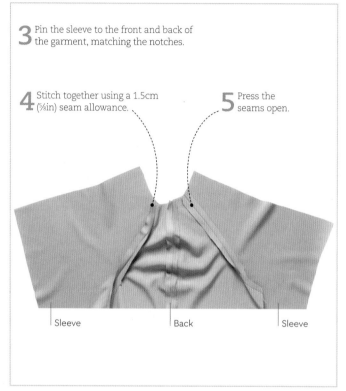

3 Pin the sleeve to the front and back of the garment, matching the notches.

4 Stitch together using a 1.5cm (⅝in) seam allowance.

5 Press the seams open.

Sleeve

Back

Sleeve

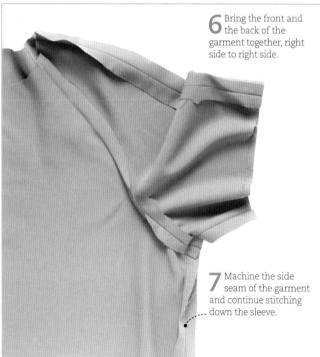

6 Bring the front and the back of the garment together, right side to right side.

7 Machine the side seam of the garment and continue stitching down the sleeve.

8 Press the seam open, then turn the sleeve through the armhole to the right side.

INSERTING A SET-IN SLEEVE

A set-in sleeve should feature a smooth sleeve head that fits on the end of your shoulder accurately. This is achieved by the use of ease stitches, which are long stitches used to tighten the fabric but not gather it.

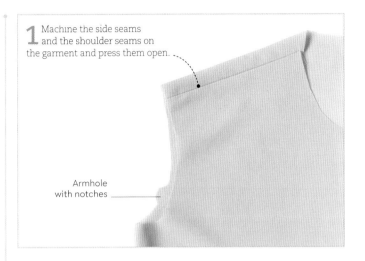

1 Machine the side seams and the shoulder seams on the garment and press them open.

Armhole with notches

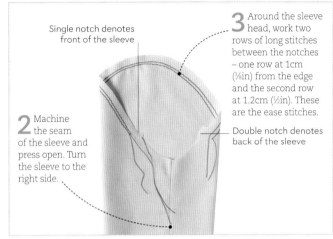

Single notch denotes front of the sleeve

3 Around the sleeve head, work two rows of long stitches between the notches – one row at 1cm (⅜in) from the edge and the second row at 1.2cm (½in). These are the ease stitches.

Double notch denotes back of the sleeve

2 Machine the seam of the sleeve and press open. Turn the sleeve to the right side.

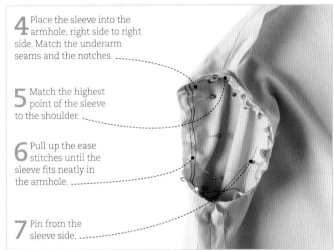

4 Place the sleeve into the armhole, right side to right side. Match the underarm seams and the notches.

5 Match the highest point of the sleeve to the shoulder.

6 Pull up the ease stitches until the sleeve fits neatly in the armhole.

7 Pin from the sleeve side.

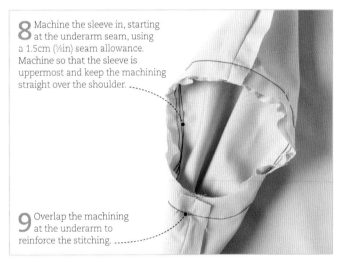

8 Machine the sleeve in, starting at the underarm seam, using a 1.5cm (⅝in) seam allowance. Machine so that the sleeve is uppermost and keep the machining straight over the shoulder.

9 Overlap the machining at the underarm to reinforce the stitching.

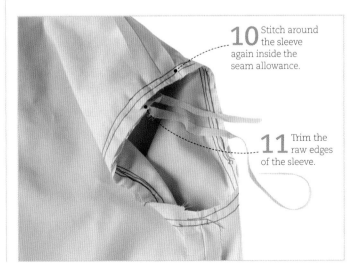

10 Stitch around the sleeve again inside the seam allowance.

11 Trim the raw edges of the sleeve.

12 Neaten the seam with a zigzag or overlock stitch, then turn the sleeve through the armhole.

Smooth sleeve head

RIGHT SIDE OF GARMENT

SET SLEEVE USING A RUN AND FELL SEAM

It is traditional to construct a tailored shirt using run and fell seams. This applies to the sleeve insertion as well, where the armhole seam is worked a little differently.

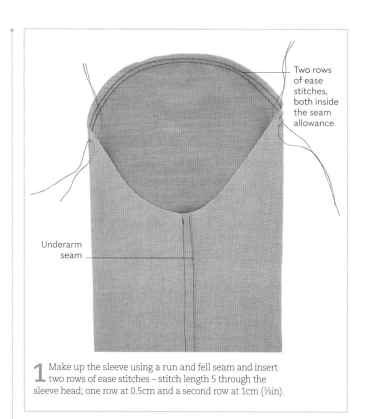

Two rows of ease stitches, both inside the seam allowance

Underarm seam

1 Make up the sleeve using a run and fell seam and insert two rows of ease stitches – stitch length 5 through the sleeve head; one row at 0.5cm and a second row at 1cm (⅜in).

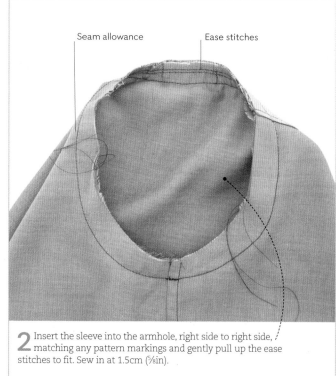

Seam allowance

Ease stitches

2 Insert the sleeve into the armhole, right side to right side, matching any pattern markings and gently pull up the ease stitches to fit. Sew in at 1.5cm (⅝in).

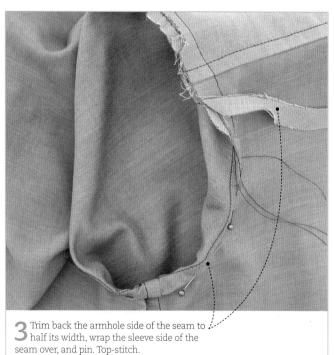

3 Trim back the armhole side of the seam to half its width, wrap the sleeve side of the seam over, and pin. Top-stitch.

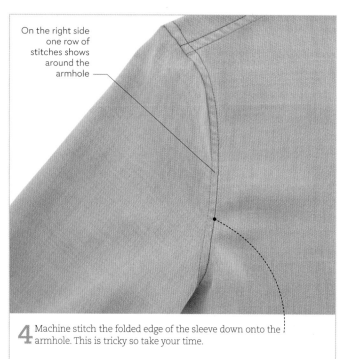

On the right side one row of stitches shows around the armhole

4 Machine stitch the folded edge of the sleeve down onto the armhole. This is tricky so take your time.

COVERING A SHOULDER PAD

An unlined jacket or coat may require a shoulder pad to give shape and structure. A covered shoulder pad will give your garment a more professional touch.

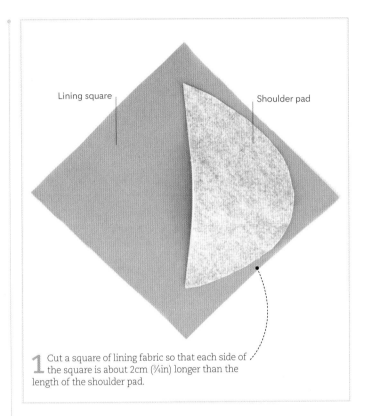

Lining square

Shoulder pad

1 Cut a square of lining fabric so that each side of the square is about 2cm (¾in) longer than the length of the shoulder pad.

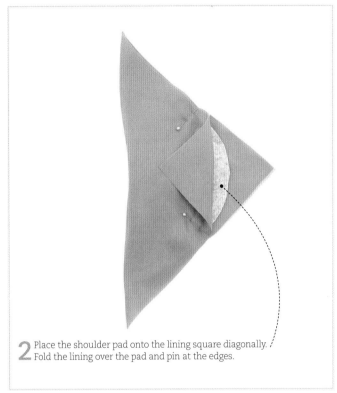

2 Place the shoulder pad onto the lining square diagonally. Fold the lining over the pad and pin at the edges.

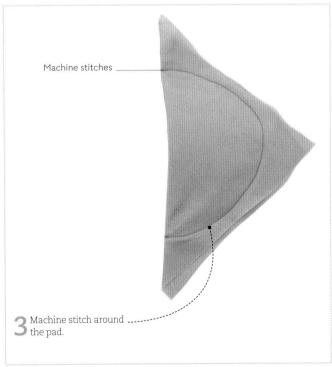

Machine stitches

3 Machine stitch around the pad.

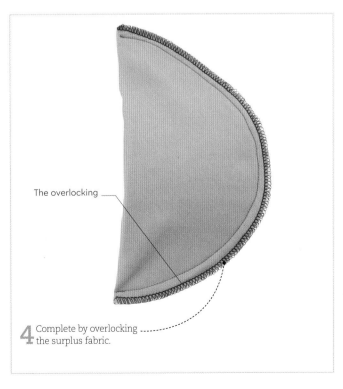

The overlocking

4 Complete by overlocking the surplus fabric.

INSERTING A TAILORED SLEEVE PLUS SLEEVE ROLL

This is a technique for tailored jacket and coats. Use this method where a more substantial sleeve head is required.

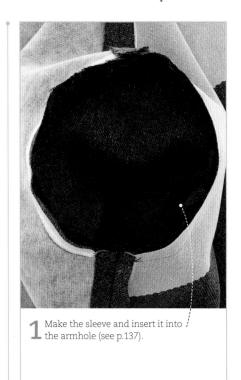

1 Make the sleeve and insert it into the armhole (see p.137).

2 Cut a piece of sleeve heading approximately 18cm (7in) long. Pin it into the armhole at the sleeve head so that the stitching in the sleeve head corresponds to the seam line of the sleeve.

Sleeve roll

3 Fold back the edge of the sleeve roll and slip stitch by hand to the armhole stitching.

SET-IN SLEEVE

On a tailored jacket, the sleeve needs to be set in to have a rounded sleeve head, which is created with polyester wadding. The sleeve head will ensure that the sleeve hangs perfectly.

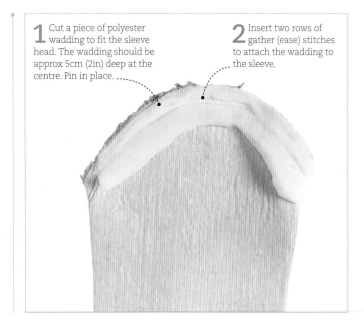

1 Cut a piece of polyester wadding to fit the sleeve head. The wadding should be approx 5cm (2in) deep at the centre. Pin in place.

2 Insert two rows of gather (ease) stitches to attach the wadding to the sleeve.

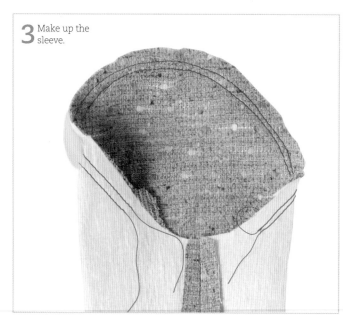

3 Make up the sleeve.

4 Insert the sleeve into the armhole, right side to right side. Pin in place.

5 Pull up the ease stitches to fit. The sleeve head will absorb the fullness.

6 Machine in place. Make a second row of machining close to the first stitching.

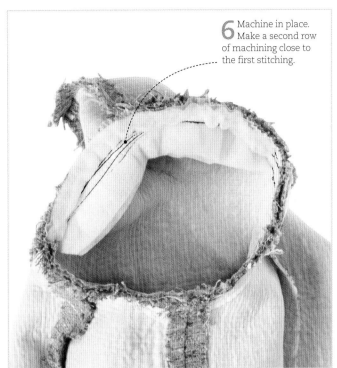

7 The shoulder pad can now be inserted. The back slope of the shoulder pad is longer than the front slope. The concave side will face the jacket lining.

Concave side

Back slope

Front slope

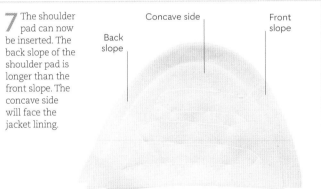

9 On the right side, the finished sleeve has a rounded sleeve head.

8 Attach the shoulder pad at the edge of the sleeve seam using a firm running stitch.

Concave side of shoulder pad

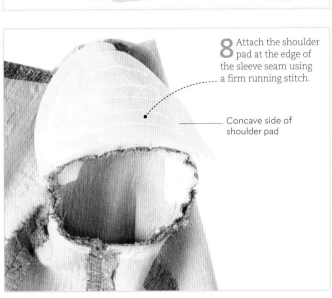

Sleeve edge finishes

The lower edge of a sleeve has to be finished according to the style of the garment being made. Some sleeves are finished tight into the arm or wrist, while others may have a more decorative or functional finish.

SLEEVE HEMS

The simplest way to finish a sleeve is to make a small hem, which can be part of the sleeve or additional fabric that is attached to turn up. A self hem is where the edge of the sleeve is turned up on to itself. If there is insufficient fabric to turn up, a bias binding can be used to create the hem. You can use purchased bias binding or make your own bias strips.

SELF HEM

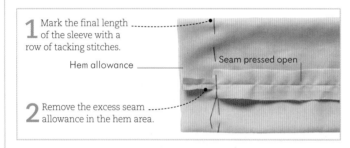

1 Mark the final length of the sleeve with a row of tacking stitches.

Hem allowance

Seam pressed open

2 Remove the excess seam allowance in the hem area.

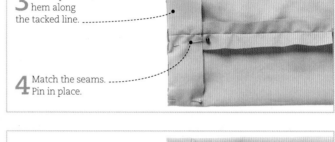

3 Turn up the hem along the tacked line.

4 Match the seams. Pin in place.

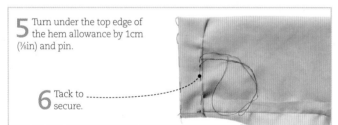

5 Turn under the top edge of the hem allowance by 1cm (⅜in) and pin.

6 Tack to secure.

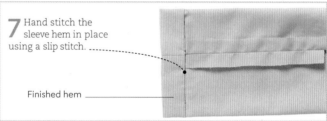

7 Hand stitch the sleeve hem in place using a slip stitch.

Finished hem

BIAS-BOUND HEM

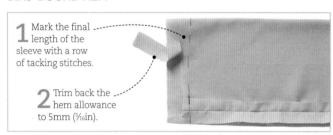

1 Mark the final length of the sleeve with a row of tacking stitches.

2 Trim back the hem allowance to 5mm (³⁄₁₆in).

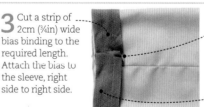

3 Cut a strip of 2cm (¾in) wide bias binding to the required length. Attach the bias to the sleeve, right side to right side.

4 Turn under the end of the bias, placing the fold of the bias to the sleeve seam.

5 Machine in place using a 5mm (³⁄₁₆in) seam allowance.

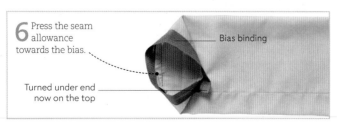

6 Press the seam allowance towards the bias.

Bias binding

Turned under end now on the top

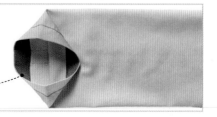

7 Turn the bias to the inside of the sleeve and machine in place, stitching along the upper edge of the bias.

Cuffs and openings

A cuff and an opening are ways of producing a sleeve finish that will fit neatly around the wrist. The opening enables the hand to fit through the end of the sleeve, and it allows the sleeve to be rolled up. There are various types of cuffs – single or double, and with pointed or curved edges. All cuffs are interfaced, with the interfacing attached to the upper cuff. The upper cuff is sewn to the sleeve.

ONE-PIECE CUFF

A one-piece cuff is cut out from the fabric in one piece, and in most cases only half of it is interfaced. The exception is the one-piece double cuff (see p.151).

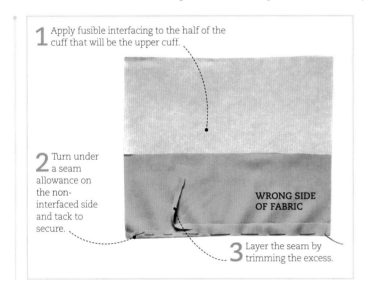

1 Apply fusible interfacing to the half of the cuff that will be the upper cuff.

2 Turn under a seam allowance on the non-interfaced side and tack to secure.

3 Layer the seam by trimming the excess.

WRONG SIDE OF FABRIC

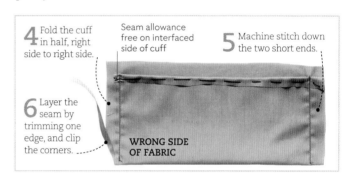

4 Fold the cuff in half, right side to right side.

Seam allowance free on interfaced side of cuff

5 Machine stitch down the two short ends.

6 Layer the seam by trimming one edge, and clip the corners.

WRONG SIDE OF FABRIC

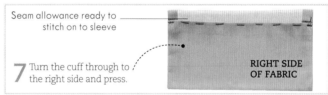

Seam allowance ready to stitch on to sleeve

7 Turn the cuff through to the right side and press.

RIGHT SIDE OF FABRIC

TWO-PIECE CUFF

Some cuffs are cut in two pieces: an upper cuff and an under cuff. The upper cuff piece is interfaced.

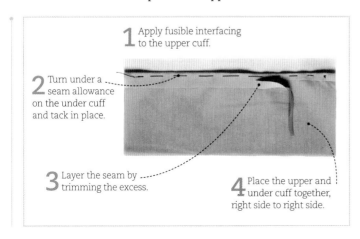

1 Apply fusible interfacing to the upper cuff.

2 Turn under a seam allowance on the under cuff and tack in place.

3 Layer the seam by trimming the excess.

4 Place the upper and under cuff together, right side to right side.

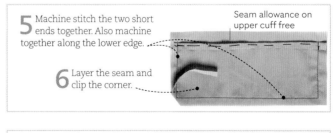

5 Machine stitch the two short ends together. Also machine together along the lower edge.

Seam allowance on upper cuff free

6 Layer the seam and clip the corner.

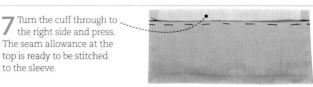

7 Turn the cuff through to the right side and press. The seam allowance at the top is ready to be stitched to the sleeve.

FACED OPENING

Adding a facing to the area of the sleeve where the opening is to be is a neat method of finishing. This type of opening is ideal to use with a one-piece cuff.

1 Turn under the long edges and one short edge on the facing by about 3mm (⅛in). Machine stitch to secure.

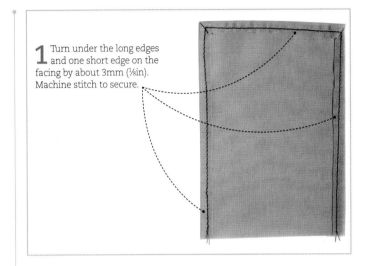

2 Place the right side of the facing to the right side of the sleeve at the appropriate sleeve markings.

3 Stitch vertically up the centre of the facing. Take one stitch across the top and then stitch straight down the other side. Keep a distance of about 5mm (³⁄₁₆in) between the stitching lines at the raw edge.

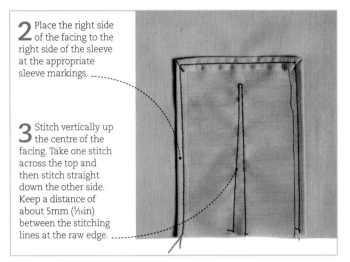

4 Slash between the stitching lines.

5 Snip with small scissors into the corners.

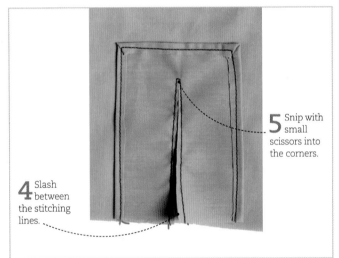

6 Turn the facing to the wrong side of the sleeve and press.

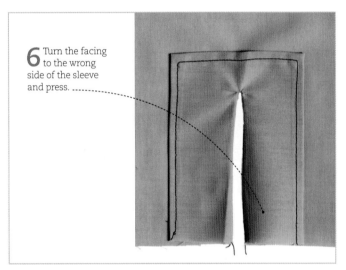

7 The finished opening on the right side.

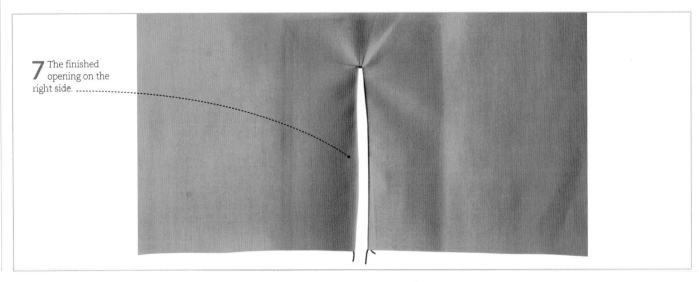

BOUND OPENING

On a fabric that frays badly or a sleeve that may get a lot of wear, a strong bound opening is a good idea. It involves binding a slash in the sleeve with a matching bias strip.

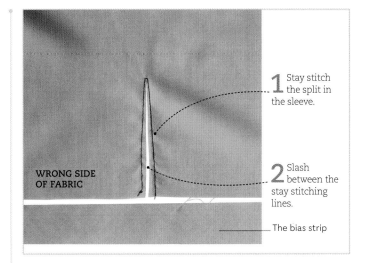

WRONG SIDE OF FABRIC

1 Stay stitch the split in the sleeve.

2 Slash between the stay stitching lines.

The bias strip

WRONG SIDE OF FABRIC

3 Working on the right side of the sleeve, pin the bias strip along the stay stitching lines. To stitch around the top of the split, open the split out into a straight line.

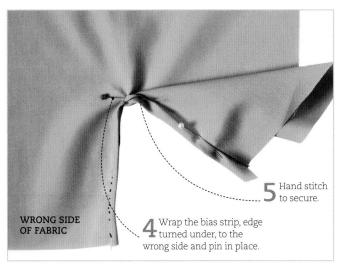

WRONG SIDE OF FABRIC

5 Hand stitch to secure.

4 Wrap the bias strip, edge turned under, to the wrong side and pin in place.

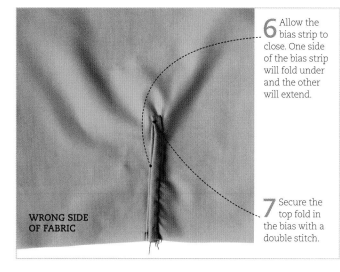

WRONG SIDE OF FABRIC

6 Allow the bias strip to close. One side of the bias strip will fold under and the other will extend.

7 Secure the top fold in the bias with a double stitch.

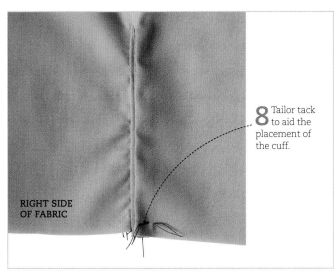

RIGHT SIDE OF FABRIC

8 Tailor tack to aid the placement of the cuff.

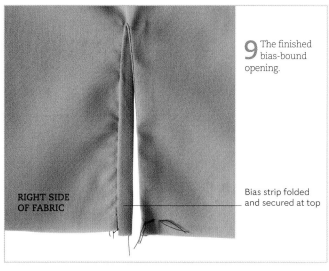

RIGHT SIDE OF FABRIC

9 The finished bias-bound opening.

Bias strip folded and secured at top

SHIRT SLEEVE PLACKET

This is the opening that is found on the sleeves of tailored shirts. It looks complicated but is straightforward if you take it one step at a time.

1 Cut out the placket and mark the pattern dots with tailor's tacks. Only these four tailor's tacks are required.

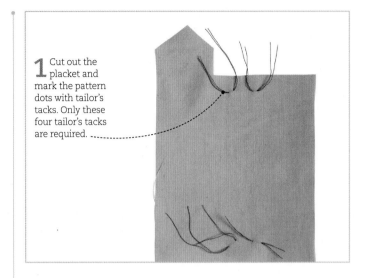

2 Place the placket to the shirt sleeve, right side of the placket to the wrong side of the sleeve, matching the tailor's tacks.

3 Pin in place.

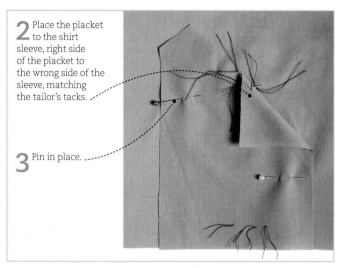

4 Machine a rectangular box, joining the tailor's tacks together. Make sure the rows of stitching are parallel. Remove the tacks.

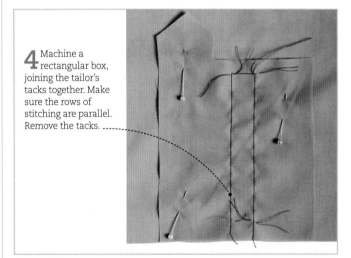

5 Slash through the placket and sleeve straight down the centre, between the rows of stitching.

6 Slash into the corners of the rectangle.

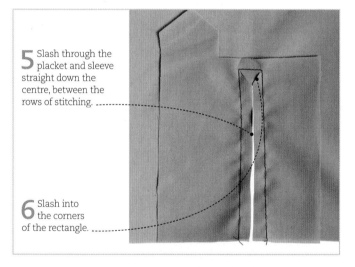

7 Open up the placket to the right side of the fabric and press. You will have a rectangular gap with sharp corners.

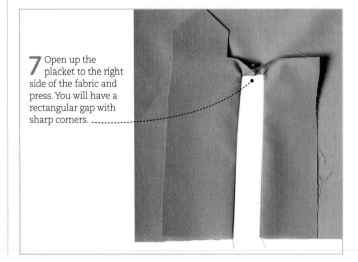

8 Fold back the long edge of the shorter side of the placket.

9 Place the folded edge on top of the machine stitching and pin in place.

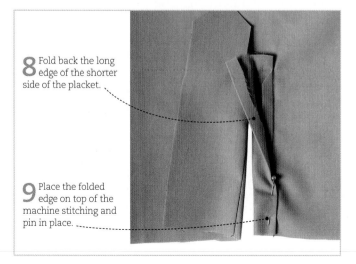

10 Machine the folded edge. Stop the machining at the top of the gap.

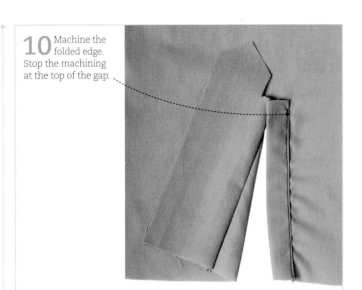

11 Fold the other side of the placket across the shorter side.

12 Press under the long edge. Fold back so that the pressed-under edge is on the machining line. Pin in place.

13 Fold under the top pointed end, following the cut edge, and press.

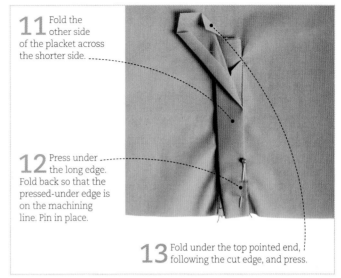

14 Machine the long folded edge in place. Make sure the underside of the placket is not caught in the stitching.

15 Continue the machining around the point.

16 Stitch an X through the point.

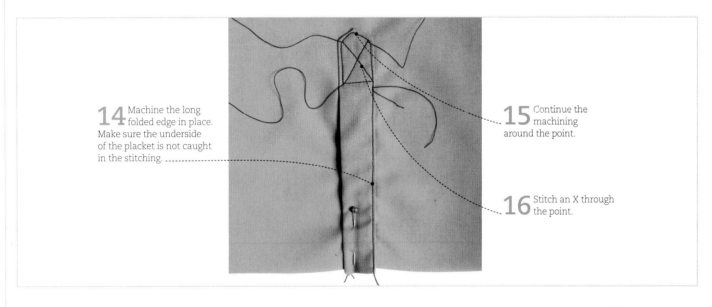

17 Pull all the ends of the machining threads through to the reverse and tie off.

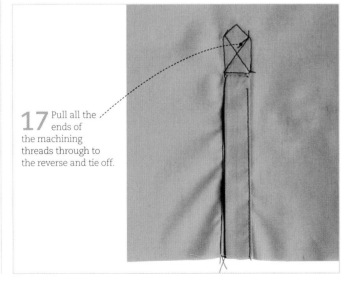

18 On the right side, the completed placket will be neatly stitched.

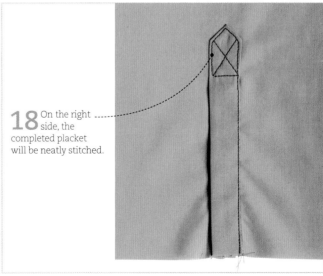

ATTACHING A CUFF

There are various types of cuff that can be attached to sleeve openings. The one-piece lapped cuff works well with a bound or faced opening. A two-piece shirt cuff is usually on a sleeve with a placket opening, but works equally well on a bound opening. The double cuff, or French cuff, is used for tailored shirts, and may be cut in one or two sections. It usually has a placket or bound opening.

LAPPED CUFF

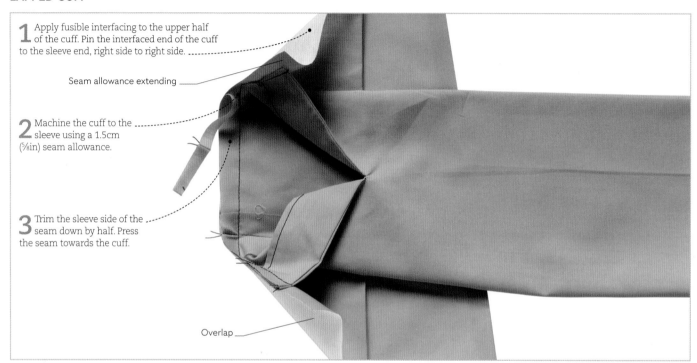

1 Apply fusible interfacing to the upper half of the cuff. Pin the interfaced end of the cuff to the sleeve end, right side to right side.

Seam allowance extending

2 Machine the cuff to the sleeve using a 1.5cm (⅝in) seam allowance.

3 Trim the sleeve side of the seam down by half. Press the seam towards the cuff.

Overlap

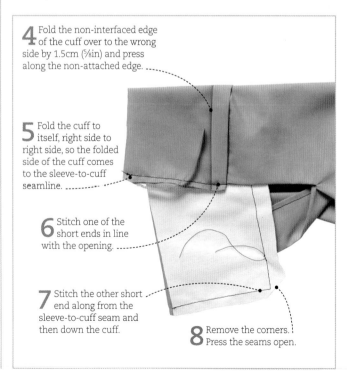

4 Fold the non-interfaced edge of the cuff over to the wrong side by 1.5cm (⅝in) and press along the non-attached edge.

5 Fold the cuff to itself, right side to right side, so the folded side of the cuff comes to the sleeve-to-cuff seamline.

6 Stitch one of the short ends in line with the opening.

7 Stitch the other short end along from the sleeve-to-cuff seam and then down the cuff.

8 Remove the corners. Press the seams open.

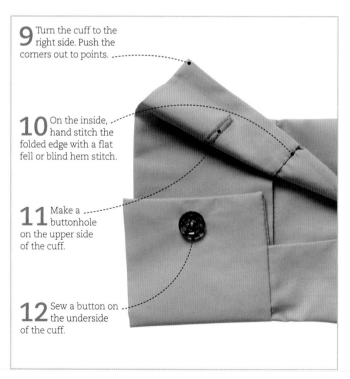

9 Turn the cuff to the right side. Push the corners out to points.

10 On the inside, hand stitch the folded edge with a flat fell or blind hem stitch.

11 Make a buttonhole on the upper side of the cuff.

12 Sew a button on the underside of the cuff.

SHIRT CUFF

1 Apply fusible interfacing to the upper cuff. Place it to the sleeve end, right side to right side, with a seam allowance extending at either end. Pin in place.

Upper cuff

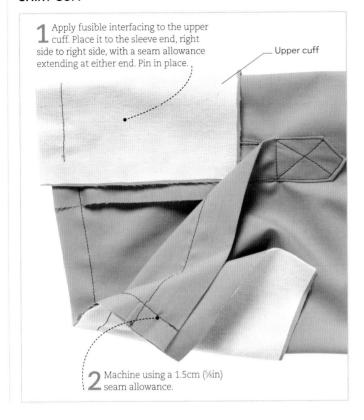

2 Machine using a 1.5cm (⅝in) seam allowance.

3 Place the right side of the under cuff to the right side of the upper cuff. Machine together around three sides, stitching in line with the sleeve opening.

Under cuff

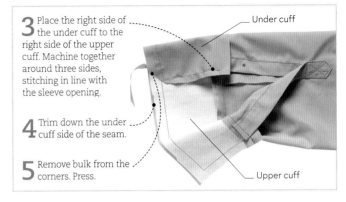

4 Trim down the under cuff side of the seam.

5 Remove bulk from the corners. Press.

Upper cuff

6 Turn the cuff to the right side and press.

7 Turn under the raw edge of the under cuff and place to the end of the sleeve. With this type of cuff, the edge is machined in place.

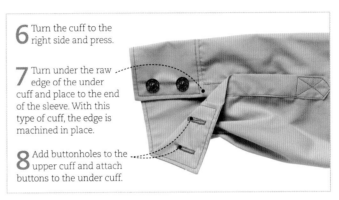

8 Add buttonholes to the upper cuff and attach buttons to the under cuff.

DOUBLE CUFF

1 Apply interfacing to the whole of the cuff. Attach the cuff to the sleeve end, right side to right side, using a 1.5cm (⅝in) seam allowance.

2 Fold the cuff back on to itself, right side to right side.

3 Machine stitch the two sides in line with the sleeve opening.

4 Trim the bulk from the seams and corners.

5 Press, then turn the cuff through to the right side.

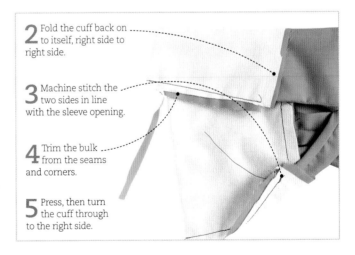

6 Fold the cuff up in half so that it is doubled.

7 Hand stitch inside to finish the other edge of the cuff.

8 Insert a buttonhole through the top two layers of the cuff and sew a button on to the under cuff.

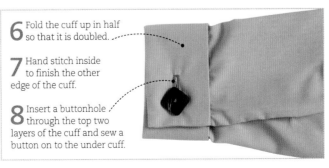

Waistlines

Waistlines can be formed where a bodice and skirt join together or at the waist edge of a skirt or pair of trousers. Some waistlines are attached to the garment to create a feature and others are more discreet. They may be shaped to follow the contours of the body.

A WAIST WITH A FACING

Many waistlines on skirts and trousers are finished with a facing, which will follow the contours of the waist but will have had the dart shaping removed to make it smooth. A faced waistline always sits comfortably to the body. The facing is attached after all the main sections of the skirt or trousers have been constructed.

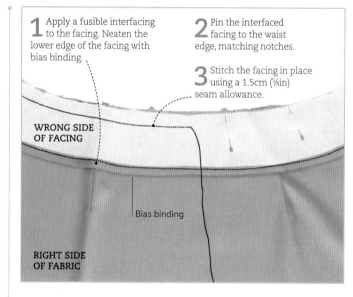

1 Apply a fusible interfacing to the facing. Neaten the lower edge of the facing with bias binding.

2 Pin the interfaced facing to the waist edge, matching notches.

3 Stitch the facing in place using a 1.5cm (⅝in) seam allowance.

WRONG SIDE OF FACING

Bias binding

RIGHT SIDE OF FABRIC

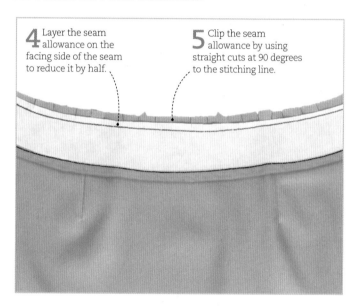

4 Layer the seam allowance on the facing side of the seam to reduce it by half.

5 Clip the seam allowance by using straight cuts at 90 degrees to the stitching line.

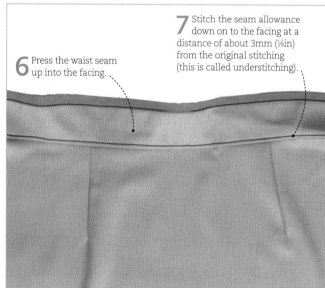

6 Press the waist seam up into the facing.

7 Stitch the seam allowance down on to the facing at a distance of about 3mm (⅛in) from the original stitching (this is called understitching).

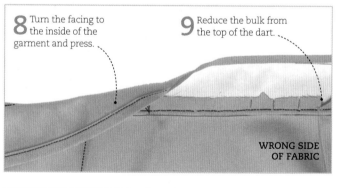

8 Turn the facing to the inside of the garment and press.

9 Reduce the bulk from the top of the dart.

WRONG SIDE OF FABRIC

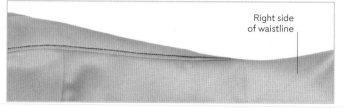

Right side of waistline

PETERSHAM-FACED WAIST

Petersham is an alternative finish to a facing if you do not have enough fabric to cut a facing. Available in black and white, it is a stiff, ridged tape that is 2.5cm (1in) wide and curved – the tighter curve is the top edge. Like a facing, petersham is attached to the waist after the skirt or trousers have been constructed.

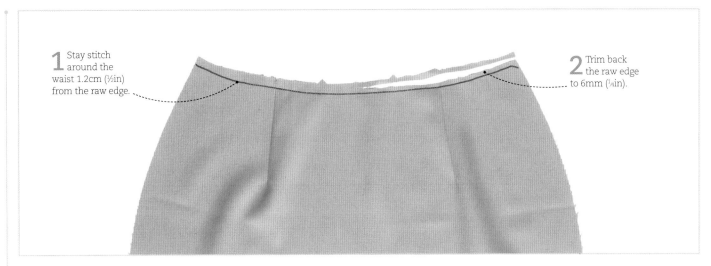

1 Stay stitch around the waist 1.2cm (½in) from the raw edge.

2 Trim back the raw edge to 6mm (¼in).

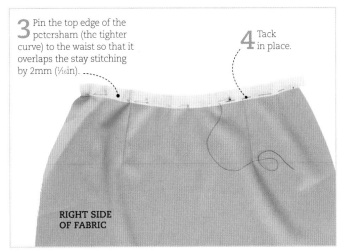

3 Pin the top edge of the petersham (the tighter curve) to the waist so that it overlaps the stay stitching by 2mm (⅛in).

4 Tack in place.

RIGHT SIDE OF FABRIC

5 Machine the petersham in place, stitching about 2mm (⅛in) from the edge of the petersham. Do not worry if the other edge looks wavy.

WRONG SIDE OF FABRIC

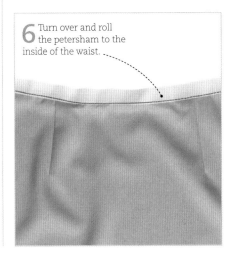

6 Turn over and roll the petersham to the inside of the waist.

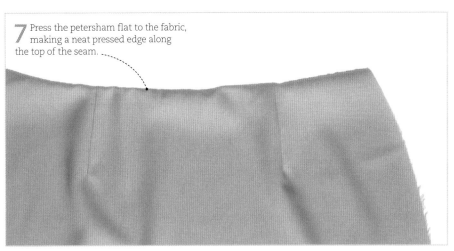

7 Press the petersham flat to the fabric, making a neat pressed edge along the top of the seam.

ATTACHING A STRAIGHT WAISTBAND

A waistband is designed to fit snugly but not tight to the waist. Whether it is straight or slightly curved, it will be constructed and attached in a similar way. Every waistband will require a fusible interfacing to give it structure and support. Special waistband interfacings are available, usually featuring slot lines that will guide you where to fold the fabric. Make sure the slots on the outer edge correspond to a 1.5cm (⅝in) seam allowance. If a specialist waistband fusible interfacing is not available you can use a medium-weight fusible interfacing.

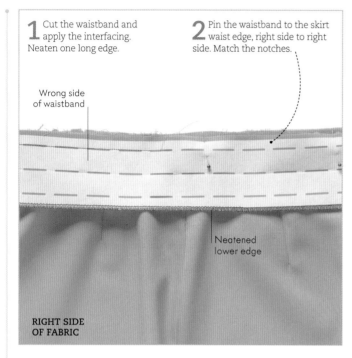

1 Cut the waistband and apply the interfacing. Neaten one long edge.

2 Pin the waistband to the skirt waist edge, right side to right side. Match the notches.

Wrong side of waistband

Neatened lower edge

RIGHT SIDE OF FABRIC

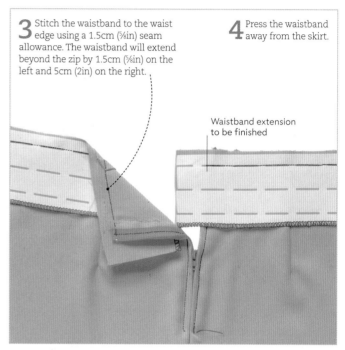

3 Stitch the waistband to the waist edge using a 1.5cm (⅝in) seam allowance. The waistband will extend beyond the zip by 1.5cm (⅝in) on the left and 5cm (2in) on the right.

4 Press the waistband away from the skirt.

Waistband extension to be finished

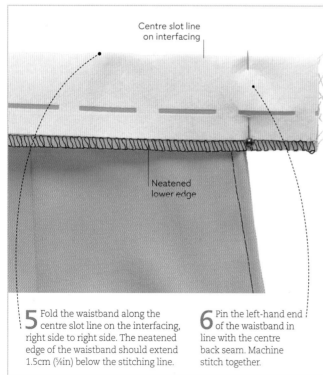

Centre slot line on interfacing

Neatened lower edge

5 Fold the waistband along the centre slot line on the interfacing, right side to right side. The neatened edge of the waistband should extend 1.5cm (⅝in) below the stitching line.

6 Pin the left-hand end of the waistband in line with the centre back seam. Machine stitch together.

7 On the right-hand end of the waistband, extend the waist to skirt stitching line into the waistband and along the short end.

8 Clip the corners and turn the ends of the waistband to the right side. The extension on the waistband should be on the right-hand back.

9 Add your chosen fasteners.

10 To complete the waistband, stitch through the band to the skirt seam. This is known as stitching in the ditch.

11 The finished straight waistband.

RIBBON-FACED WAISTBAND

On a bulky fabric, you can replace the inner side of the waistband with a ribbon. This will not affect the structure and stability of the waistband, but will produce a less bulky finish. Use a grosgrain ribbon that is 2.5cm (1in) wide. Grosgrain ribbon looks like petersham (see p.153) but is ribbed and much softer.

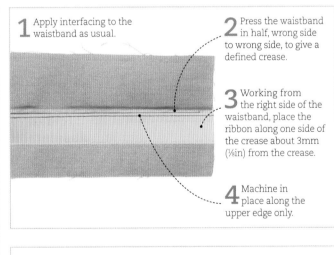

1 Apply interfacing to the waistband as usual.

2 Press the waistband in half, wrong side to wrong side, to give a defined crease.

3 Working from the right side of the waistband, place the ribbon along one side of the crease about 3mm (⅛in) from the crease.

4 Machine in place along the upper edge only.

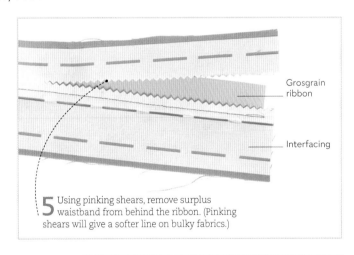

Grosgrain ribbon

Interfacing

5 Using pinking shears, remove surplus waistband from behind the ribbon. (Pinking shears will give a softer line on bulky fabrics.)

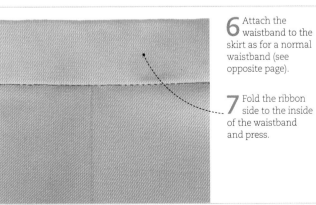

6 Attach the waistband to the skirt as for a normal waistband (see opposite page).

7 Fold the ribbon side to the inside of the waistband and press.

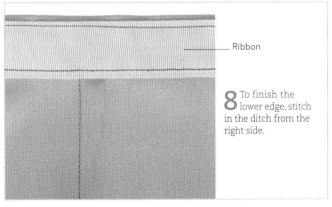

Ribbon

8 To finish the lower edge, stitch in the ditch from the right side.

ATTACHING A SPLIT WAISTBAND

A trouser waistband is often split at the centre back. This allows the waist to be easily altered from the back and so helps to ensure your tailored garment has the perfect fit.

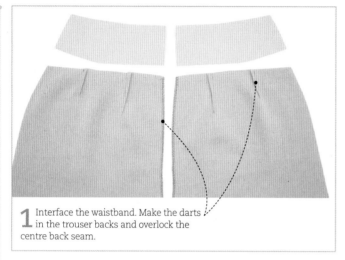

1 Interface the waistband. Make the darts in the trouser backs and overlock the centre back seam.

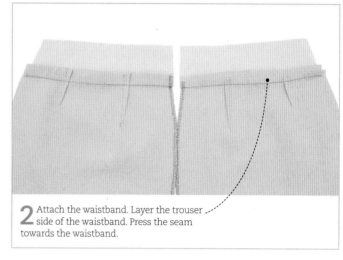

2 Attach the waistband. Layer the trouser side of the waistband. Press the seam towards the waistband.

3 Join the centre back seam, matching at the waistband seam. Press just the very top part of the centre back seam open.

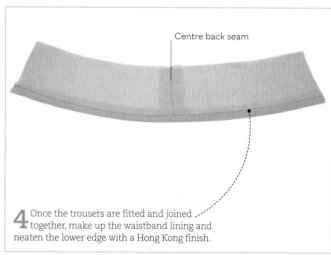

Centre back seam

4 Once the trousers are fitted and joined together, make up the waistband lining and neaten the lower edge with a Hong Kong finish.

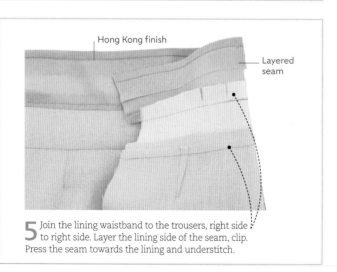

Hong Kong finish

Layered seam

5 Join the lining waistband to the trousers, right side to right side. Layer the lining side of the seam, clip. Press the seam towards the lining and understitch.

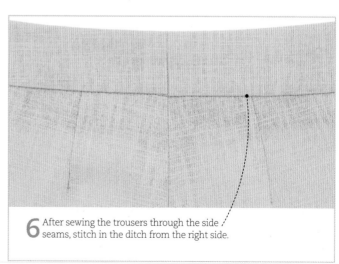

6 After sewing the trousers through the side seams, stitch in the ditch from the right side.

WAISTBAND GRIPPER TAPE

On tailored trousers the waistband often features a gripper to hold a shirt in place. This waistband is in two pieces – fabric on the outside and gripper on the inside.

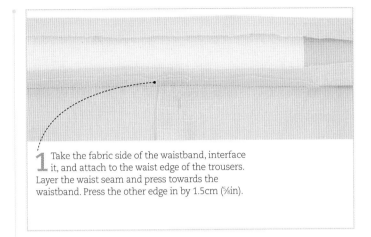

1 Take the fabric side of the waistband, interface it, and attach to the waist edge of the trousers. Layer the waist seam and press towards the waistband. Press the other edge in by 1.5cm (⅝in).

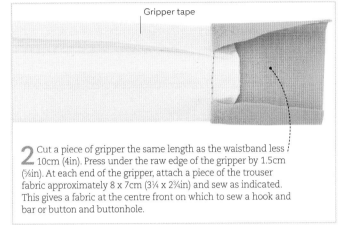

Gripper tape

2 Cut a piece of gripper the same length as the waistband less 10cm (4in). Press under the raw edge of the gripper by 1.5cm (⅝in). At each end of the gripper, attach a piece of the trouser fabric approximately 8 x 7cm (3¼ x 2¾in) and sew as indicated. This gives a fabric at the centre front on which to sew a hook and bar or button and buttonhole.

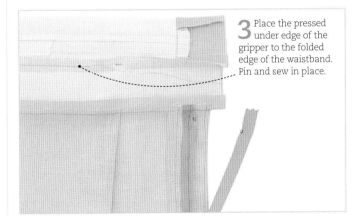

3 Place the pressed under edge of the gripper to the folded edge of the waistband. Pin and sew in place.

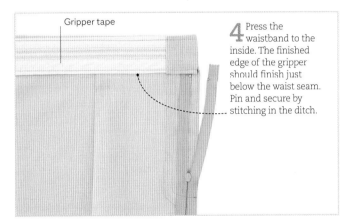

Gripper tape

4 Press the waistband to the inside. The finished edge of the gripper should finish just below the waist seam. Pin and secure by stitching in the ditch.

FINISHING THE EDGE OF A WAISTBAND

One long edge of the waistband will be stitched to the garment waist. The other edge will need to be finished, to prevent fraying and reduce bulk inside.

TURNING UNDER

This method is suitable for fine fabrics only. Turn under 1.5cm (⅝in) along the edge of the waistband and press in place. After the waistband has been attached to the garment, hand stitch the pressed-under edge in place.

OVERLOCK STITCHING

This method is suitable for heavier fabrics as it is left flat inside the garment after construction. Neaten one long edge of the waistband with a 3-thread overlock stitch.

BIAS BINDING

This method is ideal for fabrics that fray badly and can add a feature inside the garment. It is left flat inside the garment after construction. Apply a 2cm (¾in) bias binding to one long edge of the waistband.

Belt carriers

A belted garment will need belt carriers to support the belt and prevent it from drooping. Belt carriers can be made from fabric strips and machined to the garment, or they can be made more simply from thread loops fashioned by hand stitching. Fabric carriers are designed to support a heavier belt.

HAND-STITCHED BELT LOOPS

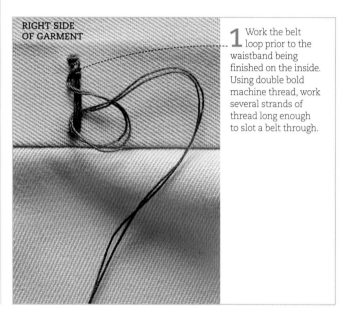

RIGHT SIDE OF GARMENT

1 Work the belt loop prior to the waistband being finished on the inside. Using double bold machine thread, work several strands of thread long enough to slot a belt through.

2 Use a buttonhole stitch and work the stitches across the loops.

3 When the loops are covered with buttonhole stitches, take the thread to the reverse and finish securely.

MACHINE-STITCHED BELT CARRIERS

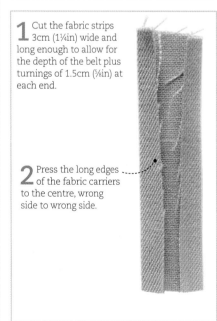

1 Cut the fabric strips 3cm (1¼in) wide and long enough to allow for the depth of the belt plus turnings of 1.5cm (⅝in) at each end.

2 Press the long edges of the fabric carriers to the centre, wrong side to wrong side.

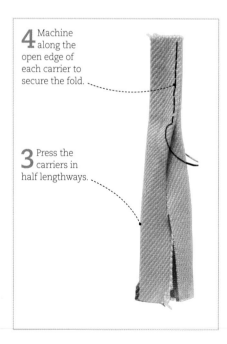

4 Machine along the open edge of each carrier to secure the fold.

3 Press the carriers in half lengthways.

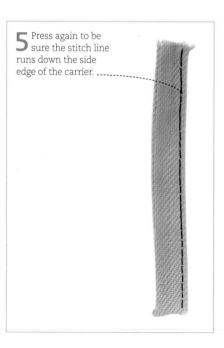

5 Press again to be sure the stitch line runs down the side edge of the carrier.

6 Starting at each side seam and then at regular intervals between, place the carriers to the waist of the garment, on the right side. Stitch to secure at the waist inside the seam allowance.

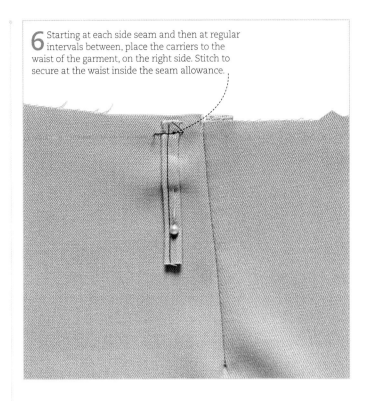

7 Apply the waistband to the garment, stitching across the carriers as you do so.

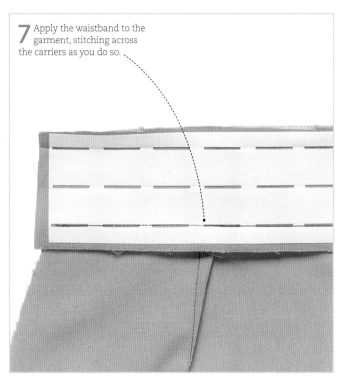

8 Press the waistband in half lengthways to give a centre crease.

9 Bring the carriers up on to the waistband.

10 Secure the end of each carrier to the inner edge of the waistband using a small, close zigzag stitch.

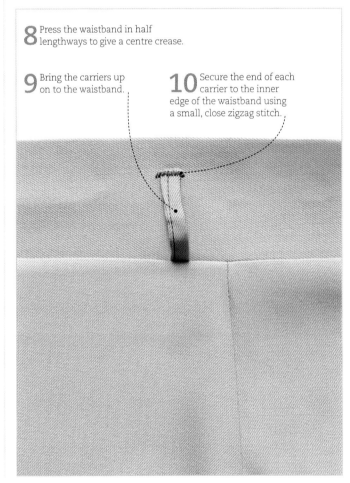

11 When the waistband is completed, the carrier will sit on it with no visible stitching.

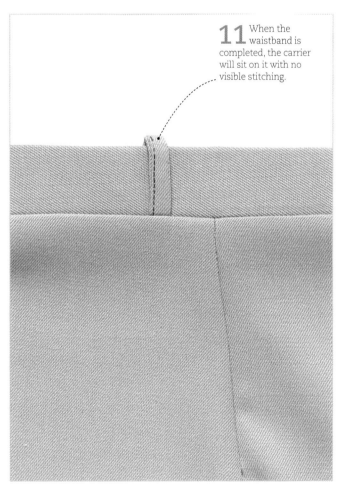

Pockets

Pockets come in lots of shapes and formats. Some, such as patch pockets, paper bag pockets, and jetted pockets with a flap, are external and can be decorative, while others, including front hip pockets, are more discreet and hidden from view. They can be made from the same fabric as the garment or in a contrasting fabric. Whether casual or tailored, all pockets are functional.

SELF-LINED PATCH POCKET

If a patch pocket is to be self-lined, it needs to be cut with the top edge of the pocket on a fold. Like an unlined pocket, if you are using a lightweight fabric an interfacing may not be required, but for medium-weight fabrics it's best to use a fusible interfacing. A self-lined patch pocket is not suitable for heavy fabrics.

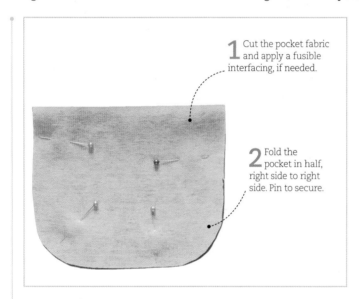

1 Cut the pocket fabric and apply a fusible interfacing, if needed.

2 Fold the pocket in half, right side to right side. Pin to secure.

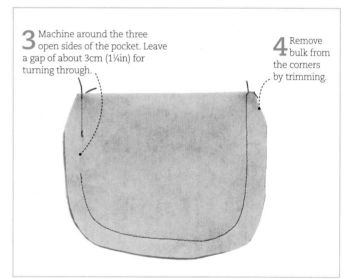

3 Machine around the three open sides of the pocket. Leave a gap of about 3cm (1¼in) for turning through.

4 Remove bulk from the corners by trimming.

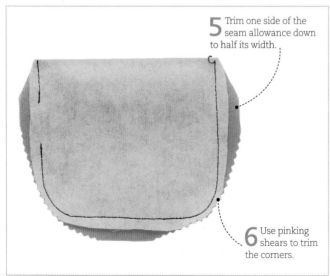

5 Trim one side of the seam allowance down to half its width.

6 Use pinking shears to trim the corners.

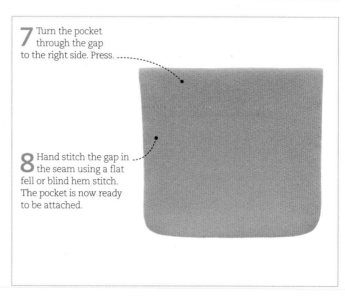

7 Turn the pocket through the gap to the right side. Press.

8 Hand stitch the gap in the seam using a flat fell or blind hem stitch. The pocket is now ready to be attached.

LINED PATCH POCKET

If a self-lined patch pocket is likely to be too bulky, then a lined pocket
is the answer. It is a good idea to interface the pocket fabric.

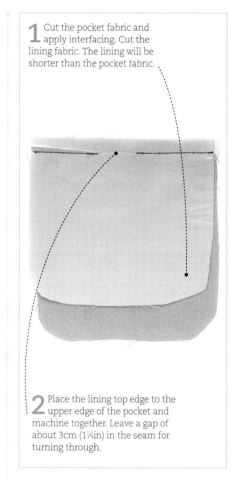

1 Cut the pocket fabric and apply interfacing. Cut the lining fabric. The lining will be shorter than the pocket fabric.

2 Place the lining top edge to the upper edge of the pocket and machine together. Leave a gap of about 3cm (1¼in) in the seam for turning through.

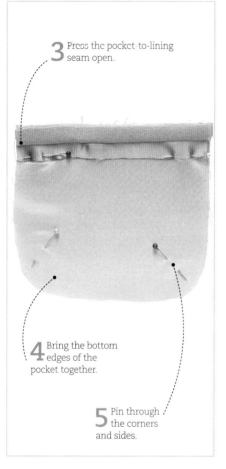

3 Press the pocket-to-lining seam open.

4 Bring the bottom edges of the pocket together.

5 Pin through the corners and sides.

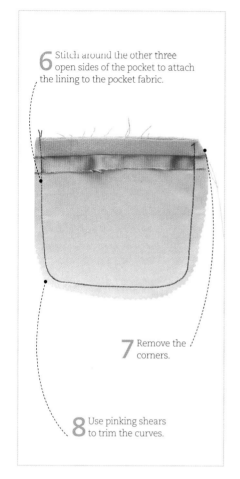

6 Stitch around the other three open sides of the pocket to attach the lining to the pocket fabric.

7 Remove the corners.

8 Use pinking shears to trim the curves.

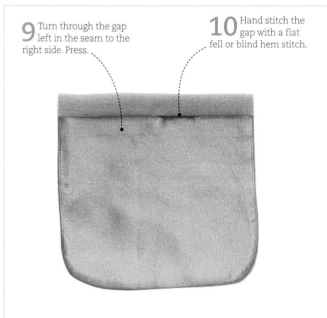

9 Turn through the gap left in the seam to the right side. Press.

10 Hand stitch the gap with a flat fell or blind hem stitch.

11 The lined patch pocket is ready to be attached.

SQUARE PATCH POCKET

It is possible to have a patch pocket with square corners. This requires mitring the corners to reduce the bulk. Use a fusible interfacing on medium-weight fabrics.

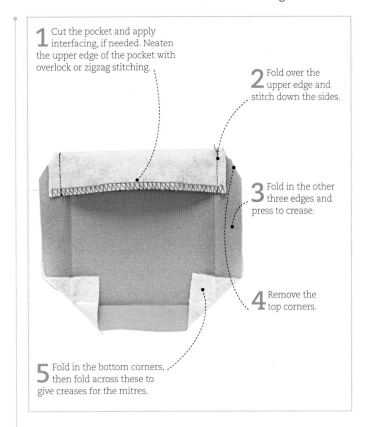

1 Cut the pocket and apply interfacing, if needed. Neaten the upper edge of the pocket with overlock or zigzag stitching.

2 Fold over the upper edge and stitch down the sides.

3 Fold in the other three edges and press to crease.

4 Remove the top corners.

5 Fold in the bottom corners, then fold across these to give creases for the mitres.

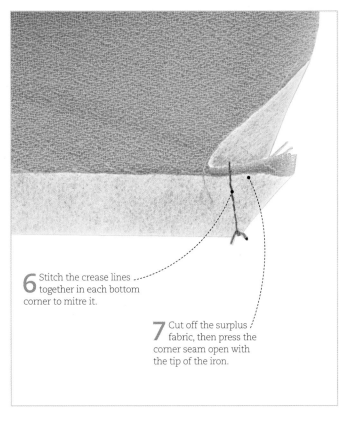

6 Stitch the crease lines together in each bottom corner to mitre it.

7 Cut off the surplus fabric, then press the corner seam open with the tip of the iron.

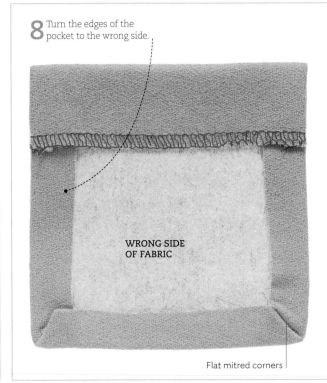

8 Turn the edges of the pocket to the wrong side.

WRONG SIDE OF FABRIC

Flat mitred corners

9 The finished pocket is now ready to be attached.

ATTACHING A PATCH POCKET

To attach a pocket successfully, accurate pattern marking is essential. It is best to do this by means of tailor's tacks or even trace tacking. If you are using a check or stripe fabric, take care to align the pocket fabric with the checks or stripes on the garment.

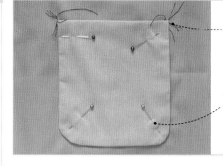

1 Mark the pocket placement lines on the garment with tailor's tacks.

2 Take the completed pocket and place it to the fabric, matching the corners with the tailor's tacks. Pin in position.

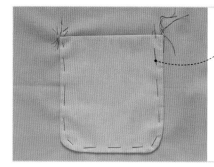

3 To make sure the pocket remains in the correct position, tack around the edge along the sides and bottom. Keep the tacking stitches close to the finished edge of the pocket.

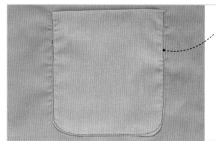

4 Machine stitch about 1mm (¹⁄₃₂in) from the edge of the pocket.

5 Remove the tacking stitches. Press.

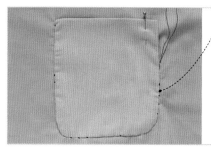

6 Alternatively, the pocket can be hand stitched in place, using a slip hem stitch into the underside of the pocket seam. Do not pull on the thread too tightly or the pocket will wrinkle.

REINFORCING POCKET CORNERS

On any patch pocket it is essential to reinforce the upper corners as these take all the strain when the pocket is being used. There are several ways to do this, some of which are quite decorative.

REVERSE STITCH

1 Reinforce the corner with a reverse stitch. Make sure the stitches lie on top of one another.

2 Pull the threads to the reverse to tie off.

DIAGONAL STITCH

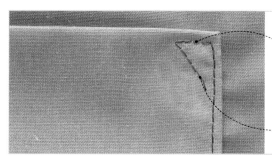

1 This is a technique used primarily on shirts. When machining the pocket in place, stitch along horizontally for four stitches.

2 Turn and stitch diagonally back to the side, to create a triangular shape in the corner.

ZIGZAG STITCH

1 Using a small zigzag stitch, stitch diagonally across the corner.

2 Make a feature of this stitch by using a thread in a contrasting colour.

PARALLEL ZIGZAG STITCH

1 Place a patch on the wrong side of the garment, behind the pocket corner, to stitch into for strength.

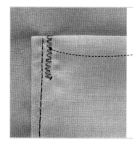

2 Using a small zigzag stitch, width 1.0 and length 1.0, machine a short vertical line next to the straight stitching.

WELT POCKET

A welt pocket features a small, straight flap that faces upwards on a garment, with the pocket opening behind the flap. This kind of pocket is found on waistcoats and is the usual breast pocket on tailored jackets, as well as being used on coats.

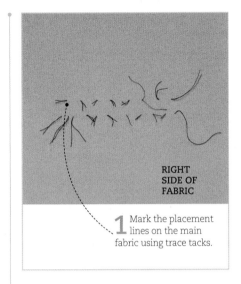

1 Mark the placement lines on the main fabric using trace tacks.

RIGHT SIDE OF FABRIC

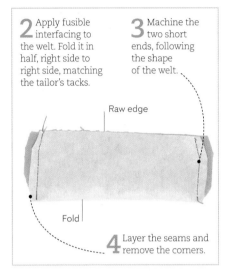

2 Apply fusible interfacing to the welt. Fold it in half, right side to right side, matching the tailor's tacks.

Raw edge

Fold

4 Layer the seams and remove the corners.

3 Machine the two short ends, following the shape of the welt.

RIGHT SIDE OF FABRIC

5 Turn the welt to the right side and press.

6 Align the top of the welt with the top line of tacks. Machine along the lower line of tacks. Trim away the bulk.

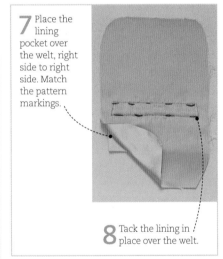

7 Place the lining pocket over the welt, right side to right side. Match the pattern markings.

8 Tack the lining in place over the welt.

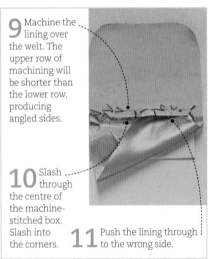

9 Machine the lining over the welt. The upper row of machining will be shorter than the lower row, producing angled sides.

10 Slash through the centre of the machine-stitched box. Slash into the corners.

11 Push the lining through to the wrong side.

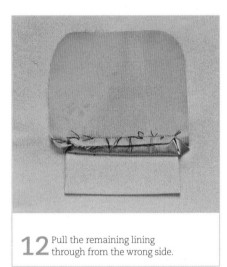

12 Pull the remaining lining through from the wrong side.

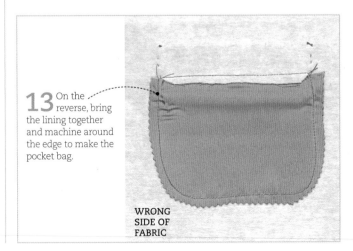

13 On the reverse, bring the lining together and machine around the edge to make the pocket bag.

WRONG SIDE OF FABRIC

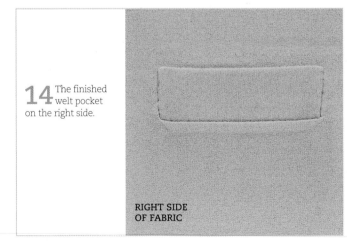

14 The finished welt pocket on the right side.

RIGHT SIDE OF FABRIC

WELT POCKET ON TROUSER BACK

A welt pocket on the back of a pair of trousers features a slim, elegant welt. For this reason, its construction is slightly different and you will need to reinforce the finished welt with stitches on the right side.

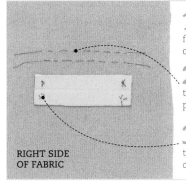

1 Reinforce the wrong side of the pocket area with fusible interfacing (not shown on these samples).

2 On the right side, mark parallel stitching lines for the welt according to your pattern with tacks.

3 Apply fusible interfacing to the welt. Use tailor's tacks to transfer the dot markings on the welt pattern.

RIGHT SIDE OF FABRIC

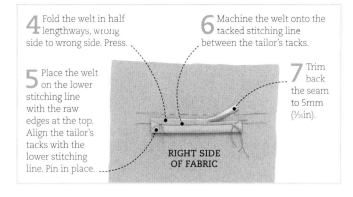

4 Fold the welt in half lengthways, wrong side to wrong side. Press.

5 Place the welt on the lower stitching line with the raw edges at the top. Align the tailor's tacks with the lower stitching line. Pin in place.

6 Machine the welt onto the tacked stitching line between the tailor's tacks.

7 Trim back the seam to 5mm (³⁄₁₆in).

RIGHT SIDE OF FABRIC

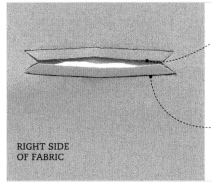

8 Place the pocket fabric on the upper stitching line and pin in place.

9 Place the pocket lining on the lower stitching line over the welt. Pin in place.

RIGHT SIDE OF FABRIC

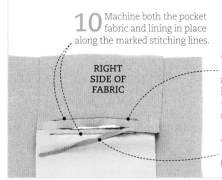

10 Machine both the pocket fabric and lining in place along the marked stitching lines.

RIGHT SIDE OF FABRIC

11 The two rows must be parallel and exactly the same length as the stitched welt. Do not stitch across the short ends.

12 Trim away the bulk from both seams.

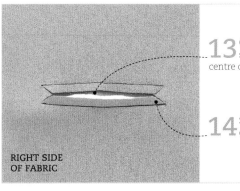

13 On the wrong side, slash through the centre of the welt.

14 Slash into the corners as shown.

RIGHT SIDE OF FABRIC

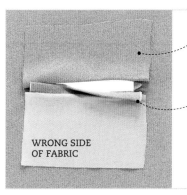

15 Pull both pocket pieces and the welt through to the wrong side.

16 Make sure the triangles at the short ends are also on the wrong side.

17 Press in place with the welt over the triangles.

WRONG SIDE OF FABRIC

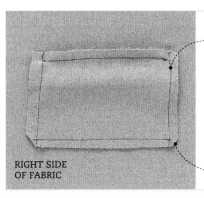

18 Fold the pocket fabric down onto the pocket lining. Stitch the two pocket sections together on three sides to make a pocket sack or bag. Make sure you catch in the triangle end of the slash and the end of the welts.

19 Trim the corners to reduce bulk.

RIGHT SIDE OF FABRIC

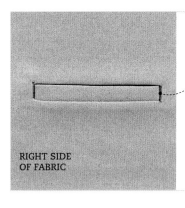

20 On the right side, set the machine to a zigzag stitch, width 2.5 and length 0.5, and stitch across the short ends of the welt to reinforce.

RIGHT SIDE OF FABRIC

JETTED POCKET WITH A FLAP

This type of pocket is found on tailored jackets and coats. It is straightforward to make. The main components are the welts (the strips that make the edges of the pocket), the flap, and the lining that makes the pocket bag.

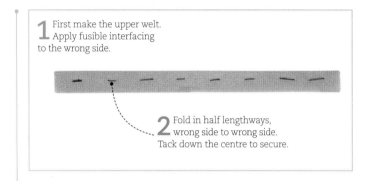

1 First make the upper welt. Apply fusible interfacing to the wrong side.

2 Fold in half lengthways, wrong side to wrong side. Tack down the centre to secure.

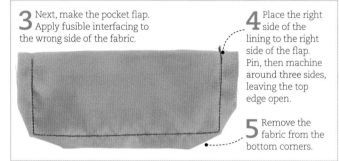

3 Next, make the pocket flap. Apply fusible interfacing to the wrong side of the fabric.

4 Place the right side of the lining to the right side of the flap. Pin, then machine around three sides, leaving the top edge open.

5 Remove the fabric from the bottom corners.

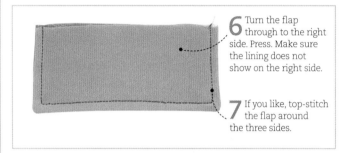

6 Turn the flap through to the right side. Press. Make sure the lining does not show on the right side.

7 If you like, top-stitch the flap around the three sides.

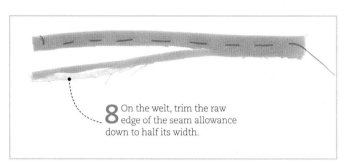

8 On the welt, trim the raw edge of the seam allowance down to half its width.

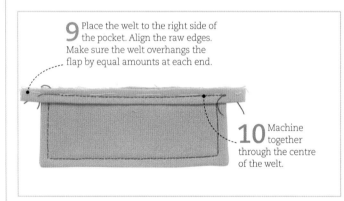

9 Place the welt to the right side of the pocket. Align the raw edges. Make sure the welt overhangs the flap by equal amounts at each end.

10 Machine together through the centre of the welt.

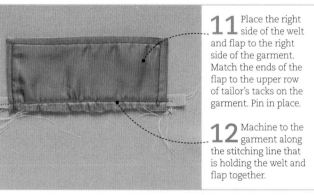

11 Place the right side of the welt and flap to the right side of the garment. Match the ends of the flap to the upper row of tailor's tacks on the garment. Pin in place.

12 Machine to the garment along the stitching line that is holding the welt and flap together.

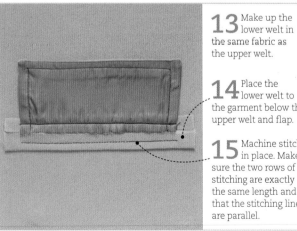

13 Make up the lower welt in the same fabric as the upper welt.

14 Place the lower welt to the garment below the upper welt and flap.

15 Machine stitch in place. Make sure the two rows of stitching are exactly the same length and that the stitching lines are parallel.

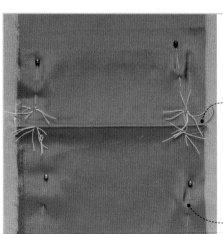

16 Take the lining and press in half, right side to right side, matching the tailor's tacks, to produce a centre crease.

17 Place the right side of the lining over the welt and flaps, matching the tailor's tacks. The crease line should be sitting between the two welts. Pin in place.

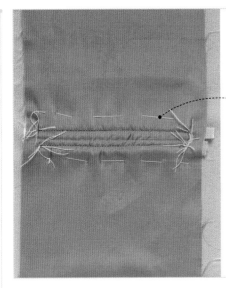

18 Tack the lining in position. Keep the tacking stitches about 1.5cm (⅝in) from the tailor's tacks that mark the welts.

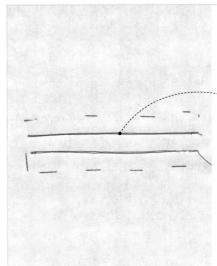

19 Working from the wrong side, machine the lining in place by stitching over the stitching lines that are holding the welts in place. The two rows of stitching should be exactly the same length. Secure at both ends.

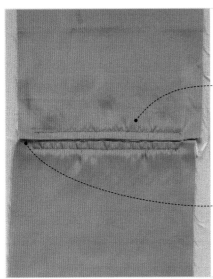

20 Turn to the right side and remove the tacking.

21 Slash through just the lining along the pressed crease line. Cut through to the edge of the lining.

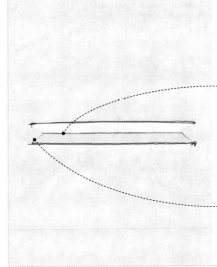

22 On the reverse, slash through the fabric of the garment. The slash line should cut through just the fabric and not the welts or flaps.

23 Slash into the corners right to the stitching lines.

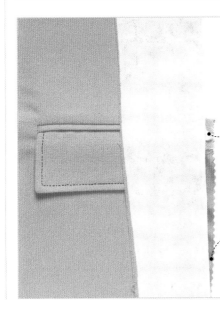

24 Pull the lining through the slash to the wrong side. Push through the ends of the welts. The pocket flap will turn down.

25 To make the pocket, pull the ends of the welts out away from the slash lines. A small triangle of fabric should be on top of these welts.

26 Stitch across the welts and the triangle and around the pocket. Use pinking shears to neaten the seams on the lining.

27 Press everything in place, using a pressing cloth if necessary.

FRONT HIP POCKET

On many trousers and casual skirts, the pocket is placed on the hipline. It can be low on the hipline or cut quite high as on jeans. The construction is the same for all types of hip pockets. When inserted at an angle, hip pockets can slim the figure.

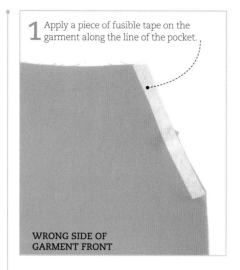

1 Apply a piece of fusible tape on the garment along the line of the pocket.

WRONG SIDE OF GARMENT FRONT

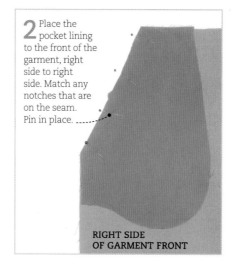

2 Place the pocket lining to the front of the garment, right side to right side. Match any notches that are on the seam. Pin in place.

RIGHT SIDE OF GARMENT FRONT

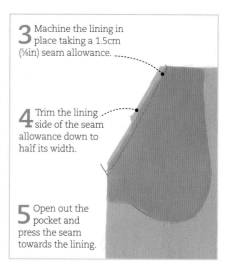

3 Machine the lining in place taking a 1.5cm (⅝in) seam allowance.

4 Trim the lining side of the seam allowance down to half its width.

5 Open out the pocket and press the seam towards the lining.

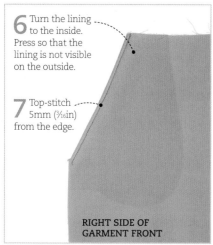

6 Turn the lining to the inside. Press so that the lining is not visible on the outside.

7 Top-stitch 5mm (³⁄₁₆in) from the edge.

RIGHT SIDE OF GARMENT FRONT

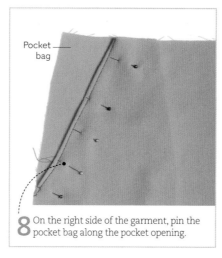

Pocket bag

8 On the right side of the garment, pin the pocket bag along the pocket opening.

9 Take the side front section that incorporates the pocket bag and place to the lining pocket section, right side to right side. Match any seams and tailor's tacks. Pin in place.

WRONG SIDE OF GARMENT

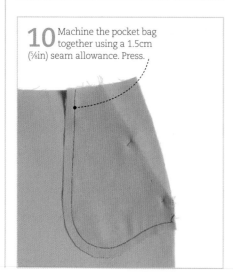

10 Machine the pocket bag together using a 1.5cm (⅝in) seam allowance. Press.

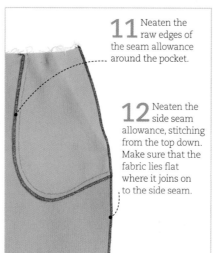

11 Neaten the raw edges of the seam allowance around the pocket.

12 Neaten the side seam allowance, stitching from the top down. Make sure that the fabric lies flat where it joins on to the side seam.

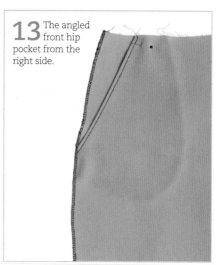

13 The angled front hip pocket from the right side.

CHINO POCKET

This is the style of pocket found on the front of chino trousers and jeans, but it can also be applied to skirts. The pocket is sometimes curved in shape rather than angular, as shown here. This pocket features a facing, which gives it a neat finish at the opening edge.

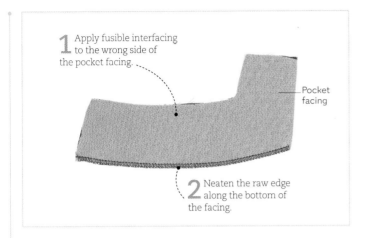

1 Apply fusible interfacing to the wrong side of the pocket facing.

Pocket facing

2 Neaten the raw edge along the bottom of the facing.

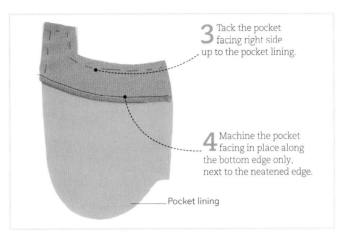

3 Tack the pocket facing right side up to the pocket lining.

4 Machine the pocket facing in place along the bottom edge only, next to the neatened edge.

Pocket lining

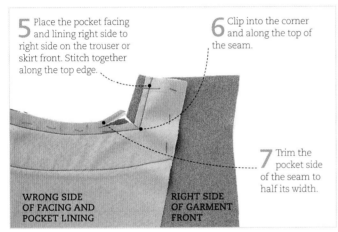

5 Place the pocket facing and lining right side to right side on the trouser or skirt front. Stitch together along the top edge.

6 Clip into the corner and along the top of the seam.

7 Trim the pocket side of the seam to half its width.

WRONG SIDE OF FACING AND POCKET LINING

RIGHT SIDE OF GARMENT FRONT

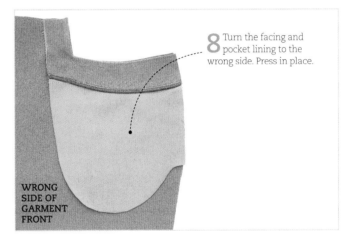

8 Turn the facing and pocket lining to the wrong side. Press in place.

WRONG SIDE OF GARMENT FRONT

9 On the right side of the garment, top-stitch using a 3.0 stitch length.

RIGHT SIDE OF GARMENT FRONT

10 On the wrong side of the garment front, place the pocket fabric over the facing and lining.

11 Stitch around the pocket sack to join the lining to the pocket fabric.

Pocket fabric

WRONG SIDE OF GARMENT FRONT

12 Stitch the side seam together, through the garment and pocket, using an overlock or zigzag stitch. The seam is left loose in order to allow extra room for the pocket.

MAKING A POCKET FLAP

On some styles of garment, there is no pocket, just a flap for decorative purposes.
The flap is sewn where the pocket would be, but there is no opening under the flap.
This is to reduce the bulk that would arise from having the rest of the pocket.

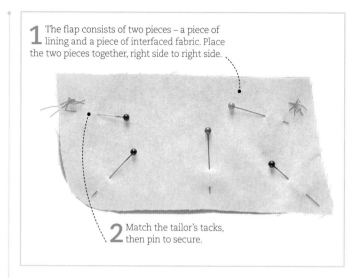

1 The flap consists of two pieces – a piece of lining and a piece of interfaced fabric. Place the two pieces together, right side to right side.

2 Match the tailor's tacks, then pin to secure.

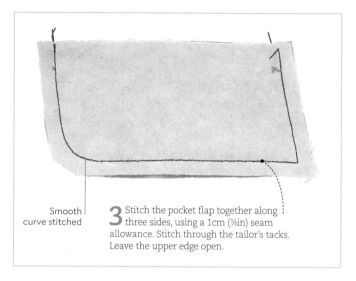

Smooth curve stitched

3 Stitch the pocket flap together along three sides, using a 1cm (⅜in) seam allowance. Stitch through the tailor's tacks. Leave the upper edge open.

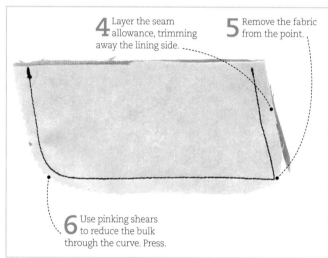

4 Layer the seam allowance, trimming away the lining side.

5 Remove the fabric from the point.

6 Use pinking shears to reduce the bulk through the curve. Press.

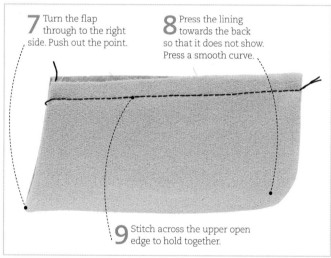

7 Turn the flap through to the right side. Push out the point.

8 Press the lining towards the back so that it does not show. Press a smooth curve.

9 Stitch across the upper open edge to hold together.

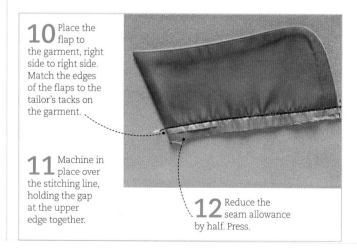

10 Place the flap to the garment, right side to right side. Match the edges of the flaps to the tailor's tacks on the garment.

11 Machine in place over the stitching line, holding the gap at the upper edge together.

12 Reduce the seam allowance by half. Press.

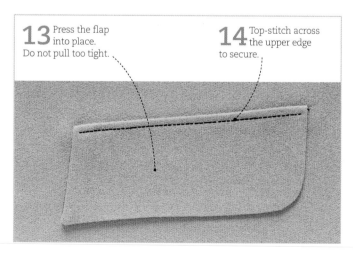

13 Press the flap into place. Do not pull too tight.

14 Top-stitch across the upper edge to secure.

SINGLE WELT POCKET WITH A FLAP

This is a stylish pocket that combines functionality with elegance – the pocket is useable but the flap hides the opening and gives a smart finish. It is usually found on tailored jackets and blazers.

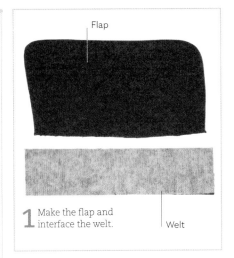

1 Make the flap and interface the welt.

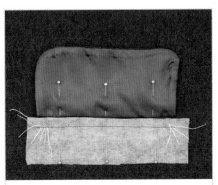

2 Place the flap and welt to the fabric, matching at the pattern markings. Sew in place. Make sure both rows of stitching are parallel and exactly the same length.

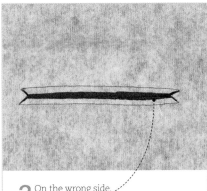

3 On the wrong side, slash between the two stitching lines and cut V shapes into the corners.

4 Gently pull the welt and the flap seam allowance through the slash.

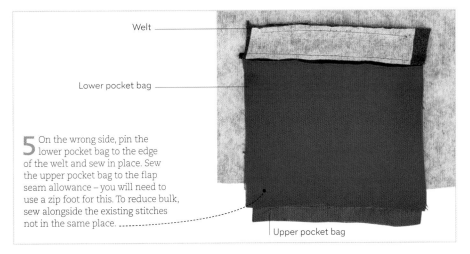

5 On the wrong side, pin the lower pocket bag to the edge of the welt and sew in place. Sew the upper pocket bag to the flap seam allowance – you will need to use a zip foot for this. To reduce bulk, sew alongside the existing stitches not in the same place.

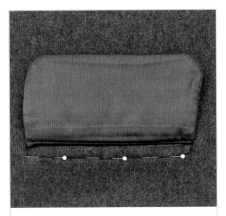

6 Fold the welt so it fills the gap. Pin along the stitch line and stitch in the ditch. Be careful not to sew through the pocket lining.

7 To complete, sew the pocket bag together stitching across the little V shapes to make the pocket ends square. Press.

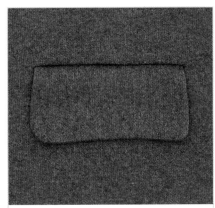

8 The completed pocket on the right side.

DOUBLE WELT POCKET WITH FLAP

This type of pocket is usually found on coats and tailored jackets. It requires slashing the fabric prior to construction. It is normal to have a dart finishing in the area too.

1 On the wrong side of the front, add a piece of interfacing approximately 5cm (2in) wide where the pocket will be sewn.

2 Insert the pattern marking for the dart and pocket. Slash as indicated in the pattern and sew the dart. Slash the dart and press open.

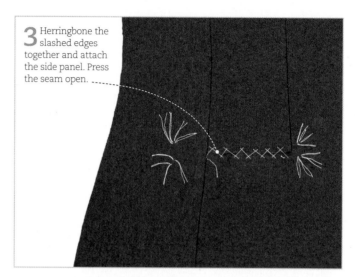

3 Herringbone the slashed edges together and attach the side panel. Press the seam open.

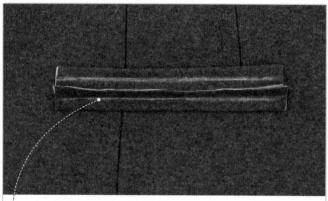

4 Chalk the stitching lines on the welts and stitch in place. Make sure they are lining up with the slash in the jacket.

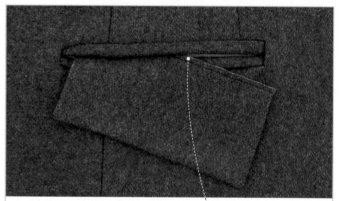

5 Remove the herringbone stitches and slash between the stitch line making V shapes into the corners. Turn the welt to the inside and press.

6 Make up the flap. Insert the flap between the welts.

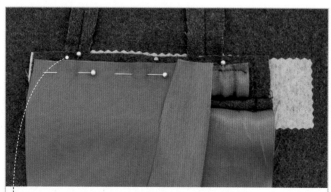

7 Insert the flap and put it to the edge of the welt. Pin to secure. Place the upper pocket lining over the flap and welt and sew to the edge of the welt. On the lower welt, pin and sew the lower pocket lining.

8 The completed pocket.

FAUX WELT POCKET

Sometimes a faux welt pocket is added to a garment as a fashion detail. It can give a plain garment of clothing some welcome texture and detail and makes a sleek addition to a tailored jacket.

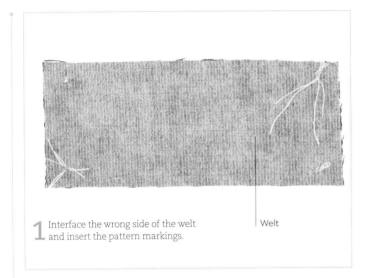

1 Interface the wrong side of the welt and insert the pattern markings.

Welt

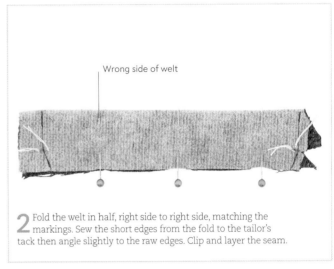

Wrong side of welt

2 Fold the welt in half, right side to right side, matching the markings. Sew the short edges from the fold to the tailor's tack then angle slightly to the raw edges. Clip and layer the seam.

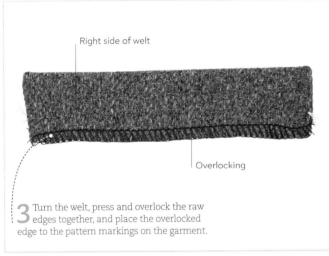

Right side of welt

Overlocking

3 Turn the welt, press and overlock the raw edges together, and place the overlocked edge to the pattern markings on the garment.

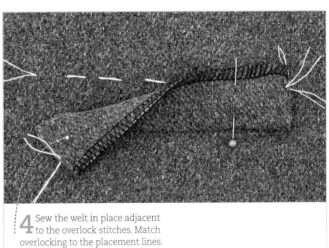

4 Sew the welt in place adjacent to the overlock stitches. Match overlocking to the placement lines.

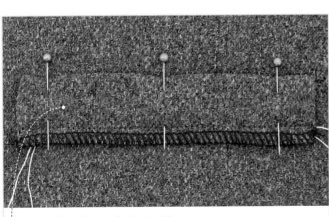

5 Press the welt towards the shoulder of the garment and hand stitch at the sides to secure. Press again.

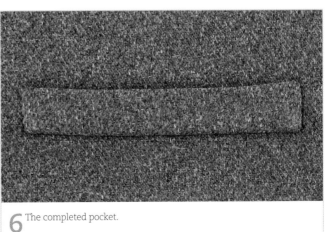

6 The completed pocket.

JETTED POCKET

This is a professional pocket found on many suit jackets. Great care has to be taken when making this pocket because there is no flap for it to hide behind!

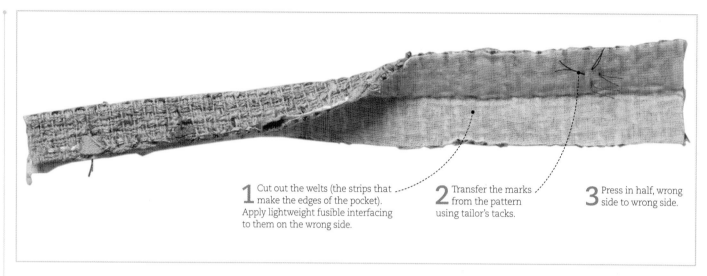

1 Cut out the welts (the strips that make the edges of the pocket). Apply lightweight fusible interfacing to them on the wrong side.

2 Transfer the marks from the pattern using tailor's tacks.

3 Press in half, wrong side to wrong side.

4 Mark the pocket position on the fabric, as indicated on your pattern, using tailor's tacks.

RIGHT SIDE OF FABRIC

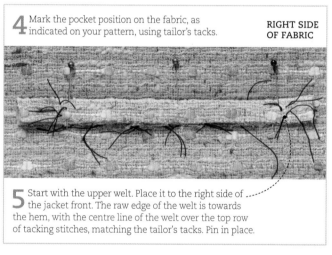

5 Start with the upper welt. Place it to the right side of the jacket front. The raw edge of the welt is towards the hem, with the centre line of the welt over the top row of tacking stitches, matching the tailor's tacks. Pin in place.

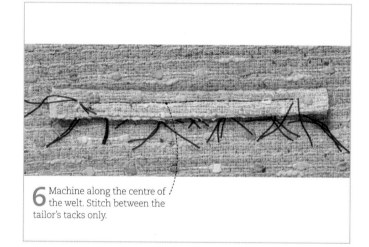

6 Machine along the centre of the welt. Stitch between the tailor's tacks only.

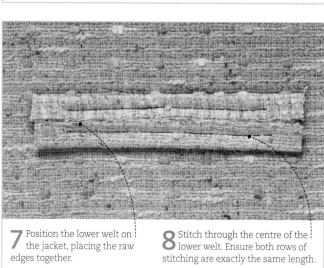

7 Position the lower welt on the jacket, placing the raw edges together.

8 Stitch through the centre of the lower welt. Ensure both rows of stitching are exactly the same length.

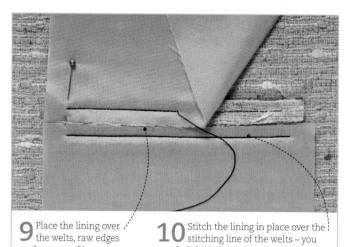

9 Place the lining over the welts, raw edges to the centre. Pin to secure.

10 Stitch the lining in place over the stitching line of the welts – you can feel the indentation of welt stitching.

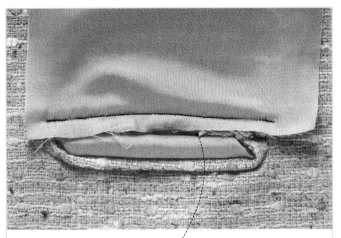

11 Slash through the jacket fabric between the welts (see Jetted pocket with flap, pp.166–167).

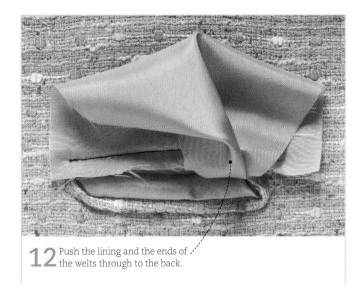

12 Push the lining and the ends of the welts through to the back.

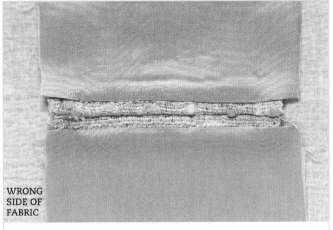

WRONG SIDE OF FABRIC

13 Press the lining and welts on the wrong side as shown.

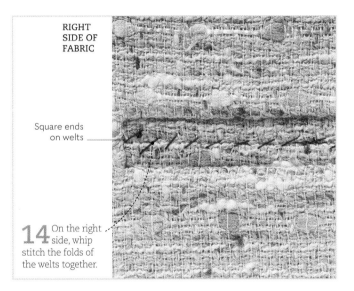

RIGHT SIDE OF FABRIC

Square ends on welts

14 On the right side, whip stitch the folds of the welts together.

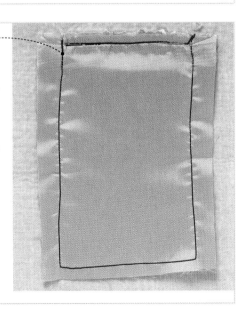

15 On the reverse, fold the top layer of the pocket lining down to meet the bottom layer. Make the pocket bag by stitching from one end of the welts, around the bottom, to the other end of the welts.

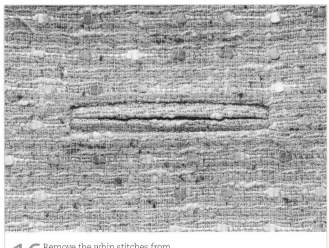

16 Remove the whip stitches from across the pocket opening.

Hems

The edge of a garment can be finished with a hem, which involves folding and stitching the fabric's edge to prevent fraying. A well-constructed hem provides a neat and refined finishing touch to a garment. Sometimes it is the style of garment that dictates the method that is used, and sometimes it is the fabric.

MARKING A HEMLINE

On a garment such as a skirt or a dress it is important that the hemline is level all around. Even if the fabric has been cut straight, some styles of skirt – such as A-line or circular – will "drop", which means that the hem edge is longer in some places. This is due to the fabric stretching where it is not on the straight of the grain. Poor posture will also cause a hem to hang unevenly.

USING A RULER

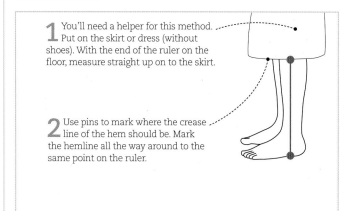

1 You'll need a helper for this method. Put on the skirt or dress (without shoes). With the end of the ruler on the floor, measure straight up on to the skirt.

2 Use pins to mark where the crease line of the hem should be. Mark the hemline all the way around to the same point on the ruler.

USING A DRESSMAKER'S DUMMY

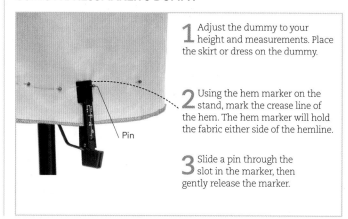

Pin

1 Adjust the dummy to your height and measurements. Place the skirt or dress on the dummy.

2 Using the hem marker on the stand, mark the crease line of the hem. The hem marker will hold the fabric either side of the hemline.

3 Slide a pin through the slot in the marker, then gently release the marker.

TURNING UP A STRAIGHT HEM

Once the crease line for the hem has been marked by the pins, you need to trim the hem allowance to a reasonable amount. Most straight hems are about 4cm (1½in) deep.

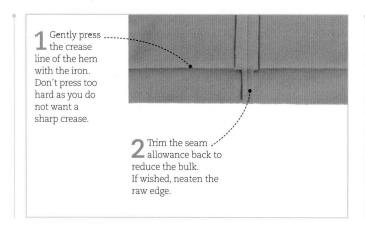

1 Gently press the crease line of the hem with the iron. Don't press too hard as you do not want a sharp crease.

2 Trim the seam allowance back to reduce the bulk. If wished, neaten the raw edge.

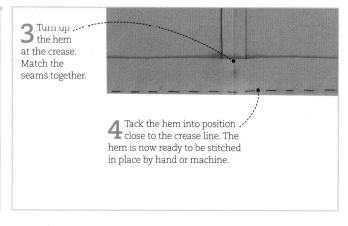

3 Turn up the hem at the crease. Match the seams together.

4 Tack the hem into position close to the crease line. The hem is now ready to be stitched in place by hand or machine.

HAND-STITCHED HEMS

One of the most popular ways to secure a hem edge is by hand. Hand stitching is discreet and, if a fine hand sewing needle is used, the stitching should not show on the right side of the work.

TIPS FOR SEWING HEMS BY HAND

1 Always use a single thread in the needle – a polyester all-purpose thread is ideal for hemming.

2 Once the raw edge of the hem allowance has been neatened by one of the methods below, secure it using a slip hem or catch stitch. For this, take half of the stitch into the neatened edge and the other half into the wrong side of the garment fabric.

3 Start and finish the hand stitching with a double stitch, not a knot, because knots will catch and pull on the hem.

4 It is a good idea to take a small backstitch every 10cm (4in) or so to make sure that if the hem does come loose in one place it will not all unravel.

CLEAN FINISH

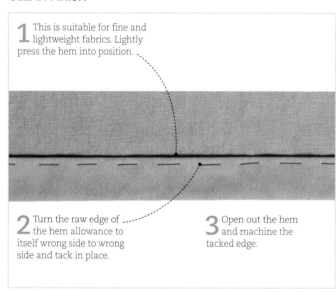

1 This is suitable for fine and lightweight fabrics. Lightly press the hem into position.

2 Turn the raw edge of the hem allowance to itself wrong side to wrong side and tack in place.

3 Open out the hem and machine the tacked edge.

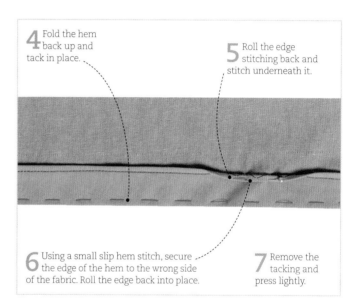

4 Fold the hem back up and tack in place.

5 Roll the edge stitching back and stitch underneath it.

6 Using a small slip hem stitch, secure the edge of the hem to the wrong side of the fabric. Roll the edge back into place.

7 Remove the tacking and press lightly.

OVERLOCKED FINISH

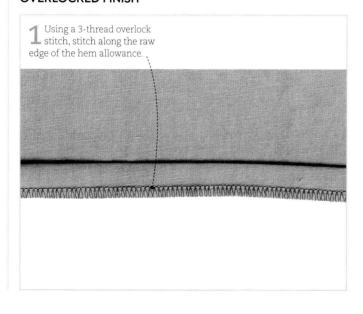

1 Using a 3-thread overlock stitch, stitch along the raw edge of the hem allowance.

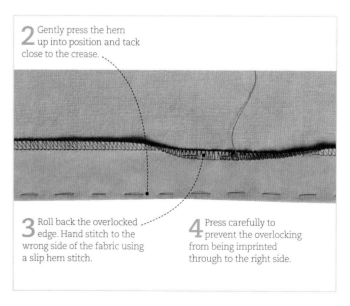

2 Gently press the hem up into position and tack close to the crease.

3 Roll back the overlocked edge. Hand stitch to the wrong side of the fabric using a slip hem stitch.

4 Press carefully to prevent the overlocking from being imprinted through to the right side.

BIAS-BOUND FINISH

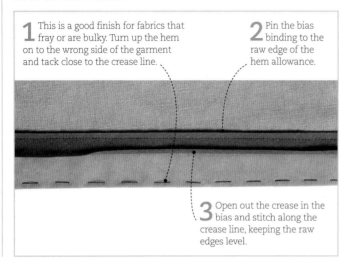

1 This is a good finish for fabrics that fray or are bulky. Turn up the hem on to the wrong side of the garment and tack close to the crease line.

2 Pin the bias binding to the raw edge of the hem allowance.

3 Open out the crease in the bias and stitch along the crease line, keeping the raw edges level.

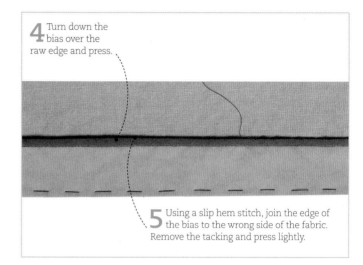

4 Turn down the bias over the raw edge and press.

5 Using a slip hem stitch, join the edge of the bias to the wrong side of the fabric. Remove the tacking and press lightly.

ZIGZAG FINISH

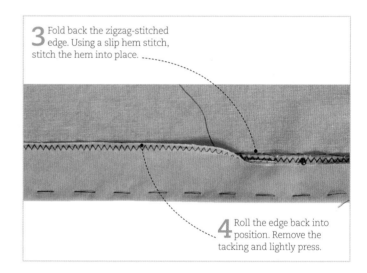

1 Use this to neaten the edge of the hem on fabrics that do not fray too badly. Set the sewing machine to a zigzag stitch, width 4.0 and length 3.0. Machine along the raw edge. Trim the fabric edge back to the zigzag stitch.

2 Turn the hem on to the wrong side of the garment and tack in place close to the crease line.

3 Fold back the zigzag-stitched edge. Using a slip hem stitch, stitch the hem into place.

4 Roll the edge back into position. Remove the tacking and lightly press.

PINKED FINISH

1 Pinking shears can give an excellent hem finish on difficult fabrics. Machine a row of straight stitching along the raw edge, 1cm (⅜in) from the edge. Pink the raw edge.

2 Turn up the hem to the wrong side of the garment and tack in place close to the crease line.

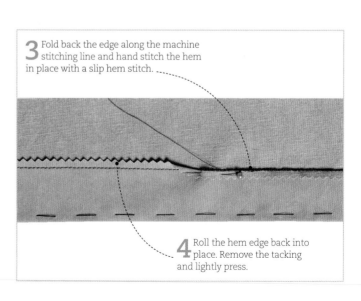

3 Fold back the edge along the machine stitching line and hand stitch the hem in place with a slip hem stitch.

4 Roll the hem edge back into place. Remove the tacking and lightly press.

MACHINED HEMS

On many occasions, the hem or edge of a garment is turned up and secured using the sewing machine. It can be stitched with a straight stitch, a zigzag stitch, or a blind hem stitch. Hems can also be made on the overlocker.

SINGLE-TURN HEM

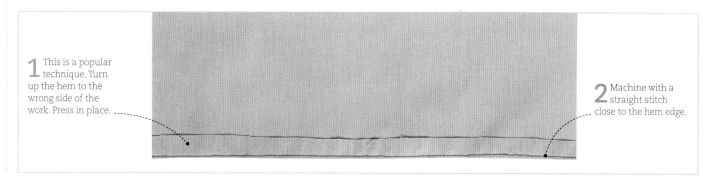

1 This is a popular technique. Turn up the hem to the wrong side of the work. Press in place.

2 Machine with a straight stitch close to the hem edge.

BLIND HEM

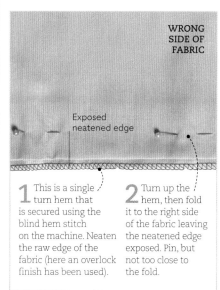

WRONG SIDE OF FABRIC

Exposed neatened edge

1 This is a single turn hem that is secured using the blind hem stitch on the machine. Neaten the raw edge of the fabric (here an overlock finish has been used).

2 Turn up the hem, then fold it to the right side of the fabric leaving the neatened edge exposed. Pin, but not too close to the fold.

WRONG SIDE OF FABRIC

Fold

3 Using the blind hem foot and the blind hem stitch, secure the hem to the fabric. The stitch line should be just below the neatened edge with only the points of the stitch going through the fold.

WRONG SIDE OF FABRIC

4 Fold the hem back into position and press lightly on the right side. The stitches will be barely visible on the right side.

DOUBLE-TURN HEM

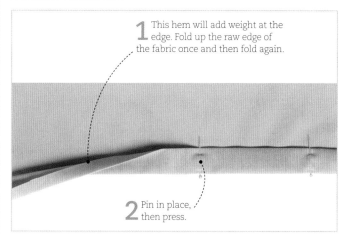

1 This hem will add weight at the edge. Fold up the raw edge of the fabric once and then fold again.

2 Pin in place, then press.

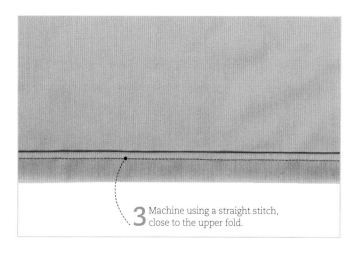

3 Machine using a straight stitch, close to the upper fold.

ADDING A HEM WITH KICK TAPE

Kick tape is often added to the back trouser hem. This is to give some extra weight and strength, and to prevent wear as the trouser hem rubs against the shoe.

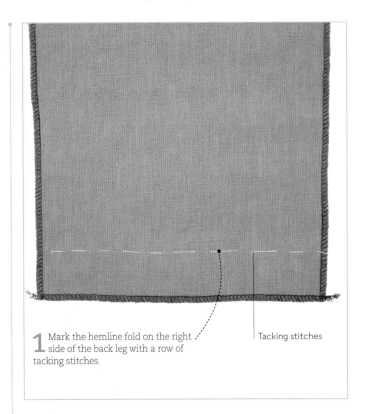

1 Mark the hemline fold on the right side of the back leg with a row of tacking stitches.

Tacking stitches

2 Working from the right side of the trousers, pin the kick tape adjacent to the tacked line, with the wider finished edge against the tacked line.

Kick tape

3 Machine the tape in place close to either edge.

4 Make up the trouser leg by joining the front to the back, press the seams open, and slip stitch the hem in place.

Side seam

FUSIBLE INTERFACED HEM

On a straight skirt or trouser hem the addition of a fusible interfacing is advantageous. It adds weight and will help the hem to hang straight.

1 Cut a strip of a lightweight fusible interfacing the width of the hem plus 1.5cm (⅝in). Cut one edge straight and the other with pinking shears to feather the edge. Fuse in place.

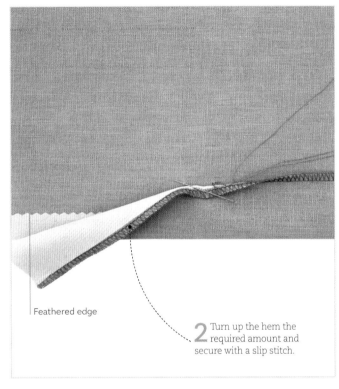

Feathered edge

2 Turn up the hem the required amount and secure with a slip stitch.

HEM AND LINING

When making a jacket, the jacket hem is turned up and then the lining is hemmed. The jacket hem needs to be reinforced first with a fusible strip. Make sure that the hem edge is parallel to the ground.

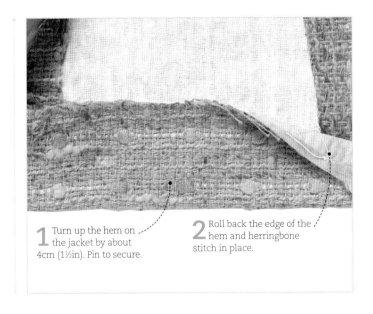

1 Turn up the hem on the jacket by about 4cm (1½in). Pin to secure.

2 Roll back the edge of the hem and herringbone stitch in place.

3 Bring the lining down over the jacket hem. Turn up the hem of the lining so that it is level to the jacket hem, then push up to 2cm (¾in) from the hem edge. At the facing edge, the lining is level with the hem edge. Pin.

4 Use a slip hem stitch to secure the lining in place.

Zips

The zip is probably the most used of all fastenings. There are a great many types available, in a variety of lengths, colours, and materials, but they all fall into one of five categories: skirt or trouser zips, metal or jeans zips, concealed zips, open-ended zips, and decorative zips. Before attaching any zip, apply 2cm (¾in)-wide strips of fusible interfacing to the zip seam allowances on the wrong side of the fabric.

HOW TO SHORTEN A ZIP

Zips do not always come in the length that you need, but it is easy to shorten them. Skirt or trouser zips and concealed zips are all shortened by stitching across the teeth or coils, whereas an open-ended zip is shortened at the top and not at the bottom.

SHORTENING A SKIRT/TROUSER OR CONCEALED ZIP

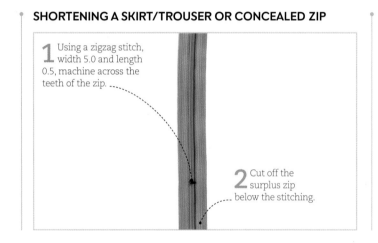

1 Using a zigzag stitch, width 5.0 and length 0.5, machine across the teeth of the zip.

2 Cut off the surplus zip below the stitching.

SHORTENING AN OPEN-ENDED ZIP

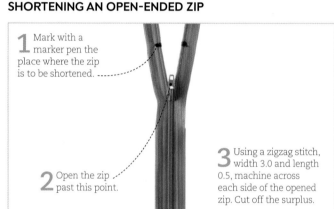

1 Mark with a marker pen the place where the zip is to be shortened.

2 Open the zip past this point.

3 Using a zigzag stitch, width 3.0 and length 0.5, machine across each side of the opened zip. Cut off the surplus.

MARKING FOR ZIP PLACEMENT

For a zip to sit accurately in the seam, the seam allowances where the zip will be inserted need to be marked. The upper seam allowance at the top of the zip also needs marking to ensure the zip pull sits just fractionally below the stitching line.

1 Stitch the seam, leaving a gap for the zip.

2 Secure the end of the stitching.

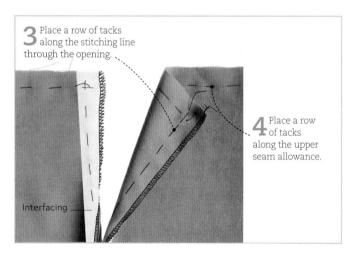

3 Place a row of tacks along the stitching line through the opening.

4 Place a row of tacks along the upper seam allowance.

Interfacing

LAPPED ZIP

A zip in a skirt or a dress is usually put in by means of a lapped technique or a centred zip technique (see p.186). For both of these techniques you will require the zip foot on the sewing machine. A lapped zip features one side of the seam – the left-hand side – covering the teeth of the zip to conceal them.

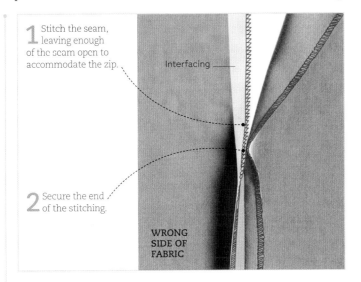

1 Stitch the seam, leaving enough of the seam open to accommodate the zip.

2 Secure the end of the stitching.

Interfacing

WRONG SIDE OF FABRIC

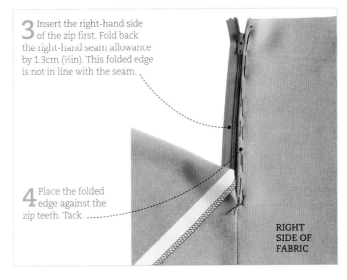

3 Insert the right-hand side of the zip first. Fold back the right-hand seam allowance by 1.3cm (½in). This folded edge is not in line with the seam.

4 Place the folded edge against the zip teeth. Tack.

RIGHT SIDE OF FABRIC

5 Using the zip foot, stitch along the tack line to secure the zip tape to the fabric. Stitch from the bottom of the zip to the top.

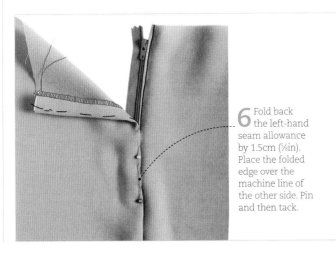

6 Fold back the left-hand seam allowance by 1.5cm (⅝in). Place the folded edge over the machine line of the other side. Pin and then tack.

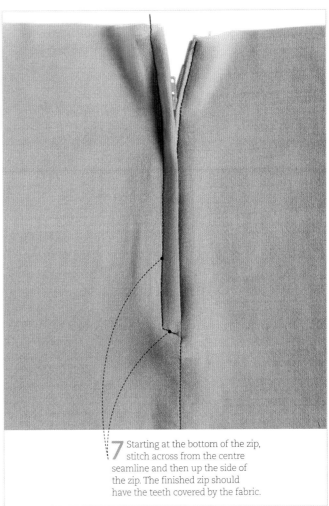

7 Starting at the bottom of the zip, stitch across from the centre seamline and then up the side of the zip. The finished zip should have the teeth covered by the fabric.

FACED FLY-FRONT ZIP

Whether it be for a classic pair of trousers or a pair of jeans, a fly front is the most common technique for inserting a trouser zip. The zip usually has a facing behind it to prevent the zip teeth from catching.

1 Interface the centre front with straight grain fusible tape. Overlock the edges. Sew the centre front seam, leaving a gap to insert the zip.

Fusible tape

Overlocking

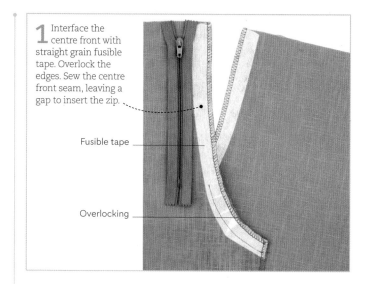

2 Interface the fly extension and overlock all edges.

Overlocked edges

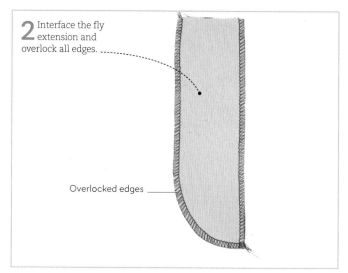

3 Sew the extension to the right-hand side as worn for womenswear, or the left-hand side as worn for menswear, right side to right side. Ensure your stitching lines up with the centre front seam. Press the seam towards the fly extension and understitch.

4 Tack the stitching line on the other front piece.

Tacking stitches

Centre front seam

5 Place the zip, right side to right side, onto the left front for womenswear, right front for menswear. Align the edge of the zip tape to the overlocked edge. Tack in place. Make sure you have left 17mm (11/16in) clearance at the waist edge.

6 Make up the zip guard – place two pieces of fabric, wrong side to wrong side, and overlock the edges.

7 Place the zip guard over the zip. Match at the overlocked edge and using the zip foot on your machine, sew through all layers. Press.

8 Fold the zip guard out of the way and bring the other front over the zip onto the tacked stitching line.

Tacking stitches

9 Working from the wrong side, pin the other edge of the zip to the extension only. Sew the zip tape to the extension.

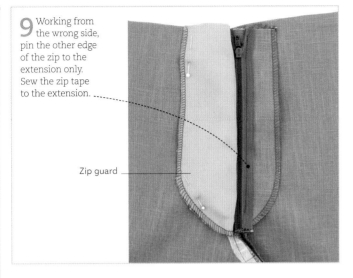

Zip guard

10 Turn to the right side and top-stitch. Start at the centre front and sew towards the waist; just sew through the two layers of fabric, not the zip tape. Press.

11 Unpin the zip guard and secure to the zip extension with a few stitches.

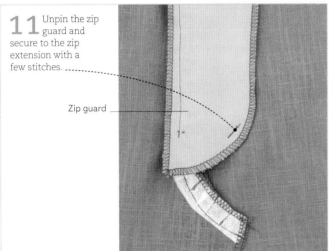

Zip guard

12 Attach the waistband at the waist edge.

13 Trim the trouser side of the seam down to half its width. Press the seams up towards the waistband.

14 Finish the other edge of the waistband using the overlocker. Fold the waistband right side to right side and sew the short ends.

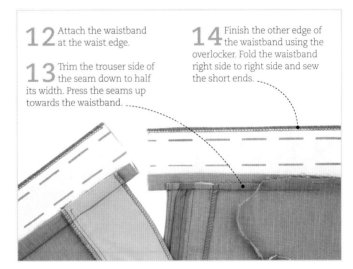

15 Fold the waistband in half, right side to right side. Ensure the seam allowance on the attached edge is pressed towards the waistband and the overlocked edge extends 1.5cm (⅝in) below the stitching line

Overlocked edge

16 Press the waistband and stitch in the ditch to finish.

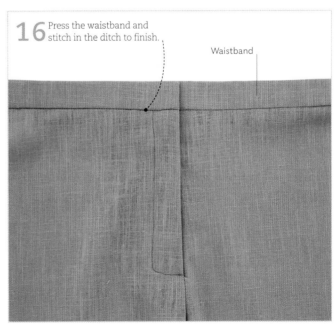

Waistband

CENTRED ZIP

With a centred zip, the two folded edges of the seam allowances meet over the centre of the teeth, to conceal the zip completely.

1 Stitch the seam, leaving a gap for the zip.

2 Tack the rest of the seam allowance.

3 Press the seam open lightly.

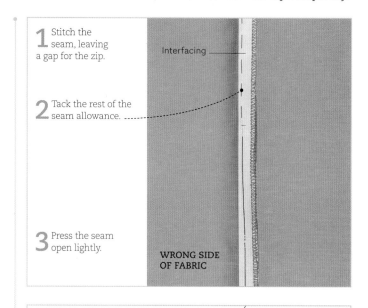

Interfacing

WRONG SIDE OF FABRIC

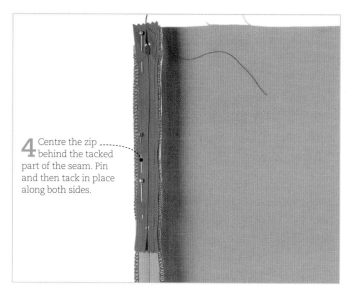

4 Centre the zip behind the tacked part of the seam. Pin and then tack in place along both sides.

5 On the wrong side, lift the seam allowance and the zip tape away from the main fabric. Pin.

6 Machine the zip tape to the seam allowance. Make sure both sides of the zip tape are secured to the seam allowances. Stitch through to the end of the zip tape.

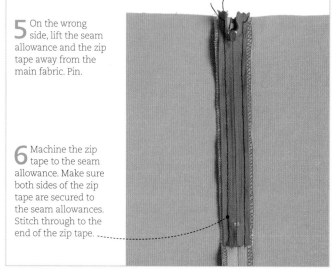

7 Working from the right side of the work, stitch down one side, across the bottom, and up the other side of the zip.

8 Remove the tacks.

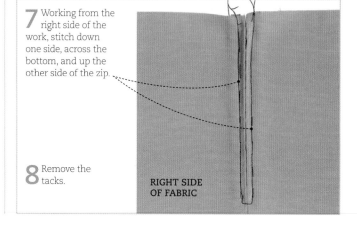

RIGHT SIDE OF FABRIC

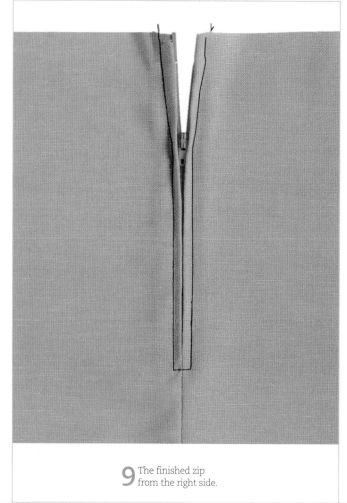

9 The finished zip from the right side.

CONCEALED OR INVISIBLE ZIP

This type of zip looks different from other zips because the teeth are on the reverse and nothing except the pull is seen on the front. The zip is inserted before the seam is stitched. A special concealed zip foot is required.

1 Mark the seam allowance with tacking stitches.

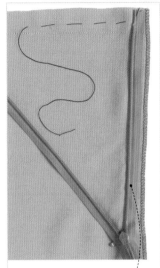

2 On the left-hand back place the centre of the zip over the tack line, right side of zip to right side of fabric. Pin in place.

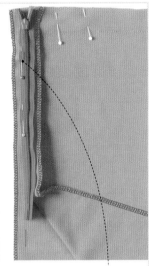

3 Undo the zip. Using the concealed zip foot, stitch from the top of the zip down as far as possible. Stitch under the teeth. Stop when the foot hits the zip pull.

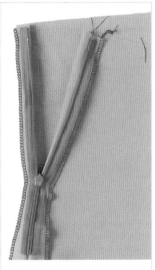

4 Do the zip up. Place the other piece of fabric to the zip. Match along the upper edge. Pin the other side of the zip tape in place.

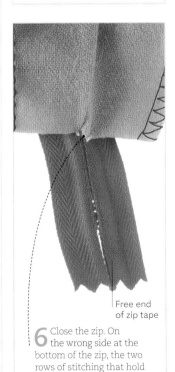

Free end of zip tape

6 Close the zip. On the wrong side at the bottom of the zip, the two rows of stitching that hold in the zip should finish at the same place.

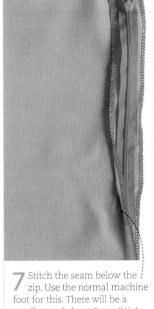

7 Stitch the seam below the zip. Use the normal machine foot for this. There will be a small gap of about 3mm (⅛in) between the stitching line for the zip and that for the seam.

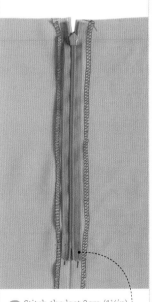

8 Stitch the last 3cm (1¼in) of the zip tape to just the seam allowances. This will stop the zip pulling loose.

5 Open the zip again. Using the concealed zip foot, stitch down the other side of the zip to attach to the right-hand side. Remove any tacking stitches.

9 On the right side, the zip is completely concealed, with just the pull visible at the top. Apply waistband or facing.

ZIP PLACKET

The zip placket, or zip guard, can be placed behind any of the zips that are covered in this chapter. This type of placket sits behind the zip on the inside of the garment, and prevents the zip from catching on you or on your clothes.

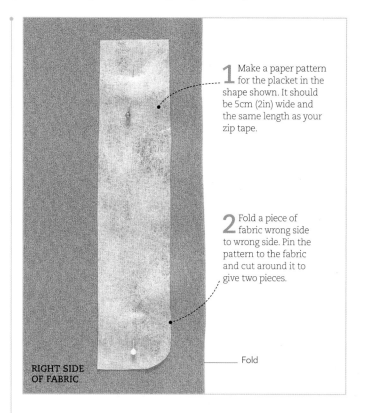

1 Make a paper pattern for the placket in the shape shown. It should be 5cm (2in) wide and the same length as your zip tape.

2 Fold a piece of fabric wrong side to wrong side. Pin the pattern to the fabric and cut around it to give two pieces.

Fold

RIGHT SIDE OF FABRIC

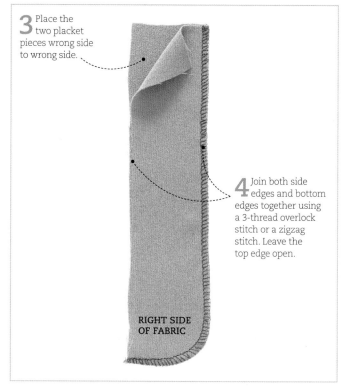

3 Place the two placket pieces wrong side to wrong side.

4 Join both side edges and bottom edges together using a 3-thread overlock stitch or a zigzag stitch. Leave the top edge open.

RIGHT SIDE OF FABRIC

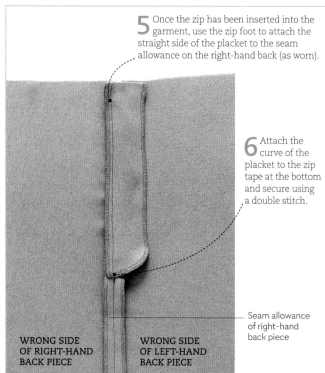

5 Once the zip has been inserted into the garment, use the zip foot to attach the straight side of the placket to the seam allowance on the right-hand back (as worn).

6 Attach the curve of the placket to the zip tape at the bottom and secure using a double stitch.

Seam allowance of right-hand back piece

WRONG SIDE OF RIGHT-HAND BACK PIECE

WRONG SIDE OF LEFT-HAND BACK PIECE

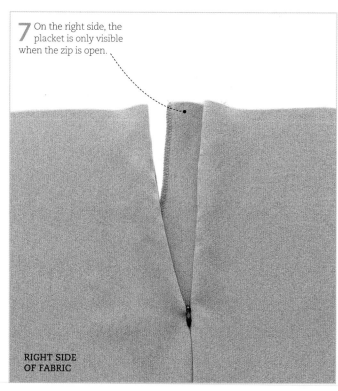

7 On the right side, the placket is only visible when the zip is open.

RIGHT SIDE OF FABRIC

Buttons

Buttons are sewn to the fabric either through holes on their face, or through a hole in a stalk called a shank, which is on the back. They are normally sewn on to garments by hand, although a 2-hole button can also be sewn on by machine.

SEWING ON A 2-HOLE BUTTON

This is the most popular type of button and requires a thread shank to be made when sewing in place. A cocktail stick will help hold your stitches in position.

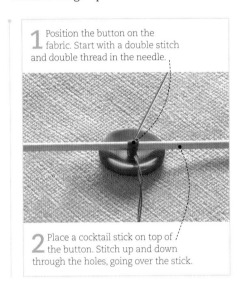

1 Position the button on the fabric. Start with a double stitch and double thread in the needle.

2 Place a cocktail stick on top of the button. Stitch up and down through the holes, going over the stick.

3 Remove the cocktail stick.

4 Wrap the thread around the thread loops under the button to make a shank.

5 Take the thread through to the back of the fabric.

6 Buttonhole stitch over the loop of threads on the back of the work.

SEWING ON A 4-HOLE BUTTON

This is stitched in the same way as for a 2-hole button except that the threads make an "X" over the button on the front.

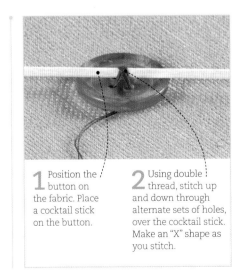

1 Position the button on the fabric. Place a cocktail stick on the button.

2 Using double thread, stitch up and down through alternate sets of holes, over the cocktail stick. Make an "X" shape as you stitch.

3 Remove the cocktail stick.

4 Wrap the thread around the thread loops under the button to make the shank.

5 On the reverse of the fabric, buttonhole stitch over the thread loops in an "X" shape.

SEWING ON A SHANKED BUTTON

When sewing this type of button in place, use a cocktail stick under the button
to enable you to make a thread shank on the underside of the fabric.

 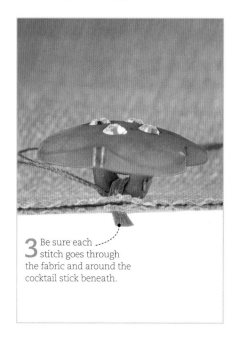 

1 Position the button on the fabric. Hold a cocktail stick on the other side of the fabric, behind the button.

2 Using double thread, stitch the button to the fabric, through the shank.

3 Be sure each stitch goes through the fabric and around the cocktail stick beneath.

4 Remove the cocktail stick. Work buttonhole stitch over the looped thread shank.

SEWING ON A REINFORCED BUTTON

A large, heavy button often features a second button sewn to it on the wrong
side and stitched on with the same threads that secure the larger button.
The smaller button helps support the weight of the larger button.

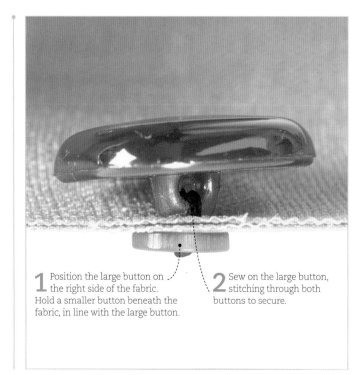 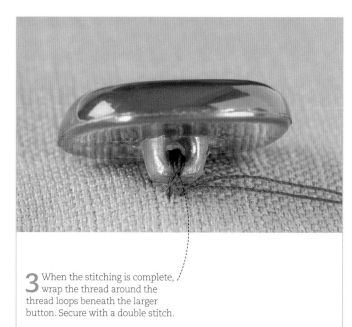

1 Position the large button on the right side of the fabric. Hold a smaller button beneath the fabric, in line with the large button.

2 Sew on the large button, stitching through both buttons to secure.

3 When the stitching is complete, wrap the thread around the thread loops beneath the larger button. Secure with a double stitch.

COVERED BUTTONS

Covered buttons are often found on expensive clothes and will add a professional finish to any jacket or other garment that you make. A purchased button-making gadget will enable you to create covered buttons very easily.

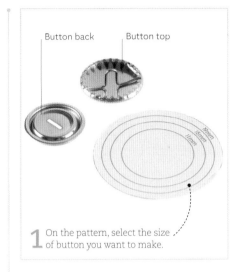

Button back   Button top

1 On the pattern, select the size of button you want to make.

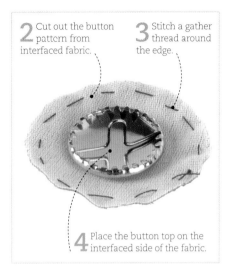

2 Cut out the button pattern from interfaced fabric.

3 Stitch a gather thread around the edge.

4 Place the button top on the interfaced side of the fabric.

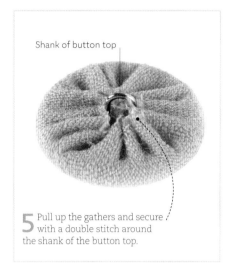

Shank of button top

5 Pull up the gathers and secure with a double stitch around the shank of the button top.

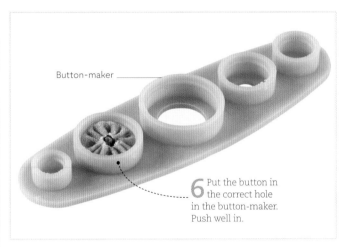

Button-maker

6 Put the button in the correct hole in the button-maker. Push well in.

7 Place the button back on top of the button.

8 Take the other side of the button-maker and press down on the button back until it clicks into position.

9 Remove the button from the button-maker and check to be sure the back is firmly in place.

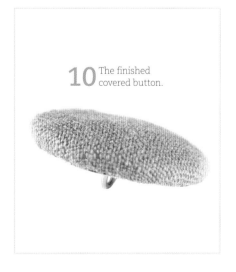

10 The finished covered button.

Buttonholes

A buttonhole is essential if a button is to be truly functional, although for many oversized buttons a snap fastener on the reverse is a better option, because the buttonhole would be just too big and could cause the garment to stretch.

STAGES OF A BUTTONHOLE

A sewing machine stitches a buttonhole in four stages. The stitch can be slightly varied in width and length to suit the fabric or item, but the stitches need to be tight and close together.

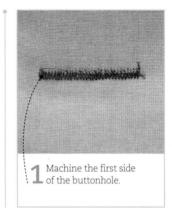

1 Machine the first side of the buttonhole.

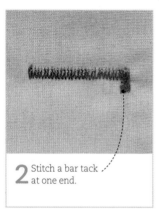

2 Stitch a bar tack at one end.

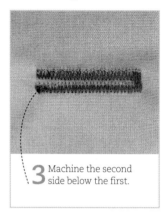

3 Machine the second side below the first.

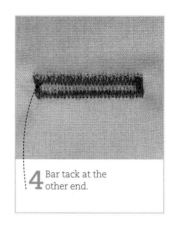

4 Bar tack at the other end.

POSITIONING BUTTONHOLES

The size and position of the buttonhole is determined by the button size and needs to be worked out prior to any type of buttonhole being made.

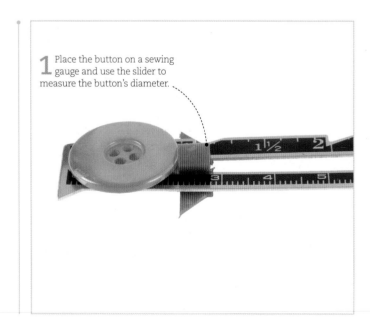

1 Place the button on a sewing gauge and use the slider to measure the button's diameter.

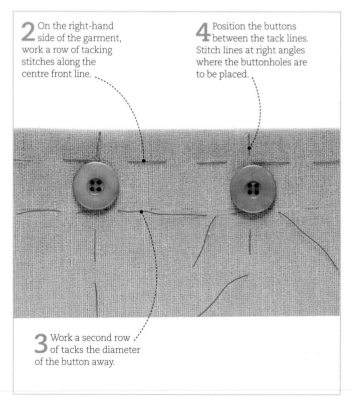

2 On the right-hand side of the garment, work a row of tacking stitches along the centre front line.

4 Position the buttons between the tack lines. Stitch lines at right angles where the buttonholes are to be placed.

3 Work a second row of tacks the diameter of the button away.

VERTICAL OR HORIZONTAL?

As a general rule, buttonholes are only vertical on a garment when there is a placket or a strip into which the buttonhole fits. All other buttonholes should be horizontal. Any strain on the buttonhole will then pull to the end stop and prevent the button from coming undone.

HORIZONTAL BUTTONHOLES

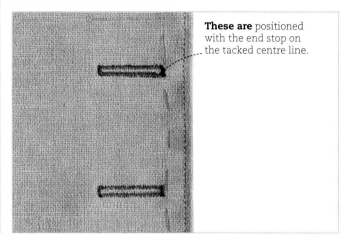

These are positioned with the end stop on the tacked centre line.

VERTICAL BUTTONHOLES

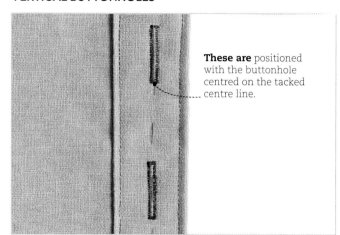

These are positioned with the buttonhole centred on the tacked centre line.

HAND-STITCHED BUTTONHOLE

A hand-worked buttonhole is a real couture choice to finish that tailored jacket or coat.

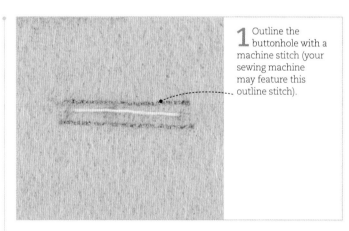

1 Outline the buttonhole with a machine stitch (your sewing machine may feature this outline stitch).

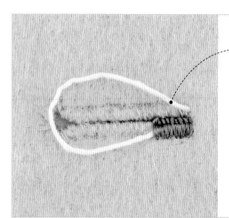

2 Cut through the machine outline and whip stitch around the buttonhole. If you want a keyhole effect, create a hole with an awl. Lay a length of buttonhole gimp thread along the outline.

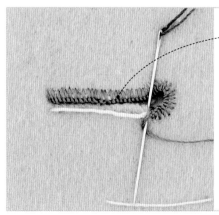

3 Using a silk buttonhole twist thread work buttonhole stitch around the outline, ensuring the stitches are worked over the gimp thread.

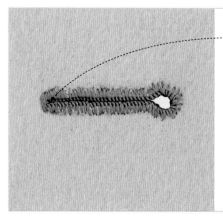

4 Secure all the thread ends between the two layers to complete the buttonhole.

MACHINE-MADE BUTTONHOLES

Modern sewing machines can stitch various types of buttonhole, suitable for all kinds of garments. On many machines the button fits into a special foot, and a sensor on the machine determines the correct size of buttonhole. The width and length of the stitch can be altered to suit the fabric. Once the buttonhole has been stitched, always slash through with a buttonhole chisel, to ensure that the cut is clean.

BASIC BUTTONHOLE

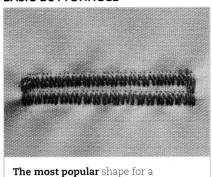

The most popular shape for a buttonhole is square on both ends.

ROUND-END BUTTONHOLE

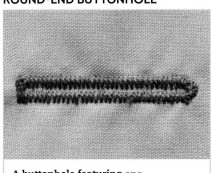

A buttonhole featuring one rounded end and one square end is used on lightweight jackets.

KEYHOLE BUTTONHOLE

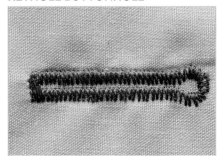

This is also called a tailor's buttonhole. It has a square end and a keyhole end, and is used on jackets and coats.

MACHINE-CORDED BUTTONHOLE

This buttonhole has a cord of heavier sewing thread running through it. You may have to refer to your sewing machine manual for the positioning of the cord.

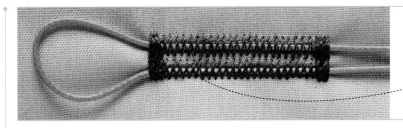

1 Place the cord into the buttonhole foot as directed by your machine manual.

2 Work the buttonhole on the machine – the machine will stitch the buttonhole over the cord.

3 Gently pull on the ends of the cord to eliminate the loop.

4 Thread the ends of the cord into a large needle.

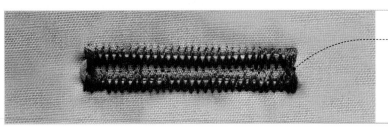

5 Take the cord to the back of the fabric. Secure with a hand stitch.

PIPED BUTTONHOLE

A buttonhole can also be made using piping cord. This is a type of buttonhole that is worked early in the construction of the garment. Very narrow piping cord needs to be used, otherwise the buttonhole will be too bulky.

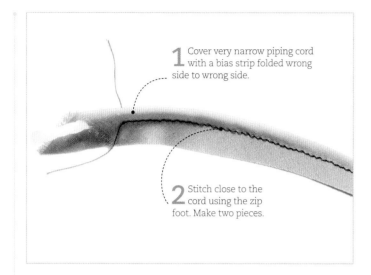

1 Cover very narrow piping cord with a bias strip folded wrong side to wrong side.

2 Stitch close to the cord using the zip foot. Make two pieces.

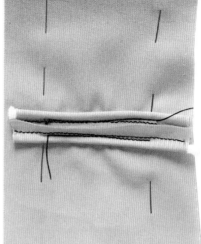

3 Align the machine stitches on the cord pieces with the buttonhole markings on the right side of the fabric, with the raw edges towards each other. Make sure the distance between the two rows of stitches is twice the diameter of the piping. If not, adjust until it is.

4 Use the zip foot to machine close to the cord. Stop stitching at the markings on the garment.

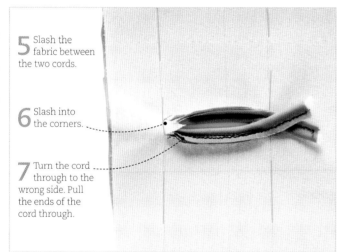

5 Slash the fabric between the two cords.

6 Slash into the corners.

7 Turn the cord through to the wrong side. Pull the ends of the cord through.

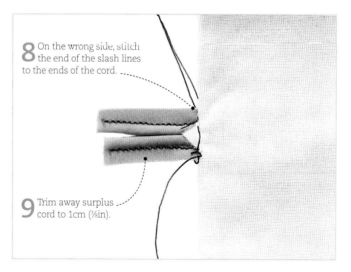

8 On the wrong side, stitch the end of the slash lines to the ends of the cord.

9 Trim away surplus cord to 1cm (⅜in).

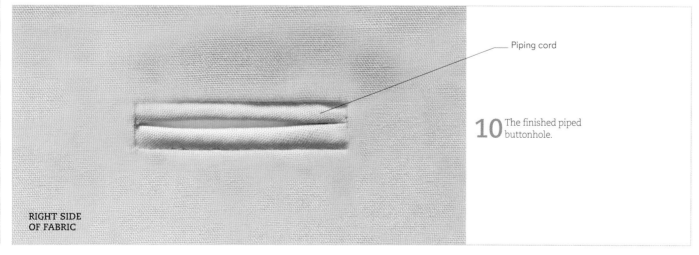

Piping cord

10 The finished piped buttonhole.

RIGHT SIDE
OF FABRIC

PATCH METHOD BOUND BUTTONHOLE

Another method of creating a buttonhole is to use a patch of fabric stitched on to the main fabric.
The technique is ideal for jackets and coats. A contrast fabric can be used for an attractive detail.
This is known as a bound buttonhole.

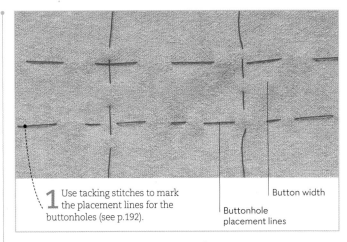

1 Use tacking stitches to mark the placement lines for the buttonholes (see p.192).

Button width

Buttonhole placement lines

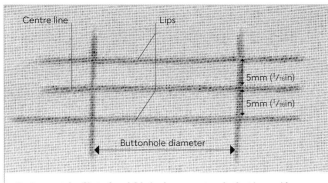

Centre line

Lips

5mm (³/₁₆in)

5mm (³/₁₆in)

Buttonhole diameter

2 On a patch of interfaced fabric, draw a rectangle that is as wide as the diameter of the button. The depth of the rectangle represents the two sides of the buttonhole. These two edges are known as lips.

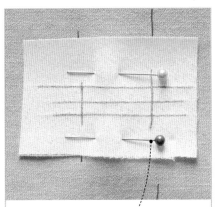

3 Place the patch with the buttonhole markings on to the fabric. Align the buttonhole shape with the markings. Pin in place.

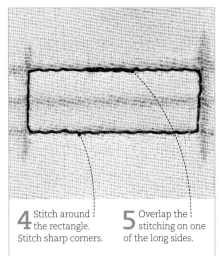

4 Stitch around the rectangle. Stitch sharp corners.

5 Overlap the stitching on one of the long sides.

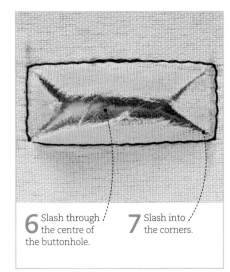

6 Slash through the centre of the buttonhole.

7 Slash into the corners.

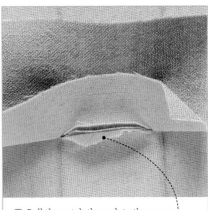

8 Pull the patch through to the wrong side. The patch should make a rectangular hole in the fabric.

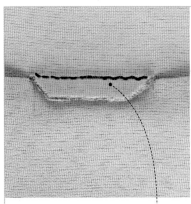

9 Press down the lip on one side of the buttonhole, then press the patch back over the lip.

10 Repeat on the other side of the buttonhole. The patch will fold over the lips to meet in the centre.

11 Turn to the right side and press.

12 On the wrong side, stitch the end of the slash lines over the folded patch.

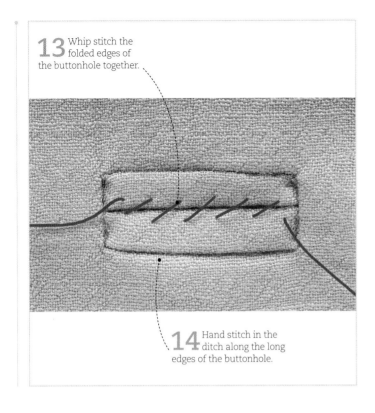

13 Whip stitch the folded edges of the buttonhole together.

14 Hand stitch in the ditch along the long edges of the buttonhole.

15 Press the finished buttonhole. Remove the whip stitches.

MACHINE BUTTONHOLE ON A CHUNKY FABRIC

Working a machine buttonhole on a textured or chunky fabric can be a challenge, as the buttonhole foot can get stuck in the weave. Try this method using some tear-away stabilizer to help the process.

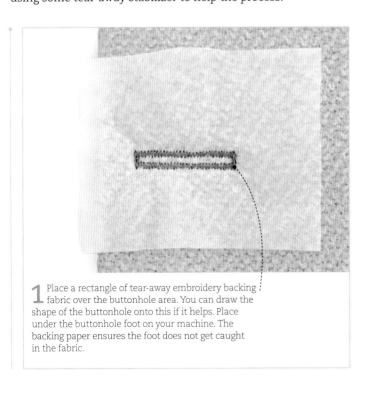

1 Place a rectangle of tear-away embroidery backing fabric over the buttonhole area. You can draw the shape of the buttonhole onto this if it helps. Place under the buttonhole foot on your machine. The backing paper ensures the foot does not get caught in the fabric.

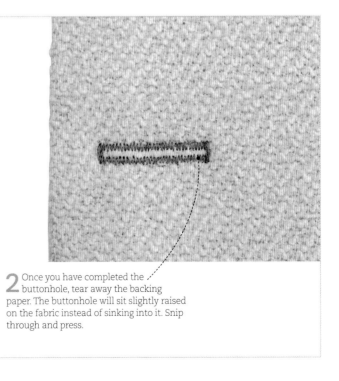

2 Once you have completed the buttonhole, tear away the backing paper. The buttonhole will sit slightly raised on the fabric instead of sinking into it. Snip through and press.

Other fastenings

Beyond zips, there are many ways to fasten garments, some of which can be used instead of or in conjunction with other fasteners. These include hooks and eyes, snaps, tape fasteners, and laced eyelets.

HOOKS AND EYES

There are a multitude of different types of hook and eye fasteners. Purchased hooks and eyes are made from metal and are normally silver or black in colour. Different-shaped hooks and eyes are used on different garments – large, broad hooks and eyes can be decorative and stitched to show on the outside, while the tiny fasteners are meant to be discreet. A hook that goes into a hand-worked eye produces a neat, close fastening.

ATTACHING HOOKS AND EYES

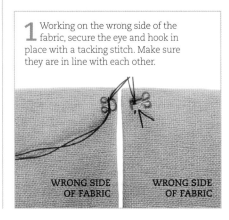

1 Working on the wrong side of the fabric, secure the eye and hook in place with a tacking stitch. Make sure they are in line with each other.

WRONG SIDE OF FABRIC   WRONG SIDE OF FABRIC

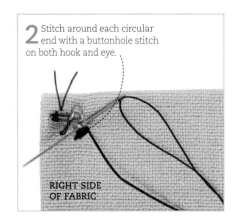

2 Stitch around each circular end with a buttonhole stitch on both hook and eye.

RIGHT SIDE OF FABRIC

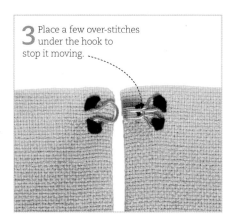

3 Place a few over-stitches under the hook to stop it moving.

HAND-WORKED EYE

1 Using a double thread, work several small loops into the edge of the fabric.

RIGHT SIDE OF FABRIC

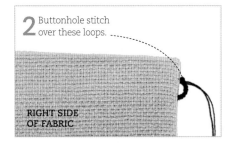

2 Buttonhole stitch over these loops.

RIGHT SIDE OF FABRIC

3 The completed loop will have a neat row of tight buttonhole stitches.

RIGHT SIDE OF FABRIC

TROUSER HOOK AND BAR

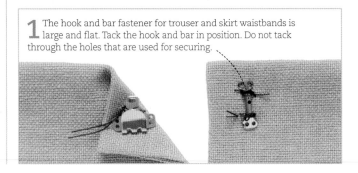

1 The hook and bar fastener for trouser and skirt waistbands is large and flat. Tack the hook and bar in position. Do not tack through the holes that are used for securing.

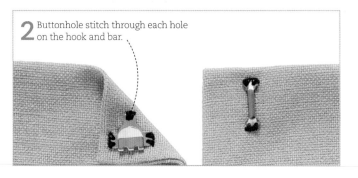

2 Buttonhole stitch through each hole on the hook and bar.

SNAPS

A snap is a ball and socket fastener that is used to hold two overlapping edges closed. The ball side goes on top and the socket side underneath. Snaps can be round or square and can be made from metal or plastic.

METAL SNAPS

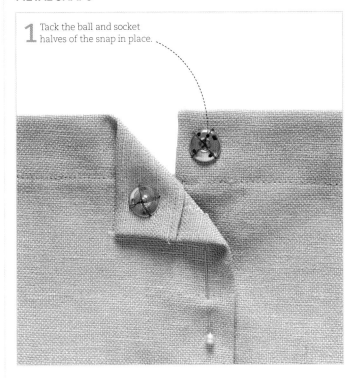

1 Tack the ball and socket halves of the snap in place.

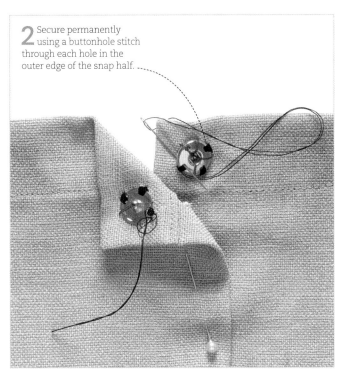

2 Secure permanently using a buttonhole stitch through each hole in the outer edge of the snap half.

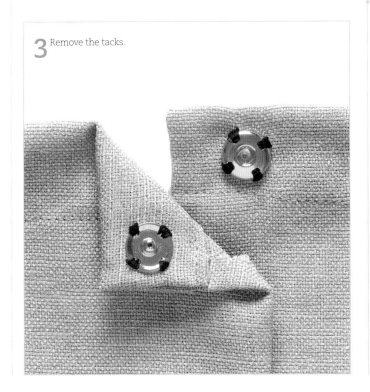

3 Remove the tacks.

PLASTIC SNAPS

A plastic snap may be white or clear plastic and is usually square in shape. Stitch in place as for a metal snap (see above).

Mending

Repairing a tear in fabric, patching a worn area, or fixing a zip or a buttonhole can add extra life to a garment. Repairs like these may seem tedious, but they are very easy to do and worthwhile. For some of the mending techniques shown here, a contrast colour thread has been used so that the stitching can be seen clearly. However, when making a repair, be sure to use a matching thread.

UNPICKING STITCHES

All repairs involve unpicking stitches. This must be done carefully to avoid damaging the fabric because the fabric will have to be re-stitched. There are three ways you can unpick stitches.

SMALL SCISSORS

Pull the fabric apart and, using very small, sharply pointed scissors, snip through the stitches that have been exposed.

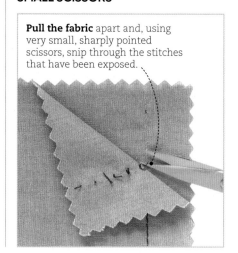

SEAM RIPPER

Slide a seam ripper carefully under a stitch and cut it. Cut through every fourth or fifth stitch, and the seam will unravel easily.

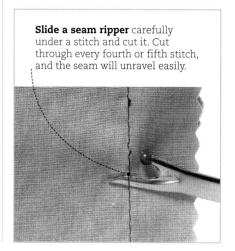

PIN AND SCISSORS

On difficult fabrics or on very small, tight stitches, slide a pin under the stitch first to lift it away from the fabric, then snip through with a pair of sharply pointed scissors.

MENDING A SPLIT IN A SEAM

A split seam can be very quickly remedied with the help of some fusible mending tape and new stitching.

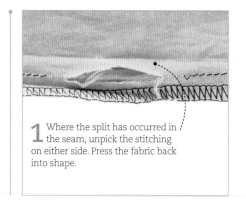

1 Where the split has occurred in the seam, unpick the stitching on either side. Press the fabric back into shape.

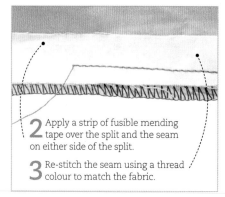

2 Apply a strip of fusible mending tape over the split and the seam on either side of the split.

3 Re-stitch the seam using a thread colour to match the fabric.

4 On the other side, the repair will not be visible.

REPAIRING FABRIC UNDER A BUTTON

A button under strain can sometimes be pulled off a garment. This will leave a hole in
the fabric, which needs fixing before a new button can be stitched on.

1 On the right side of the fabric,
the hole where the button has
been pulled off is clearly visible.

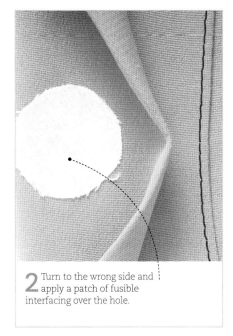

2 Turn to the wrong side and
apply a patch of fusible
interfacing over the hole.

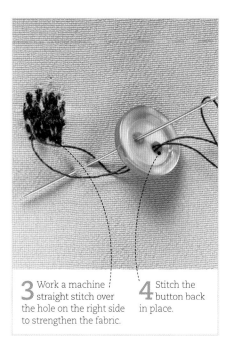

3 Work a machine
straight stitch over
the hole on the right side
to strengthen the fabric.

4 Stitch the
button back
in place.

REPAIRING A DAMAGED BUTTONHOLE

A buttonhole can sometimes rip at the end, or the stitching on the buttonhole can come unravelled.
When repairing, use a thread that matches the fabric so the repair will be invisible.

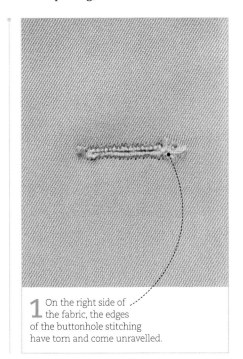

1 On the right side of
the fabric, the edges
of the buttonhole stitching
have torn and come unravelled.

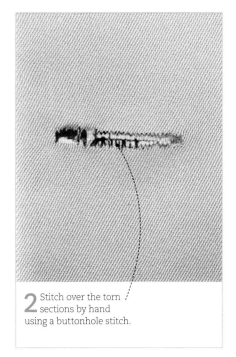

2 Stitch over the torn
sections by hand
using a buttonhole stitch.

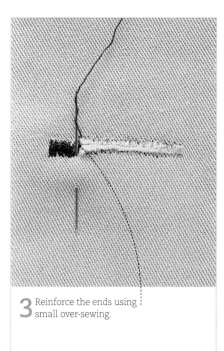

3 Reinforce the ends using
small over-sewing.

VISIBLE FUSED PATCH

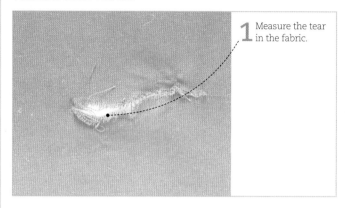

1 Measure the tear in the fabric.

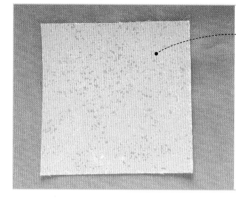

2 Cut a piece of fusible mending fabric that is slightly longer and wider than the tear.

3 Fuse the fabric in place on the right side.

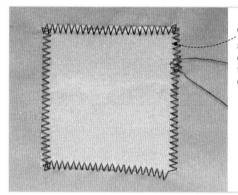

4 Using a zigzag stitch, machine all around the edge of the patch on the right side of the work.

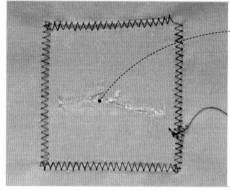

5 On the reverse side of the fabric, the tear will be firmly stuck to the mending patch, which will prevent the tear getting any bigger.

FUSED PATCH ON THE WRONG SIDE

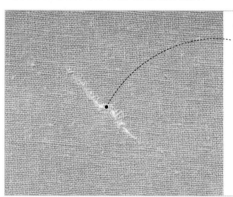

1 Measure the length of the tear. Cut a piece of fusible mending tape to fit.

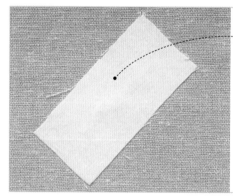

2 On the wrong side of the fabric, fuse the mending tape over the tear.

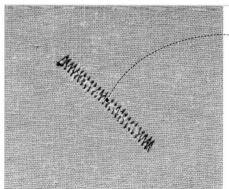

3 Using a zigzag stitch, width 5.0 and length 0.5, stitch over the tear, working from the right side.

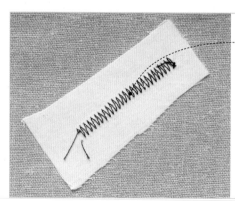

4 On the wrong side, the zigzag stitching will have gone through the fusible tape.

MENDING A TEAR WITH A MATCHING PATCH

On a patterned fabric, such as a check or a stripe, it is possible to mend a tear almost invisibly by using a patch that matches the pattern.

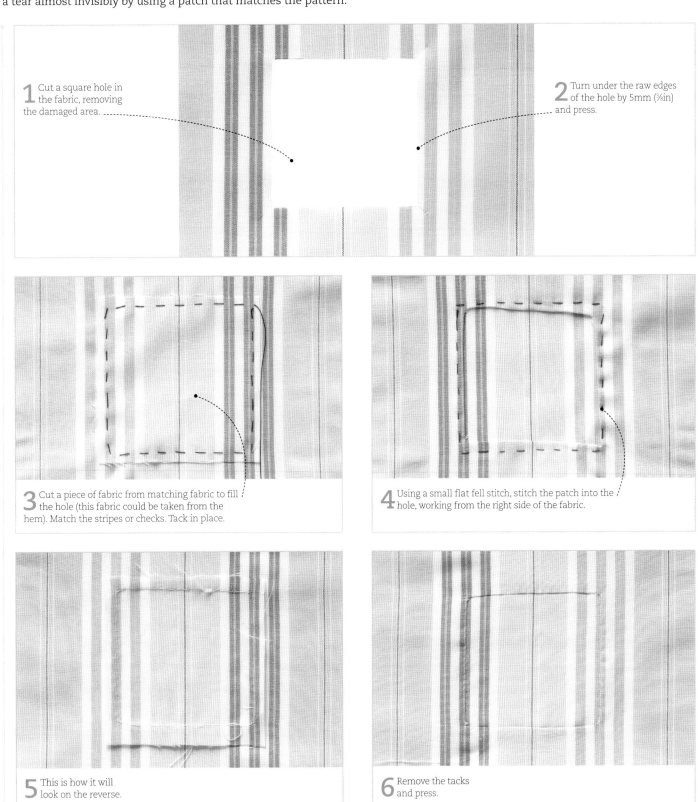

1 Cut a square hole in the fabric, removing the damaged area.

2 Turn under the raw edges of the hole by 5mm (⅜in) and press.

3 Cut a piece of fabric from matching fabric to fill the hole (this fabric could be taken from the hem). Match the stripes or checks. Tack in place.

4 Using a small flat fell stitch, stitch the patch into the hole, working from the right side of the fabric.

5 This is how it will look on the reverse.

6 Remove the tacks and press.

Tailoring methods

There are various methods you can use to create a tailored garment. If this is your first project then try speed tailoring, which is simpler and quicker than other approaches as it uses fusible interfacings. If, however, you wish to stretch your skill base, consider the more complex couture canvas method, which gives a beautifully professional finish. For coats, a hybrid approach, combining fusible techniques and machine pad stitching, works well.

Speed tailoring

Speed tailoring is the term given to modern tailoring techniques that use fusible interfacings to give shape and structure to a jacket or coat (see the princess-line jacket on pp.252–259). Choose woven fusible interfacings and cut on the same grain as the jacket fabric pieces. If possible, use two different interfacings – one a medium weight and one a light weight – in conjunction with fusible tapes to stabilize the edges of the jacket. If interfacings of different weights are not available, choose a lightweight product and use two layers if required.

COMPONENTS OF A JACKET

Here we show where to place the fusible interfacing on a jacket or coat. Your pattern may be cut differently to this – the front and back may be one piece, not two as shown here, and you may have a one-piece sleeve – but the same principle will apply, of a heavier interfacing at the front and a lighter one at the back, with reinforcement through the shoulder.

JACKET FRONT

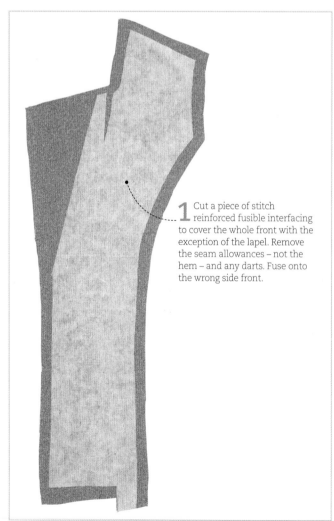

1 Cut a piece of stitch reinforced fusible interfacing to cover the whole front with the exception of the lapel. Remove the seam allowances – not the hem – and any darts. Fuse onto the wrong side front.

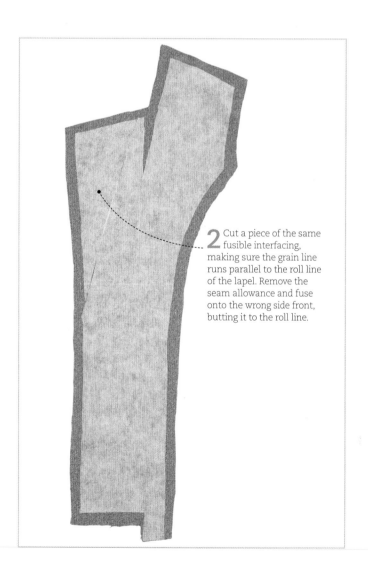

2 Cut a piece of the same fusible interfacing, making sure the grain line runs parallel to the roll line of the lapel. Remove the seam allowance and fuse onto the wrong side front, butting it to the roll line.

FLOATING SHOULDER

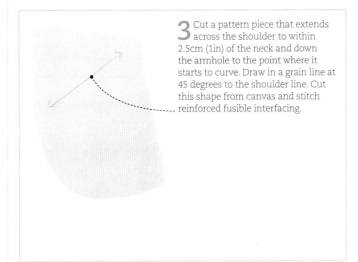

3 Cut a pattern piece that extends across the shoulder to within 2.5cm (1in) of the neck and down the armhole to the point where it starts to curve. Draw in a grain line at 45 degrees to the shoulder line. Cut this shape from canvas and stitch reinforced fusible interfacing.

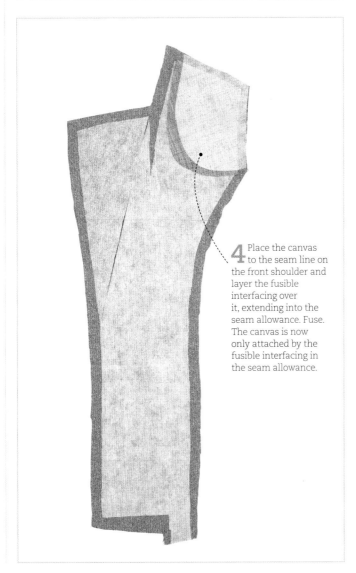

4 Place the canvas to the seam line on the front shoulder and layer the fusible interfacing over it, extending into the seam allowance. Fuse. The canvas is now only attached by the fusible interfacing in the seam allowance.

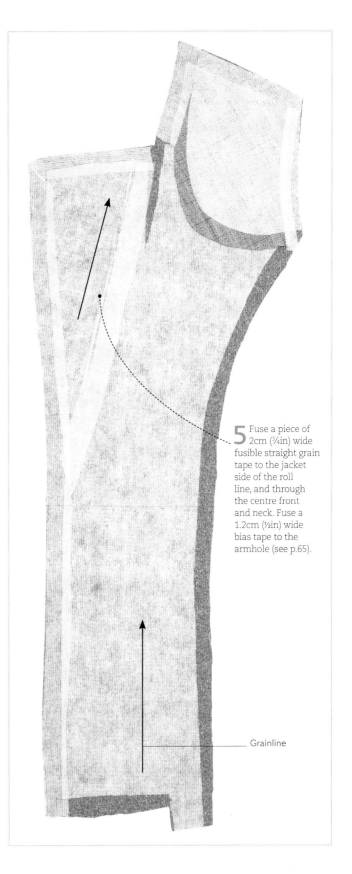

5 Fuse a piece of 2cm (¾in) wide fusible straight grain tape to the jacket side of the roll line, and through the centre front and neck. Fuse a 1.2cm (½in) wide bias tape to the armhole (see p.65).

Grainline

SIDE FRONT

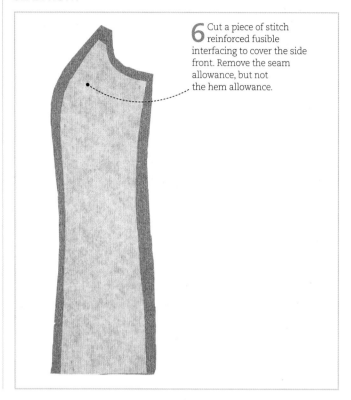

6 Cut a piece of stitch reinforced fusible interfacing to cover the side front. Remove the seam allowance, but not the hem allowance.

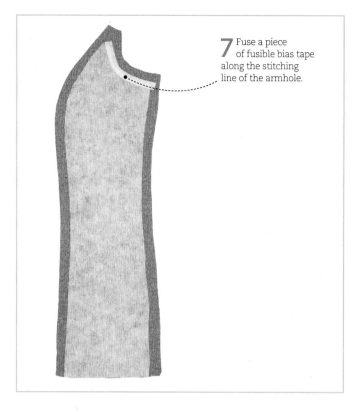

7 Fuse a piece of fusible bias tape along the stitching line of the armhole.

THE BACK AND SIDE BACK

8 Fuse a lightweight woven interfacing over both pieces, covering them completely.

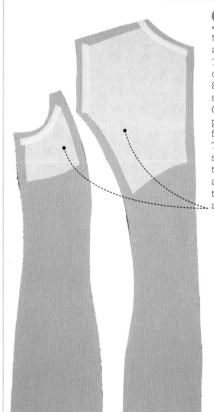

9 Use a reinforced fusible interfacing to cover the shoulder and armhole, about 15cm (6in) down the centre back, and about 8cm (3in) down the side seam. Join with a curve. Cut the curve with pinking shears to feather the edge. Fuse. Then fuse pieces of straight grain tape to the back shoulder and a fusible bias tape to the back neck and armhole.

THE FRONT FACING

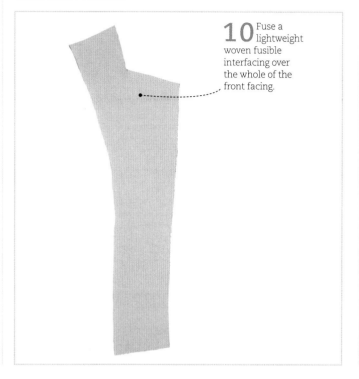

10 Fuse a lightweight woven fusible interfacing over the whole of the front facing.

THE UPPER COLLAR AND BACK FACING

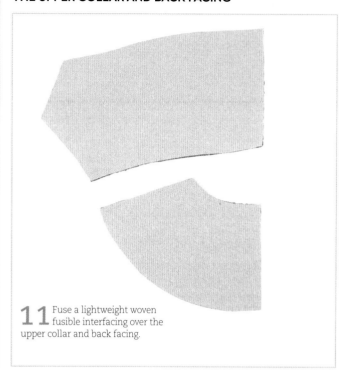

11 Fuse a lightweight woven fusible interfacing over the upper collar and back facing.

THE UNDER COLLAR

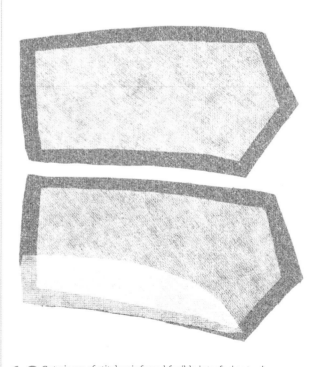

12 Cut pieces of stitch reinforced fusible interfacing to size. Remove the seam allowances. Cut a strip of fusible interfacing on the straight grain to fit from the neck edge to the roll line on the pattern. Leave seam allowances in place as above.

THE SLEEVE

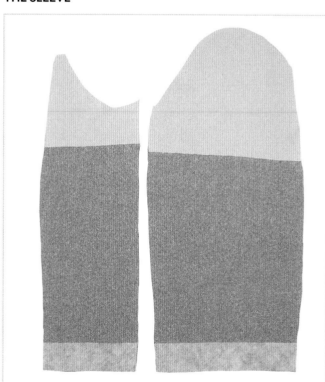

13 Using a lightweight woven fusible interfacing, interface the upper part of the sleeve to approximately 4cm (1½in) below the armhole to form a sleeve head. Interface the sleeve hem with a 4cm (1½in) wide bias strip of the stitch reinforced fusible.

Couture canvas tailoring

Couture canvas tailoring is the traditional way to tailor a jacket, which is given shape and structure by the use of canvas that has been hand-stitched, steamed, and moulded into shape (see the blazer on pp.266–275). This is the most complex of all the tailoring methods.

CANVAS COUTURE TAILORING ON A JACKET WITH PRINCESS SEAMS

On a princess-line pattern, which features in womenswear, the pattern pieces are often interlined prior to applying the canvas, particularly when the fabric is a loose weave.

1 Cut the body of the jacket from an interlining fabric such as butter muslin or silk organza. Pin the interlining to the wrong side of the fabric. Smooth out towards the edges and press the two layers together with an iron – this gets the fibres "friendly", so they sort of cling to each other. Pin at the edges, trim back any interlining that has stretched out during pressing, and tack around each piece inside the seam allowance.

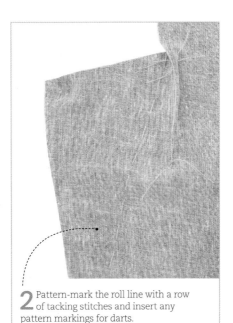

2 Pattern-mark the roll line with a row of tacking stitches and insert any pattern markings for darts.

Front

Side front

3 Stitch the darts and press and join the side front to the front. Press the seam open.

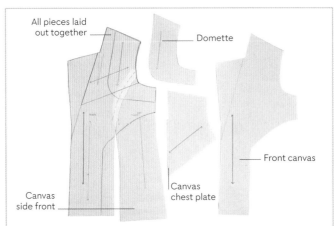

All pieces laid out together

Domette

Canvas side front

Front canvas

Canvas chest plate

4 To make the pattern pieces for the canvas, pin the front and side front pattern pieces together, matching the stitching lines. Trace off a shape that follows the pattern outline, through the centre front, neck, shoulder, armhole, and about 10–15cm (4–6in) down the side seam depending upon pattern size. Join the side to the centre front section with a curve over the top of the bust point. Draw in the roll line.

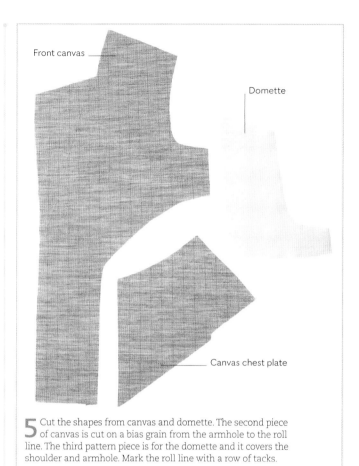

Front canvas

Domette

Canvas chest plate

5 Cut the shapes from canvas and domette. The second piece of canvas is cut on a bias grain from the armhole to the roll line. The third pattern piece is for the domette and it covers the shoulder and armhole. Mark the roll line with a row of tacks.

6 Place the bias-cut shoulder plate to the front canvas. Match at the edges, and mark stitching lines. Pad stitch the layers together, following the straight grain on the bias strip. Keep your stitches 2–2.5cm (¾ –1in) long and the rows 2.5cm (1in) apart.

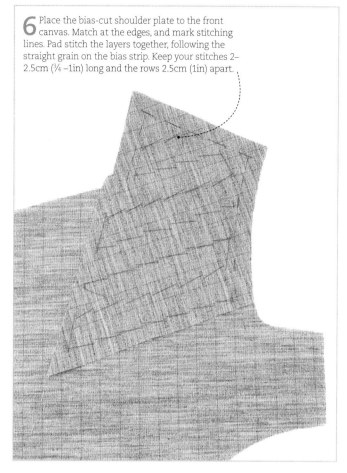

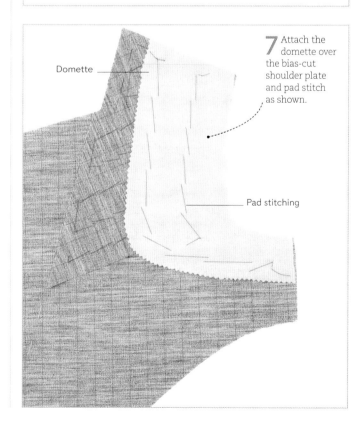

Domette

7 Attach the domette over the bias-cut shoulder plate and pad stitch as shown.

Pad stitching

8 Pin this piece to the jacket front. Match along the roll line and the raw edges. The canvas will form a "bubble" where the fullness of the princess line seam is. Slash through the fullness and overlap the canvas. Mould it over a tailor's ham to shape the canvas. Pin the canvas overlap in place.

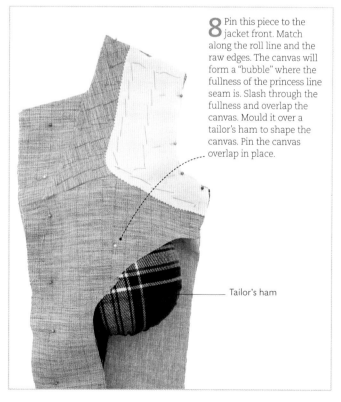

Tailor's ham

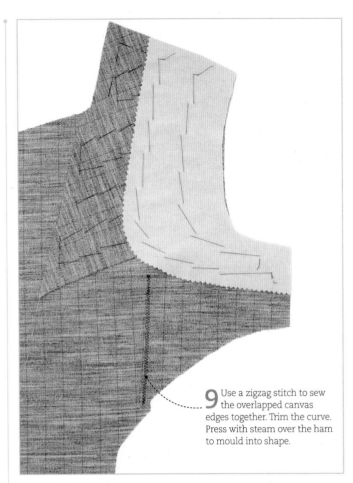

9 Use a zigzag stitch to sew the overlapped canvas edges together. Trim the curve. Press with steam over the ham to mould into shape.

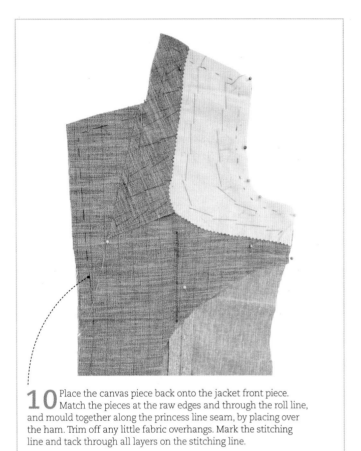

10 Place the canvas piece back onto the jacket front piece. Match the pieces at the raw edges and through the roll line, and mould together along the princess line seam, by placing over the ham. Trim off any little fabric overhangs. Mark the stitching line and tack through all layers on the stitching line.

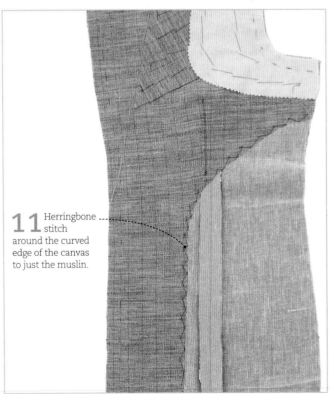

11 Herringbone stitch around the curved edge of the canvas to just the muslin.

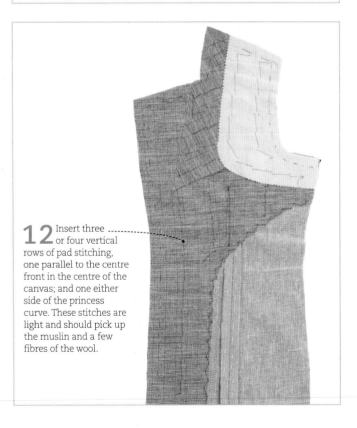

12 Insert three or four vertical rows of pad stitching, one parallel to the centre front in the centre of the canvas; and one either side of the princess curve. These stitches are light and should pick up the muslin and a few fibres of the wool.

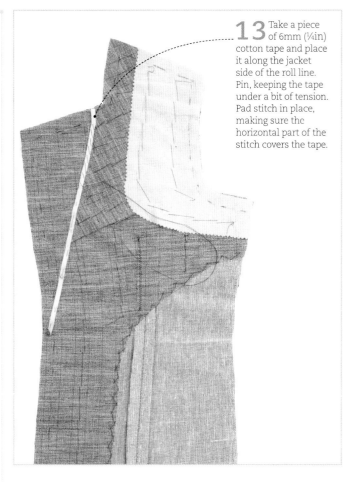

13 Take a piece of 6mm (¼in) cotton tape and place it along the jacket side of the roll line. Pin, keeping the tape under a bit of tension. Pad stitch in place, making sure the horizontal part of the stitch covers the tape.

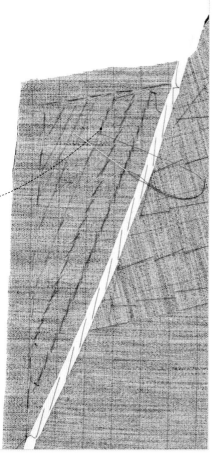

14 Using a water-soluble pen, draw lines on the canvas lapel piece, parallel to the roll line at 1cm (⅜in) intervals. As you get closer to the corner the space between the lines should narrow to 5mm (³⁄₁₆in). Pad stitch along these lines. The stitches here should be much shorter and deeper to pick up the back of the wool. This causes dimples on the right side of the fabric.

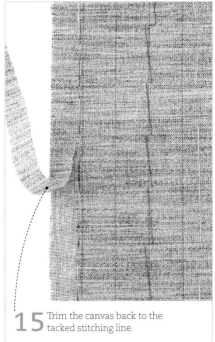

15 Trim the canvas back to the tacked stitching line.

16 Place the cotton tape onto the edge of the canvas, pin and stitch down both sides of the tape. Your stitches should just pick up the canvas and muslin.

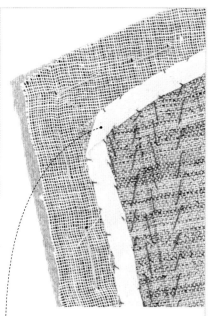

17 At the corner of the lapel, fold the tape as shown and stitch in place.

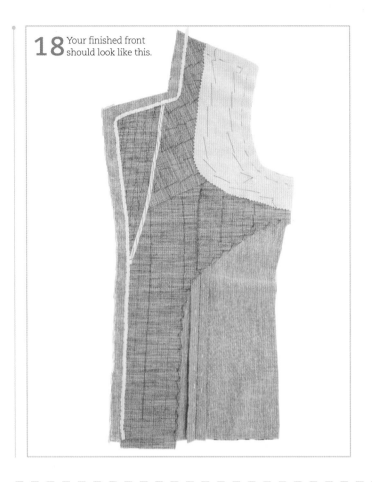

18 Your finished front should look like this.

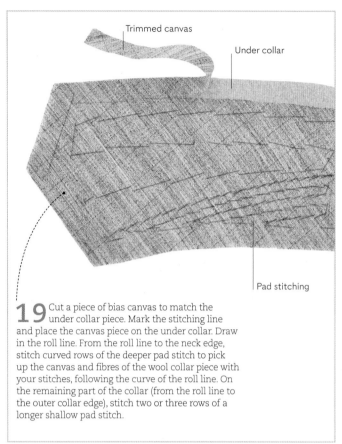

Trimmed canvas

Under collar

Pad stitching

19 Cut a piece of bias canvas to match the under collar piece. Mark the stitching line and place the canvas piece on the under collar. Draw in the roll line. From the roll line to the neck edge, stitch curved rows of the deeper pad stitch to pick up the canvas and fibres of the wool collar piece with your stitches, following the curve of the roll line. On the remaining part of the collar (from the roll line to the outer collar edge), stitch two or three rows of a longer shallow pad stitch.

CANVAS COUTURE TAILORING ON A JACKET WITHOUT BUST SEAMS

The application of the canvas to a menswear jacket is slightly different, in that the jacket fabric is not underlined. Why? Firstly, menswear jackets tailored in this style are traditionally made from wool suiting, which clings to the canvas. Secondly, for this style of garment the canvas is cut to cover more of the front of the chest.

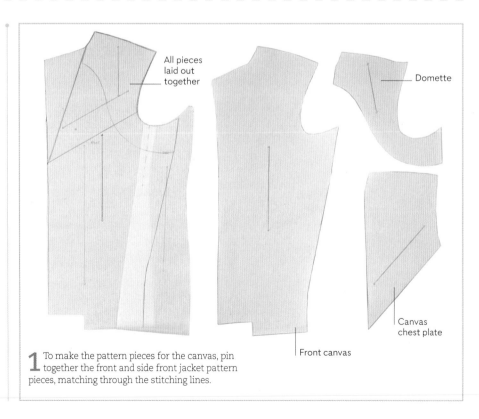

All pieces laid out together

Domette

Canvas chest plate

Front canvas

1 To make the pattern pieces for the canvas, pin together the front and side front jacket pattern pieces, matching through the stitching lines.

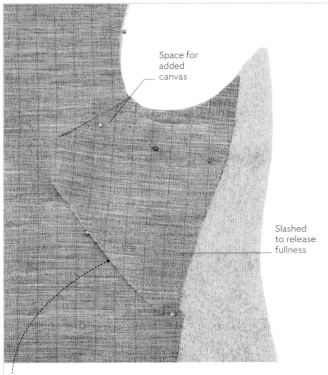

Space for added canvas

Slashed to release fullness

2 Cut out your canvas pieces, and place the canvas to the jacket front and side front. Pin at the edges. The "bubble" will be in a different place to the princess line jacket (see p.211), but you can use the same technique to mould the canvas bubble to the front piece over the tailor's ham with the iron. Slash the canvas to release the fullness. If necessary, fill in any slashed space with an additional overlapped piece of canvas.

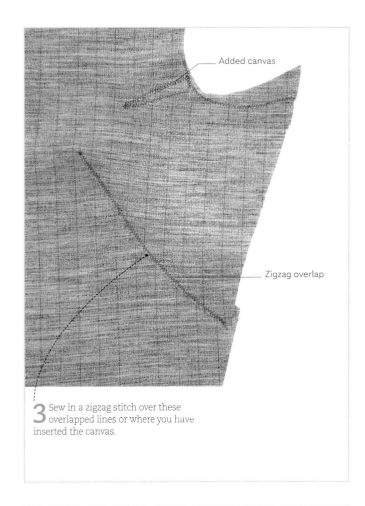

Added canvas

Zigzag overlap

3 Sew in a zigzag stitch over these overlapped lines or where you have inserted the canvas.

4 Place the bias-cut canvas to the shoulder and pad stitch as for step 6 of the princess line jacket (see p.211). Follow steps 7 to 10 of the princess line jacket canvas application (see pp.211–212).

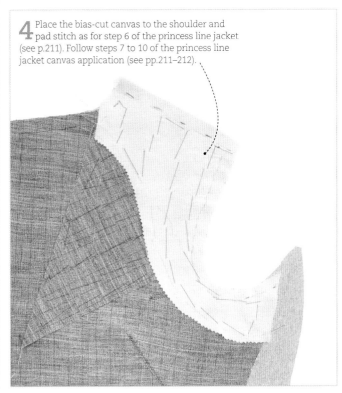

5 Follow steps 13 to 16 of the princess line jacket (see p.213). The insertion of the pockets will further anchor the canvas pieces to the front wool piece of the jacket.

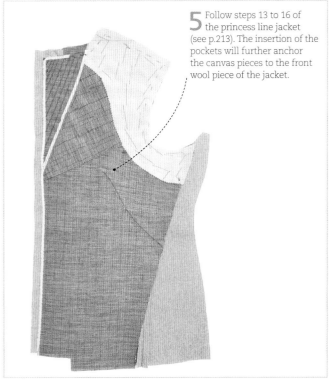

Hybrid tailoring

Hybrid tailoring combines many speed tailoring techniques with a couture canvas technique. This method is used primarily in coats – like the two in this book (see pp.276–291) – and is widely used in ready-to-wear garments. Choose your interfacings carefully, as they need to be lighter in weight than the fashion fabric.

FOR COATS AND JACKETS WITH A LAPEL

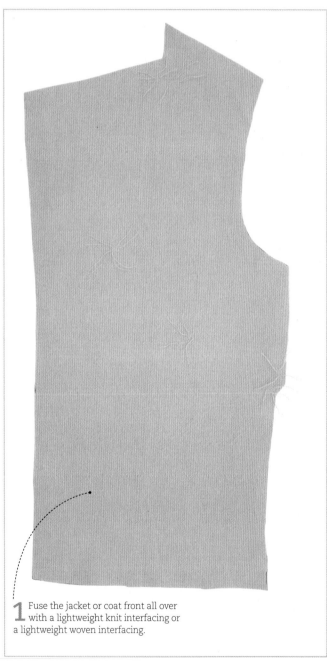

1 Fuse the jacket or coat front all over with a lightweight knit interfacing or a lightweight woven interfacing.

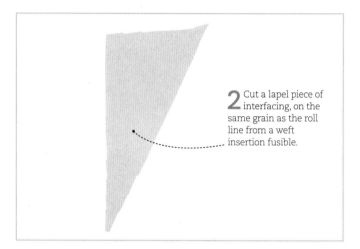

2 Cut a lapel piece of interfacing, on the same grain as the roll line from a weft insertion fusible.

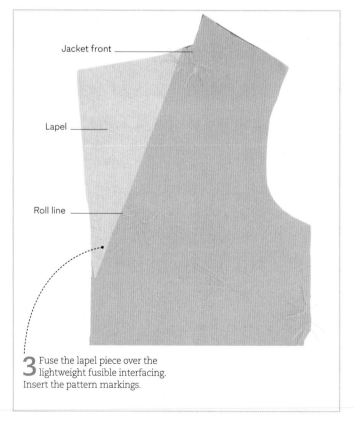

Jacket front

Lapel

Roll line

3 Fuse the lapel piece over the lightweight fusible interfacing. Insert the pattern markings.

4 Fuse straight grain tape to the jacket side of the roll line and leading front edge. Sew the darts and press.

5 Cut a pattern piece for the canvas shoulder plate that reaches over the shoulder seam, down the armhole to the point it starts to curve, and across to the roll line. This piece of canvas should be cut on a bias grain.

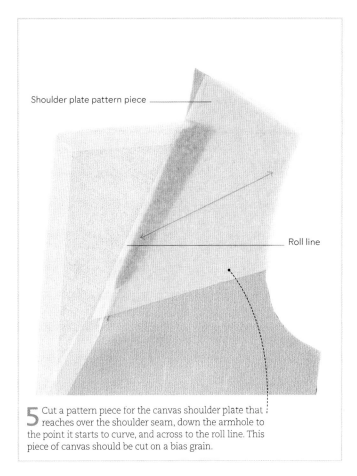

Shoulder plate pattern piece

Roll line

6 Cut a second pattern piece that is slightly smaller and curved at the lower edge. This should be cut on a straight grain from domette.

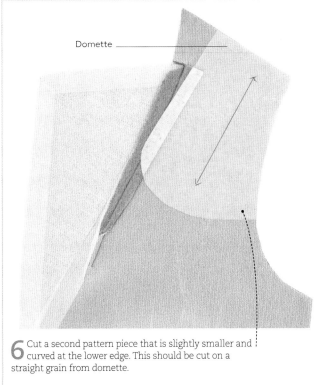

Domette

7 Join these two pieces together with evenly spaced vertical rows of machine stitching.

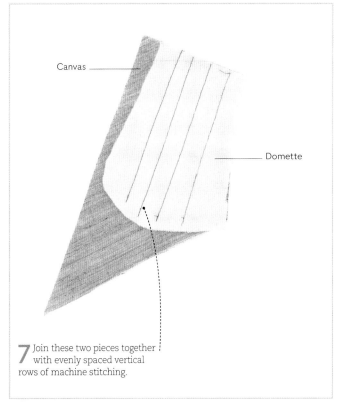

Canvas

Domette

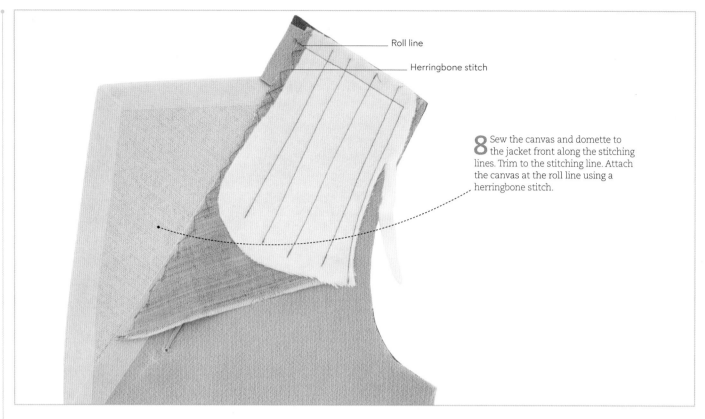

Roll line

Herringbone stitch

8 Sew the canvas and domette to the jacket front along the stitching lines. Trim to the stitching line. Attach the canvas at the roll line using a herringbone stitch.

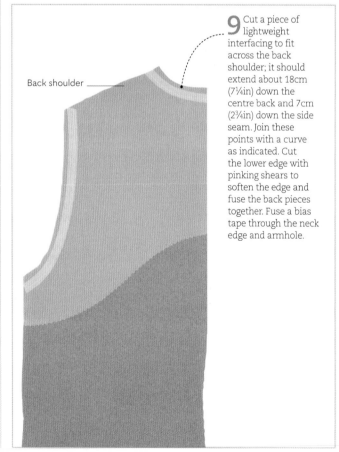

Back shoulder

9 Cut a piece of lightweight interfacing to fit across the back shoulder; it should extend about 18cm (7¼in) down the centre back and 7cm (2¾in) down the side seam. Join these points with a curve as indicated. Cut the lower edge with pinking shears to soften the edge and fuse the back pieces together. Fuse a bias tape through the neck edge and armhole.

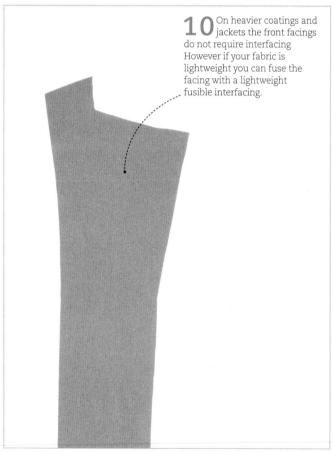

10 On heavier coatings and jackets the front facings do not require interfacing However if your fabric is lightweight you can fuse the facing with a lightweight fusible interfacing.

FOR JACKETS AND COATS WITHOUT A LAPEL OR ROLL LINE

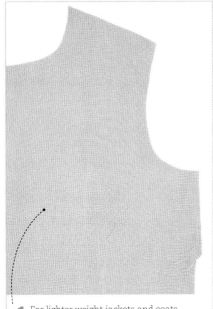

1 For lighter weight jackets and coats with no lapel and roll line, fuse a lightweight knit or woven fusible interfacing all over the front and insert pattern markings.

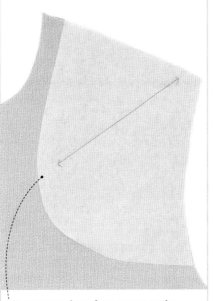

2 Cut out a shape from canvas, on the bias, that extends across the shoulder to within 2cm (¾in) of the neck and down the armhole to the point at which it starts to curve. Join the two points with a curve.

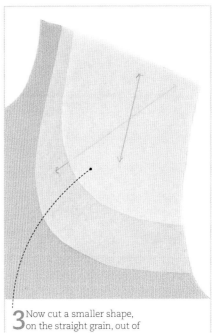

3 Now cut a smaller shape, on the straight grain, out of domette and place it on top of the canvas.

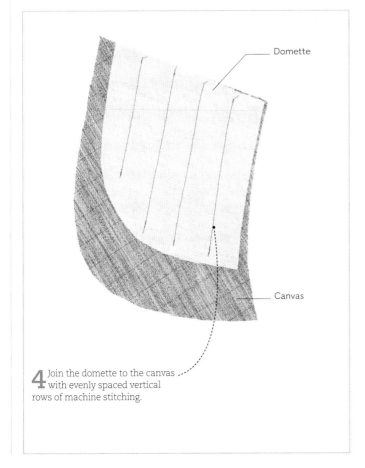

Domette

Canvas

4 Join the domette to the canvas with evenly spaced vertical rows of machine stitching.

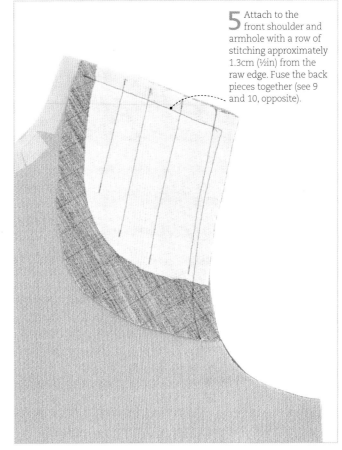

5 Attach to the front shoulder and armhole with a row of stitching approximately 1.3cm (½in) from the raw edge. Fuse the back pieces together (see 9 and 10, opposite).

The garments

Here you'll find step-by-step instructions for crafting ten classic garments that form the basis of a well-tailored wardrobe. These patterns vary in their complexity and encompass a wide range of tailoring techniques covered in earlier chapters.

PENCIL SKIRT PATTERN
Pencil skirt

A straight, well-fitting tailored skirt is an essential garment in a polished, well put-together wardrobe. This pattern is fully lined, with a waistband and a centre back zip. There is a back vent for walking ease and most importantly, chino-style pockets! Back darts help to create a flattering silhouette when paired with a tucked-in top or shirt (see pp.240–245). Consider crafting this classic in a fashion tweed or tartan, or maybe a plain wool or corduroy.

TECHNIQUES USED Applying fusible interfacing **p.59**, Plain dart **p.114**, Inserting a concealed zip **p.187**, Making a chino pocket **p.169**, Lining around a vent **pp.120–121**, Attaching a straight waistband **pp.154–155**, Hook and bar **p.198**

LEVEL OF DIFFICULTY
Intermediate This is a great first tailoring project, but take care with lining around the vent.

YOU WILL NEED
- Pattern template (see pp.12–13 for instructions on how to download your size)
- 1.2m (47¼in) x 150cm (59in) fabric
- 1m (39¼in) x 150cm (59in) lining
- 1 x 22cm (8½in) concealed zip
- 1 x reel all-purpose thread
- 1m (39¼in) waistband interfacing
- 1m (39¼in) bias binding
- 20cm (8in) lightweight fusible interfacing
- 1 x hook and bar fastener

GARMENT CONSTRUCTION
This straight skirt has front and back darting at the waist, generous chino pockets, a concealed zip at the back, and a back vent for ease of movement.

FRONT   BACK

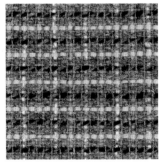

LINTON TWEED

ACETATE TAFFETA LINING

◀ Using a heavy tweed material makes this skirt ideal for the cooler seasons, while the acetate taffeta lining provides the perfect slip for ease of dressing as well as comfort while wearing.

CREPE

ACETATE LINING

▲ If you'd prefer to craft a lighter weight skirt, a crepe material would provide a flattering drape.

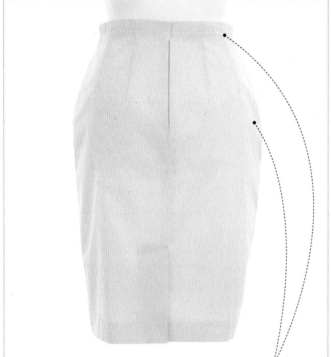

1 Make the toile of the skirt (see pp.86–87) and try on. Check the fit at the waist and hips. Do you have swayback (folds of excess fabric at the centre back)? Is the finished length correct? Adjust your pattern as necessary.

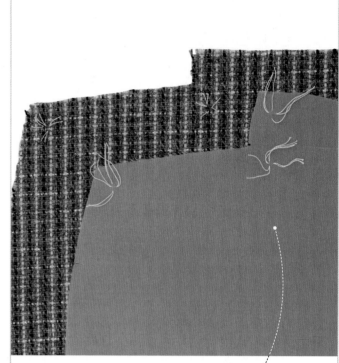

2 Cut out all the pattern pieces in your skirt and lining fabric. Add tailor's tacks to insert the pattern markings.

Back side seam

3 Make the darts in the skirt back and press towards the centre back (see p.114). Fuse a straight grain strip of interfacing 2 x 25cm (¾ x 10in) to the centre back seam where the zip is to be inserted. Overlock the centre back seam and the back side seams.

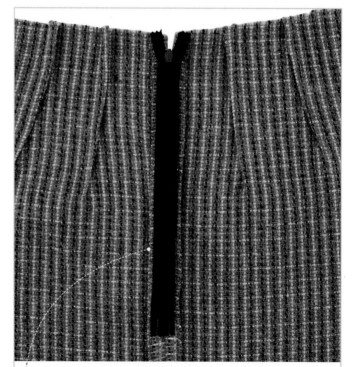

4 Insert a concealed zip at the centre back (see p.187). Stitch the rest of the seam, stopping at the dot above the vent. Secure the end of the zip tape to the centre back seam allowance.

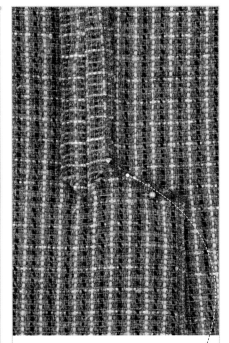

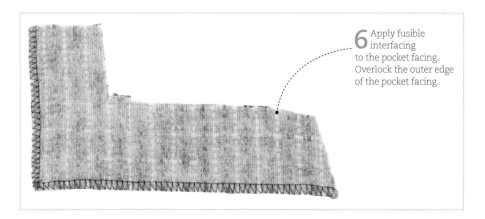

6 Apply fusible interfacing to the pocket facing. Overlock the outer edge of the pocket facing.

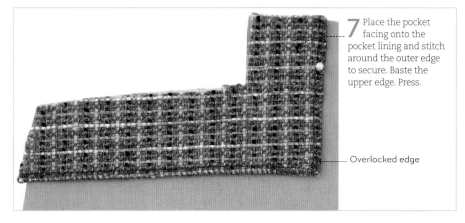

7 Place the pocket facing onto the pocket lining and stitch around the outer edge to secure. Baste the upper edge. Press.

Overlocked edge

5 On the centre back seam, clip the seam allowance on the right-hand side as worn above the vent. Fold the fabric extension towards the left-hand side as worn and press.

Centre front   Side front dart

8 Stitch the dart in the side front. Press towards the centre front.

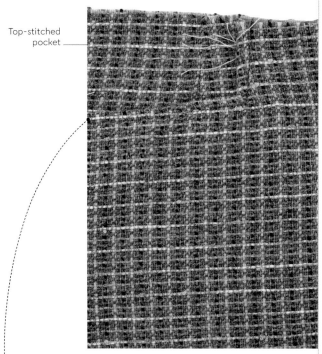

Top-stitched pocket

9 Place the pocket facing and lining to the skirt front as indicated. Stitch, layer, turn to the right side, and top-stitch (see p.169).

RIGHT SIDE

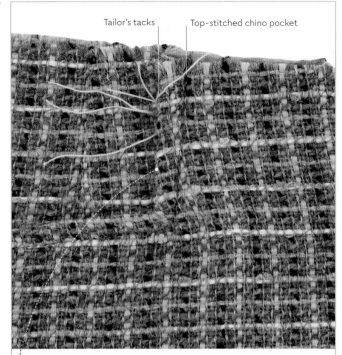

Tailor's tacks   Top-stitched chino pocket

10 On the right side of the skirt, make sure the edges of the pocket align with the pattern dots. The pocket is not flat – there is a bit of ease to allow for your hand. Tack to secure at the side seam. Top-stitch over the existing top-stitches at the waist.

Overlocked pocket

11 Overlock the side seams through all the layers.

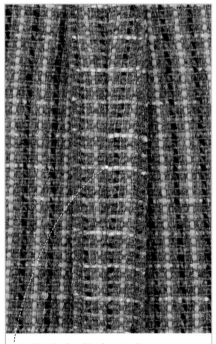

12 Join the skirt front to the skirt back at the side seams. Press open.

13 Overlock the centre back seams and the side seams of the lining. Join the centre back seam on the lining between the dots. Reinforce the corners on the vent. Press the seam open.

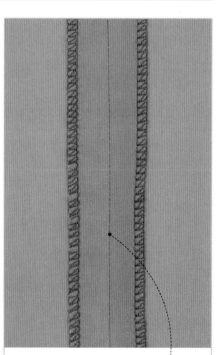

14 Join the front and back lining at the side seams. Press open.

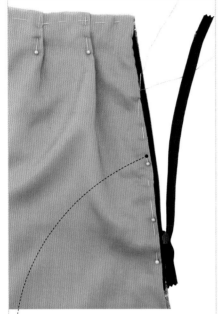

15 Place the lining and skirt together, wrong side to wrong side. Pin and tack or baste together at the waist, making tucks in the lining over the darts to avoid bulk. At the centre back zip, turn under the lining seam allowance onto the centre of the zip tape. Pin and flat fell stitch in place.

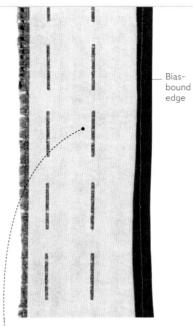

Bias-bound edge

16 Interface the waistband. Bind one long edge. Attach the waistband through both the skirt fabric and lining (see p.154).

RIGHT-HAND BACK AS WORN   LEFT-HAND BACK AS WORN

17 Overlock the skirt hem. Turn up the hem 4cm (1½in) and catch stitch in place. At the centre back vent, mitre the hem on the left-hand back as worn and turn under the seam allowance on the right-hand back.

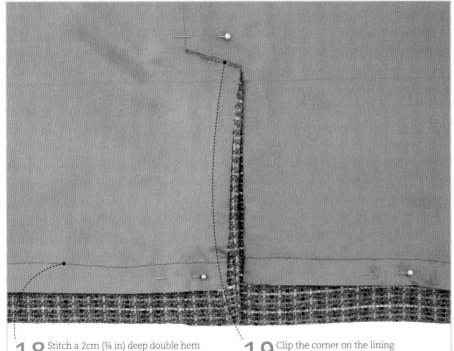

18 Stitch a 2cm (¾ in) deep double hem on the lining. Turn 2cm (¾in), press, then turn 2cm (¾in) again and press.

19 Clip the corner on the lining and pin in place around the vent. Flat fell the stitch in place (see pp.120–121).

20 Sew a flat hook and bar onto the waistband (see p.198) and your skirt is finished.

STRAIGHT-LEG TROUSER PATTERN
Straight-leg trousers

Classic ankle-grazing straight-leg trousers that can be dressed up or down to take you from the office to a more casual day away. With front and back darts and functional front hip pockets, these trousers are a must in any tailored wardrobe. To ensure they hang beautifully, skimming the frame and stopping just at the ankles, choose the pattern size closest to your measurements and make a toile to perfect the fit. I will also show you a wide-leg version of these trousers on pages 236 to 239.

TECHNIQUES USED Applying fusible interfacing **p.59**, Plain dart **p.114**, Welt pocket **p.165**, Adding a front tuck on trouser legs **p.117**, Front hip pocket **p.168**, Split waistband **p.156**, Faced fly front zip **pp.184–185**, Hand-stitched hems **p.177**, Hook and bar **p.198**

LEVEL OF DIFFICULTY
Intermediate Why not leave out the back welt pockets if these are your first trousers.

YOU WILL NEED
- Pattern template (see pp.12–13 for instructions on how to download your size)
- 1–1.5m (39¼–59in) x 150cm (59in) fabric
- 50cm (20in) lining fabric
- 50cm (20in) fusible interfacing
- 50cm (20in) fusible straight grain tape
- 1 x 20cm (8in) trouser zip
- 1 x reel all-purpose thread
- 1m (39¼in) bias binding
- 1 x hook and bar fastener

GARMENT CONSTRUCTION
Ankle-grazing slim leg trousers with darts at the front and back, and a shaped waistband that has a centre seam to aid fitting. Hip pockets and a faced fly complete the trouser front, while back welt pockets add a flattering line and enhance the trouser's sleek symmetry.

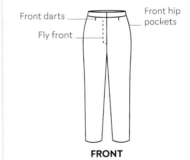

Front darts

Front hip pockets

Fly front

FRONT

Back welt pockets

Back darts

Ankle-grazing length

BACK

TWILL WEAVE WOOL

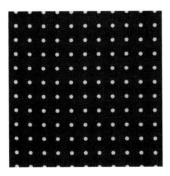

SILK TWILL LINING

◀ These trousers are made from a twill weave wool that drapes elegantly while also being durable and warm. Silk twill lining in a chic polka dot pattern has been used to line the waistband and for the fly front placket.

FASHION TWEED

FASHION TWEED

▲ Bring a contemporary edge to your trousers by choosing a fashion tweed to complement your wardrobe.

1 Make a toile of the trousers (see pp.86–87). Check the fit – is the waist and hip size correct? Do you need a longer crotch seam? Have you got any wrinkles? Check the length and width at the hem edge. Adjust the pattern as necessary.

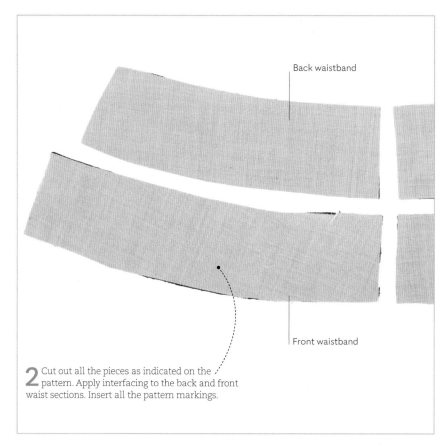

Back waistband

Front waistband

2 Cut out all the pieces as indicated on the pattern. Apply interfacing to the back and front waist sections. Insert all the pattern markings.

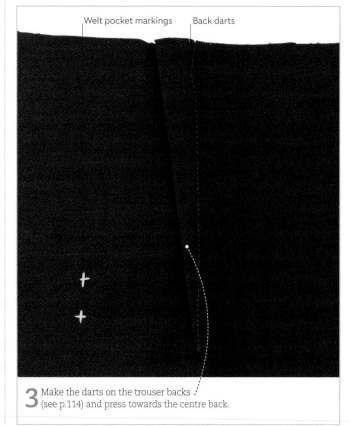

Welt pocket markings Back darts

3 Make the darts on the trouser backs (see p.114) and press towards the centre back.

4 Make the back welt pockets (see p.165).

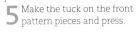

Front tuck

5 Make the tuck on the front pattern pieces and press.

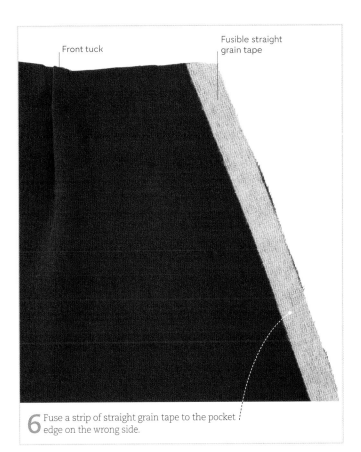

Front tuck

Fusible straight grain tape

6 Fuse a strip of straight grain tape to the pocket edge on the wrong side.

Pocket facing

7 Overlock the long, straight edge on the trouser pocket facing. Place the wrong side facing the right side pocket bag, matching at the sloped edge. Diagonally baste and machine to secure alongside the overlocking.

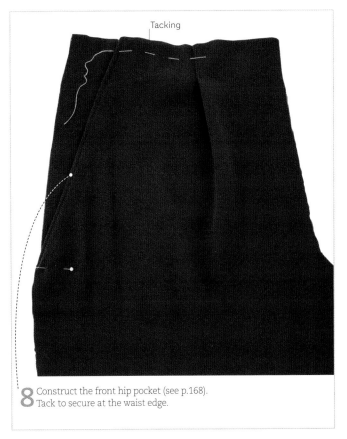

Tacking

8 Construct the front hip pocket (see p.168). Tack to secure at the waist edge.

In leg seam

9 Overlock the side seam and in leg seam on the trouser front and back pattern pieces and join a front leg to a back leg, right side to right side, at the in leg seam. Press the seam open.

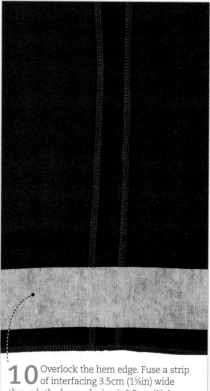

10 Overlock the hem edge. Fuse a strip of interfacing 3.5cm (1⅜in) wide through the hem, placing it 2.5cm (1in) from the overlocked edge.

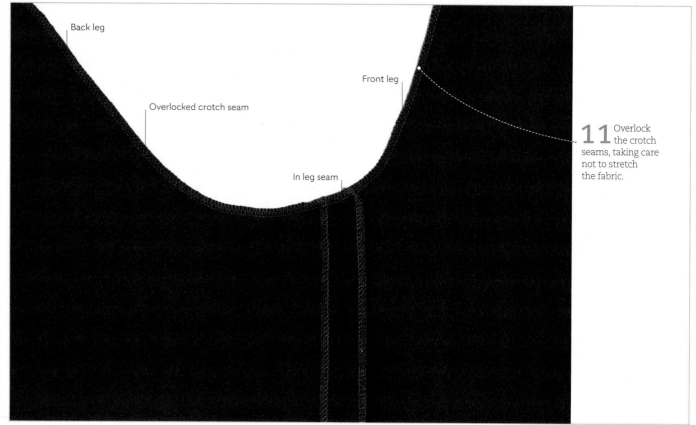

Back leg

Overlocked crotch seam

Front leg

In leg seam

11 Overlock the crotch seams, taking care not to stretch the fabric.

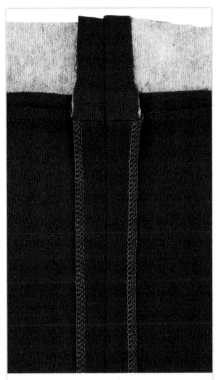

Waistband seam

12 Attach the waistband sections to the back legs. Layer the seam and press towards the waistband.

13 Join the trousers together through the crotch seam from the dot on the centre front through to the back waistband.

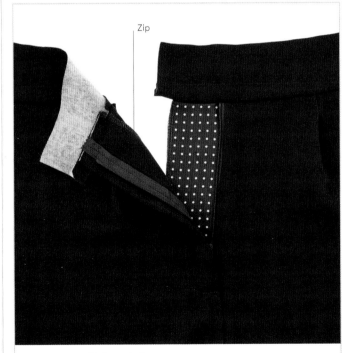

Zip

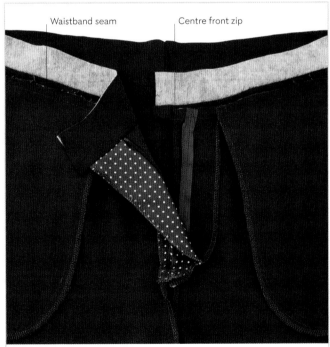

Waistband seam   Centre front zip

14 Insert a fly front zip (see pp.184–185) and attach the front waistbands.

15 Layer the seam and press towards the waistband.

Fly front facing

Tacking

16 Bring the trousers together right side to right side. Tack or baste down the side seams to make the two legs. Try on. Adjust the fit if necessary. Stitch permanently and press the seam open over a seam roll.

Bias bound edge

17 Join the waistband lining pieces together and bind or overlock the lower edge of the lining waistband. Pin the lining to the fabric waistbands, right side to right side, matching through the side seams and centre back.

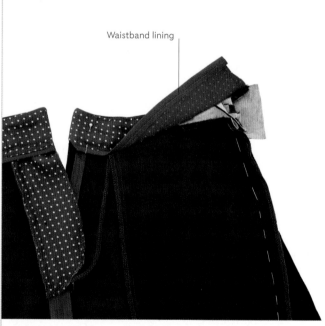

Waistband lining

18 Join the lining waistbands to the trouser waistband at the upper edge. Stitch at the upper edge and centre front. Layer and understitch.

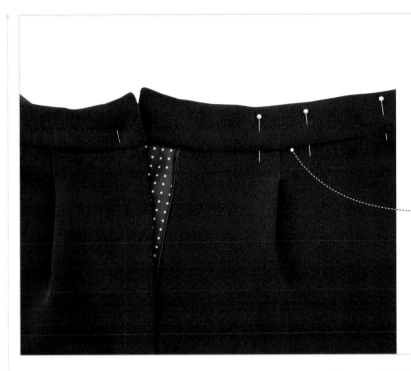

19 Pin the waistband lining to the trouser-waistband seam as shown and stitch in the ditch.

20 Sew one or two flat trouser hooks and bars at the centre front (see p.198).

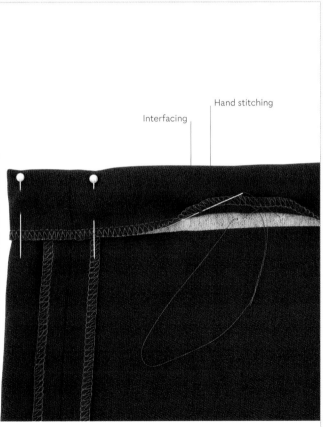

Hand stitching

Interfacing

21 Turn up your trouser hem 3.5cm (1⅜in) and slip stitch the hem in place (see p.177). Press.

WIDE-LEG TROUSER PATTERN
Wide-leg trousers

These wide-leg trousers are a variation on the straight-leg trousers (see pp.228–235), where the front darts have been replaced by pleats and the fly front zip is now a concealed zip in the side seam. With a relaxed fit from waist to hem, they offer effortless elegance and can be dressed up or down to suit any occasion. To ensure they hang beautifully, choose a fabric with a heavy drape such as a linen, crepe, or a twill weave. Pair with a fitted top, such as the classic shirt (pp.240–245), or wear with the jacket (pp.252–259) for a smart look.

TECHNIQUES USED Applying fusible interfacing **p.59**, Plain dart **p.114**, Concealed zip **p.187**, Front hip pockets **p.168**, Split waistband **p.156**, Hand-stitched hems **p.177**

LEVEL OF DIFFICULTY
Beginner A super simple pair of trousers, ideal for a first tailoring project.

YOU WILL NEED
- Pattern template (see pp.12–13 for instructions on how to download your size)
- 2.5m (98in) x 150cm (59in) wide fabric
- 50cm (20in) fusible interfacing
- 50cm (20in) lining fabric
- 1 x reel all-purpose thread
- 1 x 20cm (8in) concealed zip

GARMENT CONSTRUCTION
These wide-leg trousers are constructed from a vibrant linen and feature pleats from the waistband, a concealed zip in the side seam, and shaping darts on the trouser backs.

Front pleats

Concealed zip and front hip pockets

FRONT

Back darts

Split waistband

BACK

LINEN

SATIN WEAVE LINING

◄ These wide-leg trousers have been made from a medium weight linen fabric, great for summer dressing as the natural, breathable fibres will keep you cool. The waistband has been lined with a satin weave lining.

HEAVY CREPE

ACETATE TAFFETA LINING

▲ These trousers would also look great in a heavy crepe or triple crepe fabric, which would hang beautifully due to its weight. Pair with a lighter acetate taffeta lining.

1 Make a toile of the trousers (see pp.86–87). Check the fit – is the waist and hip size correct? Do you need a longer crotch seam? Have you got any wrinkles? Check the length and width at the hem edge. Adjust the pattern as necessary.

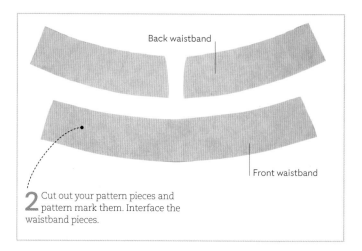

Back waistband

Front waistband

2 Cut out your pattern pieces and pattern mark them. Interface the waistband pieces.

3 Make the darts on the trouser backs (see p.114) and press towards the centre back.

4 Follow steps 6–11 of the straight-leg trousers (see pp.231–232).

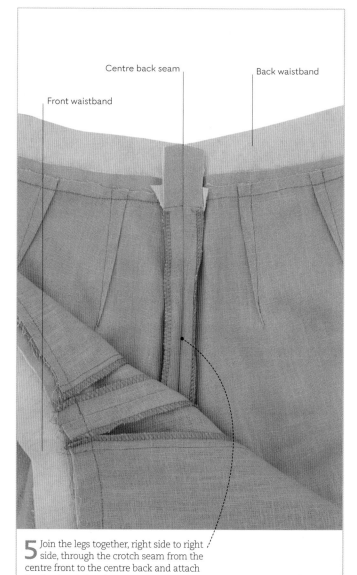

Centre back seam

Back waistband

Front waistband

5 Join the legs together, right side to right side, through the crotch seam from the centre front to the centre back and attach the front waistband.

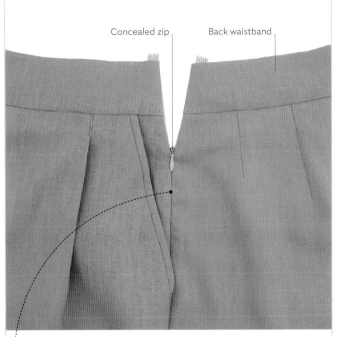

Concealed zip   Back waistband

6 Bring the trousers together, right side to right side (see step 16 of the straight-leg trousers, p.234). Insert a concealed zip in the left-hand side of the trousers through the waistband and side front (see p.187).

7 Follow steps 17–19 of the straight-leg trousers (see pp.234–235) to attach the waistband lining.

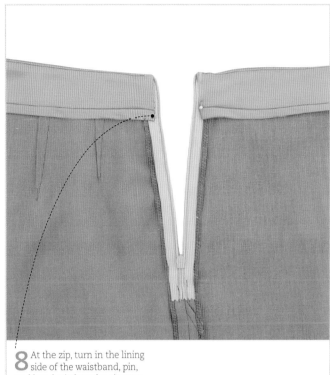

8 At the zip, turn in the lining side of the waistband, pin, and hand stitch to the zip tape.

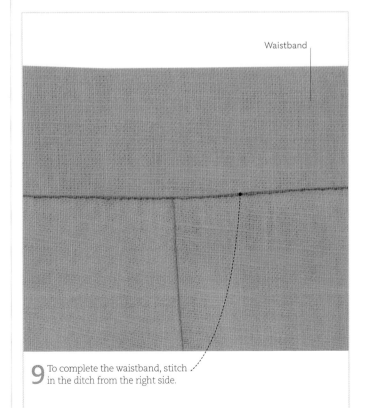

Waistband

9 To complete the waistband, stitch in the ditch from the right side.

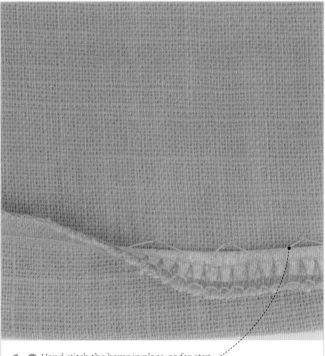

10 Hand stitch the hems in place, as for step 21 of the straight-leg trousers (see p.235).

CLASSIC SHIRT PATTERN
Classic shirt

A fitted shirt is a timeless garment that exudes sophistication. So versatile it can be worn both casually or as more formal attire, this traditionally tailored shirt, with run and fell seams, a two-piece collar, and a sleeve placket and cuff will enhance any wardrobe. It would coordinate well with other projects in this book, such as the straight-leg trousers (pp.228–235) and the princess-line jacket (pp.252–259).

TECHNIQUES USED Plain dart **p.114**, Adding a tuck on a shirt back **p.117**, The burrito method, **pp.126–127**, Run and fell seam **p.107**, Shirt sleeve placket **pp.148–149**, Attaching a cuff **pp.150–151**, Inserting a set-in sleeve **p.139**, Two-piece shirt collar **pp.132–133**, Buttons **p.189**, Buttonholes **pp.192–197**

LEVEL OF DIFFICULTY
Advanced Discover how to apply a two-piece collar and create a sleeve with a placket and cuff.

YOU WILL NEED
* Pattern template (see pp.12–13 for instructions on how to download your size)
* 2.5–3m (98–118in) x 150cm (59in) fabric
* 10–12 x shirt buttons
* 1 x reel all-purpose thread
* 1m (39¼in) interfacing

GARMENT CONSTRUCTION
The shirt has bust darts, subtle side seam shaping, and a dart on the back. It is constructed with run and fell seams, but you could use a plain seam and overlock the seam allowances together.

Two-piece collar

Bust darts

Tuck

FRONT

BACK

◀ This shirt is constructed in striped shirting, giving a timeless look to this tailored piece.

STRIPED SHIRTING

◀ For a softer look, a floral fabric such as this liberty print cotton lawn would work well.

COTTON LAWN

1 Make a toile of the shirt (see pp.86–87). Check the fit at the bust, the sleeve length, and neck size.

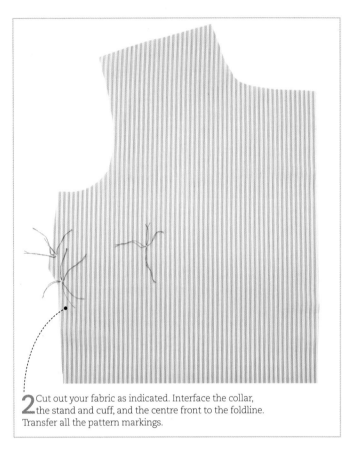

2 Cut out your fabric as indicated. Interface the collar, the stand and cuff, and the centre front to the foldline. Transfer all the pattern markings.

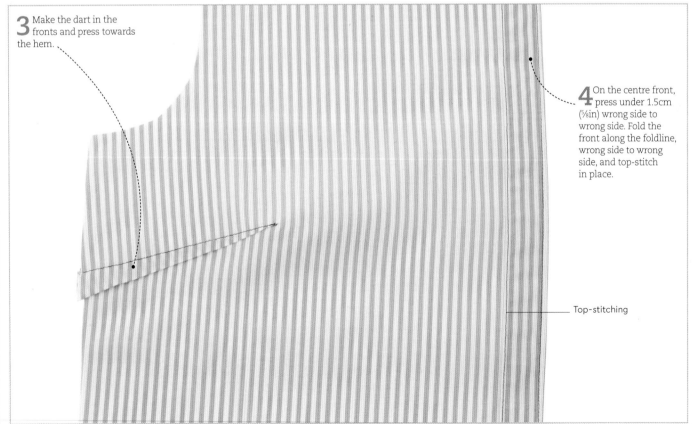

3 Make the dart in the fronts and press towards the hem.

4 On the centre front, press under 1.5cm (⅝in) wrong side to wrong side. Fold the front along the foldline, wrong side to wrong side, and top-stitch in place.

Top-stitching

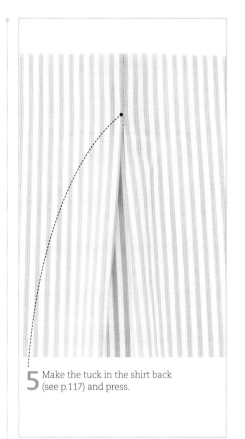

5 Make the tuck in the shirt back (see p.117) and press.

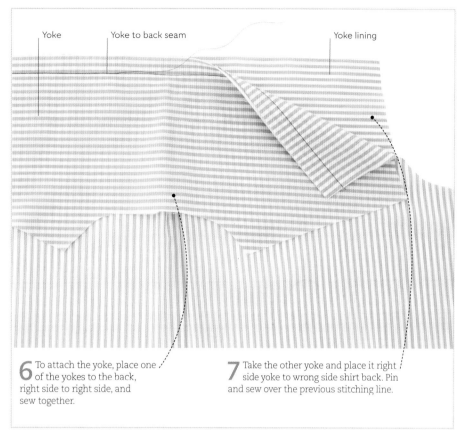

Yoke

Yoke to back seam

Yoke lining

6 To attach the yoke, place one of the yokes to the back, right side to right side, and sew together.

7 Take the other yoke and place it right side yoke to wrong side shirt back. Pin and sew over the previous stitching line.

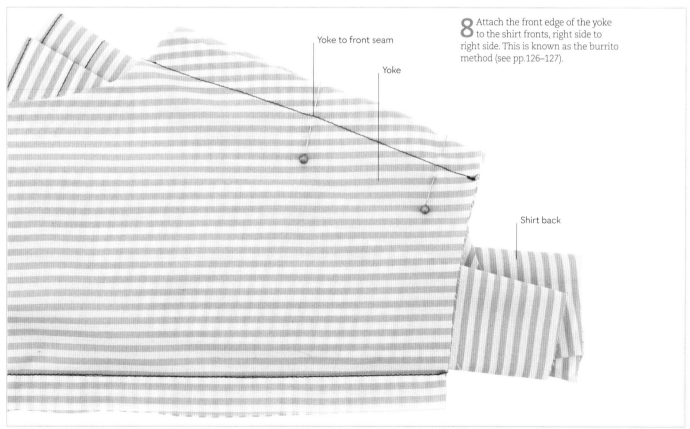

Yoke to front seam

Yoke

Shirt back

8 Attach the front edge of the yoke to the shirt fronts, right side to right side. This is known as the burrito method (see pp.126–127).

9 Press the seams and top-stitch.

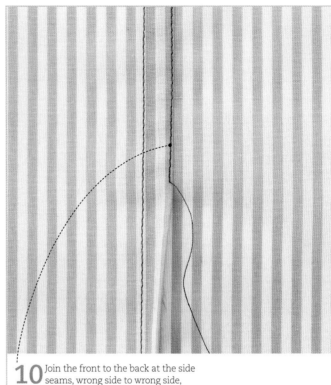

10 Join the front to the back at the side seams, wrong side to wrong side, with a run and fell seam (see p.107).

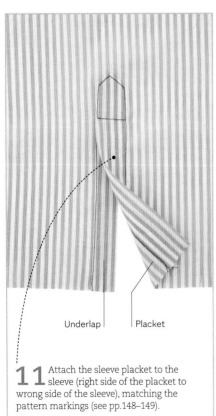

Underlap | Placket

11 Attach the sleeve placket to the sleeve (right side of the placket to wrong side of the sleeve), matching the pattern markings (see pp.148–149).

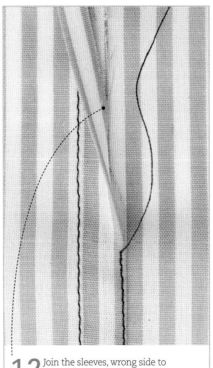

12 Join the sleeves, wrong side to wrong side, with a run and fell seam (see p.107).

13 Attach the cuff (see pp.150–151) and top-stitch.

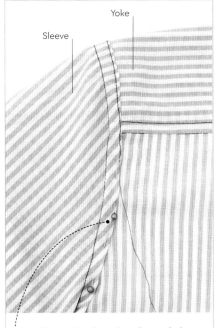

Sleeve

Yoke

14 Insert the sleeve into the armhole, right side to right side (see p.139). Attach using a run and fell seam, pressing the seam towards the body of the shirt, from the underarm up to the shoulder and back round to the underarm (matching all seams in a cross under the arm).

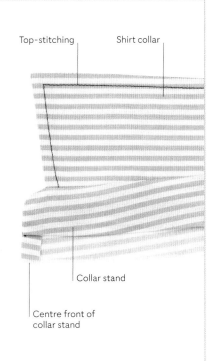

Top-stitching

Shirt collar

Collar stand

Centre front of collar stand

15 Attach the collar to the collar stand. Press under the 1.5cm (⅝in) seam allowance on the non-interfaced side of the collar stand.

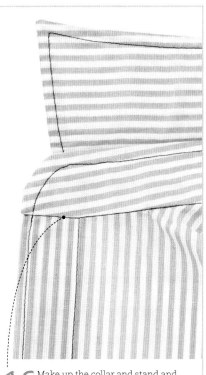

16 Make up the collar and stand and attach to the neck edge of the shirt (see pp.132–133).

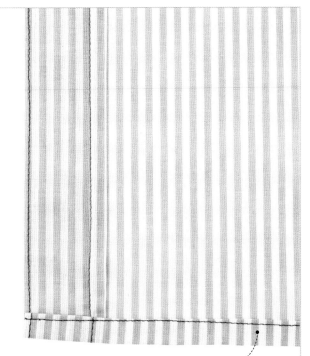

17 Make a double hem – stitch around the hem 1.5cm (⅝in) from the raw edge. Fold the centre front hem edge right side to right side, and stitch 1.5cm (⅝in) from the raw edge. Clip, turn to the right side and press.

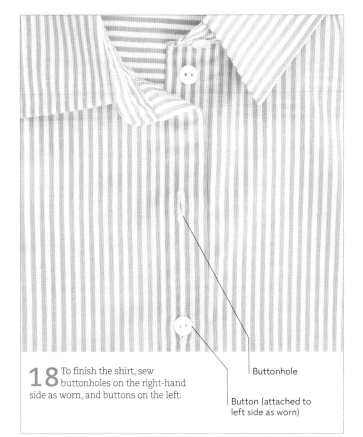

Buttonhole

Button (attached to left side as worn)

18 To finish the shirt, sew buttonholes on the right-hand side as worn, and buttons on the left.

FIVE-BUTTON WAISTCOAT PATTERN

Five-button waistcoat

A waistcoat can be a stand-alone garment, capable of elevating any outfit, or it can be the item that completes a three-piece suit. This classic menswear version features a working chest pocket and faux lower welts. A traditional back lining with a buckle and belt fastener completes the look. For the more adventurous dresser, add some panache by bringing in a patterned fabric for the back – too good to be hidden under a suit jacket!

TECHNIQUES USED Applying fusible interfacing **p.59**, Plain dart **p.114**, Faux welt pocket **p.173**, Welt pocket **p.164**, Buttons **p.189**, Buttonholes **pp.192–197**

LEVEL OF DIFFICULTY

Intermediate This waistcoat will teach you how to "bag out" through the shoulders.

YOU WILL NEED

- Pattern template (see pp.12–13 for instructions on how to download your size)
- 1m (39¼in) x 150cm (59in) fabric
- 1m (39¼in) x 150cm (59in) satin lining
- 1m (39¼in) stitch reinforced fusible interfacing
- 2m (79in) fusible straight grain tape
- 1.5m (59in) bias grain tape
- 1 x reel all-purpose thread
- 1 x waistcoat buckle
- 5 x buttons 18mm (¾in) diameter

GARMENT CONSTRUCTION

This menswear waistcoat has a functional breast pocket and two faux pockets. Here, it has been made with a lining back, but you could use a fabric back in any pattern of your choice.

Upper welt pocket

Dart

Faux welt pocket

FRONT

Lining back

Buckle fastener

BACK

HARRIS TWEED

VISCOSE LINING

◀ This waistcoat is made from Harris Tweed with a satin weave viscose lining. The same lining has been used for the back of the waistcoat.

WOOL TWEED

DOBBY WEAVE LINING

▲ A traditional wool tweed with coordinating lining would also be a smart choice for this waistcoat.

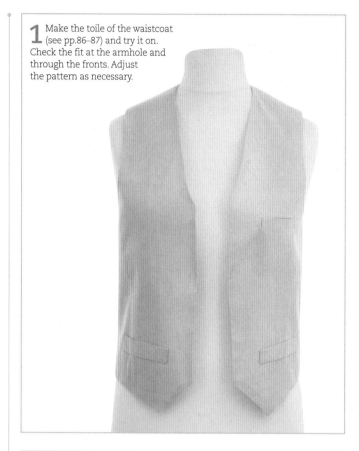

1 Make the toile of the waistcoat (see pp.86–87) and try it on. Check the fit at the armhole and through the fronts. Adjust the pattern as necessary.

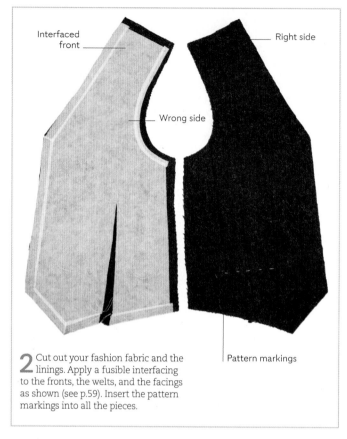

Interfaced front

Right side

Wrong side

Pattern markings

2 Cut out your fashion fabric and the linings. Apply a fusible interfacing to the fronts, the welts, and the facings as shown (see p.59). Insert the pattern markings into all the pieces.

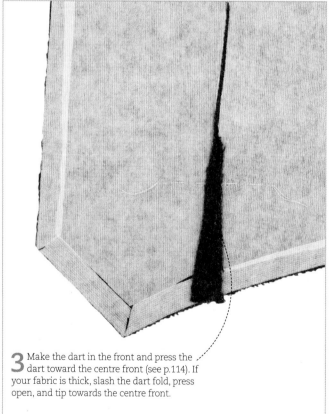

3 Make the dart in the front and press the dart toward the centre front (see p.114). If your fabric is thick, slash the dart fold, press open, and tip towards the centre front.

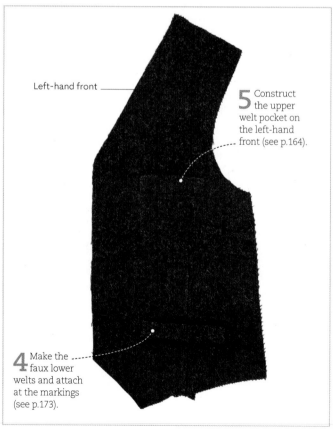

Left-hand front

5 Construct the upper welt pocket on the left-hand front (see p.164).

4 Make the faux lower welts and attach at the markings (see p.173).

6 Join the waistcoat centre back sections between the neck and the dot. Press the seam open.

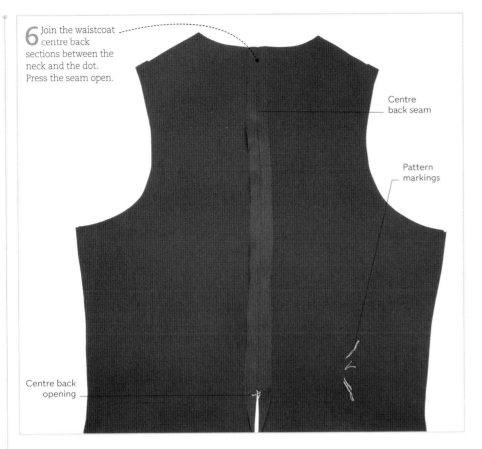

Centre back seam

Pattern markings

Centre back opening

7 Make up the lining belt. Press the strip in half, wrong side to wrong side. Press the edges to the centre.

8 Turn in one short end and top-stitch.

Top-stitching

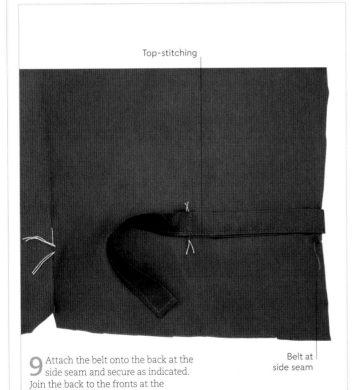

9 Attach the belt onto the back at the side seam and secure as indicated. Join the back to the fronts at the shoulders and press open.

Belt at side seam

Back neck facing

10 Sew the centre back seam between the neck and the dot on the lining. Press open and attach the back neck facing. Clip the lining side of the seam and press towards the lining.

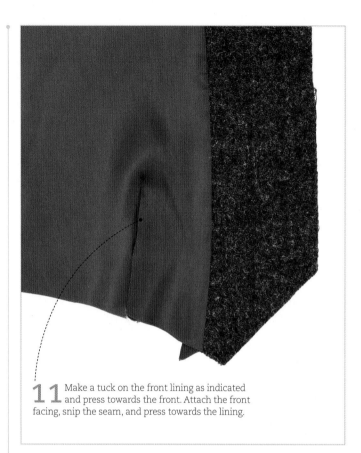

11 Make a tuck on the front lining as indicated and press towards the front. Attach the front facing, snip the seam, and press towards the lining.

12 Join the front to the back at the shoulder seam and press the seam open.

13 Place the lining and waistcoat fronts together, right side to right side. Match the raw edges around the armholes, the neck, the front, and the back hems. Stitch together.

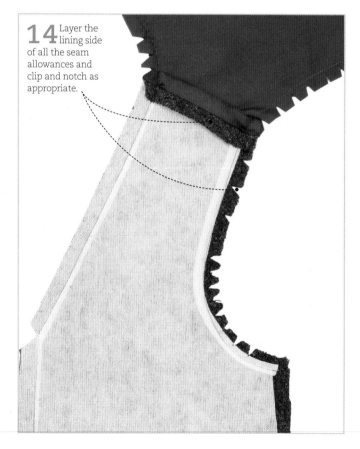

14 Layer the lining side of all the seam allowances and clip and notch as appropriate.

Front

Back

15 Insert your hand through the back side seam and pull the fronts through each shoulder in turn, and then turn to the right side.

16 Press all the edges, rolling them so the seam edge is slightly to the wrong side.

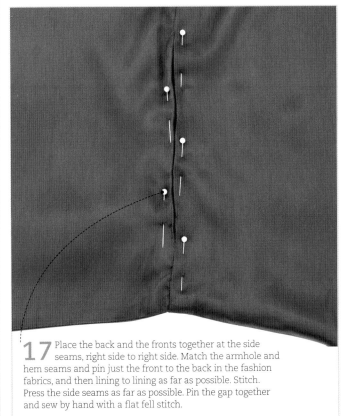

17 Place the back and the fronts together at the side seams, right side to right side. Match the armhole and hem seams and pin just the front to the back in the fashion fabrics, and then lining to lining as far as possible. Stitch. Press the side seams as far as possible. Pin the gap together and sew by hand with a flat fell stitch.

18 To finish, make buttonholes on the left-hand front and sew on buttons on the right-hand front to match.

19 Attach the waistcoat buckle at the back.

PRINCESS-LINE JACKET PATTERN

Princess-line jacket

This princess-line jacket is the perfect introduction to working on a tailored jacket, as the construction features fusible underlinings, jetted pockets, and a bound buttonhole – all essential tailoring techniques. With its curved lapels and collar, this garment will coordinate well with other projects in this book, such as the shirt (pp.240–245), trousers (pp.228–235), and skirt (pp.222–227).

TECHNIQUES USED Speed tailoring **pp.206–209**, Applying fusible interfacing **p.59**, Plain dart **p.114**, Jetted pocket **p.174**, Bound buttonhole **pp.196–197**, Collar application **p.136**, Inserting a tailored sleeve plus sleeve roll **p.142**, Hand inserted sleeve lining **p.118**, Hand-stitched hems **p.177**, Buttons **p.189**

LEVEL OF DIFFICULTY

Advanced This project uses speed tailoring techniques. The jetted pockets are challenging.

YOU WILL NEED

- Pattern template (see pp.12–13 for instructions on how to download your size)
- 2m (79in) x 150cm (59in) fabric
- 2m (79in) medium weight fusible interfacing
- 2m (79in) lightweight fusible woven interfacing
- 3m (118in) x 2cm (¾in) fusible edge tape
- 2m (79in) fusible bias tape
- 40cm (16in) square of non-fusible tailoring canvas
- Pair of shoulder pads
- Small piece of ice wool, knitted domette, or a flat domette for sleeve heads
- 5 x buttons 2.5cm (1in) diameter

GARMENT CONSTRUCTION

This princess line hip-length jacket, with jetted pockets, features collar and revers with a contemporary curved finish. The two-piece sleeve has a faux vent also featuring the curved finished edge. The jacket fastens with a single button and bound buttonhole.

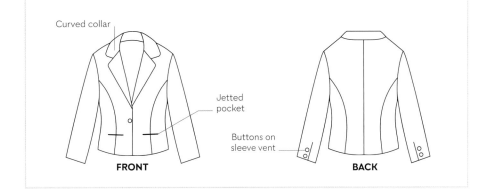

Curved collar

Jetted pocket

Buttons on sleeve vent

FRONT

BACK

WOOL SUITING

VISCOSE LINING

◄ This jacket is made from a wool suiting fabric 80% wool, 18% polyester 2% spandex for movement. The coordinated lining is 100% viscose.

FASHION TWEED

LINING

▲ This jacket would also look great in a fashion tweed, a silk/wool mix, a linen, or even a pinstripe.

1 Make the toile of the jacket (see pp.86–87) and try it on. Check the fit – how is the shoulder width? Does the sleeve length look right? Is it too tight or loose over the bust? Is the finished length correct? Adjust the pattern as necessary.

2 Cut out all the fashion fabric and lining as indicated. Interface all the jacket pieces (see pp.206–209). Insert the pattern markings into all the pieces.

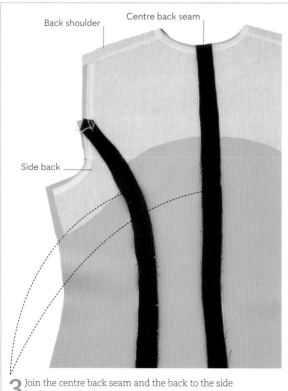

Back shoulder Centre back seam

Side back

3 Join the centre back seam and the back to the side backs. Press the seams open over a ham, clipping and notching as necessary.

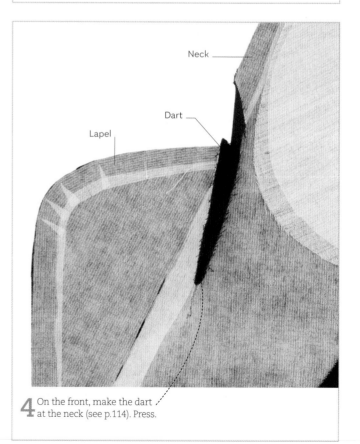

Neck

Dart

Lapel

4 On the front, make the dart at the neck (see p.114). Press.

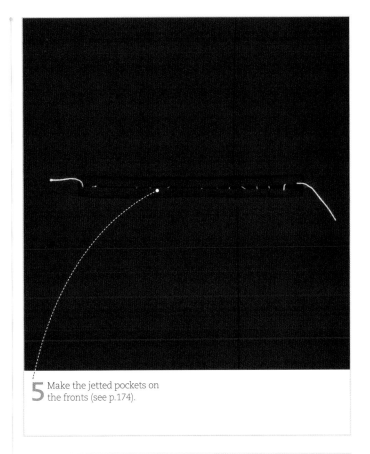

5 Make the jetted pockets on the fronts (see p.174).

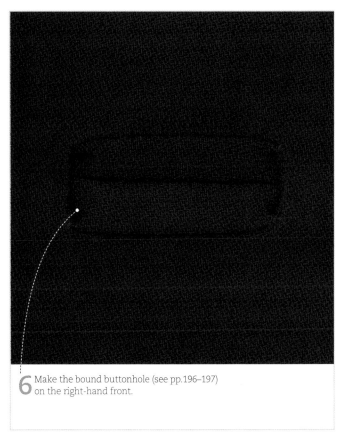

6 Make the bound buttonhole (see pp.196–197) on the right-hand front.

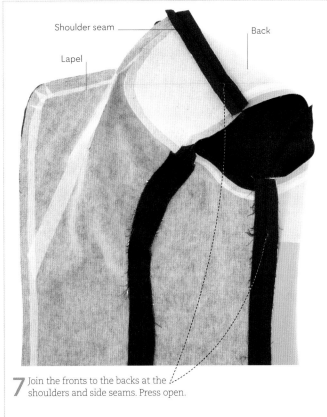

Shoulder seam

Back

Lapel

7 Join the fronts to the backs at the shoulders and side seams. Press open.

8 Join the under collar at the centre back and attach to the neck edge of the jacket (see p.136).

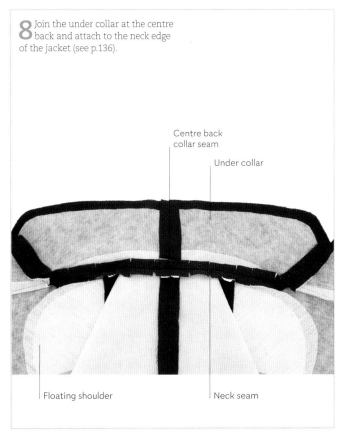

Centre back collar seam

Under collar

Floating shoulder

Neck seam

9 Join the under and upper sleeve as shown and press the seam open.

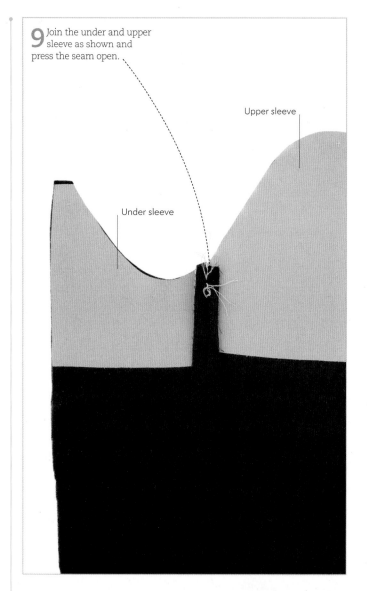

Upper sleeve

Under sleeve

10 Attach the sleeve facing. Layer the seam, notching through the curve. Press and understitch.

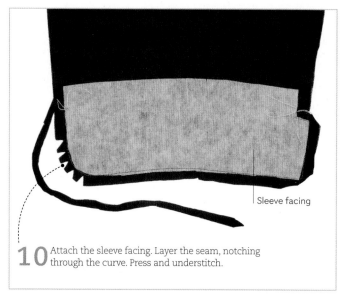

Sleeve facing

11 Join the other sleeve seam and press open. Pin a domette sleeve head in place and insert two rows of ease stitches.

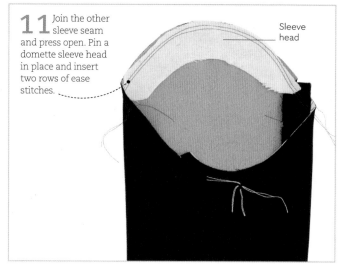

Sleeve head

12 Pin the sleeve into the armhole, matching notches (see p.142).

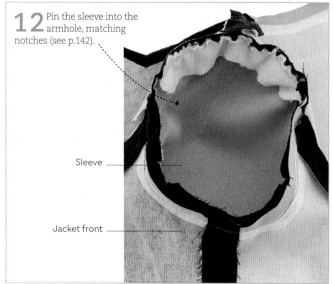

Sleeve

Jacket front

13 Sew the shoulder pad in place.

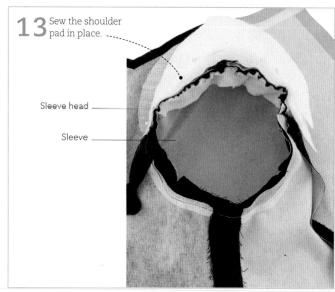

Sleeve head

Sleeve

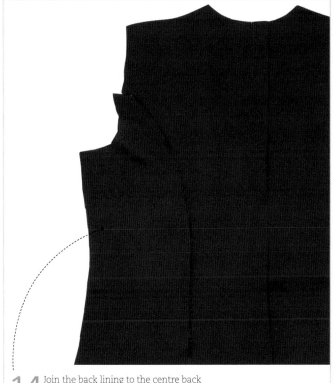

14 Join the back lining to the centre back seam and stitch in a pleat between the dots. Join the side back, and press all seams towards the centre back.

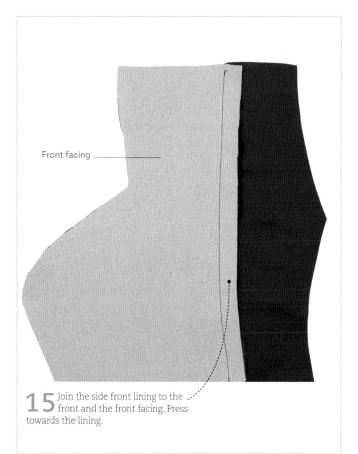

Front facing

15 Join the side front lining to the front and the front facing. Press towards the lining.

Shoulder seam

Back lining

Front facing

16 Join the lining front to the back at the shoulder and side seams. Press the shoulder seam open and the side seam towards the back.

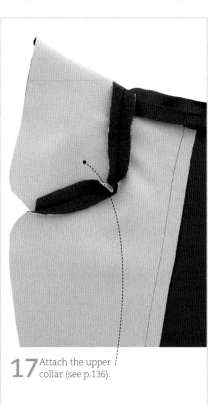

17 Attach the upper collar (see p.136).

18 Make up the lining sleeves (see p.118), and press the seams towards the under sleeve. Put to one side.

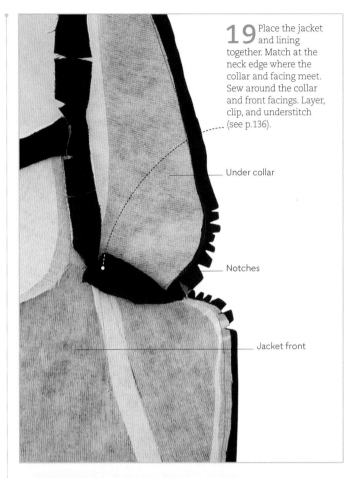

19 Place the jacket and lining together. Match at the neck edge where the collar and facing meet. Sew around the collar and front facings. Layer, clip, and understitch (see p.136).

Under collar

Notches

Jacket front

20 At the back neck, pin the seam allowances together and stitch to secure.

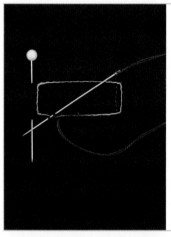

21 On the facing, mark the position of the buttonhole. Place a piece of silk organza or lining fabric on the facing over the pattern marking. Stitch a rectangle on the organza and the facing to match the size of the buttonhole. Slash through the organza and the facing within the rectangle. Push the organza through the hole to the wrong side of the facing, to create a little box in the facing. Secure with hand stitches to the edges of the bound buttonhole.

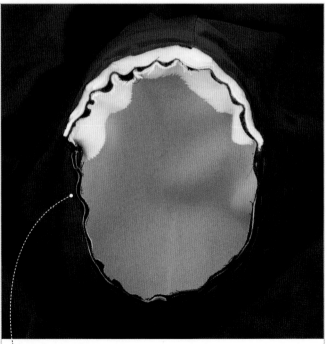

22 Bring the lining armhole to the jacket armhole and baste or tack the armhole together. Make sure they are not pulling.

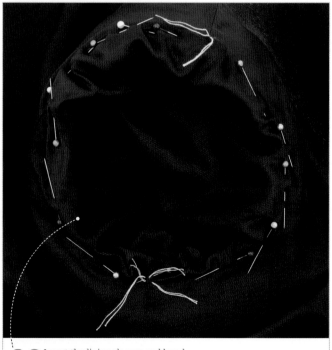

23 Insert the lining sleeves and hand stitch in place (see p.118).

24 Fuse a 5cm (2in) bias strip of interfacing through the jacket hem.

25 Catch stitch the hem in place (see p.177).

26 Level the jacket lining to the finished hem. Fold up a 1.5cm (⅝) lining hem and push up the completed hem to form a jump pleat. Pin. Check it is not pulling anywhere.

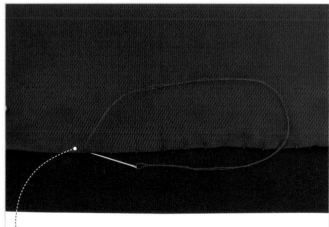

27 Hem the lining in place with a flat fell stitch.

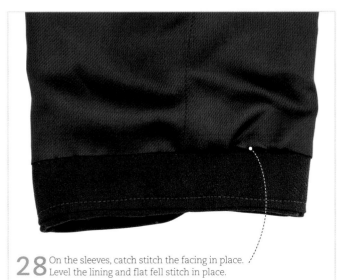

28 On the sleeves, catch stitch the facing in place. Level the lining and flat fell stitch in place.

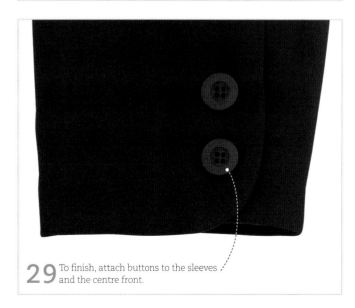

29 To finish, attach buttons to the sleeves and the centre front.

UNLINED SUMMER JACKET PATTERN
Unlined summer jacket

This lighter weight version of the classic fitted jacket (pp.252–259) exudes casual elegance and is perfect for warmer weather. This time the jacket is finished with a back neck facing and a Hong Kong finish on the seams. There is a lining on the sleeves only, for ease of wear. Linen or ramie are both great fabric choices for this jacket – naturally breathable yet with enough weight to drape beautifully.

TECHNIQUES USED Speed tailoring **pp.206–209**, Applying fusible interfacing **p.59**, Hong Kong finish **p.109**, Lined patch pockets **p.161**, Collar application **p.136**, Inserting a tailored sleeve plus sleeve roll **p.142**, Hand inserted sleeve lining **p.118**, Hand-stitched hems **p.177**, Buttons **p.189**, Machine-made buttonhole **p.197**

LEVEL OF DIFFICULTY

Intermediate–advanced A hip-length jacket with patch pockets using fusible tailoring techniques.

YOU WILL NEED

- Pattern template (see pp.12–13 for instructions on how to download your size)
- 2m (79in) x 150cm (59in) fabric
- 1m (39¼in) stitch reinforced fusible
- 3m (118in) fusible straight grain tape
- 2m (79in) fusible bias tape
- 1m (39¼in) pre-folded bias binding or 50cm (20in) fabric to make your own
- 1 x reel all-purpose thread
- 5 x buttons 2.5cm (1in) diameter
- 1m (39¼in) lining fabric
- Small piece of ice wool, knitted domette, or a flat domette for sleeve heads

GARMENT CONSTRUCTION

This princess line summer-weight jacket has a curved collar and revers for a neat, contemporary finish. The jacket features patch pockets and lined sleeves, and fastens with a single button.

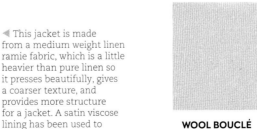

Curved collar

Patch pockets

Sleeve buttons

FRONT

BACK

LINEN RAMIE

VISCOSE LINING

◀ This jacket is made from a medium weight linen ramie fabric, which is a little heavier than pure linen so it presses beautifully, gives a coarser texture, and provides more structure for a jacket. A satin viscose lining has been used to create the sleeve lining and to make the bias strips for the Hong Kong finish.

WOOL BOUCLÉ

COTTON LAWN

▲ This jacket would also work well in a wool bouclé, which would add textural interest and be a little warmer for spring or autumn. Or a floral cotton lawn would be perfect for summer dressing.

1 Make the toile for the jacket (see pp.86–87) and try it on. Check the fit – how is the shoulder width? Does the sleeve length look right? Is it too tight or loose across the bust? Is the finished length correct? Adjust the pattern as necessary.

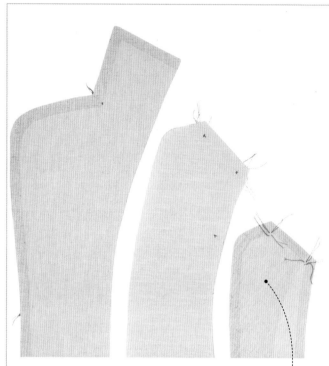

2 Cut out all the fashion fabric and sleeve and pocket linings as indicated. Interface the front facing, back neck facing, upper and lower collar, and sleeve facing (see pp.206–209). Insert the pattern markings into all the pieces.

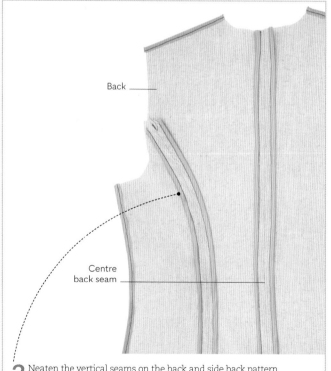

Back

Centre back seam

3 Neaten the vertical seams on the back and side back pattern pieces using a Hong Kong finish (see p.109). Join the centre back seam and then the back to the side backs. Press the seams open. Hong Kong finish the shoulder seam.

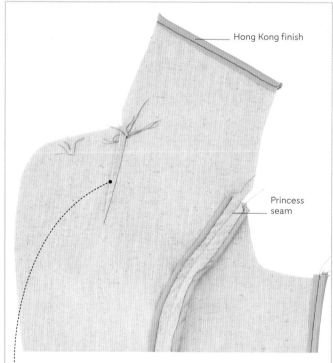

Hong Kong finish

Princess seam

4 On the front, make the dart at the neck. Press. Hong Kong finish the vertical seams on the side front and the front–side front seam on the front piece. Join the front to the side front. Press the seams open. Hong Kong finish the shoulder seam.

5 Make the lined patch pockets (see p.161) and attach to the fronts following the pattern markings.

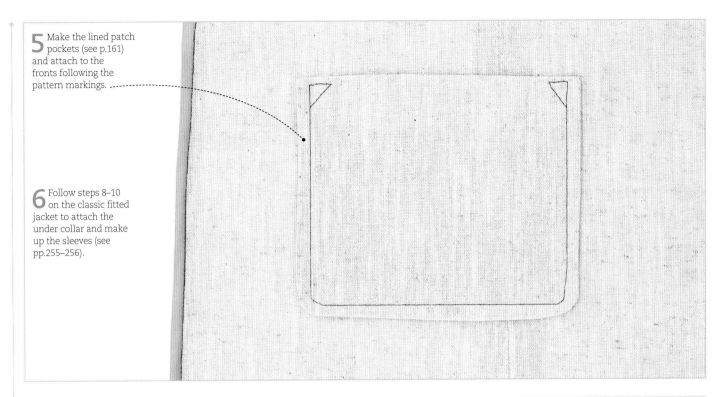

6 Follow steps 8–10 on the classic fitted jacket to attach the under collar and make up the sleeves (see pp.255–256).

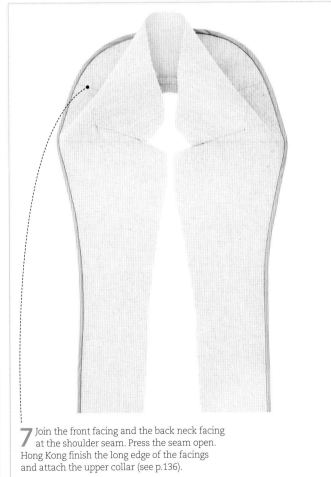

7 Join the front facing and the back neck facing at the shoulder seam. Press the seam open. Hong Kong finish the long edge of the facings and attach the upper collar (see p.136).

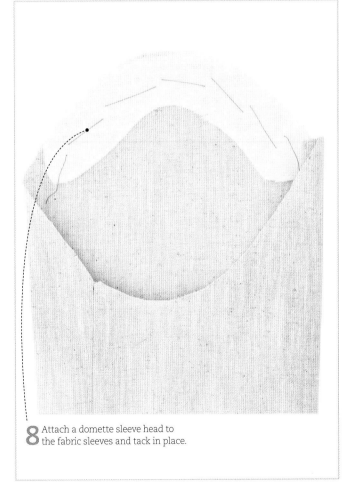

8 Attach a domette sleeve head to the fabric sleeves and tack in place.

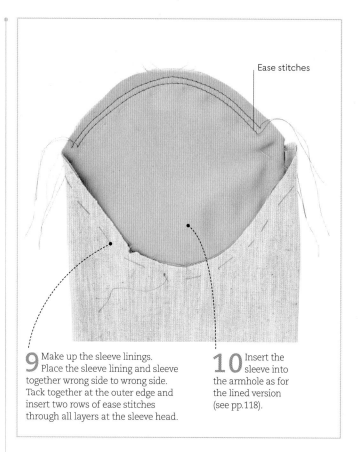

Ease stitches

9 Make up the sleeve linings. Place the sleeve lining and sleeve together wrong side to wrong side. Tack together at the outer edge and insert two rows of ease stitches through all layers at the sleeve head.

10 Insert the sleeve into the armhole as for the lined version (see pp.118).

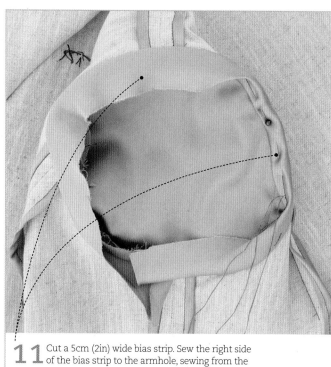

11 Cut a 5cm (2in) wide bias strip. Sew the right side of the bias strip to the armhole, sewing from the jacket side, following the sewing line used to insert the sleeve. Trim back by approximately 3mm and wrap the bias strip over the armhole seam. Pin and tack in place.

12 Wrap the bias strip over the armhole seam. Pin and tack in place. Secure with a flat fell stitch.

Bias bound armhole

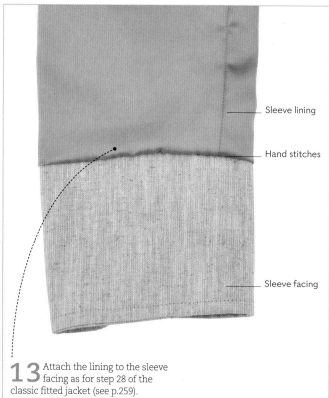

Sleeve lining

Hand stitches

Sleeve facing

13 Attach the lining to the sleeve facing as for step 28 of the classic fitted jacket (see p.259).

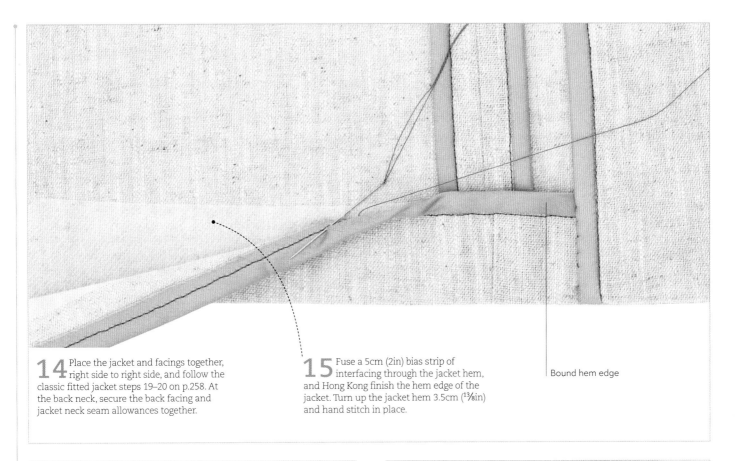

Bound hem edge

14 Place the jacket and facings together, right side to right side, and follow the classic fitted jacket steps 19–20 on p.258. At the back neck, secure the back facing and jacket neck seam allowances together.

15 Fuse a 5cm (2in) bias strip of interfacing through the jacket hem, and Hong Kong finish the hem edge of the jacket. Turn up the jacket hem 3.5cm (1⅜in) and hand stitch in place.

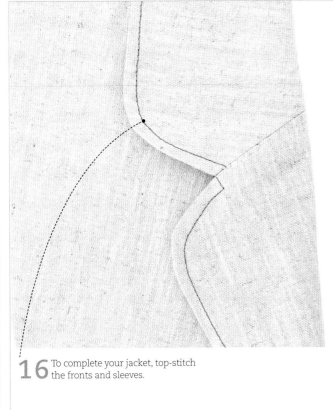

16 To complete your jacket, top-stitch the fronts and sleeves.

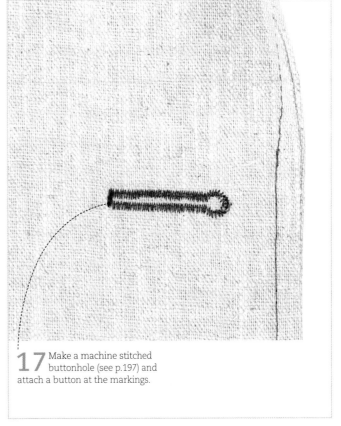

17 Make a machine stitched buttonhole (see p.197) and attach a button at the markings.

DARTED BLAZER PATTERN
Darted blazer

This time we turn our attention to a classic menswear blazer, tailored using the couture technique of canvas interfacing, shaped by hand stitches. I can't make you into a Savile Row tailor, but why not try the methods and techniques that they use (see pp.214–219)? This will elevate your blazer, providing structure, shaping, durability, and an impressive professional finish that you won't find in ready-to-wear styles.

TECHNIQUES USED Couture canvas tailoring **pp.214–219**, Melton under collar **pp.134–135**, Buttons **p.189**, Buttonholes **pp.192–197**, Lining around a vent **pp.120–121**, Inserting a tailored sleeve plus sleeve roll **p.142**, Welt pocket **p.164**, Double welt pocket with flap **p.172**, Hand inserted sleeve lining **p.118**

LEVEL OF DIFFICULTY
Advanced A challenging jacket with a lot of hand stitching and shaping that will take time.

YOU WILL NEED
- Pattern template (see pp.12–13 for instructions on how to download your size)
- 2.5m (98in) x 150cm (59in) wool fabric
- 2m (79in) x 150cm (59in) lining fabric
- 2m (79in) canvas interfacing
- 50cm (20in) domette
- 3m (118in) x 6mm wide cotton tape
- 75cm (30in) ready pad stitched collar Melton
- 1 x pair shoulder pads
- 1 x reel all-purpose thread
- 3 x buttons 2.5cm (1in) diameter
- 8 x buttons 1.5cm (⅝in) diameter

GARMENT CONSTRUCTION

This menswear blazer jacket uses couture tailoring techniques. The darted front has double welt pockets with a flap and a functional breast pocket. The jacket back has a flattering vent, complemented by the sleeve vents, and fastens with three buttons.

Welt pocket

Dart

Welt pocket with flap

Sleeve vent

Back vent

FRONT

BACK

WOOL SUITING

VISCOSE LINING

◀ This jacket is made from wool tweed and lined with an acetate taffeta lining. Choose a fabric that has a high wool content to get the most from the couture canvas tailoring technique.

FASHION TWEED

SATIN WEAVE LINING

▲ This blazer would also look good in a wool check or plain wool fabric and could be paired with a satin weave lining.

1 Make a toile of the blazer (see pp.86–87) and check the fit at the shoulder, the chest, and the hip, and make sure the finished length is right. Adjust the pattern as necessary.

2 Cut out all the pieces in fabric and lining as indicated on the pattern piece, and pattern mark. Trace tack the roll line.

Dart

Pocket opening

3 Make the dart in the jacket front. Slash open and press. Herringbone the pocket opening together.

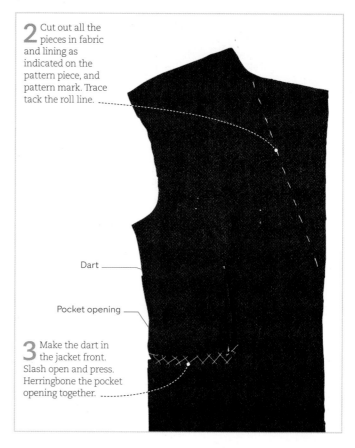

4 Pin the side to the front and sew together. Press open.

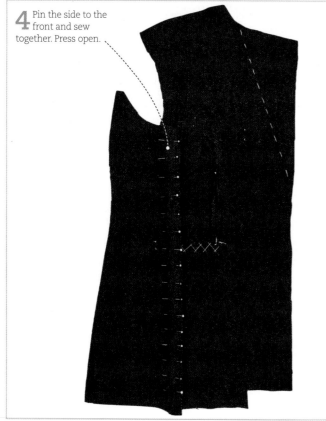

5 Prepare the canvas following the instructions on p.214 and place to the front.

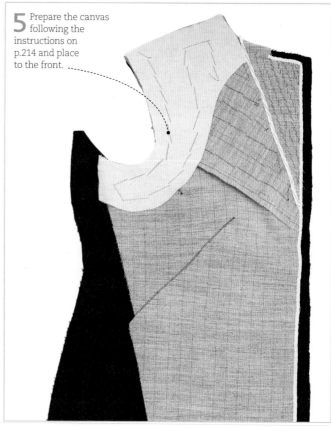

6 Make the welt pockets with flap (see p.172).

7 Make the welt pocket on the upper left front (see p.164).

Pocket bag

Canvas

8 Join the centre back seam. Snip the right-hand side of the seam at the extension and press the seam open. Apply interfacing to the left hand side of the vent as shown.

9 Join the jacket fronts to the back at the side.

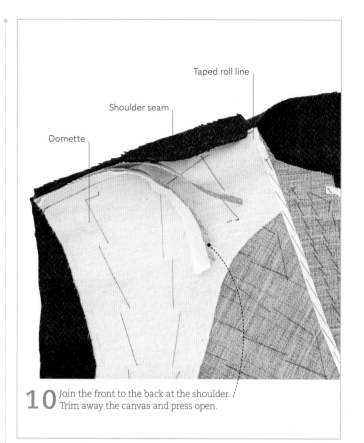

Domette

Shoulder seam

Taped roll line

10 Join the front to the back at the shoulder. Trim away the canvas and press open.

Sleeve head

Under sleeve

11 Join the sleeves on the short seam. Press open and attach a 4cm (1½in) wide bias strip of canvas through the hem.

12 Join the long sleeve seam and press open. Turn up the sleeve hem, mitring the corner.

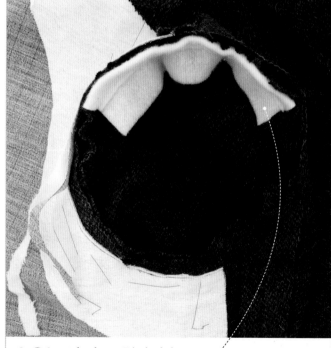

13 Insert the sleeves. Trim back the canvas and domette in the armhole seam. Apply sleeve head roll (see p.142).

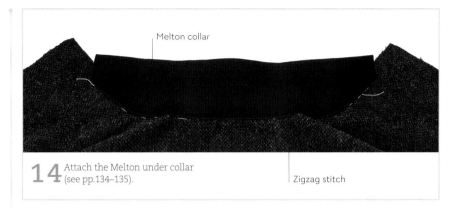

14 Attach the Melton under collar (see pp.134–135).

Melton collar

Zigzag stitch

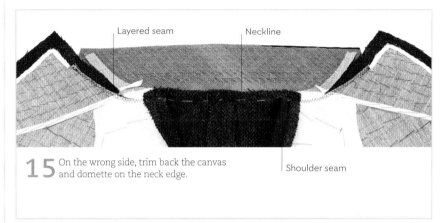

15 On the wrong side, trim back the canvas and domette on the neck edge.

Layered seam

Neckline

Shoulder seam

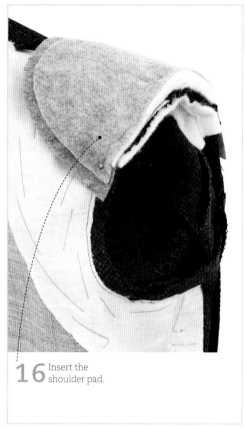

16 Insert the shoulder pad.

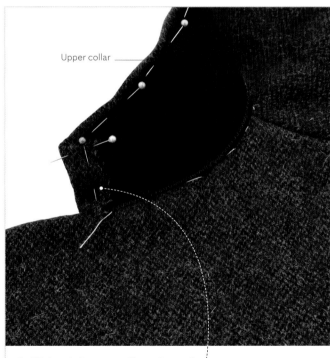

17 Attach the upper collar and wrap the centre front edge around the Melton collar (see pp.134–135). Pin in place.

Upper collar

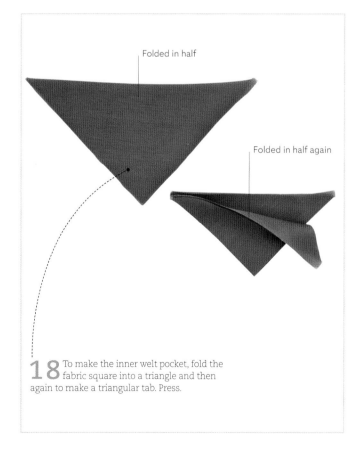

18 To make the inner welt pocket, fold the fabric square into a triangle and then again to make a triangular tab. Press.

Folded in half

Folded in half again

19 Make the inner welt pocket on the left-hand facing as worn (see p.164).

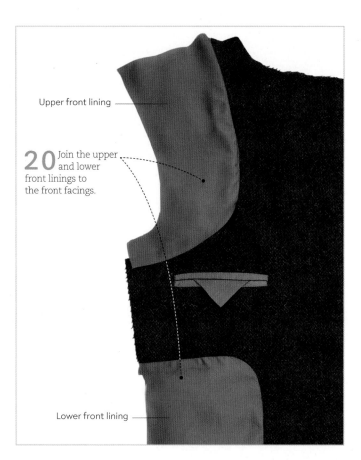

Upper front lining

20 Join the upper and lower front linings to the front facings.

Lower front lining

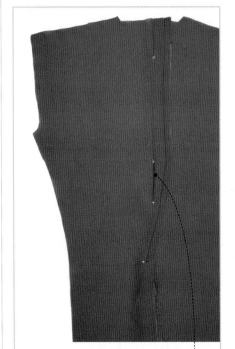

21 Join the centre back seam in the lining, stopping at the lower dot. Stitch between the other dots to create a pleat.

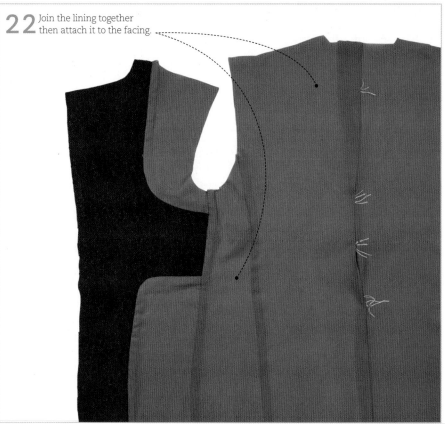

22 Join the lining together then attach it to the facing.

23 Join the shoulder seam.

Front facing

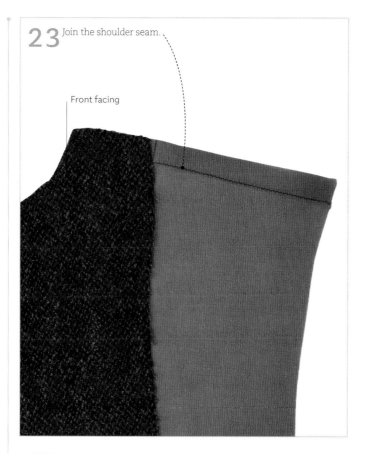

24 Place the lining and the jacket together, wrong side to wrong side. Match at the seams and tack together around the armhole.

Upper front lining

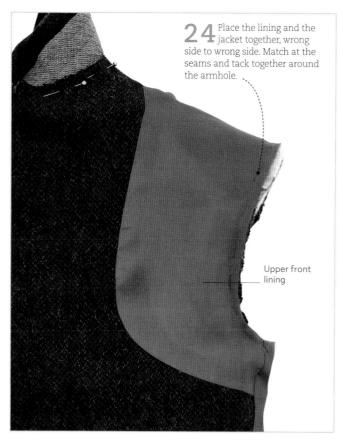

Folded edge of upper collar

25 Tack the lining and jacket together at the neck edge.

Herringboned seam

26 Turn in the leading front edges of the jacket and facing and sew together.

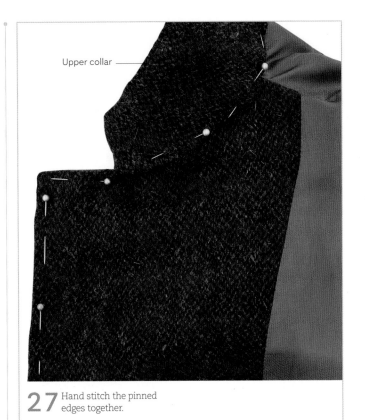

Upper collar

27 Hand stitch the pinned edges together.

Sleeve lining

28 Insert the lining sleeve by hand (see p.118).

29 Apply a 4cm (1½in) bias strip of interfacing through the hem of the jacket and turn up the hem.

Folded lining hem

30 At the centre front, fold under the facing hem and hand stitch. Push the folded hem of the lining up the hem and pin and stitch in place. This will form a jump pleat for wearing ease.

31 Turn in the edges of the centre back vent. Mitre the left-hand side and stitch up the hem. Machine across the top of the vent.

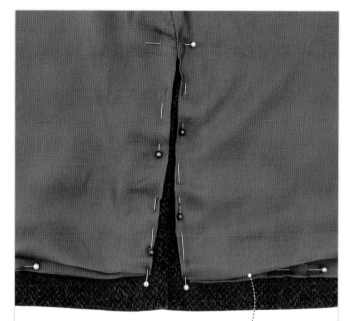

32 Bring the lining down to the vent. Turn under the seam allowance on the lining and pin around the vent. Follow the lining hem through from the front and create a little pleat at the edges to make the jump pleat for wearing ease. Hem in place (see pp.120–121).

33 Before finishing the sleeve lining, sew buttonholes on the sleeve opening and attach the smaller buttons.

Flat fell stitch

34 Attach the lining to the sleeve hem using a flat fell stitch.

35 Stitch buttonholes on left front as worn. Sew on buttons to match. Give your jacket a final press.

CAMEL COAT PATTERN
Camel coat

A full-length camel coat never goes out of fashion! Why not try this single-breasted version crafted in wool coating, and create a timeless classic that will elevate your winter style. It's constructed using hybrid tailoring techniques; a combination of fusible methods and machine pad stitching. With a simple shape, a deep back vent, and flap pockets, this fully lined coat is a wonderful addition to any wardrobe.

TECHNIQUES USED Hybrid tailoring **pp.216–219**, Plain dart **p.114**, Collar application **p.136,** Lining around a vent **pp.120–121,** Inserting a tailored sleeve plus sleeve roll **p.142**, Single welt pocket with a flap **p.171** Hand inserted sleeve lining **p.118**, Hand-stitched hems **p.177**, Buttons **p.189**, Buttonholes **pp.192–197**

LEVEL OF DIFFICULTY

Advanced This is a great project to practise using hybrid tailoring techniques.

YOU WILL NEED

- Pattern template (see pp.12–13 for instructions on how to download your size)
- 3.5–4m (138–157½in) x 150cm (59in) coat fabric
- 2.5–3m (98–118in) x 150cm (59in) lining fabric
- 2m (79in) fusible knit interfacing
- 50cm (20in) weft insertion fusible interfacing
- 50cm (20in) canvas
- 4m (157½in) straight grain tape
- 2m (79in) bias tape
- 1 x reel all-purpose thread
- Pair of shoulder pads
- Small piece of ice wool, knitted domette, or a flat domette for sleeve heads
- 3 x buttons 38mm (¾in) diameter

GARMENT CONSTRUCTION

This straight, below-the-knee, single-breasted camel coat has a front dart and a single welt pocket with a flap. There is a generous back vent to aid ease of walking. It fastens with three buttons.

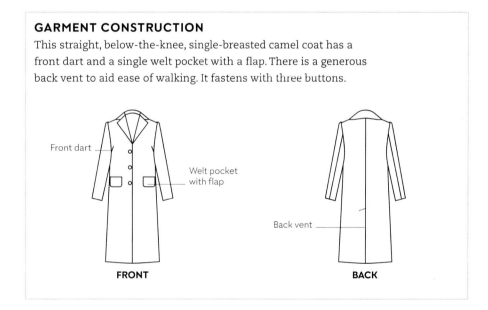

Front dart

Welt pocket with flap

Back vent

FRONT

BACK

WOOL COATING

VISCOSE LINING

◀ We used a pure wool coating in a classic camel, a neutral colour that never dates and goes with everything. This warm, hard-wearing fabric doesn't crease or mark easily, so your coat will be durable as well as stylish. We lined the coat with a lighter coloured viscose lining.

BOILED WOOL

ACETATE LINING

▲ The coat would also look great in a boiled wool, which is a cheaper option that comes in many fashion colours. This would be a good choice for your first coat as it's easy to sew. Pair with a similarly toned acetate lining.

1 Make a toile for the coat (see pp.86–87) and try it on. Check the fit – is it too long? Is the sleeve length correct? Can you fit a sweater under it? Adjust the pattern as necessary.

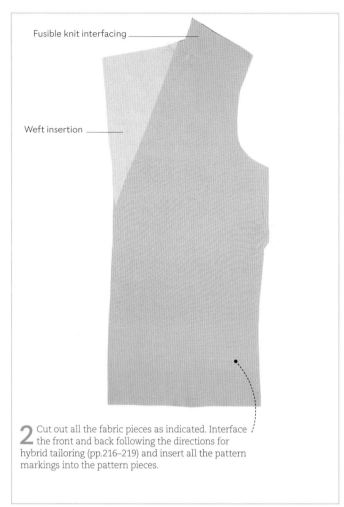

Fusible knit interfacing

Weft insertion

2 Cut out all the fabric pieces as indicated. Interface the front and back following the directions for hybrid tailoring (pp.216–219) and insert all the pattern markings into the pattern pieces.

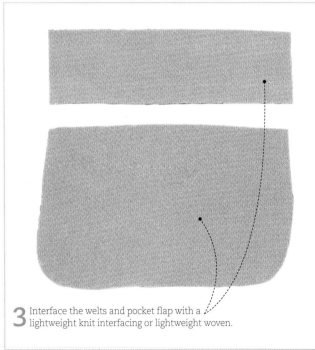

3 Interface the welts and pocket flap with a lightweight knit interfacing or lightweight woven.

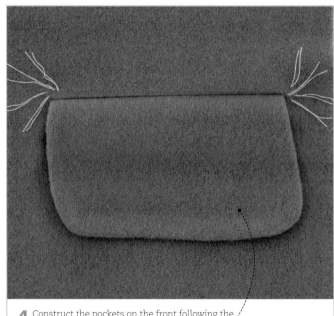

4 Construct the pockets on the front following the instructions for a single welt pocket with a flap (p.171).

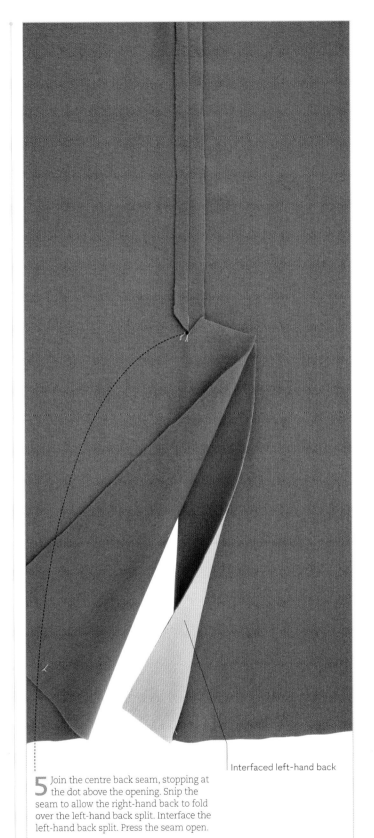

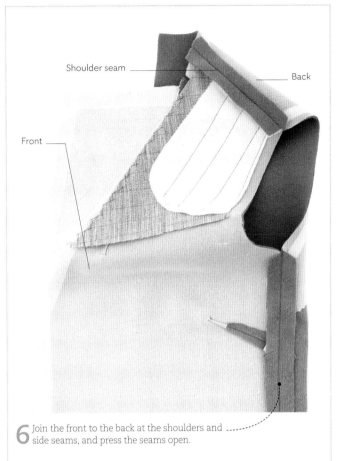

Shoulder seam

Back

Front

6 Join the front to the back at the shoulders and side seams, and press the seams open.

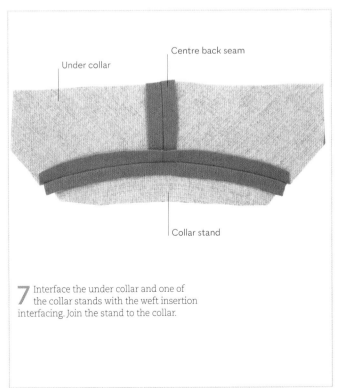

Under collar

Centre back seam

Collar stand

5 Join the centre back seam, stopping at the dot above the opening. Snip the seam to allow the right-hand back to fold over the left-hand back split. Interface the left-hand back split. Press the seam open.

Interfaced left-hand back

7 Interface the under collar and one of the collar stands with the weft insertion interfacing. Join the stand to the collar.

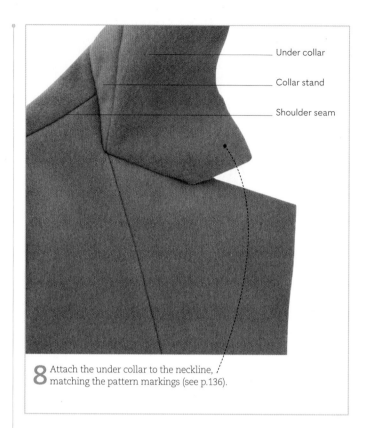

Under collar

Collar stand

Shoulder seam

8 Attach the under collar to the neckline, matching the pattern markings (see p.136).

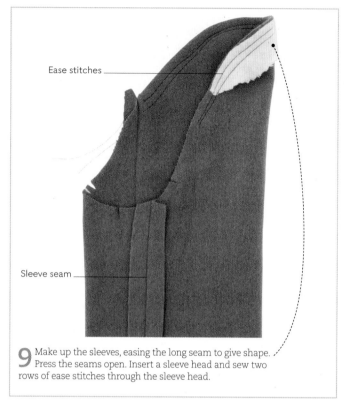

Ease stitches

Sleeve seam

9 Make up the sleeves, easing the long seam to give shape. Press the seams open. Insert a sleeve head and sew two rows of ease stitches through the sleeve head.

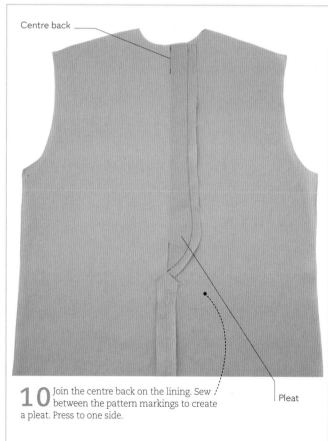

Centre back

Pleat

10 Join the centre back on the lining. Sew between the pattern markings to create a pleat. Press to one side.

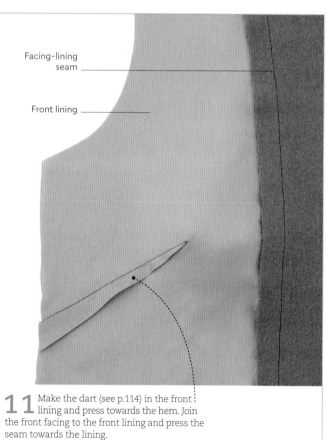

Facing-lining seam

Front lining

11 Make the dart (see p.114) in the front lining and press towards the hem. Join the front facing to the front lining and press the seam towards the lining.

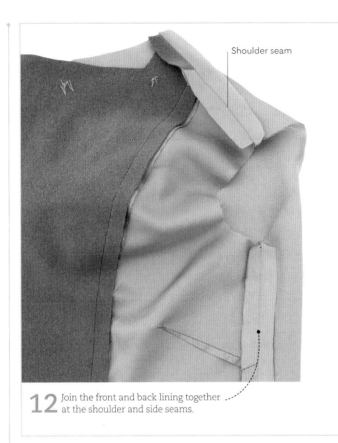

Shoulder seam

12 Join the front and back lining together at the shoulder and side seams.

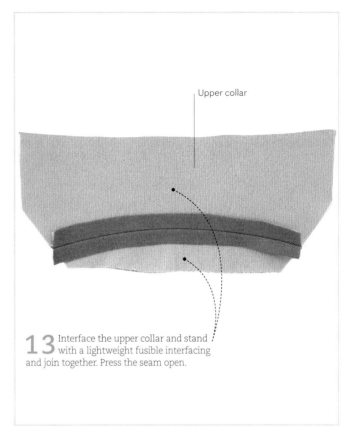

Upper collar

13 Interface the upper collar and stand with a lightweight fusible interfacing and join together. Press the seam open.

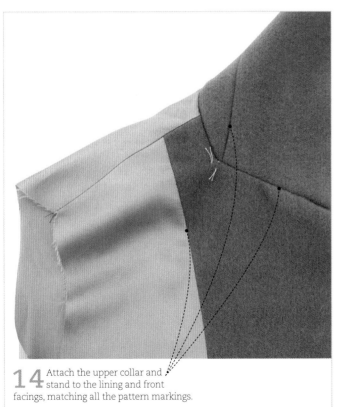

14 Attach the upper collar and stand to the lining and front facings, matching all the pattern markings.

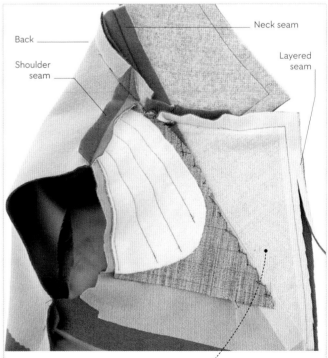

Neck seam

Back

Shoulder seam

Layered seam

15 Place the collars and the front facings together, right side to right side. Join the coat together sewing first the collars and then the facings. Clip and layer the seam, turn to the right side and press. Secure the neck seams together (see p.136).

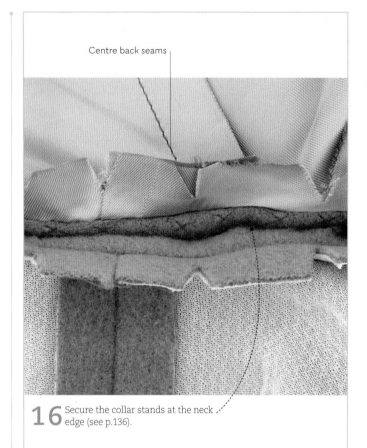

Centre back seams

16 Secure the collar stands at the neck edge (see p.136).

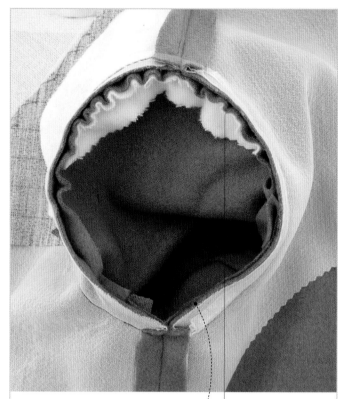

Sleeve head

17 Insert the sleeves into the armholes (see p.142), then insert the shoulder pads (see p.143).

18 Make up the sleeve linings and insert into the armholes (see p.118).

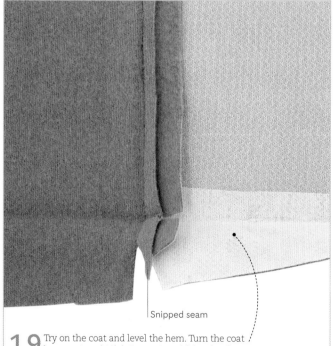

Snipped seam

19 Try on the coat and level the hem. Turn the coat hem up 4cm (1½in). Fuse a 5cm (2in) strip of interfacing through the hem. At the centre front, snip to reduce the bulk at the facing-coat seam.

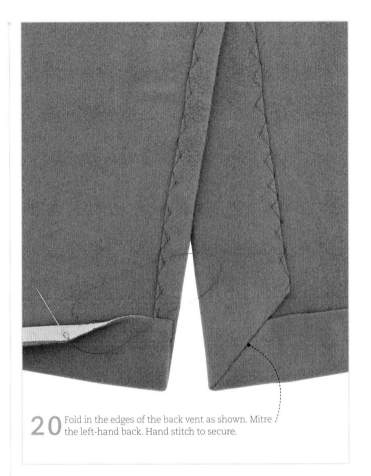

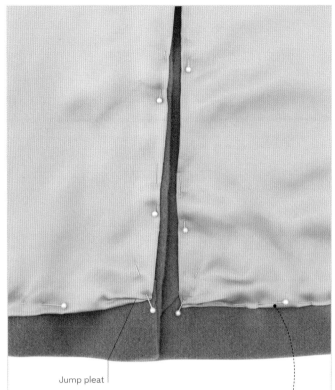

Jump pleat

20 Fold in the edges of the back vent as shown. Mitre the left-hand back. Hand stitch to secure.

21 Bring the lining over the vent, turn in the edges and hand stitch in place. At the hem, turn the lining up 1.5cm (⅝in) and push the fold up by 3cm (1½in). Slip stitch to secure (see p.88).

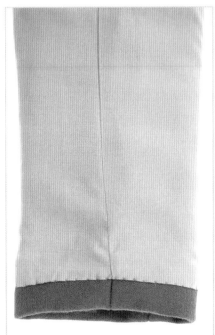

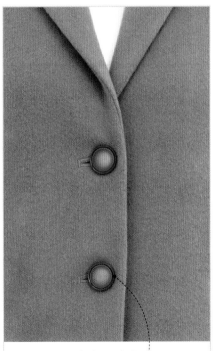

22 Attach the lining to the sleeve hem using a flat fell stitch.

23 Create the buttonholes and attach the buttons at the centre front markings.

24 Give the collar and lapels a final press on the right side.

KNEE-LENGTH COAT PATTERN
Knee-length coat

This short coat is great for everyday wear and will coordinate well with the skirt (pp.222–227) and trousers (pp.228–239). The deep patch pockets lend the coat a casual look, while a velvet collar and buttons add a touch of opulance, their texture contrasting beautifully with the wool fabric. This coat is best constructed in a heavyweight fabric such as wool coating, tweed, or flannel to ensure great drape and shaping, as well as warmth.

TECHNIQUES USED Hybrid tailoring **pp.216–219**, Plain dart **p.114**, Flat collar **p.130**, Inserting a tailored sleeve plus sleeve roll **p.142**, Patch pockets **pp.160–163**, Hand inserted sleeve lining **p.118**, Hand-stitched hems **p.177**, Covered buttons **p.191**, Snaps **p.199**

LEVEL OF DIFFICULTY

Intermediate This shorter version encompasses all the techniques of the camel coat, minus the tricky element of lining around a vent.

YOU WILL NEED

- Pattern template (see pp.12–13 for instructions on how to download your size)
- 2.5–3m (98–118in) x 150cm (59in) fabric
- 2.5–3m (98–118in) x 150cm (59in) lining
- 2m (79in) fusible knit interfacing
- 1m (39¼in) weft insertion fusible interfacing
- 50cm (20in) canvas
- 50cm (20in) domette
- 75cm (30in) x 115cm (46in) cotton velvet
- 3m (118in) fusible straight grain tape
- 2m (79in) bias tape
- 1 x reel all-purpose thread
- Pair of shoulder pads
- 4 x covered buttons 5cm (2in) diameter

GARMENT CONSTRUCTION

This straight, knee-length coat has deep patch pockets that are sewn into the side seam. A Peter Pan style velvet collar and velvet buttons complete the look.

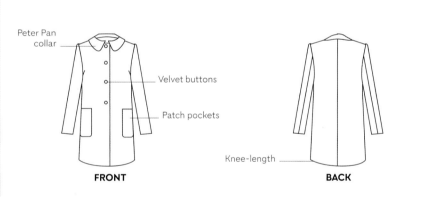

Peter Pan collar

Velvet buttons

Patch pockets

Knee-length

FRONT

BACK

WOOL COATING

VISCOSE LINING

COTTON VELVET

◀ This coat is made in a pure wool coating fabric with cotton velvet collar and buttons for a luxurious touch. Be sure not to use silk velvet, which is very hard to sew! The acetate taffeta lining is a similar tone to the wool coating.

TEXTURED WOOL COATING

ACETATE LINING

▲ This coat would work well in textured wool coating. Alternatively, a tweed, flannel, or heavy cord would also look great. Try using fake fur for a fashion collar with impact.

1 Make a toile of the coat (see pp.86–87) and try on. Check the pocket position, the shoulder width, and the sleeve length.

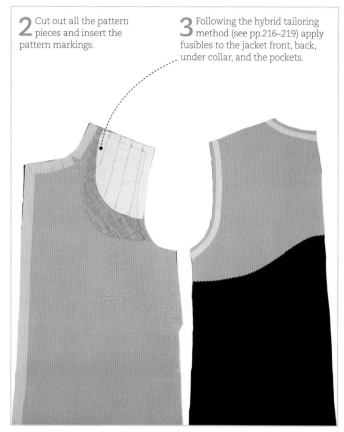

2 Cut out all the pattern pieces and insert the pattern markings.

3 Following the hybrid tailoring method (see pp.216–219) apply fusibles to the jacket front, back, under collar, and the pockets.

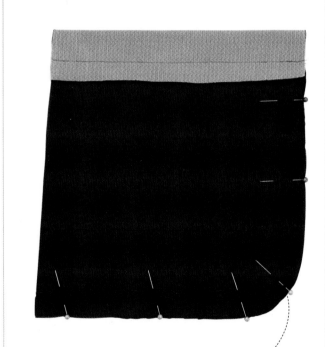

4 The patch pocket on this coat is constructed in a slightly different way to the usual method, as it is sewn into the side seam. Sew the lining to the top of the pocket. Press as shown and pin the lining around the curved edge.

5 Stitch around the curved edge. Clip the corner and notch through the curve. Keep the long, straight edge open.

6 Turn the pocket to the right side and press.

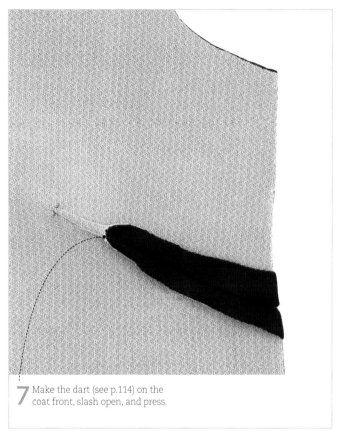

7 Make the dart (see p.114) on the coat front, slash open, and press.

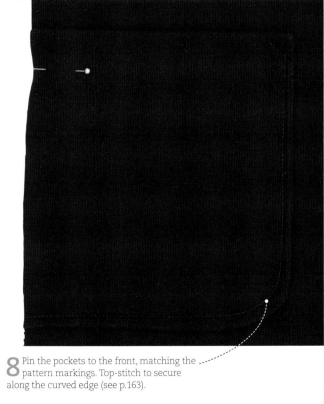

8 Pin the pockets to the front, matching the pattern markings. Top-stitch to secure along the curved edge (see p.163).

9 Join the centre back seam.

10 Join the front to the back at the shoulders and side seams and press the seams open.

11 Follow steps 9, 17, and 18 on the camel coat to construct and insert the sleeves (see pp.280 and 282).

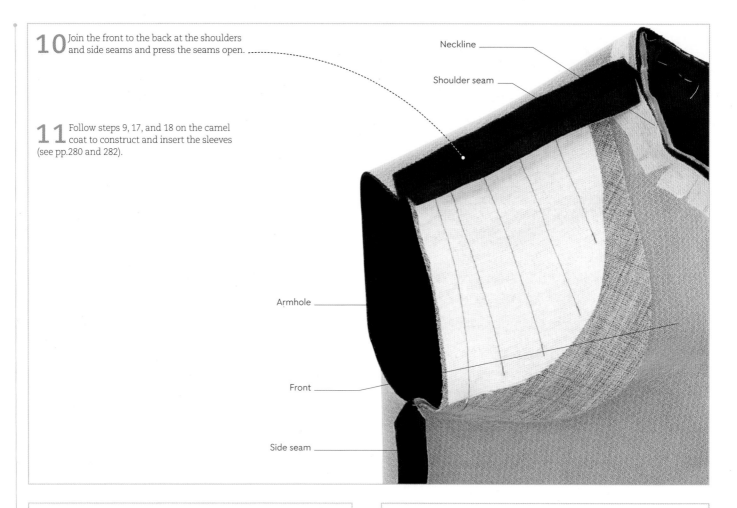

Neckline

Shoulder seam

Armhole

Front

Side seam

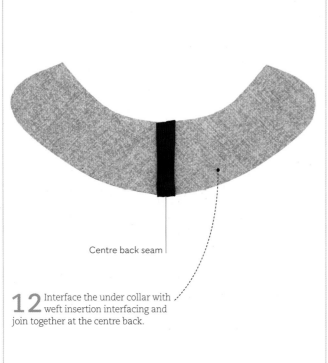

Centre back seam

12 Interface the under collar with weft insertion interfacing and join together at the centre back.

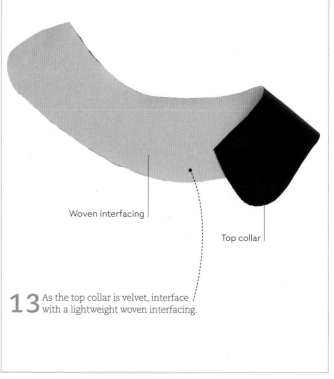

Woven interfacing

Top collar

13 As the top collar is velvet, interface with a lightweight woven interfacing.

14 Join the upper and under collar together, and clip away the seam allowance. Layer the under collar side of the seam and notch through the curves so that the collar turns out nicely.

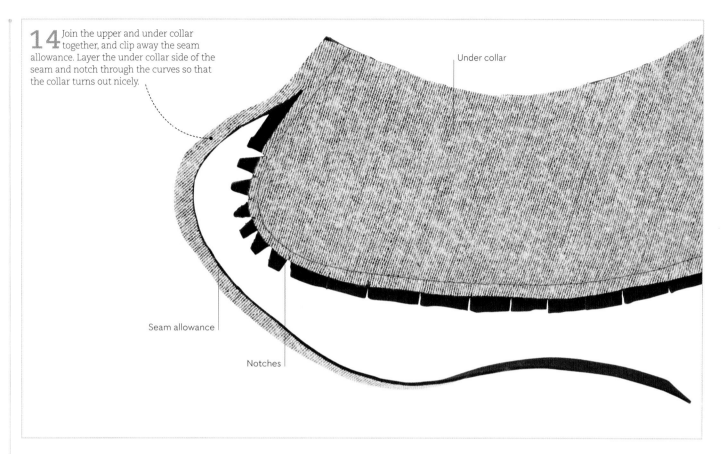

Under collar

Seam allowance

Notches

15 Turn to the right side and press.

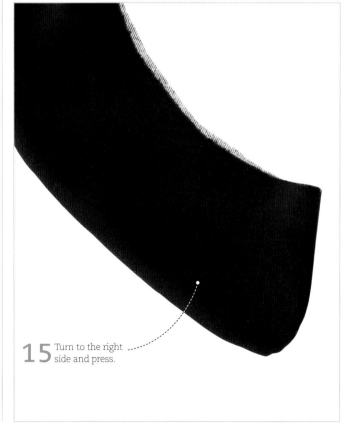

16 Tack the collar to the neck of the coat.

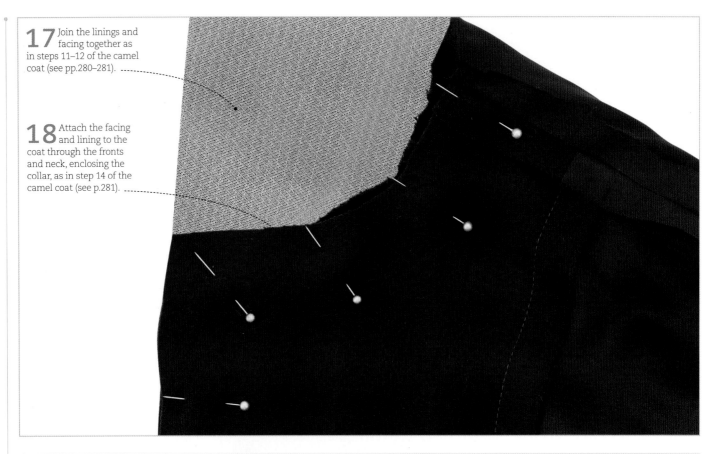

17 Join the linings and facing together as in steps 11–12 of the camel coat (see pp.280–281).

18 Attach the facing and lining to the coat through the fronts and neck, enclosing the collar, as in step 14 of the camel coat (see p.281).

19 Clip and layer the collar seam at the neck.

20 Turn to the right side and press.

21 Attach the lining to the sleeve hem and coat hem using a flat fell stitch.

22 If your coat fabric is thick then try using snaps to fasten your coat (see p.199). Cover your buttons (see p.191) to match the collar and sew them on top of the snaps.

23 Press your coat carefully to finish. Wear and enjoy!

Glossary

Acetate Man-made fabric widely used for linings.

Acrylic Man-made fabric resembling wool.

Armhole Opening in a garment for the sleeve and arm.

Back stitch A strong hand stitch with a double stitch on the wrong side, used for outlining and seaming.

Belt carrier Loop made from a strip of fabric, which is used to support a belt at the waist edge of a garment.

Bias 45-degree line on fabric that falls between the lengthways and the crossways grain. Fabric cut on the bias drapes well. *See also* Grain.

Bias binding Narrow strips of fabric cut on the bias. Used to give a neat finish to hems and seam allowances.

Binding Method of finishing a raw edge by wrapping it in a strip of bias-cut fabric.

Blind hem stitch Tiny hand stitch used to attach one piece of fabric to another, mainly to secure hems. Also a machine stitch consisting of two or three straight stitches and one wide zigzag stitch.

Bobbin Round holder beneath the needle plate of a sewing machine on which the thread is wound.

Bodice Upper body section of a garment.

Buttonhole Opening through which a button is inserted to form a fastening. Buttonholes are usually machine stitched but may also be worked by hand or piped for reinforcement or decorative effect.

Buttonhole chisel Very sharp, small chisel that cuts cleanly through a machine-stitched buttonhole.

Buttonhole stitch Hand stitch that wraps over the raw edges of a buttonhole to neaten and strengthen them. Machine-stitched buttonholes are worked with a close zigzag stitch.

Button shank Stem of a button that allows room for the buttonhole to fit under the button when joined.

Calico A plain weave, usually unbleached fabric.

Cashmere The most luxurious of all wools.

Catch stitch *See* Slip hem stitch.

Centre back The vertical line of symmetry of a garment back piece. Often marked as CB.

Centre front The vertical line of symmetry of a garment front piece. Often marked as CF.

Challis Fine woollen fabric with uneven surface texture.

Chambray A light cotton with a coloured warp thread.

Chiffon Strong, fine, transparent silk.

Clapper Wooden aid that is used to pound creases into heavy fabric after steaming.

Contour dart Also known as double-pointed dart, this is used to give shape at the waist of a garment. It is like two darts joined together. *See also* Dart.

Corduroy A soft pile fabric with distinctive stripes.

Cotton Soft, durable, and inexpensive fabric widely used in dressmaking. Made from the fibrous hairs covering the seed pods of the cotton plant.

Crease Line formed in fabric by pressing a fold.

Crepe Soft fabric made from twisted yarn.

Cross stitch A temporary hand stitch used to hold pleats in place and to secure linings. It can also be used for decoration.

Cutting line Solid line on a pattern piece used as a guide for cutting out fabric.

Darning Mending holes or worn areas in a knitted garment by weaving threads in rows along the grain of the fabric.

Dart Tapered stitched fold of fabric used on a garment to give it shape so that it can fit around the contours of the body. There are different types of dart, but all are used mainly on women's clothing.

Darted tuck A tuck that can be used to give fullness of fabric at the bust or hip. *See also* Tuck.

Denim Hard-wearing twill weave fabric with coloured warp and white weft.

Double-pointed dart *See* Contour dart

Drape The way a fabric falls into graceful folds; drape varies with each fabric.

Dressmaker's carbon paper Used together with a tracing wheel to transfer pattern markings to fabric. Available in a variety of colours.

Ease Distributing fullness in fabric when joining two seams together of slightly different lengths, for example a sleeve to an armhole.

Ease stitch Long machine stitch, used to ease in fullness where the distance between notches is greater on one seam edge than on the other.

Edge to edge A garment, such as a jacket, in which the edges meet at the centre front without overlapping.

Enclosed edge Raw fabric edge that is concealed within a seam or binding.

Facing Layer of fabric placed on the inside of a garment and used to finish off raw edges of an armhole or neck of a garment. Usually a separate piece of fabric, the facing can sometimes be an extension of the garment itself.

Flannel Wool or cotton with a lightly brushed surface.

Flat fell seam *See* Run and fell seam.

Flat fell stitch A strong, secure stitch used to hold two layers together permanently. Often used to secure linings and bias bindings.

Fusible tape Straight grain tape used to stabilize edges and also replace stay stitching. The heat of the iron fuses it into position.

Gabardine Hard-wearing fabric with a distinctive weave.

Gimp A thread over which handworked buttonholes are stitched.

Gingham Two-colour, checked cotton fabric.

Grain Lengthways and crossways direction of threads in a fabric. Fabric grain affects how a fabric hangs and drapes.

Grosgrain Synthetic, ribbed fabric often used to make ribbons.

Haberdashery Term that covers all the bits and pieces needed to complete a pattern, such as fasteners, elastics, ribbons, and trimmings.

Habutai Smooth, fine silk originally from Japan.

Hem The edge of a piece of fabric neatened and stitched to prevent unravelling. There are several methods of doing this, both by hand and by machine.

Hem allowance Amount of fabric allowed for turning under to make the hem.

Hemline Crease or foldline along which a hem is marked.

Herringbone stitch Hand stitch used to secure hems and interlinings. This stitch is worked from left to right.

Herringbone weave A zigzag weave where the weft yarn goes under and over warp yarns in a staggered pattern.

Hong Kong finish A method of neatening raw edges particularly on wool and linen. Bias-cut strips are wrapped around the raw edge.

Hook and eye fastening Two-part metal fastening used to fasten overlapping edges of fabric where a neat join is required. Available in a wide variety of styles.

Interfacing A fabric placed between garment and facing to give structure and support. Available in different thicknesses, interfacing can be fusible (bonds to the fabric by applying heat) or non-fusible (needs to be sewn to the fabric).

Interlining Layer of fabric attached to the main fabric prior to construction, to cover the inside of an entire garment to provide extra warmth or bulk. The two layers are then treated as one. Often used in jackets and coats.

Jersey Cotton or wool yarn that has been knitted to give stretch.

Keyhole buttonhole stitch A machine buttonhole stitch characterized by having one square end while the other end is shaped like a loop to accommodate the button's shank without distorting the fabric. Often used on jackets.

Layering Trimming one side of the seam allowance to half its width to reduce bulk at the seam.

Linen Natural fibre derived from the stem of the flax plant, linen is available in a variety of qualities and weights.

Lining Underlying fabric layer used to give a neat finish to an item, as well as concealing the stitching and seams of a garment.

Locking stitch A machine stitch where the upper and lower threads in the machine "lock" together at the start or end of a row of stitching.

Madras Brightly coloured, unevenly checked cotton fabric from India.

Matka A silk suiting fabric with uneven yarn.

Mitre The diagonal line made where two edges of a piece of fabric meet at a corner, produced by folding. *See also* Mitred corner.

Mitred corner Diagonal seam formed when fabric is joined at a corner. Excess fabric is cut away before or after stitching.

Mohair Fluffy wool yarn cloth used for sweaters, jackets, and soft furnishings.

Multi-size pattern Paper pattern printed with cutting lines for a range of sizes on each pattern piece.

Muslin Fine, plain, open-weave cotton.

Nap The raised pile on a fabric made during the weaving process, or a print pointing one way. When cutting out pattern pieces, ensure the nap runs in the same direction.

Needle threader Gadget that pulls thread through the eye of a needle. Useful for needles with small eyes.

Notch V-shaped marking on a pattern piece used for aligning one piece with another. Also V-shaped cut taken to reduce seam bulk.

Notion An item of haberdashery, other than fabric, needed to complete a project, such as a button, zip, or elastic. Notions are normally listed on the pattern envelope.

Organza Thin, sheer fabric made from silk or polyester.

Overedge stitch Machine stitch worked over the edge of a seam allowance and used for neatening the edges of fabric.

Overlocker Machine used for quick stitching, trimming, and edging of fabric in a single action; it gives a professional finish to a garment. There are a variety of accessories that can be attached to an overlocker, which enable it to perform a greater range of functions.

Overlock stitch A machine stitch that neatens edges and prevents fraying. It can be used on all types of fabric.

Pad stitch A hand-worked stitch used in couture tailoring to shape the canvas and jacket front.

Pattern markings Symbols printed on a paper pattern to indicate the fabric grain, foldline, and construction details, such as darts, notches, and tucks. These should be transferred to the fabric using tailor's chalk or tailor's tacks.

Pile Raised loops on the surface of a fabric, for example velvet.

Pinking A method of neatening raw edges of fray-resistant fabric using pinking shears. This will leave a zigzag edge.

Pinking shears Cutting tool with serrated blades, used to trim raw edges of fray-resistant fabrics to neaten seam edges.

Pivoting Technique used to machine stitch a corner. The machine is stopped at the corner with the needle in the fabric, then the foot is raised, the fabric turned following the direction of the corner, and the foot lowered for stitching to continue.

Placket An opening in a garment that provides support for fasteners, such as buttons, snaps, or zips.

Plain weave The simplest of all the weaves; the weft yarn passes under one warp yarn, then over another one.

Pleat An even fold or series of folds in fabric, often partially stitched down. Commonly found in skirts to shape the waistline, but also in soft furnishings for decoration.

Pocket flap A piece of fabric that folds down to cover the opening of a pocket.

Polyester Man-made fibre that does not crease.

Presser foot The part of a sewing machine that is lowered on to the fabric to hold it in place over the needle plate while stitching. There are different feet available.

Pressing cloth Muslin or organza cloth placed over fabric to prevent marking or scorching when pressing.

Prick stitch Small spaced hand stitch with large spaces between each stitch. Often used to highlight the edge of a completed garment.

Raw edge Cut edge of fabric that requires finishing, for example using zigzag stitch, to prevent fraying.

Rayon Also known as viscose, rayon is often blended with other fibres.

Reverse stitch Machine stitch that simply stitches back over a row of stitches to secure the threads.

Right side The outer side of a fabric, or the visible part of a garment.

Round-end buttonhole stitch Machine stitch characterized by one end of the buttonhole being square and the other being round, to allow for the button shank.

Run and fell seam Also known as a flat fell seam, this seam is made on the right side of a garment and is very strong. It uses two lines of stitching and conceals all the raw edges, reducing fraying.

Running stitch A simple, evenly spaced straight stitch separated by equal-sized spaces, used for seaming and gathering.

Satin A fabric with a satin weave.

Satin weave A weave with a sheen, where the weft goes under four warp yarns, then over one.

Seam Stitched line where two edges of fabric are joined together.

Seam allowance The amount of fabric allowed for on a pattern where sections are to be joined together by a seam; usually this is 1.5cm (⅝in).

Seam edge The cut edge of a seam allowance.

Seamline Line on paper pattern designated for stitching a seam; usually this is 1.5cm (⅝in) from the seam edge.

Seam ripper A small, hooked tool used for undoing seams and unpicking stitches.

Seam roll Tubular pressing aid for pressing seams open on fabrics that mark.

Selvedge Finished edge on a woven fabric. This runs parallel to the warp (lengthways) threads.

Set-in sleeve A sleeve that fits into a garment smoothly at the shoulder seam.

Sewing gauge Measuring tool with adjustable slider for checking small measurements, such as hem depths and seam allowances.

Sharps General purpose needle used for hand sewing.

Shirting Closely woven, fine cotton with coloured warp and weft yarns.

Silk Threads spun by the silkworm and used to create cool, luxurious fabrics.

Slip hem stitch Similar to herringbone stitch but is worked from right to left. It is used mainly for securing hems.

Snaps Also known as press studs, these fasteners are used as a lightweight hidden fastener.

Snips Spring-loaded cutting tool used for cutting off thread ends.

Staple fibres These include both natural and manufactured fibres such as cotton, wool, flax, and polyester. They are short in length, and relatively narrow in thickness.

Stay stitch Straight machine stitch worked just inside a seam allowance to strengthen it and prevent it from stretching or breaking.

Stitch in the ditch A line of straight stitches sewn on the right side of the work, in the ditch created by a seam. Used to secure waistbands and facings.

Stitch ripper *See* Seam ripper.

Straight stitch Plain machine stitch, used for most applications. The length of the stitch can be altered to suit the fabric.

Stretch stitch Machine stitch used for stretch knits and to help control difficult fabrics. It is worked with two stitches forwards and one backwards so that each stitch is worked three times.

Swayback Horizonal folds of excess fabric which gather at the centre back of a garment if the pattern pieces are too long for the body.

Tacking stitch A temporary running stitch used to hold pieces of fabric together or for transferring pattern markings to fabric.

Taffeta Smooth plain-weave fabric with a crisp appearance.

Tailor's buttonhole A buttonhole with one square end and one keyhole-shaped end, used on jackets and coats.

Tailor's canvas A coarse woven fabric that contains wool for couture tailoring

Tailor's chalk Square- or triangular-shaped piece of chalk used to mark fabric. Available in a variety of colours, tailor's chalk can be removed easily by brushing.

Tailor's ham A ham-shaped pressing cushion that is used to press shaped areas of garments.

Tailor's tacks Loose thread markings used to transfer symbols from a pattern to fabric.

Tape maker Tool for evenly folding the edges of a fabric strip, which can then be pressed to make binding.

Tape measure Flexible form of ruler made from plastic or fabric.

Tartan Fabric made using a twill weave from worsted yarns. Traditionally used for kilts.

Thimble Metal or plastic cap that fits over the top of a finger to protect it when hand sewing.

Toile A test or dry run of a paper pattern using calico. The toile helps you analyse the fit of the garment.

Top-stitch Machine straight stitching worked on the right side of an item, close to the finished edge, for decorative effect. Sometimes stitched in a contrasting colour.

Top-stitched seam A seam finished with a row of top-stitching for decorative effect. This seam is often used on crafts and soft furnishings as well as garments.

Trace tacking A method of marking fold and placement lines on fabric. Loose stitches are sewn along the lines on the pattern to the fabric beneath, then the thread loops are cut and the pattern removed.

Tracing wheel Tool used together with dressmaker's carbon paper to transfer pattern markings on to fabric.

Tuck Fold or pleat in fabric that is sewn in place, normally on the straight grain of the fabric. Often used to provide a decorative addition to a garment.

Tweed Traditional tweed is a rough fabric with a distinctive warp and weft. Modern tweed is a mix of chunky and bobbly wool yarns, often in bright colours.

Twill weave Diagonal patterned weave.

Understitch Machine straight stitching through facing and seam allowances that is invisible from the right side; this helps the facing to lie flat.

Velvet Luxurious pile-weave fabric.

Waistband Band of fabric attached to the waist edge of a garment to provide a neat finish.

Warp Lengthways threads or yarns of a woven fabric.

Weft Threads or yarns that cross the warp of a woven fabric.

Wool A natural animal fibre, available in a range of weights, weaves, and textures. It is comfortable to wear, crease-resistant, and ideal for tailoring.

Wool worsted A light, strong cloth made from good quality fibres.

Wrong side Reverse side of a fabric; the inside of a garment or other item.

Yoke The top section of a dress or skirt from which the rest of the garment hangs.

Zigzag stitch Machine stitch used to neaten and secure seam edges and for decorative purposes. The width and length of the zigzag can be altered.

Zip Fastening widely used on garments consisting of two strips of fabric tape, carrying specially shaped metal or plastic teeth that lock together by means of a pull or slider. Zips are available in different colours and weights.

Zip foot Narrow machine foot with a single toe that can be positioned on either side of the needle.

Index

Acknowledgments

AUTHOR'S ACKNOWLEDGMENTS

No book could ever be written without help and encouragement. I would like to say a huge thank you to Jackie Boddy and Linda Walters for their help with toiles and samples and especially my husband Nigel for his support. Thanks also go to Deborah Shepherd at Janome UK Ltd, Vliesline, Prym, Linton tweed, Fabworks, Misan and Marvic, Emma and Tom Forge, and Emma Hill. I would also like to thank the wonderful team at DK, especially Lucy Sienkowska, Zara Anvari and Glenda Fisher.

ABOUT THE AUTHOR

Alison Smith trained as a fashion and textiles teacher, and taught for many years at one of the largest schools in Birmingham, where she was Head of Department. In 1992 she set up the School of Sewing – the first of its kind in the UK – teaching all aspects of sewing, including dressmaking, tailoring, and corsetry. Alison has also taught at the Liberty Sewing School in London and at Janome's sewing school in Stockport.

In 2004, Alison opened a fabric shop in Ashby de la Zouch to complement the School of Sewing, and in 2013, she was awarded an MBE for her services to sewing and corsetry. In 2019 Alison started her own online teaching platform – School of Sewing Members Club – where she releases a new video every Friday. This online platform covers everything from sewing techniques, to fitting, to sew-alongs. She also teaches online for Craftsy.com and writes for various sewing magazines. She has written books for DK including *The Sewing Book* and *The Dressmaking Book*.

Alison has given up her shop to concentrate on her teaching and writing. She lives in Leicestershire with her husband and has two adult children.

www.schoolofsewing.co.uk
www.schoolofsewingmembersclub.co.uk

PUBLISHER'S ACKNOWLEDGMENTS

DK would like to thank Kathryn Glendenning for proofreading, Vanessa Bird for creating the index, Eleanor Ridsdale for design development work, XAB Design for additional photography organisation and art direction, and MIG Pattern Cutting for creating the project patterns.

The publisher would also like to thank the following companies for providing sewing machines, haberdashery, and fabrics: Janome UK Ltd, EQS, Vliesline, Prym, Linton tweed, Fabworks, Misan and Marvic, Adjustoform, Guttermann threads, The Button Company, YKK zips, Graham Smith Fabrics, Fabulous Fabric, Simplicity patterns, and Freudenberg Nonwovens LP.

For their work on *The Sewing Book*, DK would like to thank: Alice Chadwick-Jones, Alice Horne, Alison Gardner, Amy Child, Anjali Sachar, Ankita Sharma, Anukriti Arora, Anurag Trivedi, Arani Sinha, Ariane Durkin, Arunesh Talapatra, Beki Lamb, Bob Bridle, Caroline de Souza, Charlotte Johnson, Chhaya Sajwan, Christine Keilty, Dawn Henderson, Devangana Ojha, Elaine Hewson, Elma Aquino, Hansa Babra, Heather Haynes, Ishita Sareen, Janashree Singha, Jomin Johny, Kanupriya Lal, Karen Constanti, Katie Hardwicke, Laura Knox, Louise Brigenshaw, Madhurika Bhardwaj, Manish Chandra Upreti, Mary-Clare Jerram, Meenal Goel, Nisha Shaw, Nityanand Kumar, Nonita Saha, Norma MacMillan Peter Anderson, Priyadarshini Gogoi, Rajdeep Singh, Rajesh Singh Adhikari, Roshni Kapur, Ruth Jenkinson, Satish Gaur, Shashwati Tia Sarkar, Shipra Jain, Soma B. Chowdhury, Sourabh Challariya, Syed Md Farhan, Victoria Charles, Vikas Sachdeva, and Virien Chopra.

For their work on *The Dressmaking Book*, DK would like to thank: Alicia Ingty, Alison Shackleton, Amy Slack, Angela Baynham, Ankita Gupta, Anurag Trivedi, Charlotte Johnson, Christine Keilty, Claire Cross, Glenda Fernandes, Glenda Fisher, Hannah Moore, Hilary Mandleberg, Ira Sharma, Janashree Singha, Jane Bull, Jane Ewart, Jennifer Murray, Laura Palosuo, Lucy Philpott, Manish Chandra Upreti, Mansi Nagdev, Marianne Markham, Marie Lorimer, Mary Ling, Mary-Clare Jerram, Maxine Pedliham, Millie Andrew, Nand Kishor Archarya, Navidita Thapa, Neha Ruth Samuel, Nicola Powling, Pankaj Sharma, Paula Keogh, Penny Smith, Peter Stephens, Rajdeep Singh, Rebecca Fallowfield, Ruth Jenkinson, Ruth O'Rourke, Satish Gaur, Seyhan Esen, Soma B. Chowdhury, Sunil Sharma, Tarun Sharma, and Zaurin Thoidingjam.

DK LONDON
Senior Acquisitions Editor Zara Anvari
Editorial Manager Clare Double
Senior Editor Lucy Sienkowska
Senior Designer Glenda Fisher
Design Assistant Izzy Poulson
Production Editor David Almond
Senior Production Controller Luca Bazzoli
Jacket and Sales Material Coordinator Emily Cannings
Art Director Maxine Pedliham
Publishing Director Katie Cowan

Editorial Emma Hill
Design Emma Forge and Tom Forge
Jacket Design Eleanor Ridsdale
Photography Ruth Jenkinson

DK DELHI
Editor Ankita Gupta
Managing Editor Saloni Singh
Assistant Art Editors Devina Pagay, Rajoshi Chakraborty
Project Art Editor Roshni Kapoor
Senior Art Editors Bhavika Mathur, Devika Awasthi
Managing Art Editor Neha Ahuja Chowdhry
DTP Designers Satish Gaur, Manish Upreti, Nityanand Kumar
DTP Coordinator Pushpak Tyagi
Pre-production Manager Balwant Singh
Production Manager Pankaj Sharma
Creative Head Malavika Talukder

This edition published in 2024
First published in Great Britain in 2024 by
Dorling Kindersley Limited
DK, One Embassy Gardens, 8 Viaduct Gardens,
London, SW11 7BW

The authorised representative in the EEA is
Dorling Kindersley Verlag GmbH. Arnulfstr. 124,
80636 Munich, Germany

A CIP catalogue record for this book
is available from the British Library.
ISBN: 978-0-2416-4125-5

Printed and bound in China

www.dk.com

This book was made with Forest
Stewardship Council™ certified
paper – one small step in DK's
commitment to a sustainable future.
Learn more at **www.dk.com/uk/
information/sustainability**